Treating Children's Fears and Phobias
(PGPS-114)

Pergamon Titles of Related Interest

Apter TROUBLED CHILDREN/TROUBLED SYSTEMS
Cartledge/Milburn TEACHING SOCIAL SKILLS TO CHILDREN:
INNOVATIVE APPROACHES
Gelfand/Hartmann CHILD BEHAVIOR ANALYSIS AND THERAPY,
Second Edition
Karoly/Steffen/O'Grady CHILD HEALTH PSYCHOLOGY:
Concepts and Issues
Morris/Kratochwill PRACTICE OF THERAPY WITH CHILDREN:
A Textbook of Methods
Schwartz/Johnson PSYCHOPATHOLOGY OF CHILDHOOD:
A Clinical-Experimental Approach

Related Journals*

ANALYSIS AND INTERVENTION IN
DEVELOPMENTAL DISABILITIES
APPLIED RESEARCH IN MENTAL RETARDATION
JOURNAL OF CHILD PSYCHOLOGY AND PSYCHIATRY

*Free specimen copies available upon request.

PERGAMON GENERAL PSYCHOLOGY SERIES
EDITORS
Arnold P. Goldstein, *Syracuse University*
Leonard Krasner, *SUNY at Stony Brook*

Treating Children's Fears and Phobias
A Behavioral Approach

Richard J. Morris
University of Arizona

Thomas R. Kratochwill
University of Arizona

PERGAMON PRESS
New York   Oxford   Toronto   Sydney   Paris   Frankfurt

Pergamon Press Offices:

U.S.A.   Pergamon Press Inc., Maxwell House, Fairview Park,
                Elmsford, New York 10523, U.S.A.

U.K.   Pergamon Press Ltd., Headington Hill Hall,
                Oxford OX3 0BW, England

CANADA   Pergamon Press Canada Ltd., Suite 104, 150 Consumers Road,
                Willowdale, Ontario M2J 1P9, Canada

AUSTRALIA   Pergamon Press (Aust.) Pty. Ltd., P.O. Box 544,
                Potts Point, NSW 2011, Australia

FRANCE   Pergamon Press SARL, 24 rue des Ecoles,
                75240 Paris, Cedex 05, France

FEDERAL REPUBLIC   Pergamon Press GmbH, Hammerweg 6,
OF GERMANY   D-6242 Kronberg-Taunus, Federal Republic of Germany

Library of Congress Cataloging in Publication Data

Morris, Richard J.

　　Treating children's fears and phobias.

　　(Pergamon general psychology series ; 114)
　　Bibliography: p.
　　Includes indexes.
　　1. Phobias in children. 2. Fear in children.
3. Behavior therapy. I. Kratochwill, Thomas R.
II. Title. III. Series. [DNLM: 1. Fear—In
infancy and childhood. 2. Phobic disorders—In
infancy and childhood. 3. Behavior therapy—In
infancy and childhood. WM 178 M877t]
RJ506.P38M67　1982　618.92′85225　82-10186
ISBN 0-08-025999-5
ISBN 0-08-025998-7 (soft)

Printed in the United States of America

To our wives, Vinnie Morris and Carol Kratochwill, and our children, Stephanie, Michael, Jacqueline, and Tyler.

Contents

Preface

The clinical and research literature on children's fears and phobias has grown at an exponential rate over the past 15 years. What has emerged from this literature is a major change in the direction of treatment and the understanding of the development of children's fears and phobias. Coinciding with this change has been the development of a systematic measurement approach for the diagnosis and assessment of this and other forms of childhood behavior disorders. In addition, this recent literature has shown that many fear reduction intervention procedures now have sufficient empirical support to merit their utilization in clinical and other applied settings, and that such procedures can be used effectively by psychologists, psychiatrists, teachers, social workers, aides, and parents.

The major change in the literature on children's fears and phobias has been away from the psychoanalytic treatment and etiological orientation emphasized by Sigmund Freud and toward more behavioral conceptualizations of this disorder as conceived by Albert Bandura, B. F. Skinner, and Joseph Wolpe, among others. Consistent with this trend, there have been changes in terms of the focus of therapy. Instead of treating the child *in vacuo* in the therapist's office, many service providers have begun to modify the child's environment as well as his/her behavior within that environment.

This is not to say that mental health professionals and teachers have totally abandoned such psychological theorizing as psychoanalysis and client-centered approaches to childhood fears and phobias or have discounted the possible contribution of biological factors. What we are suggesting here is that there has been a substantial shift in the clinical and research literature in the past 15 years away from the strict psychodynamic and phenomenological theorizing and treatment orientation that dominated this area previously and toward a more behavioral orientation. It was because of our interest in the area of children's fears and phobias, as well as our finding that there was no systematic review of the behavioral literature in this area, that we decided to write this book.

The book is designed to present a comprehensive review of the behavior therapy research and clinical literature on the diagnosis, assessment, and treatment of children's fears and phobias. The book was written for those individuals who work with these children in clinic, school, and home settings to assist them in assessing and treating this behavior problem. Our secondary purpose is to present to the reader a systematic approach for evaluating the effectiveness of behavioral interventions and for conducting clinical and laboratory research in this area. Our ultimate hope is that individuals from diverse fields will extend research and practice in this area as a function of the material presented in this book.

Many people have contributed a significant amount of time in preparing this book for publication. Special appreciation is due Jerry Frank at Pergamon Press for his support throughout the preparation of this book. We would also like to express our appreciation to Jesse Fryer, Judy Landrum, Louis Pavelka, Alice Schoenberger, Mary Shubart, Naomi VanGilder, and Elvira Vega for their secretarial assistance during various phases of this project. Appreciation is also due Becky McReynolds and Kathy Campbell for their assistance in the preparation of the manuscript and Dr. Billy A. Barrios for his very helpful comments on the initial draft of this book.

Finally, special thanks are due our wives, Vinnie Morris and Carol Kratochwill, whose support, patience, and love have been ever present during the many long hours we put into the writing of this book.

Treating Children's Fears and Phobias
(PGPS-114)

CHAPTER 1

Introduction to Children's Fears and Phobias

At one time or another every human experiences fear. Fear, as Jersild (1968) suggests, "is both an inevitable and an essential emotion . . . it augments energies in times of danger and it provides an impetus to caution and prudence" (p. 327). For children, fear is an integral part of normal development. Many fears are transitory, appear in children of similar age, and generally do not interfere with everyday functioning. In addition, experiences and emotions associated with "developmental" fears often provide children with a means of adapting to various life stressors. Fears therefore often involve "normal" reactions to those stimuli that are construed by the child as either directly threatening or associated with threatening stimuli.

Fears typically involve three types of reactions in people: *motoric reactions* involving the avoidance of the feared stimulus, object, event, or at least the very cautious and prudent approach toward such stimuli; *cognitive reactions* involving unpleasant subjective feelings or cognitions about the feared situation, including feelings of muscular tenseness, irritability, panic and/or losing control (they include such self-verbalizations as "I'm scared," "I don't want to stay here," "I'm going to run away fast," along with dizziness, nausea, butterflies in the stomach, inability to concentrate on a particular task(s), feelings of unreality or detachment from reality, and extremely weak or paralyzing feelings in the arms and legs); *physiological reactions* involving pallor, an increased heart rate (often reported by people as a "pounding heart"), perspiration and sweat, pupillary dilation, rapid breathing, and desire to urinate (e.g., Marks, 1969).

Concern with children's fears on the part of mental health professionals and educators has increased tremendously over the past 20 years, although there has been a strong tradition in psychology of study and interest in this area (see, for example, Freud, 1909; Haslam, 1915; Jersild, 1968; Jersild & Holmes, 1935a, b; Jones, 1924a, b; Watson & Rayner, 1920).

1

NORMATIVE DATA ON CHILDREN'S FEARS

Fears are found in children from infancy through adolescence. Those seen in infancy typically occur as a reaction to something taking place in the infant's environment. As the child grows older into the early school years, his/her fears broaden and involve dark, supernatural figures, and particular persons, objects, and events. With increasing age, the child's fears turn more toward imaginary figures, objects, and events as well as the future (e.g., school, etc.) (Jersild, 1968).

Some of the fears that are often found in children at various age levels are presented below:

0–6 months: Loss of support, loud noises;

7–12 months: Fear of strangers, fear of sudden, unexpected, and looming objects;

1 year: Separation from parent, toilet, injury, strangers;

2 years: A multitude of fears including loud noises (vacuum cleaners, sirens/alarms, trucks, and thunder), animals (e.g., large dog), dark room, separation from parent, large objects/machines, change in personal environment;

3 years: Masks, dark, animals, separation from parent;

4 years: Parent separation, animals, dark, noises (including at night);

5 years: Animals, "bad" people, dark, separation from parent, bodily harm;

6 years: Supernatural beings (e.g., ghosts, witches, "Darth Vader"), bodily injuries, thunder and lightning, dark, sleeping or staying alone, separation from parent;

7–8 years: Supernatural beings, dark, fears based on media events, staying alone, bodily injury;

9–12 years: Tests and examinations in school, school performance, bodily injury, physical appearance, thunder and lightning, death, dark (low percentage).

Source: Ilg & Ames, 1955; Jersild & Holmes, 1935a; Kellerman, 1981, Lapouse & Monk, 1959; Scarr & Salapatek, 1970.

As we mentioned earlier, these "age-related" fears are typically transitory in nature, of short duration, and vary in intensity both *intra-* and *inter-* children.

A number of studies have also examined the incidence rates of children's fears within particular age ranges. For example, Jersild and Holmes (1935) studied children ranging in age from 24 to 71 months and found that they had an average of 4.6 fears. As Table 1.1 shows, they also calculated the percentage of children who demonstrated specific fears within their experimental setting by children's age range. The results show the fading out of

Table 1.1. Fears Shown by Children at Yearly Age Levels from 24 to 71 Months in Various Experimental Situations

Situation	Percentage of children showing fear			
	24–35 months	36–47 months	48–59 months	60–71 months
1. Being left alone	12.1	15.6	7.0	0
2. Falling boards	24.2	8.9	0	0
3. Dark room	46.9	51.1	35.7	0
4. Strange person	31.3	22.2	7.1	0
5. High boards	35.5	35.6	7.1	0
6. Loud sound	22.6	20.0	14.3	0
7. Snake	34.8	55.6	42.9	30.8
8. Large dog	61.9	42.9	42.9	· · ·
Total	32.0	30.2	18.1	4.5

Source: Jersild, A. T. *Child Psychology.* (6th ed.) Englewood Cliffs, N.J.: Prentice-Hall, 1968. Reprinted with permission.

some high percentage fears over increasing age (e.g., dark room, large dog, strange person, and walking across high boards) and the variability and maintenance of other fears (e.g., snakes).

In another study, Lapouse and Monk (1959) studied the fears and worries of a group of 482 children between the ages of 6 and 12. They also found a clear prevalence of children's fears within this older age group. Incidence data on adolescent fears have also been studied. For example, Croake and Knox (1971) asked 212 ninth-grade students from the southeastern United States about their fears. Their results, reported in Table 1.2, show that girls have more fears than boys, supporting the findings of other researchers (e.g., Angelino & Shedd, 1953; Croake, 1967; Russell & Sarason, 1965). In addition, the boys in their study indicated more fears related to the "future." Generally, fears related to personal relations, politics, and the home were frequently mentioned by all of the adolescents, with those from the upper socioeconomic classes reporting more fears than the lower-class youth (especially in the area of fears related to family functioning).

Although these and other studies are discussed in more detail later (see Chapter 2), these findings suggest that there are "normal" age ranges for certain children's fears, and consequently, that the developmental nature and appropriateness of a child's fear should be assessed before any direct intervention is planned. However, if the particular fear is found to be age appropriate, but is also found to be (1) excessive, (2) last over a relatively long period of time, and (3) create problems in living for the parent(s) and/or child, then therapeutic intervention should be considered.

Table 1.2. What Adolescents Fear

	Sex		Socioeconomic Level		
Category	Male	Female	Upper	Lower	Total Sample
Animals	9.04%	10.55%	10.22%	9.73%	9.79%
Future	10.97	8.62	9.88	9.79	9.79
Supernatural phenomena	8.39	9.68	9.45	8.93	9.03
Natural phenomena	6.62	10.87	7.11	11.40	8.74
Personal appearance	8.47	9.17	9.23	8.68	8.82
Personal relations	10.56	10.56	11.06	10.30	10.56
School	10.37	10.05	10.86	10.64	10.21
Home	11.71	10.21	10.40	9.67	10.95
Safety	8.77	8.46	8.52	9.02	8.61
Political	13.02	12.35	13.24	12.32	12.68

Source: Croake, J. W., & Knox, F. H. A second look at adolescent fears. *Adolescence*, 1971, **6**, 279–284. Reprinted with permission.

Fears Versus Phobias

As noted earlier, fear in children is a very strong emotion and is associated with behavioral, cognitive, and physiological indicators of anxiety. Generally speaking, when a child experiences fear that is not age-related in a setting where there is no obvious external danger, the fear is irrational, and the child is said to have a *phobia*. When the person begins to avoid the nondangerous feared situation, even though maintaining that such action is "silly" or foolish, the phobia is commonly referred to as a *phobic reaction* (e.g., Knopf, 1979; Morris, 1980).

Although the meaning of the constructs "phobia" and "phobic reaction" appear somewhat clear, the literature reveals a good deal of confusion in the interchanging of these constructs with such terms as "fear," "anxiety," "stress," and "avoidance behavior." To add to the confusion, however, at times these latter terms are also used differently from "phobia" or "phobic reaction." The term "fear," for example, is often used in the child development literature to refer to a *normal* reaction to a real or perceived threat. On the other hand, in the child behavior disorders/psychopathology literature, the term "fear" is sometimes used within the context of a normal developmental reaction and at other times as a clinical problem (see, for example, Kessler, 1972; Lippman, 1967). This problem will be discussed further in Chapter 2. Suffice it to say that there is not total agreement among researchers and/or practitioners as to what constitutes a fear or phobia, although some attempts to differentiate between these terms will be presented in subsequent pages.

Separating the meaning of these two terms is further compounded by the construct "courage." Rachman (1978), for example, discusses two possible conceptualizations of courage: (1) Mowrer's (1960) view that it is "simply the *absence* of fear in situations where it might well be expected to be present" (p. 435), and (2) Rachman's view of performing an activity with "considerable persistence in the face of intense fear" or fearful people coping with a particular action or activity with "perserverance in the face of stress and adversity" (Rachman, 1978, pp. 2–3). Referring to this last point, Rachman (1978) states, "One could in fact argue that it is this latter type of conduct that is the purest form of courage" (pp. 234–235). Thus, in courage we find people engaging in an activity with perserverance, even though they are also experiencing intense fear. Their motoric activities do not necessarily reveal their "fear" (e.g., through avoidance behavior), while their cognitive and physiological activity *may* reveal their intense "fearfulness." Therefore we may find individuals who are "fearful" or "phobic," but who demonstrate none or only some of the components of these terms. According to Mowrer (1960), what determines whether an individual demonstrates (at least, motorically) fear or courage is related to the relationship of "the opposing forces in a conflict."

> If much fear and little hope are associated with the stimuli which a given action produces, then, with respect to that action, the individual is 'timid', 'cowardly"; but if there is relatively little fear and much hope, then the action may be boldly executed [pp. 433–434].

It should be noted, however, that relatively little research has been performed on courage or on those factors that contribute to its development, nor has its relationship to fears and phobias been fully articulated within the experimental literature (see, for example, Mowrer, 1960; Rachman, 1978).

Although reliable incidence data are lacking regarding the prevalence of fears and phobias in children, some patterns have emerged. Generally speaking, children and their parents report significantly more fears than phobias. For example, in a study by Lapouse and Monk (1959), parents of children between the ages of 6–12 years reported that 43% of their children experienced at least seven or more fears—with significantly more girls than boys demonstrating these fears. With regard to phobias and/or severe fears, the literature is more sparse. For example, Miller, Barrett, and Hampe (1974) report that the incidence of intense or excessive fears was about 5% of their sample of children ages 7–12. Similarly, Graham (1964), as cited in Marks (1969), reported that only about 4% of the children referred for treatment had "phobias." Rutter, Tizard, and Whitmore's (1970) prevalence data were only slightly higher (about 7%), as were those of Graziano and DeGiovanni (1979) regarding those children with clinical fears or phobias who were referred to behavior therapists for treatment. With regard to "school phobia," Kennedy (1965) reports that 17 out of 1000 children (1.7%) experience this problem. Even though these various incidence studies differ on their definitions of severe fear, clinical fear, phobia, and related problems, it is interesting to note that each reports that the prevalence of intense fears (those necessitating clinical intervention) is less than 8% of the number of referrals to a clinician or in the general child population.

In differentiating between fears and phobias, Marks (1969) has suggested that phobia is a subcategory of fear which:

1. Is out of proportion to demands of the situation,
2. Cannot be explained or reasoned away,
3. Is beyond voluntary control, and
4. Leads to avoidance of the feared situation [Marks, 1969, p. 3].

To these criteria, Miller et al. (1974) added that a phobia "persists over an extended period of time . . . is unadaptive . . . [and] is not age or stage specific" (p. 90). As illustrated in the following case example, this is not to say that a young child who is afraid of dogs could not also have a phobia.[1]

When Bobby was three and one-half years old, he was playing outside with his five-year-old sister, Pam, and their medium size family dog. They took turns throwing a stick and having the dog retrieve it. After doing this a number of times, the dog tired, but Bobby and Pam did not. Pam then approached the dog and tried various ways to goad the dog into playing with them. The dog reacted by growling, then snapping at Pam. Both children thought this was "fun" and Pam continued to push and pull at the dog. The dog finally reacted by growling louder and scratching and biting Pam on the arm. Bobby watched these series of events and began crying and screaming with Pam as they both ran toward their house.

Pam recovered from the bite and scratches and was quite hesitant to play for a number of months with the family dog. She was, however, able to play with her friend's dog. Bobby, on the other hand, refused to go near the family dog or anyone else's. In fact, he refused to enter any house which had a "large dog," would repeatedly ask his parents if dogs would be wherever they were going as a family, made his parents leave any place or house in which there was a large dog, and generally avoided any open area outside his house, preferring to play in the enclosed back yard.

These behaviors on Bobby's part continued for six months before his parents sought professional help.

Here, Bobby's fear of dogs, though age-specific, is classified as a phobia because it: (1) was out of proportion to the situation (he refused to go to or insisted that he and his parents leave any place which had a "large dog"); (2) could not be reasoned away (no amount of reassurance or explanation by his parents about how he and his sister caused the dog to bite and scratch her reduced the intensity of his fear or avoidance behavior); (3) could not be controlled by him—in fact, he refused to control it; (4) led to avoidance of other settings where dogs were or might be; (5) lasted for six months; and (6) was not adaptive after the initial incident with his sister.

The next case example more clearly differentiates a childhood phobia from a fear.

Tommy is a six-year-old boy who has a severe neurological disorder causing his right leg to "give-out" and cause him to fall without warning and to have mild seizures a number of times per month. Medication did not seem to appreciably control these events. Sometimes the ataxia in his legs and his seizure activity occurred at night and at other times during the school day or in the morning before school, causing Tommy to sometimes miss the school bus. He enjoyed school tremendously and often became upset when he missed school.

He often associated getting dressed in the morning with his ataxia and seizures and blamed his missing the bus on his difficulty in getting dressed following and during his falling and seizures. In order to avoid the fear and tension he experienced each morning regarding whether he would be able to be dressed for school and meet his bus, Tommy began going to bed each night with all of his clothes on (excluding shoes) for the next morning, i.e., he changed his clothes, bathed, and dressed each evening before bedtime wearing clean clothes for the next day. He slept very still at night in order not to mess up his next day's clothes. In addition, he always made sure that he wore very long soccer socks so that they could fit over his knees. By engaging in these dressing activities at night, Tommy avoided the frustrating and unpleasant situation of possibly experiencing falling and seizures in the morning and then missing the bus because he was not dressed.

In this example, Tommy's behavior represents a phobic response because (1) it was out of proportion to the demands of the morning situation (he has no idea whether his problems will occur on any one morning so he avoids dressing in the morning completely); (2) his parents were unable to convince him of the irrationality of his bedtime activities; (3) he could or would not actively stop what he was doing each evening; (4) he avoided dressing each morning; (5) these bedtime activities lasted for a number of months without change, and (6) his bedtime and sleep behaviors were not adaptive.

The third case example described below indicates how a person can develop both fears and phobic behavior based on the same antecedent events.

Mary, a 17-year-old girl, worked part-time at night at a local restaurant in order to have some extra spending money. One night after finishing work she walked to her car in the restaurant parking lot, unlocked the driver's door, and sat down behind the wheel. Just as she sat down, a man wielding a gun opened the unlocked passenger door, sat down beside her, and told her to drive away. Mary was quite frightened and complied with the man's instructions, asking him not to hurt her. After driving through various neighborhoods for one-half hour, the man had Mary stop the car and then began hitting her with the gun. After struggling with the man for a short time, Mary was able to unlock her car door and run away from the car and the man. She knocked on various doors at different houses and finally found someone who answered, called her parents, and took her to a nearby hospital for treatment of her multiple wounds.

As a result of this assault, Mary never used her car again and finally sold it. She drove her mother's car although never at night, would not go out on a date although she would go out at night with girlfriends, and had severe nightmares about the assault three to four times per week.

Using the criteria outlined earlier, her phobic responses involved driving at night and dating, while her fears entailed going to sleep and possibly having a nightmare (she had no trouble entering her bedroom or falling asleep), trusting any male stranger (although she was quite willing to talk to male strangers during the day at school or at her new job), and entering any car that was parked in a parking lot (she would enter a car very reluctantly, scanning the outside perimeter as she entered and sat down).

Although each of these examples of phobia involved the observing of or direct involvement with a traumatic or aversive event, this is not always the case. In some cases, no actual aversive antecedent event precedes the phobic response. For example, some preadolescent children who refuse to stay alone in their house have never had an identified negative experience associated with being alone. Similarly, many adolescent children who refuse to sleep in their bedroom at night without a lamp on (*not* a small nightlight) have never had any traumatic event associated with their lights being off. In many cases, an unpleasant fantasy, image, or movie may be the antecedent factor for these youths. Again, all of these fears fall into the subcategory of phobia behavior using the Marks (1969) and Miller et al. (1974) criteria stated earlier. Controversy, however, does exist regarding the latter point, and we will detail this in Chapter 2. One writer (Kellerman, 1981) has even stated that he does not find the term "phobia" to be at all useful when dealing with children:

We have seen that children, especially young ones, may not always understand the difference between fantasy and reality. To them the shark from *Jaws* may be as real as if they had encountered it in the family bathtub. If we really wish to help the fearful child, . . . avoid labeling him as neurotic . . . [and] recognize that he is exhibiting one type of learned behavior. And no matter what causes an anxiety reaction, the child's anguish is very real [p. 31–32].

Overview of Theoretical and Therapeutic Assumptions About Fears and Phobias

The etiology and treatment of children's fears and related problems have been discussed in the literature from many theoretical perspectives. We have summarized in this section the general theoretical and therapeutic assumptions of the behavioral approach to the etiology and treatment of children's fears and phobias and have compared these to four other frequently cited theoretical or therapeutic frameworks regarding children's fears, phobias, and related problems. Specifically, the following theoretical perspectives are compared to the behavioral approach: psychoanalytic, Adlerian, Rogerian, and biological/organic positions.[2]

Generally, each of these theoretical and therapeutic positions represents a cause and effect view toward the development, maintenance, and treatment of childhood fears and phobias. Four of the theoretical/therapeutic frameworks (behavioral, psychoanalytic, Adlerian, and Rogerian positions) generally consider fears and phobias to be learned by children but differ markedly with regard to how such behaviors are learned. The fifth view (biological/organic position) considers fears and phobias to be related to biological conditions in the person, i.e., the child has a predisposition toward the development of the fear.

Fears/Phobias Are Learned.   Those individuals who identify with the behaviorally-oriented approach generally take the position that through principles of learning a person's immediate environment sets the occasion for and maintains the level of his/her fear or phobia (e.g., Bandura, 1969; Wolpe, 1958). Therefore, children learn to avoid a particular object, event, or situation through their conditioning history. On the other hand, many who follow a psychoanalytic perspective maintain that the basis for a child's fear or phobia is found in the Oedipal complex. Children become fixated in the Oedipal or pre-Oedipal stage of psychosexual development, and the object, event, or situation they fear represents a substitute on which they project their particular fears of the parent of the opposite sex (e.g., Freud, 1909).

From a Rogerian perspective, a child's fear or phobia is a result of being in a state of incongruence between his/her own perceptions of himself/herself and the actual experiences encountered. As incongruence increases, the child experiences or feels anxiety and threat. If these feelings are not incorporated into the child's perceptions of himself/herself, then avoidance of those experiences producing the threat will occur (Rogers, 1951).

Adlerians, on the other hand, generally conceptualize fears and phobias developing out of a child's life style, when there are feelings of low social interest and activity, resulting in discouragement. Although many children show a variety of transitory fears, a particular fear will only become a serious problem if the child is discouraged and the parents provide him/her with attention and sympathy (e.g., Adler, 1964; Dreikurs & Soltz; 1964).

Proponents of a biological/organic approach believe that intense fears and phobias occur independent of a person's learning and that they represent predispositions on the part of the person that are specific to his/her biological, developmental, and/or evolutionary history (e.g., Marks, 1969; Seligman, 1971).

Fears/Phobias Are Learned Separately. With respect to the development of specific fears, we also find both agreement and disagreement among these theoretical/therapeutic frameworks. Most proponents of the behavioral approach maintain that different fears/phobias are learned separately from other fears and phobias, i.e., there are different environmental contingencies and conditions that control the development of each fear/phobia. It is therefore conceivable that a therapist could intervene on one of many fears/phobias a child displays and effect a reduction in the level of one particular fear without expecting a reduction in any of the other fears/phobias.

This view is different from the other four models under review. The psychoanalytic, Adlerian, and Rogerian frameworks view the fears/phobias as interrelated and caused by the same underlying psychological conflict. The fears/phobias therefore represent an attempt by the person to resolve or reduce their underlying conflict. Although the specific nature of the underlying psychological problem differs between the various frameworks (e.g., it is typically sexual for the psychoanalytic position, while for the Adlerians it is related to distorted perceptions and the family constellation), the general belief that an underlying psychological conflict caused these behaviors is held by each position. It follows then, that each fear/phobia is *not* viewed as being learned separately; rather, because they are interrelated the successful resolvement of the underlying psychological conflict will effect a reduction in each of the fears/phobias. From a biological/organic view, each fear/phobia which is related to the same biological/organic condition will occur at the same time. Similarly, by treating the underlying biological/organic condition, the therapist would also effect a reduction in each of the child's fears/phobias.

Insight Is Not Necessary for Reducing Fear. Since proponents of the behavioral approach do not accept the belief that an underlying psychological conflict is responsible for a person's fear or phobia, it follows that they do not assume that insight is a necessary condition for effecting positive behavior change. This is not a view shared by proponents of the psychoanalytic, Adlerian, or Rogerian frameworks. They do believe that internal psychological factors are responsible for the fears/phobias. Insight, therefore, would be necessary for effecting positive change in the child. From the standpoint of the biological/organic proponents, insight is not a necessary condition for effecting positive behavior change.

Fears/Phobias Are a Sample of Child's Behavior and Are Situation Specific. Advocates of the behavioral approach generally view a child's fear(s) as a sample of how the child behaves within particular settings or whenever certain environmental stimuli are present. It therefore follows that fears are seen as situation or setting specific. This belief is not shared by the other four positions. The psychoanalytic, Adlerian, and Rogerian positions maintain that fears are not situation specific, but transcend most settings because the cause is not tied to environmental factors but to internal, psychological ones. A child's fear/phobia is therefore not a sample of his/her behavior in a particular setting, but rather a sign of an underlying psychological conflict. Proponents of the biological/organic position view a fear/phobia as a sign of an underlying biological condition and also maintain that such fears transcend situations.

Emphasis of Treatment Is on the Present.   The emphasis of therapeutic intervention for the behaviorally-oriented person, as well as for proponents of the Rogerian and biological/organic views, is on the present. The behaviorists maintain this view because they generally assume that present environmental circumstances (actual or cognitive) are maintaining the child's behavior. This is not to say that they deny that historical events may have contributed to, or were responsible for, a child's fear, but only that such events can not be manipulated. Historical conditioning events are emphasized only if they are also presently contributing to the child's fear (e.g., Kazdin & Wilson, 1978). The Rogerians maintain that the child is presently suffering (e.g., experiencing fears/phobias) because of present life circumstances and threats to his/her actual or real self-concept. Therapy, therefore, also concentrates on the present. Similarly, intervention for proponents of the biological/organic position also concentrates on the here-and-now, because it is assumed that one cannot change a person's biological or evolutionary past. The only direction one can take is to treat the person's symptoms, fears, or phobias in the present—in some cases, as almost a "symptom-relief" therapy. In contrast, the emphasis of treatment for proponents of the psychoanalytic and Adlerian positions is on past/historical events which may have contributed to the child's behavior, particularly those involving interactions with the child's parents or sibling and/or the family constellation.

Goals of Therapy Are Specific.   Because proponents of the behavioral approach assume that fears and phobias are situation specific, under the control of environmental factors, and learned independently of other fears and phobias, they view the goals of therapy as being very specific, e.g., the reduction of a particular fear/phobia within a particular setting(s). A similar specific treatment goal is also maintained by proponents of the biological/organic position. This view, however, is not shared by those individuals who follow either the psychoanalytic, Adlerian, or Rogerian models. A general goal of psychoanalytic therapy, for example, is the reorganization of the person's personality and the establishment of intrapsychic harmony. In Adlerian therapy, a major goal is to help the child, achieve self-realization, and "the enhancement of social interest" (Mosak, 1979). Therapists following a Rogerian model maintain that the goal of therapy is also general, namely, to assist the child in reaching his/her own level of self-actualization—or the child's highest level of potential functioning.

Fears/Phobias Caused by Environment; Unconscious Factors Play No Essential Role.   It follows from what has already been discussed that from a behavioral perspective "unconscious" factors do not contribute to the development, maintenance, or treatment of children's fears and related problems. The emphasis of etiological investigations and treatment is on those environmental circumstances that might contribute to an increase or decrease in the frequency of the fears. This is in contrast to the psychoanalytic and Adlerian approaches which view unconscious factors as important variables to any investigation of the etiology and treatment of children's fears. Therefore, underlying psychological conflicts are also important considerations for the therapist in dealing with a child's fear/phobia. Rogerians do not discuss in detail the concept of the unconscious but maintain that underlying psychological conflicts are major contributors to a person's fears/phobias. Proponents of the biological/organic position do not consider unconscious factors as contributors to the development and treatment of children's fears, but do maintain that biological conditions are responsible for the development of these fears.

The reader should recognize that each of the theoretical/therapeutic frameworks discussed here is comprised of a set of working assumptions regarding the development and treatment of most childhood behavior disorders. These assumptions cannot be proven directly because each is too general. We must await well-controlled and replicated research to determine objectively which set of working assumptions is more likely to effect positive behavior change under particular conditions.

OVERVIEW OF ETIOLOGICAL THEORIES
OF FEARS/PHOBIAS

As we mentioned in the previous section, there have been numerous theoretical positions presented in the literature on the etiology of fears and phobias. In addition to the behaviorally-oriented theories of fear development, four commonly discussed theories are the psychoanalytic, Adlerian, Rogerian, and biological/organic positions. In the present section, we will briefly review these various theories. We should note, however, that very little controlled research has been published in the literature that either supports or refutes these theories with regard to children.

Freud's Psychoanalytic View

Sigmund Freud articulated his theory of the etiology of phobias in children in the very detailed case of "Little Hans" (Freud, 1909). Hans was almost five years old and was very afraid of horses. His fear that a horse would bite him caused him to be reluctant to leave the house. It was on the basis of these symptoms and information revealed during therapy that Freud formulated his theory, although he never treated Hans directly. Hans' father treated him under Freud's direction and supervision.[3] Because of the detailed analysis of this case by Freud, a number of writers (Achenbach, 1974; A. Freud, 1981; Marks, 1969; Rachman, 1978) have commented on its relative importance to and impact on psychoanalytic theory. For example, Anna Freud (1981) stated:

> What the analysis of Little Hans opened up is a new branch of psychoanalysis, more than the extension of its therapy from the adult to the child — namely, the possibility of a new perspective on the development of the individual and on the successive conflicts and compromises between the demands of the drive, the ego, and the external world which accompany the child's laborious steps from immaturity to maturity [p. 278].

Achenbach (1974) commented:

> The case was of great significance because it revealed Freud's hypothesized Oedipal dynamics at work in a child rather than through reconstructions by adults during analytic treatment. It showed the child's concern with sexual matters, his concern about the absence of a penis in females, his fear of castration as a retaliation for masturbating and for having sexual desires toward his mother, and his fear and hostility toward his father [pp. 268–269].

Freud (1909) pointed out that this case was significant since it was the first published account of child analysis, and it was viewed by him as supporting his theoretical position.

At age 4¾ years, Hans developed a severe fear that a horse would bite him in the street. It seems that one day while he was walking in the street with his nursemaid, he developed "an attack of morbid anxiety." He felt that he wanted to return home and be with his mother and "to coax with her."[4] The next day his mother took him for a walk in the same vicinity as the day before to see if she could discover what had troubled him. After a while he began to cry again and was frightened. On the way back home, he related to his mother, "I was afraid a horse would bite me." (Freud, 1909, p. 167). Earlier in the week he also awoke one morning crying and said to his mother, " 'When I was asleep I thought you were gone and I had no Mummy to coax with' " (Freud, 1909, p. 166). His fear of the horse apparently generalized to horses pulling carts, horses that moved or drove fast, horses that had certain physical characteristics (e.g., horses with black around their mouths and with blinders), and horses that could possibly fall down. It also generalized to other big animals such as elephants and giraffes.

Freud's interpretation of the development of Hans' phobia centered on his Oedipal conflicts. He had hostile and jealous feelings toward his father and sexual feelings/impulses toward his mother ("premonitions, as it were, of copulation"). Freud maintained that Hans hated his father because he saw him as a rival for his mother and wanted to take "possession" of his mother. Hans also feared punishment from his father in the form of castration because of his hostile feelings toward him and his sexual attraction to his mother. Freud felt that Hans repressed these hostile feelings and castration anxiety and "transposed [displaced them] from his father on to the horses." In support the fact that his father wore eyeglasses. As mentioned earlier, Freud noted that this case clearly provided support for his theoretical statement regarding the development of a phobia. We should add, however, that little or no well-controlled research has been published to support this theory (cf. Marks, 1969).

Adlerian View

Although Alfred Adler was one of the charter members of Freud's Vienna Psychoanalytic Society and later its president, he developed ideas at variance with the group and resigned in 1911. Thereafter he formed his own group which was known as Individual Psychology. Adlerian approaches to personality can be regarded as psychodynamic, but are distinguished from Freudian psychoanalysis.[5] Mosak (1979) has listed several differences between Freud and Adler. For example, in contrast to Freud, who assumed that human behavior is motivated by inborn instincts, Adler assumed that human beings are motivated primarily by social factors. Second, Adler introduced the notion of the creative self which was perceived as a highly personalized, subjective system that directed experiences for the person. This contrasts with the Freudian concept of ego which served the ends of inborn instincts. Third, Adler emphasized the uniqueness of each individual personality. In contrast to Freud's early views which held that sexual instincts were central in personality dynamics, Adler stressed that each person is a unique configuration of social factors (e.g., motives, traits, values, interests). Fourth, in dramatic contrast to Freud's heavy emphasis on unconscious processes, Adler made consciousness the center of personality. This is not to deny the emphasis in Adlerian psychology on dynamics of personality where some unconscious processes direct the individual.

For Adler, psychopathological behavior is not regarded as a "mental illness" in the usual sense. Individuals demonstrating deviant behavior are said to be involved in mistaken ways of living. The mistaken life style involves mistakes about oneself, the world, goals of success, and a low level of social interest and activity. "The neurotic by virtue of his ability to choose, creates difficulty for himself by setting up a 'bad me' (symptoms, 'ego-alien' thoughts, 'bad behavior') that prevents him from implementing his good intentions" (Mosak, 1979, p. 46).

Pathological forms of behavior can develop also in childhood. Adler noted that the first four or five years of life lay the foundation for the life style. Adler also acknowledged the significance of the mother in positive social development, noting that three negative factors could endanger the process: imperfect organs and childhood diseases, pampering, and neglect. Adler (1964b) noted that the neglected or unwanted child tries to escape and stay a safe distance from others. Specific childhood problems (such as fears and phobias), however, are not conceptualized any differently from any other childhood behavior disorder. Fears and phobias, therefore, are considered a "neurotic" problem.

Adler (1964) discussed several interpretations of phobias and fears in both children and adults. In discussing the case, for example, of a 40-year-old man who was afraid of high buildings, Adler related the fear to the goal of superiority, stemming from the person's childhood wherein it was recollected that he was physically attacked the first day of school. Thus, it is recognized that early childhood fear-arousing situations (or the perception of these) can influence adult disturbance. Dreikurs (e.g., Dreikurs, 1972; Dreikurs & Stolz, 1964) has been very consistent in his approach to interpretation of childhood fears. The approach, best summed up in the title of a chapter devoted to the topic in Dreikurs and Stolz' (1964) book, *Children: The Challenge*, is "Be Unimpressed by Fear." Children are said to develop fears only if adults are impressed by them. Thus, a child may show a particular fear, but this becomes a serious problem when the parents provide attention and sympathy. Thus, "Children can have a shock reaction, either by sudden noise, falling down, or a threatening experience. But this reaction will not lead to continued fears if the parents do not try to make up for the 'shock' " (Dreikurs,

1971, p. 437). As in the case of Freudian theory, however, there is little or no well-controlled research with children to support this theoretical position.

Rogerian View

During his years (1928–1939) at the Rochester Guidance Center, Carl Rogers became increasingly dissatisfied with the predominant psychoanalytic approaches of that time and began developing his own approach to treatment and personality development. These views were then refined during his tenure at Ohio State University and the University of Chicago and elaborated upon in later years at the University of Wisconsin, Stanford University, Western Behavioral Sciences Institute, and the Center for Studies of the Person.[6] Although he wrote a great deal on personality development, he did not often address in detail the development of particular forms of behavior disorders in either children or adults, preferring more often to speak in such general terms as "psychological maladjustment." His "client centered therapy" and "theory of personality and behavior" were based on what Rogers (1951, 1959) considered to be "the nature of the individual." For example, he listed the following conclusions on the characteristics of the human organism:

1. The individual possesses the capacity *to experience in awareness* the factors in his *psychological maladjustment*, namely, the incongruences between his *self-concept* and the totality of his *experience*.
2. The individual possesses the capacity and has the tendency to reorganize his *self-concept* in such a way as to make it more congruent with the totality of his *experience*, thus moving himself away from a state of *psychological maladjustment* and toward a state of *psychological adjustment*.
3. These capacities and this tendency, when latent rather than evident, will be released in any interpersonal *relationship* in which the other person is *congruent* in the *relationship*, experiences *unconditional positive regard* toward, and *empathic* understanding of, the individual, and achieves some communication of these attitudes to the individual [Rogers, 1959, p. 221].

The conclusions were based on his fundamental or central hypothesis that "the individual has the capacity to guide, regulate, and control himself, providing only that certain definable conditions exist" (Rogers, 1959, p. 221). That is, when a person is provided with certain reasonable conditions for psychological growth, s/he will work toward constructive change and become self-actualized.

From Rogers' view any form of psychological maladjustment results when there is some degree of incongruence between an individual's self-structure and his/her experience. This state of incongruence, often referred to as "vulnerability", could then result in the person experiencing feelings of threat—assuming the threat was symbolized into awareness. Once the feelings of threat were in awareness, the person would then enter a state of anxiety. In order to prevent this threat from entering awareness, a process of defense may take place, thereby maintaining consistency in the person's self-structure. The process of defense, however, may not operate successfully if there is a rather large incongruence between the individual's self and experience. This state of incongruence would then be symbolized in awareness. Anxiety would result, and a state of disorganization takes place. When such a state is present, Rogers (1959) noted that the individual's tendency toward self-actualization would be blocked.

As we mentioned earlier, Rogers did not separate out particular behavior disorders and explain how his theory accounted for their development. This is the case for fears and phobias in children. One might speculate, however, that a childhood phobia would develop when a child feels threat in a particular non-dangerous situation. This would indicate that a state of incongruence had occurred between the child's experience and his/her self-structure, that the process of defense was not successful, and as a result that the incongruence had been symbolized into awareness producing anxiety/threat and avoidance of the particular situation. The state of incongruence would remain in the child until the phobic situation was accurately symbolized into his/her self-structure. The feelings of threat would then be reduced, the child would no longer be fearful, and s/he would continue toward achieving self-actualization.[7]

There is little research published on Rogers' theory of personality and behavior, although substantial process and outcome research has been conducted on his client-centered therapy approach that is consistent with his theoretical perspective (see, for example, Rogers, 1951, 1959). Rogers' personality theory is essentially a philosophical statement about the nature of individuals—their striving and potentialities—rather than a systematic set of principles concerning personality development. It therefore follows that he would not be directly concerned with the etiology of particular behavior problems like children's fears and phobias, even though advocates of this therapeutic position would treat children who manifest such behaviors.

Biological/Organic View

A great deal has been written on the biological/organic origins of fears, phobias, and related problems (see, for example, Delprato, 1980; Gray, 1971; Marks, 1969; Mathews, Gelder & Johnston, 1981; Seligman, 1971; Sluckin, 1979). These writings are typically directed toward adult fears and phobias, to the biological nature of fears in animals (e.g., Russelli, 1979;

Salzen, 1979), or to fears associated with "normal" stages of child development (see pp. 7–9), with little being written specifically about the etiology of children's "non-developmental" fears and phobias (e.g., Gray, 1971; Smith, 1979). In contrast to the dearth of literature on the biological basis of children's fears and related problems, there is a relative abundance of recent literature on the biological/psychopharmacological treatment of these behaviors (see, for example, Algozzine, 1981; Gittleman-Klein, 1975, 1978; Gittleman-Klein & Klein, 1973; Klein, Gittleman, Quitkin & Rifkin, 1980).

The general working assumption/supposition of most writers who follow a biological or constitutional perspective to the development of fears and phobias can be summarized in the following manner:

> The genes do indeed influence the predisposition to neurotic illness in a number of ways, in particular in their effect on personality and on the kind of disorder an individual is most likely to develop under stress. Neurotics should, therefore, tend to differ from non-neurotics and amongst themselves in biological variables [Shields, 1978, p. 166].

In their review of the biological model of phobias and related problems, Mavissakalian and Barlow (1981b) state that the biological predisposition to which Shields is referring can also be referred to as "anxiety-proneness." Broadly speaking, this type of conceptualization appears to be what Gittleman-Klein and Klein (1973) were referring to in their discussion of one possible etiological view of separation anxiety in school phobic children. Following Bowlby's (1969, 1973) position, they suggested that wide constitutional variations can occur in the threshold of the theorized "biological phenomenon" of separation anxiety. Assuming this may be the case, they state:

> severe separation anxiety [the type associated with school phobia] may be seen as a pathological manifestation of a normal biological developmental process, around which secondary anxieties may be learned. If such were the case, one would expect relatively little alteration of the biological anxiety threshold via verbal or management therapeutic efforts [Gittleman-Klein & Klein, 1973, p. 214].

Although some research has been reported in the adult phobia literature that supports the anxiety-proneness view (cf. Mavissakalian & Barlow, 1981a), little or no theoretical research of this nature has been conducted with children (e.g., Smith, 1979).

Another etiological view has been discussed by Seligman (1971). He suggested that human phobias are a form of "prepared" classical (Pavlovian) conditioning, i.e., biologically prepared forms of conditioning. His model emerged out of criticisms he had with the learning or behavioral views (see discussion below) of the development of phobias. Specifically, Seligman (1971) maintained the following:

(1) phobias do not extinguish under conventional procedures which reliably extinguish classically conditioned fear in the laboratory [p. 308].
(2) There is a common misconception among clinicians about the extinction of conditioned fear in the laboratory. . . . The misconception arises from a careless interpretation of the avoidance learning literature, a leap from the fact that avoidance responding does not extinguish to the mistaken inference that conditioned fear does not extinguish [p. 309].
(3) Implicit in the general process learning view of phobias is the assumption that they can be learned in one trial. . . . One-trial conditioning of fear is the exception, not the rule, in laboratory fear conditioning [p. 311].
(4) According to Pavlov's view of conditioning, the choice of CS is a matter of indifference. . . . This is the heart of the general process view of learning . . . any CS which happens to be associated with trauma should become phobic. But a neglected fact about phobias is that by and large they comprise a relatively nonarbitrary and limited set of objects . . . events related to the survival of the human species [p. 312].

Seligman therefore felt that there was a selectivity associated with the development of fears and phobias, and that this selective learning process had its basis in evolution. That is, he believed phobias were "prepared" in humans. The degree of a person or organism's preparedness for a particular fear or phobia was defined in the following manner:

The relative preparedness of an organism for learning about a situation is defined by the amount of input (e g , numbers of trials, pairings, bits of information, etc.) which must occur before that output (responses, acts, repertoire, etc.) which is construed as evidence of acquisition, reliably occurs [Seligman, 1970, p. 408].

Instinctive responding represents the (extreme) *prepared* end of the preparedness dimension; a response that occurs consistently after only a few pairings is viewed as *somewhat prepared* on the dimension; a response that takes place consistently only after many pairings is viewed as *unprepared*; and, finally, if a response occurs only after "very many" pairings or does not occur at all, it is viewed as *contraprepared* (Seligman, 1970). Seligman (1971) maintains that the prepared learning category provides a good fit for phobias because phobias (1) can be learned in one trial, (2) are selective, (3) show resistance to extinction, and (4) may be noncognitive.

Although a fair amount of systematic research has been conducted on this model with adults, college-age students, and laboratory animals, little or no research has been conducted on the preparedness of children's fears or phobias (see, for example, Clark, 1979; Delprato, 1980; de Silva, Rachman & Seligman, 1977). Although the research findings (e.g., Hugdahl, Fredrikson, & Öhman, 1977; Öhman, Eriksson, & Olofsson, 1975; Öhman, Erixon, & Lofberg, 1975) with adults are interesting, at least one writer (Delprato, 1980) has commented that the research data either have "limited" implications "for the inheritance of dispositions to acquire fear," or have "led to evidence in direct conflict with the evolutionary hypothesis" (Delprato, 1980, p. 90). Only a few studies (e.g., McNally & Reiss, 1982) have reported data which are inconsistent with the preparedness theory position.

Behavioral View

Behavioral conceptualizations of the development of fears and phobias have their roots in the learning theory positions of Pavlov (1927), Skinner (1938, 1953), Hull (1943), Mowrer (1939, 1960), and Bandura (1969, 1977; Bandura & Walters, 1963). Generally speaking, most etiological statements regarding fear development include Pavlov's classical conditioning notion in their explanation. Other views are based strictly on an operant conditioning framework or a social-learning perspective.

Perhaps, the most famous as well as the oldest fear development study in behavioral psychology was conducted by Watson and Rayner (1920) involving an 11-month-old child called Little Albert. These investigators reported that through classical conditioning they could teach a child to become afraid of a live white rat, and that this conditioned fear could be generalized to a fear of other animals and furry-like objects (e.g., a white rabbit, a dog, a piece of cotton). Initially, it was reported that the rat did not elicit any fear reaction from the child, but after its presence was paired with a loud noise, it elicited fear responses from Albert. Although few writers within the behavioral view would question the impact and relative contribution of Watson and Rayner's findings, a number of writers (e.g., Costello, 1970; Harris, 1979; Marks, 1969; Seligman, 1970) have cited later studies by other researchers who were not able to replicate or demonstrate this fear conditioning in young children when more neutral objects (e.g., wooden blocks) were used instead of a furry rat. Delprato (1980), however, questions such studies on methodological grounds and suggests that sufficient data have not yet been gathered to refute the Watson and Rayner findings.

Another view that integrated the classical and instrumental conditioning notions was developed by Mowrer (1939, 1960) and called *two-factor learning theory*. In essence, Mowrer combined classical conditioning with Hullian instrumental learning to account for the conditioning and maintenance of a fear response. He maintained that fear was a classically conditioned response (CR) that came about by the pairing of an aversive unconditioned stimulus

(UCS) with a previous neutral stimulus (CS). The conditioned fear response (CR) motivates avoidance behavior in the organism whenever the CS is present, and this avoidance behavior reduces the CR which, in turn, reinforces the organism for engaging in the avoidance behavior (Carr, 1979). This was one of the most prevailing views of fear development up through the 1960s when writers began critically evaluating and questioning this perspective (e.g., Bandura, 1969; Graziano et al., 1979; Rachman, 1976b, 1977).

Mowrer's view also assisted Wolpe (1958) in conceptualizing his theory of the development and treatment of fears, phobias, and related problems. Wolpe maintained that neurotic behavior (fears, phobias, and so forth) was a persistent, unadaptive habit which was learned and, as such, could be unlearned. He further wrote that neurotic behavior was learned through temporal contiguity of the stimulus and response (classical conditioning) and maintained by drive reduction (Hullian instrumental learning). Thus, what we have here is a conditioning paradigm where fear mediates instrumental avoidance behavior on the part of the organism. Wolpe further maintained, in marked contrast to Seligman (1970, 1971), the general process view toward learning that was described above.

> Experimentally it is possible to condition an animal to respond with anxiety to any stimulus one pleases merely by arranging for that stimulus, on a number of occasions, to appear in an appropriate time relation to the evocation of anxiety. . . . In human neuroses one can usually elicit a history of similar kinds of conditioning [Wolpe, 1964, p. 10].

Support for Mowrer's theory began to erode around the very early 1970s. Marks (1969), for example, commented after reviewing two factor theory that it does not explain the tremendous resistance to extinction found with avoidance responses. He stated:

> In theory, as avoidance responses continue the classically conditioned CER is no longer reinforced and should extinguish. This should lead in turn to extinction of the avoidance response. But in practice neither the CER nor the avoidance response are easily extinguished [Marks, 1969, p. 59].

Another weakness mentioned in the literature has been the demonstration that avoidance behavior can be learned independent of the presence of mediating fear or anxiety; fear is not apparently necessary as an antecedent factor to effect avoidance behavior (e.g., Carr, 1979; Seligman & Johnston, 1973).

A third behavioral view of the development of fears and phobias is based on operant conditioning (e.g., Skinner, 1938, 1953). One of the most articulate explanations of this view was outlined by Ayllon, Smith, and Rogers

(1970) in their article on the behavior management of a school phobic child. First, an operant approach assumes that the target behaviors associated with the "school phobia" are learned, and that aspects of the child's environment are responsible for these targeted behaviors. Even the term "school phobia" is rarely used except as a general summary term for communication/descriptive purposes (as in the title of the Ayllon et al. article). Instead, the "phobia" is defined in terms of observable behaviors—in the case of "school phobia" as low frequency school attendance. Thus, low school attendance is assumed to be a function of the child's environment. For example, when a child begins to fuss and cry about attending school, it is conceivable that the parents might let him/her stay home. If the home environment was more attractive to the child than the school environment then there would be a high probability that s/he would become "ill" again. To the extent that parents supported their child in not attending school, then his/her low frequency school attendance would be causally tied to parental consent and support (reinforcement) for this activity. Empirical support for this operant position of fear and phobia development in children is lacking at the present time. It seems that most investigators who have conducted research over the past 10 to 20 years on children's fears and phobias have not identified strongly with the operant approach. As a consequence, fewer etiological studies have been published using humans, although a substantial body of research exists using laboratory animals.

The fourth model involves social learning theory approaches (e.g., Bandura, 1969, 1977; Bandura & Walters, 1963) to the etiology of fears and phobias in children. This perspective involves the conditioning of a fear in a person through vicarious learning. Here the person acquires a fear or avoidance behavior by directly observing a model being exposed to a traumatic event in the fear situation and acquiring a symbolic representation of the modeled event. As Bandura (1971) states, "Social learning theory . . . assumes that modeling influences operate principally through their informative function, and that observers acquire mainly symbolic representations of modeled events rather than specific stimulus-response connections" (p. 16). The modeling activity, in turn, is governed by four subprocesses: observer attentional processes; observer retention processes; observer motoric reproduction processes; and reinforcement and motivational processes to regulate the observer's overt expression of the modeled behavior. Marks (1969) maintains that there is "ample experimental evidence" for the development of fears through this modeling process in both animals and people. For example, in a study by Bandura and Rosenthal (1966), observers who viewed a model receive shock associated with a buzzer as part of a conditioning experiment, showed increase levels of physiological reactivity when the buzzer was presented to them, even though they had no history of being shocked when the buzzer went on.

More recently, Bandura (1977a) has noted that behavior change procedures may serve the function of creating and strengthening "personal efficacy." A distinction is made between outcome expectations that relate to whether or not a behavior will result in a certain consequence and efficacy expectations that relate to a personal conviction that the individual can perform a particular behavior. For example, an efficacy expectation would relate to a child's expectation that he/she could enter a darkened area of the house. Outcome expectations could include such factors as reinforcement from the parents and the child's own satisfaction that this behavior can be performed. More detailed accounts of the self-efficacy construct can be found in Bandura (1977 a,b; 1978).

Of the four behavioral views presented here, the one that has a fair amount of research to support its view on the development of fears in children is the social learning position. Research in this area, however, has been on fairly focused fears (e.g., dogs, snakes, etc.). It is therefore not clear at this point whether the social learning position will be able to account for the development of more clinically-relevant fears and phobias that are seen in children (e.g., leaving the sight of one's parents; taking tests; being alone; school; using public toilets; swimming; heights; riding in cars; and so forth).

OVERVIEW OF BOOK

Subsequent chapters in this book provide the reader with detailed discussions of various components of the behavioral treatment and assessment of fears and phobias and related problems in children. Chapters 2 and 3 are concerned with the area of diagnosis and assessment and also review incidence and definitional issues. Chapters 4 and 5 concentrate on detailed descriptions of various behavioral methods for reducing fears, phobias, and related problems in children. Specifically, Chapter 4 reviews the desensitization and flooding therapies, while Chapter 5 discusses the contingency management, modeling, and self-control therapies. Each of these latter chapters also includes reviews of the therapy research supporting each method, as well as a discussion of variations in the use of these methods. Chapter 6 concentrates on methodological issues and the conduct of outcome research in the area of childhood fears, phobias, and related problems. The intended purpose of the book is to provide those students who are currently in training, as well as the practicing therapist, counselor, social worker, and teacher with the most up-to-date thinking in the area of behavioral approaches to assessing and treating childhood fears and phobias.

Note

Individuals involved as either practitioners or researchers in behavioral assessment and treatment must embrace sound ethical and legal considerations in these practices. Although we have not provided in this book a review of these various considerations in the application of behavioral approaches to the treatment of children's fears and phobias, we would like to emphasize that the Association for the Advancement of Behavior Therapy has provided guidelines for the practice of behavior therapy. These guidelines have been reproduced in Table 1.3.

Individuals unfamiliar with these guidelines should take the time to carefully study them and their implications for the research on and practice of behavior therapy. In addition to this we would emphasize that readers consider studying the behavior therapy literature that has outlined some of the major ethical and legal considerations in behavioral approaches to assessment and treatment (see, for example, Kazdin, 1980; Schwizgabel & Schwizgabel, 1980).

Table 1.3. Ethical Issues for Human Services

The questions related to each issue have deliberately been cast in a general manner that applies to all types of interventions and not solely or specifically to the practice of behavior therapy. Issues directed specifically to behavior therapists might imply erroneously that behavior therapy was in some way more in need of ethical concern than non-behaviorally-oriented therapies.

In the list of issues, the term "client" is used to describe the person whose behavior is to be changed, "therapist" is used to describe the professional in charge of the intervention; "treatment" and "problem," although used in the singular, refer to any and all treatments and problems being formulated with this checklist. The issues are formulated so as to be relevant across as many settings and populations as possible. Thus, they need to be qualified when someone other than the person whose behavior is to be changed is paying the therapist, or when that person's competence or the voluntary nature of that person's consent is questioned. For example, if the therapist has found that the client does not understand the goals or methods being considered, the therapist should substitute the client's guardian or other responsible person for "client," when reviewing the issues below.

A.   Have the goals of treatment been adequately considered?
   1. To insure that the goals are explicit, are they written?
   2. Has the client's understanding of the goals been assured by having the client restate them orally or in writing?
   3. Have the therapist and client agreed on the goals of therapy?
   4. Will serving the client's interests be contrary to the interests of other persons?
   5. Will serving the client's immediate interests be contrary to the client's long-term interest?

B.   Has the choice of treatment methods been adequately considered?
   1. Does the published literature show the procedure to be the best one available for that problem?
   2. If no literature exists regarding the treatment method, is the method consistent with generally accepted practice?

Table 1.3. (*continued*)

3. Has the client been told of alternative procedures that might be preferred by the client on the basis of significant differences in discomfort, treatment time, cost, or degree of demonstrated effectiveness?
4. If a treatment procedure is publicly, legally, or professionally controversial, has formal professional consultation been obtained, has the reaction of the affected segment of the public been adequately considered, and have the alternative treatment methods been more closely reexamined and reconsidered?

C. Is the client's participation voluntary?
1. Have possible sources of coercion on the client's participation been considered?
2. If treatment is legally mandated, has the available range of treatments and therapists been offered?
3. Can the client withdraw from treatment without a penalty or financial loss that exceeds actual clinical costs?

D When another person or an agency is empowered to arrange for therapy, have the interests of the subordinated client been sufficiently considered?
1. Has the subordinated client been informed of the treatment objectives and participated in the choice of treatment procedures?
2. Where the subordinated client's competence to decide is limited, have the client as well as the guardian participated in the treatment discussions to the extent that the client's abilities permit?
3. If the interests of the subordinated person and the superordinate persons or agency conflict, have attempts been made to reduce the conflict by dealing with both interests?

E. Has the adequacy of treatment been evaluated?
1. Have quantitative measures of the problem and its progress been obtained?
2. Have the measures of the problem and its progress been made available to the client during treatment?

F. Has the confidentiality of the treatment relationship been protected?
1. Has the client been told who has access to the records?
2. Are records available only to authorized persons?

G. Does the therapist refer the clients to other therapists when necessary?
1. If treatment is unsuccessful, is the client referred to other therapists?
2. Has the client been told that if dissatisfied with the treatment, referral will be made?

H. Is the therapist qualified to provide treatment?
1. Has the therapist had training or experience in treating problems like the client's?
2. If deficits exist in the therapist's qualifications, has the client been informed?
3. If the therapist is not adequately qualified, is the client referred to other therapists, or has supervision by a qualified therapist been provided? Is the client informed of the supervisory relation?
4. If the treatment is administered by mediators, have the mediators been adequately supervised by a qualified therapist?

Source: Association for Advancement of Behavior Therapy. Ethical issues for human services. *Behavior Therapy*, 1977, **8**, v–vi. Reproduced by permission.

NOTES

1. Throughout this book, the unquoted case descriptions have been changed to protect the anonymity of the clients involved.

2. We should note that our conceptualization of different models represents an amalgamation of many views which have been published within one of the summarized frameworks. Thus, although one might find some differences within each perspective, we believe that each view within a particular framework maintains a similar core of assumptions which on a higher order binds the differing views together into one conceptual framework.

3. Freud (1909), however, does report "It is true that I laid down the general lines of the treatment, and that on one single occasion, when I had a conversation with the boy, I took a direct share in it [i.e., the boy's treatment]; but the treatment itself was carried out by the boy's father" (p. 149).

4. Freud (1909) notes in a footnote that "to coax" was Hans' "expression for 'to carress' " (p. 166).

5. The interested reader is referred to Adler's original writing for a more extensive discussion of his theory (see, for example, Adler, 1938, 1964a, 1968).

6. The interested reader is referred to Rogers' original writings for a more extensive discussion of his theoretical and therapeutic orientation (see, for example, Rogers, 1942, 1951, 1959).

7. Portions of this analysis are based on Clark's (1979) interpretation of the application of Rogers' theory to fear development in children.

CHAPTER 2

Diagnosis, Classification, and Incidence

Throughout the history of psychology and psychiatry, various profession-als have attempted to differentiate fear, phobia, and anxiety and map their unique characteristics. For example, phobias first achieved a separate diag-nostic label in the International Classification of Diseases in 1947 and in the American Psychiatric Association in 1952 (Marks, 1969). Yet the process of classifying fear and phobia so that various events associated with these problems may be measured and communicated among professionals is still quite primitive. One reason for this likely relates to the more basic problem of diagnosis and classification in general. Indeed, it can be noted that psy-chiatry and psychology have basically failed to develop a comprehensive system of classification that unifies and transcends specialty areas (Adams, Doster, & Calhoun, 1977).

In this chapter we present an overview of some issues in diagnosis and classification of childhood fears, phobias, and related problems. Although the primary focus is on these childhood problems, we discuss them within the context of some of the major issues raised in diagnosis and classification of behavior disorders in general. Yet our discussion is far from comprehensive in this general domain. The interested reader is referred to several texts devoted to the topic of psychiatric diagnosis (e.g., Spitzer & Klein, 1978) as well as several other sources (Adams et al., 1977; Begelman, 1976; Phillips, Draguns, & Bartlett, 1975; Quay, 1979; Ullman & Krasner, 1969). In addi-tion, we discuss some major issues in the incidence of fears and phobias. Methodological and conceptual issues relevant to diagnosis, classification, and incidence are also presented.

DEFINITIONS: FEARS, PHOBIAS, AND ANXIETIES

Despite any appearance of consensus on definitions of fear, phobia, and anxiety in the professional literature, individuals within and across theoreti-cal persuasions have generally disagreed on these terms. The lack of agree-

ment stems in part from the different theoretical perspectives of those working in the field. Other reasons lie in the process of defining activities
themselves. For example, Begelman (1976) noted that there are at least 11
distinguishable activities in the clinical literature that have been associated
with developing definitions. Each of the common terms used in the field are
considered within the context of conceptual and methodological issues.

Problems of Definition

Problems of definition are somewhat of an understatement in the literature
on childhood fears. Such terms as "fear," "anxiety," "phobia," "avoidance
behavior," are used somewhat differently and sometimes interchangeably
within and among different theoretical positions. Indeed, there is a rather
extensive literature on the definition of fears that raises both genetic and
environmental learning components of this construct. It is impossible to
review all the different definitions and the bases for the differences among
them here. The interested reader is referred to several sources for a detailed
discussion of these issues (e.g., Gray, 1971; Sluckin, 1979).

Since fear has been conceptualized as one of the human emotions, one
might look to the motivation (emotion) literature to improve our analysis of
definitions of fear. Unfortunately, work in this area will not elucidate definitions in this area. We have decided to use some of the conventional terminology from the clinical literature, realizing that there are problems with this
approach. A major problem with terminology in the clinical literature is that
various terms in their descriptive functions have typically referred to *general*
conditions. Yet each of the conditions have a variety of manifestations and
involve considerable diversity in behavior (Thornson, 1979). Consider the
following conventional distinctions. Fear has been regarded as a *normal*
reaction to a real or perceived threat involving subjective feelings of discomfort, avoidance of the stimulus purported to be fear provoking, and actual
physiological change in the organism (e.g., sweating, rapid heart beat). For
example, many children experience fear of dentists due to discomfort associated with dental visits. This fear is likely to be "rational" in that actual
pain may be inflicted (Melamed, 1979). Yet there is considerable disagreement over the *manifestations* of the fear.

As we discussed in Chapter 1, a distinction is often made between fears
and phobias. Phobias have been regarded as a special form of fear, which,
according to Marks (1969) (1) *is out of proportion to demands of the situation*,
(2) *cannot be reasoned away,* (3) *is beyond voluntary control, and* (4) *leads to
avoidance of the feared situation* (p. 3). Miller et al. (1974) expanded on this
formulation, noting that a phobia is a special form of fear which:

1. Is out of proportion to demands of the situation.
2. Cannot be explained or reasoned away.
3. Is beyond voluntary control.
4. Leads to avoidance of the feared situation.
5. Persists over an extended period of time.
6. Is unadaptive.
7. Is not age or stage specific [p. 90].

Generally then, fears and phobias have been distinguished on the basis of their persistence, maladaptiveness, and magnitude (e.g., Barrios, Hartmann, & Shigetomi, 1981; Berecz & Crider, 1949; Graziano et al., 1979; Marks, 1969; Miller et al., 1974).

Phobias have sometimes been labeled *clinical fears* usually through the criteria described above. Graziano et al. (1979) suggested that some children might be classed as having fears of clinical duration. They note that "Intensity and duration might be important defining characteristics and we suggest that "clinical fears" be defined as those with a duration of over 2 years, or an intensity that is debilitating to the client's routine life style" (p. 805).

Fear and phobia have not been the only terms used in the clinical literature. The term "anxiety" has also been used across various theoretical positions. Anxiety has sometimes been distinguished from fears on the basis of the specificity of the eliciting stimuli and accompanying response (cf. Jersild, 1954). Anxiety is also sometimes regarded as more diffuse (Barrios et al., 1981), yet it has also been linked to phobias. For example, in the adult literature, Mavissakalian and Barlow (1981b) note:

> Similarly, in clinical parlance, one speaks of the two components of phobia, namely, phobic anxiety and phobic avoidance. Phobic anxiety does not differ qualitatively from nonphobic or spontaneous anxiety. It is essentially a psychophysiological response characterized by rapid heart rate, palpitation, epigastric discomfort, nausea, diarrhea, desire to urinate, dyspnea, and the feeling of choking or suffocation. The pupils are often dilated, the face is flushed, the skin perspires, and the patient suffers from parasthesias and tremulousness, feels dizzy or faint, and often has a sense of weakness and of impending death. At its extreme, this anxiety reaction is called *panic*. The only difference between phobic anxiety and spontaneous anxiety is that the former is experienced only in the actual or imagined presence of the phobic object or situation, which usually leads to escape. As a natural defense, the patient, whenever possible, avoids the phobic situation and hence, the phobic anxiety [p. 2].

Mavissakalian and Barlow (1981b) were primarily focusing on adult disorders, but these reactions might just as easily be applied to characterize child problems in this area. Indeed, the notion of "avoidance behavior" has found its way into the literature on treating children's "anxiety states". Richards and Siegel (1978) noted:

There is a good deal of overlap between anxiety states and avoidance behaviors, of course, with the choice of one or the other labels frequently reflecting a matter of emphasis. Anxiety states usually involve avoidance, and avoidance behaviors usually involve anxiety, but negative emotional states are more pronounced in the anxiety disorders [p. 276].

Some writers have made no distinction between fear and anxiety (e.g., Nietzel & Bernstein, 1981). Anxiety is occasionally treated as a construct (Borkovec, Weerts, & Bernstein, 1977), and in this regard has been used to explain behavior. A perspective on its use in the psychological field is provided by Borkovec et al. (1977):

"Anxiety" entered the psychological lexicon as the English translation of Freud's *Angst*, a word he used to describe the negative affect and physiological arousal that is analogous to the consequence of having food stuck in one's throat (McReynolds, in press; Sarbin, 1964, 1968). Although Freud never specifically defined the unique identifying characteristics of *Angst*, the construct was nevertheless emphasized in his theory of the development of behavior and behavior disorder. Consequently, psychology and psychiatry were faced with the task of measuring and modifying a vague, ill-defined, and metaphorical variable that, over time, was reified (Sarbin, 1964) into a "thing" assumed to be of vital importance in the understanding of human behavior. It is important to note that, in the reification process, anxiety developed a "multiple personality." It has been viewed as transient emotional/physiological behavior (i.e., "He is anxious today"), a dispositional trait ("She is an anxious person"), and a cause or explanation of behavior (i.e., "He overeats because of anxiety"; "Her seductiveness is a defense against anxiety") [pp. 367–368].

As an alternative to the traditional conceptualization of anxiety, Nietzel and Bernstein (1981) advanced four dimensions of the social learning conceptualization of anxiety that are useful for future empirical work in the field:

1. Anxiety is not a trait or personality characteristic that is internal to the individual.
2. Anxiety can be acquired through different learning mechanisms.
3. Anxiety consists of multiple response components.
4. Anxiety response channels are not highly correlated [pp. 216–19].

There are three important aspects of this conceptualization of anxiety that are important when considering children's behavior. First of all, it has been difficult to distinguish among the various terms that have been employed in the literature (i.e., between fears, clinical fears, phobias, anxiety, and avoidance behaviors). One might substitute any one of these various terms for anxiety in the above dimensions. The reason for this is that *labeling* a child has not been especially useful in providing information on how the child will behave (Barrios et al., 1981). Second, even if the first two dimensions are not met with general acceptance (readers from different orientations may object to a social learning formulation), the notion that anxiety, fears, or phobias consist of multiple response components has the possibility of advancing knowledge in the field *independent of theoretical persuasion*. Finally, the notion that anxiety consists of multiple response components, and that these may not be highly related, has important implications for treatment of these various problems. For example, treatment might be focused independently on each specific channel. Thus, our perspective is that the various labels used in the literature should be operationalized within the context of the multiple response components. We introduce this perspective realizing fully that there are a number of conceptual and methodological problems in this area (these issues are discussed in detail in Chapter 6).

Multiple Response Components

An increasingly popular conceptualization of anxiety in both the child and adult literature, formally developed by Lang (1968), and known as "triple response mode" (e.g., Cone, 1979), "multiple response components" (e.g., Nietzel & Bernstein, 1981), or "three response system" (e.g., Kozak & Miller, 1982) has been a view shared by many writers (e.g., Barrios et al., 1981; Hugdahl, 1981; Johnson & Melamed, 1979; Graziano et al., 1979; Marks, 1973; McReynolds, 1976; Melamed & Siegel, 1975; Miller et al., 1974; Phillips, 1977; Rachman, 1978; Richards & Siegal, 1978; Schwartz, 1978). The position is that anxiety is a complex multichannel/response pattern of behavior.

The notion that anxiety/fear can be conceptualized on more than one response dimension is not a completely new concept. An analysis of the concept of fear presented by Kenny (1963) in his book *Actions, Emotion and Will* (Chapter 3, p. 67) presents some early perspectives on how fear can be analyzed by three types of criteria:

1. Firstly, there are fearful circumstances in the human environment—dangerous and threatening objects.
2. Secondly, there are symptoms of fear: physiological changes of the kind discussed in textbooks of physiological psychology in the sections on 'emotion'.
3. Finally, there is action towards the object: intelligent, intentional actions (flight, hiding, evasion, combat, etc.). In an ideal case all three criteria can be identified and 'fear' can be applied as an appropriate classification.
   (a) If a wild animal approaches, X turns pale, breaks into a sweat, screams, runs for shelter, hides, and later says "I was scared stiff". We readily accept 'X was afraid of the lion' as a correct classification.

(b) X displays symptoms of fear and takes action to avoid an object, but there is no genuinely dangerous situation, as in the case of phobias. Here criterion 1 is absent, but 2 and 3 apply.

(c) X shows symptoms of fear but takes no appropriate action, e.g., when 'rooted' to the spot'. Here, criterion 3 is absent, but 1 and 2 apply.

(d) A dangerous situation exists and avoidance action is taken, but there are no symptoms of fear, e.g., X sees a storm approaching and quickly steers his boat into the harbor. Here, criterion 2 is absent, but 1 and 3 apply.

(e) Dangerous circumstances exist but there are no symptoms of fear, and avoidance behavior is absent, e.g., a soldier advances into an area of heavy fire. Later, he says "I was terrified but I did my duty'. Here, criteria 2 and 3 are absent, but 1 applies, supported by subsequent testimony [cited in Thornson, 1979, p. 8].

This early example presented by Kenny (1963) serves to illustrate the multiple criteria that can be used to define fear. Similar approaches have been developed in the clinical literature. For example, Lang's (1968) approach to defining anxiety was based on laboratory fear research in which variables were grouped into three categories: "Fear is a response, and further that it is expressed in three main behavioral systems: verbal (cognitive), overt-motor, and somatic" (p. 90). Similar to the Kenny (1963) analysis of fear, Lang (1968) concluded that fear is not a unitary phenomenon because responses in the three systems were not perfectly correlated.

Conceptualizing fear, phobias, or anxiety in terms of three response systems has philosophical implications (Kozak & Miller, 1982). In the view advanced by Lang (1968, 1978a) and others accepting this position, fear is not regarded as a phenomenological experience, and private events are not regarded as primary scientific data. In order to gain a perspective on this approach to defining fear we briefly review these channels. A more detailed discussion of assessment of these channels is presented in Chapter 3. Methodological and conceptual research issues in these areas are presented in Chapter 6.

Cognitive Systems. One system or channel used to define anxiety is the cognitive or self-report system. This is regarded as a subjective system in that it depends upon the self-report of the client to validate its existence. The self-report may come through direct statements to another (e.g., the child may report that "I'm afraid of dogs" or "I'm afraid to go to school") through self-monitoring data or from response to structured questionnaire items.

Virtually every therapeutic approach reviewed in this text considers self-report as an important source of data to define the concept of fear, phobia, and anxiety. There is, however, considerable variation in the *emphasis* placed on this system in definition within the behavior therapy field. For example, cognitive behaviorists have tended to place much greater emphasis on self-report data than applied behavior analysts, who have been generally critical of exclusive reliance on this data source. We regard the self-report channel as important to definition, and, as we shall later argue, essential in both assessment and treatment efforts.

Physiological Systems.   The physiological channel (also referred to as somatic or visceral) focuses on measurement of the sympathetic portion of the autonomic nervous system (e.g., Nietzel & Bernstein, 1981; Paul & Bernstein, 1973). Anxiety in this channel is assessed by a variety of measures of the autonomic nervous system (e.g., blood pressure, heart rate, galvanic skin response, temperature, muscular tension, respiration rate, etc.). Usually, more than one physiological measure is used to define anxiety in this system. The reason for this is that different physiological measures may not correlate highly (Haynes, 1978).

Motor System.   The third channel is referred to as *motor* or *overt behavior.* Measurement here focuses on the actual overt behavior of the client. This channel has been divided into *direct* and *indirect* measures (Paul & Bernstein, 1973). Direct measures refer to the overt behavioral consequences of physiological arousal. For example, if a child was trembling in the presence of a particular stimulus (e.g., dog, water), this would be a direct measure defining the presence of anxiety. Indirect measures include the class of escape and/or avoidance behaviors from certain stimuli (e.g., running away from a horse).

Considerations.   We believe that it is necessary to define children's fears, phobias, and anxiety within the context of the three systems or channels described above. Evidence for these constructs can come from one or any combination of the three systems. It is not necessary for measures taken from the three systems to correlate highly. It can also be assumed that the lack of a strong relation among the three systems may be due to a variety of factors, all of which need to be measured during assessment activities. Thus, when a fear or anxiety becomes a "problem" for the client and/or his/her providers, the client may display problems in any one or all of the systems. As we shall later argue, this has important implications for both assessment and treatment. Thus assessment will need to be broad-based and focus on each system. Moreover, treatment may be aimed at one or all of the different systems identified as problematic.

DIAGNOSIS AND CLASSIFICATION

Classification efforts go back as far as Hippocrates' division of disorders into three categories: mania, melancholia, and phrenitis (Mahoney, 1980; Yule, 1981). Contemporary diagnostic systems can be traced to the German psychiatrist Emil Kraepelin (1856–1926), who developed a system that has had a profound impact on diagnosis generally (cf. Kazdin, 1978b). For example, the major features of the Kraepelin system and his basic approach to mental disorders have been largely retained and are reflected in the past and current editions of the Diagnostic and Statistical Manual of Mental Disorders (DSM-I, DSM-II, and DSM-III). Two broad classification approaches have been employed in the child area. First, the clinically derived categories are developed such as those of the American Psychiatric Association (DSM-I, 1952; DSM-II, 1968; DSM-III, 1979), the Group for Advancement of Psychiatry, and the World Health Organization (see Rutter, Lebocici, Eisenberg, Sneznevskij, Sadoun, Brooke, & Lin, 1969; Rutter, Shaffer, & Shepherd, 1975; Yule, 1981). A second approach is developed from an empirically-oriented effort in which classification occurs through multivariate statistical procedures (e.g., Achenbach & Edelbrock, 1978; Quay, 1979).

Beyond these two systems, several specific attempts have been made to classify fears and phobias in the child literature. Finally, several attempts have been made to develop more behaviorally-oriented approaches to classification. Each of these approaches is reviewed as it relates to classification of childhood fears and related problems.

Clinically Derived Systems

The World Health Organization International Classification of Diseases 9 (WHO-ICD-9) has developed a classification system for children. The interested reader can find a full description in Rutter et al. (1975). As Yule (1981) has noted, in this system some fine discriminations are difficult to make, as reflected in attempts to discriminate between "abnormal separation anxiety" and "school refusal."

Another clinical system is that developed by the American Psychiatric Association and referred to as DSM-III. Many textbooks in abnormal psychology (e.g., Coleman & Broen, 1972; Ullman & Krasner, 1969) and psychiatry (e.g., Freedman & Kaplan, 1967) have been organized around the DSM system, which can be regarded as a clinically derived classification system (Quay, 1979). In this regard they initially evolved out of the observations of clinicians, who noted the regularity with which certain characteristics occur together. In turn, these are sorted out and serve as the basis of the diagnostic category. This is not to suggest that empirical research is lacking on the DSM systems. In fact, considerable work has been done on DSM-II, although there is a paucity of research at present on the reliability and validity of DSM-III. The DSM-III provides information for the diagnosis of mental, medical, and psychosocial conditions presented by individuals within several diagnostic "axes." That is, a multiaxial diagnostic system is used in which five axes are referenced in diagnosis of individuals:

Axis I. Clinical Syndromes
Conditions not Attributable to a Mental Disorder that are a Focus of Attention or Treatment
Additional Codes
Axis II. Personality Disorders
Specific Developmental Disorders
Axis III. Physical Disorders and Conditions
Axis IV and V are available for use in special clinical and research settings and provide information supplementing the official DSM-III diagnoses (Axes I, II, and III) that may be useful for planning treatment and predicting outcome:
Axis IV. Severity of Psychosocial Stressors
Axis V. Highest level of Adaptive Functioning Past Year [American Psychiatric Association, 1980, p. 23].

In the case of mental disorders (axes I and II), there are over 230 separate categories of disturbance, representing a 60% increase in the total number of psychiatric disorders contained in DSM-II and a 280% increase over DSM-I (McReynolds, 1978).

Anxiety Disorders of Childhood or Adolescence. The DSM-III system proposes three childhood disorders in which anxiety is the predominant clinical feature: *Separation Anxiety Disorder*, *Avoidant Disorder of Childhood or Adolescence*, and *Overanxious Disorder*. In the former two, anxiety is said to focus on specific situations, whereas in the Overanxious Disorder anxiety is said to have generalized to a variety of situations.

Separation Anxiety Disorder. In this problem "the predominant disturbance is excessive anxiety on separation from major attachment figures or from home or other familiar surroundings" (APA, 1980, p. 50). The child may experience anxiety to the point of panic. It is noted that although the disorder represents a form of phobia, it is not included in the Phobic Disorder classification because it has unique features and is typically associated with childhood. The following diagnostic criteria have been advanced by the APA (1980) for Separation Anxiety Disorder:

A. Excessive anxiety concerning separation from those to whom the child is attached, as manifested by at least three of the following:
   1. Unrealistic worry about possible harm befalling major attachment figures or fear that they will leave and not return.
   2. Unrealistic worry that an untoward calamitous event will separate the child from a major attachment figure, e.g., the child will be lost, kidnapped, killed, or be the victim of an accident.
   3. Persistent reluctance or refusal to go to school in order to stay with major attachment figures or at home.
   4. Persistent reluctance or refusal to go to sleep without being next to a major attachment figure or to go to sleep away from home.
   5. Persistent avoidance of being alone in the home and emotional upset if unable to follow the major attachment figure around the home.
   6. Repeated nightmares involving theme of separation.
   7. Complaints of physical symptoms on school days, e.g., stomach aches, headaches, nausea, vomiting.
   8. Signs of excessive distress upon separation, or when anticipating separation, from major attachment figures, e.g., temper tantrums or crying, pleading with parents not to leave (for children below the age of six, the distress must be of panic proportions).
   9. Social withdrawal, apathy, sadness, or difficulty concentrating on work or play when not with a major attachment figure.
B. Duration of disturbance of at least two weeks.
C. Not due to a Pervasive Developmental Disorder, Schizophrenia, or any other psychotic disorder.
D. If 18 or older, does not meet the criteria for Agoraphobia [p. 53].

Avoidant Disorder of Childhood or Adolescence.   In this disorder "the predominant disturbance is a persistent and excessive shrinking from contact with strangers of sufficient severity so as to interfere with social functioning in peer relationships, coupled with a clear desire for affection and acceptance, and relationships with family members and other familiar figures that are warm and satisfying" (APA, 1980, p. 53–54). The following diagnostic criteria from APA (1980) are used for Avoidant Disorder of Childhood or Adolescence:

A. Persistent and excessive shrinking from contact with strangers.
B. Desire for affection and acceptance, and generally warm and satisfying relations with family members and other familiar figures.
C. Avoidant behavior sufficiently severe to interfere with social functioning in peer relationships.
D. Age at least 2½. If 18 or older, does not meet the criteria for Avoidant Personality Disorder.
E. Duration of the disturbance of at least six months [p. 55].

Overanxious Disorder.   This disorder is characterized by excessive worrying and fearful behavior that is not focused on a specific situation or object. Moreover, this disturbance is not due to a recent psychological stressor (e.g., worry about future events). The following diagnostic criteria are used for Overanxious Disorder (APA, 1980):

A.   The predominant disturbance is generalized and persistent anxiety or worry (not related to concerns about separation), as manifested by at least four of the following:
   1.   Unrealistic worry about future events.
   2.   Preoccupation with the appropriateness of the individual's behavior in the past.
   3.   Overconcern about competence in a variety of areas, e.g., academic, athletic, social.
   4.   Excessive need for reassurance about a variety of worries.
   5.   Somatic complaints, such as headaches or stomachaches, for which no physical basis can be established.
   6.   Marked self-consciousness or susceptibility to embarrassment or humiliation.
   7.   Marked feelings of tension or inability to relax.
B.   The symptoms in A have persisted for at least six months.
C.   If 18 or older, does not meet the criteria for Generalized Anxiety Disorder.
D.   The disturbance is not due to another mental disorder, such as Separation Anxiety Disorder, Avoidant Disorder of Childhood or Adolescence, Phobic Disorder, Obsessive Compulsive Disorder, Depressive Disorder, Schizophrenia, or a Pervasive Developmental Disorder [pp. 56-7].

Sleep Terror Disorder.   The Sleep Terror Disorder is classified with "other disorders with physical manifestations" and is not regarded as an anxiety disorder as described above. Nevertheless, because the sleep terror disorder is characterized by intense anxiety, we describe its characteristics here. The disorder is said to begin between the ages of 4 and 12 years of age. The following diagnostic criteria are used for the Sleep Terror Disorder (APA, 1980):

A.   Repeated episodes of abrupt awakening (lasting 1-10 minutes) from sleep, usually occurring between 30 and 200 minutes after onset of sleep (the interval of sleep that typically contains EEG delta activity, sleep stages 3 and 4) and usually beginning with a panicky scream.
B.   Intense anxiety during the episode and at least three of the following signs of autonomic arousal:
   1.   tachycardia
   2.   rapid breathing
   3.   dilated pupils

    4. sweating

    5. piloerection

C. Relative unresponsiveness to efforts of others to comfort the individual during the episode and, almost invariably, confusion, disorientation, and perseverative motor movements (e.g., picking at pillow).

D. No evidence that the episode occurred during REM sleep or of abnormal electrical brain activity during sleep [p. 86].

The child may exhibit avoidance behavior in that situations where awareness is possible (camp, overnight visit at friends) are avoided.

Considerations in the ICD-9 and DSM-III. Several writers have discussed issues in the conception and use of the ICD-9 and/or DSM-III (e.g., Mash & Terdall, 1981; McReynolds, 1978; Quay, 1979; Schacht & Nathan, 1977; Spitzer, Sheehy, & Endicott, 1977; Skinner, 1981; Spitzer & Williams, 1980; Yule, 1981). Like the former DSM systems, DSM-III adheres to a categorical, disease-entity conception of behavior disorders. Spitzer et al. (1977) advance the following defense of this position:

> The justification for using a categorical approach in DSM-III which treats psychiatric conditions as separate entities, connoting entity status if not denoting it lies in the practical utility of such topology for communication, treatment, and research, despite theoretical limitations. Furthermore, the history of medicine attests to the value of categorical subdivision in the discovery of specific etiology and treatment [p. 6].

In some respects, the DSM-III system has carried out a tradition of diagnosis, even in the face of basic problems in defining disorders. Indeed, as Spitzer and Endicott (1978) have suggested, classification of mental disorders has existed for decades despite the lack of consensus regarding what constitutes a disorder in the first place. However, this has not been unique to the DSM systems. The official classification schemes of the World Health Organization (WHO), the International Classification of Diseases (ICD-9), the system developed by the Group for the Advancement of Psychiatry (GAP), and the California I-Level system have not effectively dealt with this issue.[1]

Many critical issues have been raised over the DSM system as well as over diagnosis generally. For example, Begelman (1976) summarized nine general criticisms of the DSM systems:

1. Excessive reliance on the medical model of abnormal behavior.
2. Facilitating the stigmatization of individuals.
3. Employing debatable theoretical notions.
4. Poor or low reliability and validity.
5. Little relevance toward prognosis, treatment, and future prediction of behavior.

6. Dehumanizing the client-therapist relationship.
7. Poor consistency of categorical groupings.
8. Promoting biases that stem from arbitrary decision rules.
9. Promoting a perception of homogeneity among individuals labeled the same [pp. 23–4].

One of the more strongly voiced criticisms of the DSM system is the heavy reliance on the medical model (e.g., Adams, 1964; Albee, 1968; Begelman, 1971; Kratochwill, 1981; McReynolds, 1978; Schacht & Nathan, 1977; Szasz, 1960; Ullman & Krasner, 1969). Within the medical model framework, the individual is considered sick and suffering from an illness that prevents normal adjustment (Phillips et al., 1975). A major problem has been to apply the disease conception of illness (in either a literal or metaphorical sense) to deviant behavior. McReynolds (1979) argued:

> The medical model is no longer heuristic in social science. What good it brought to our discipline was exhausted long ago. It now entraps our thinking and limits our research and practice. This is true not only for the disease entity conception of behavioral processes but for all categorical representations of behavior, be they mental disorders, personality types, or other notions of behavioral discontinuity. In sum, there is little reason to expect a decade of new research on DSM-III to produce findings that substantiate the categorical approach to understanding and modifying unwanted or troublesome behavior. That well is dry [p. 125].

Further criticisms of the DSM-III system has been advanced by McLermore and Benjamin (1979, p. 18). They claim, first, that diagnosis rests on impressionistic clinical judgment, such as global ratings of the severity of psychological stresses and of the client's highest level of adaptive functioning during the past year. Second, the DSM-III system is criticized for categorizing individuals in terms of broadly defined illness (as in the case of the childhood anxiety disorders). Finally, DSM-III generally neglects social psychological variables and interpersonal behavior.

The DSM-III system has also been considered imprecise (Yule, 1981). In this regard, many of the categories are not founded on the basis of epidemiological research, as this prevalence estimate shows:

Anxiety Disorders
  309.21 *Separate anxiety disorder.* "The disorder is apparently not uncommon."
  313.21 *Avoidant disorder.* "The disorder is apparently not uncommon."
  313.00 *Overanxious disorder.* "The disorder is apparently common" [Yule, 1981, p. 23].

These statements are rather meaningless in attempts to discuss prevalence rates. Yet it is the lack of good prevalence data that does not allow for alternatives (see later discussion).

In some respects, the problem with DSM-III and ICD-9 generally and their use with diagnoses and classification of childhood anxiety disorders specifically is the lack of adequate reliability and validity data. In some studies, clinicians have been asked to categorize various disorders. Generally, there is good interrater agreement on major categories (e.g., discrimination between psychoses, neurotic, or conduct disorders), but less agreement when finer discriminations are required (e.g., Matison, Cantwell, Russell, & Will, 1979; Rutter, Shaffer, & Shepherd, 1975; Sturge, Shaffer, & Rutter, 1977). Specifically in the Mattison et al. (1979) study, anxiety disorders, among others, were diagnosed with low agreement. It may very well be that future research will attest to the credibility of these systems. Some authors have suggested that DSM-III will facilitate research, possibly better than DSM-II (e.g., Skinner, 1981). Yet at this time there are few reliability and validity studies conducted with children where the anxiety disorders have been examined.

Other Traditional Classification Schemes

Attempts to classify childhood fears and phobias have been characterized by several problems (cf. Marks, 1969). First of all, a traditional procedure has been to classify based on the *feared situation*. However, this approach has the problem of a very endless classification scheme based on the numerous Greek and Latin prefixes. For example, many formal names might be employed, as is shown in Table 2.1. Although such a classification scheme potentially results in endless terminology, description and identification of the specific feared object could be quite useful (Marks, 1969). Certainly it would appear important to specify a fear stimulus if one can be identified. In behavioral assessment the stimulus would be regarded as particularly important in establishing a treatment program (see Chapter 3).

A second consideration related to classification of fears and phobias is that such problems occur with other disorders. In many cases, anxiety is present with other disorders, and it becomes the task of the clinician to determine the primary problem. In DSM-III, for example, this has usually involved making a differential diagnosis. Consider the following guidelines in differential diagnosis for Overanxious Disorder (APA, 1980):

> *Differential Diagnosis.* In *Separation Anxiety Disorder*, the anxiety is focused on situations involving separation (e.g., going to school). Children with *Attention Deficit Disorder* may appear nervous and jittery, but are not unduly concerned about the future. The two disorders, however, may coexist. In *Adjustment Dis-*

Table 2.1. Selected Phobias Which Children Experience

Technical Name	Phobia
Acrophobia	height
Agoraphobia	open spaces
Aichmophobia	sharp and pointed objects
Ailurophobia	cats
Arachnophobia	spiders
Anthophobia	flowers
Anthropophobia	people
Aquaphobia	water
Astraphobia	lightning
Brontophobia	thunder
Claustrophobia	closed spaces
Cynophobia	dogs
Equinophobia	horses
Menophobia	being alone
Mikrophobia	germs
Murophobia	mice
Numerophobia	number
Nyctophobia	darkness
Ophidiophobia	snakes
Pyrophobia	fire
Thanatophobia	death
Trichophobia	hair
Xenophobia	stranger
Zoophobia	animal

order with Anxious Mood, the anxiety is always clearly related to the recent occurrence of a psychosocial stressor.

Overanxious Disorder should not be diagnosed when the anxiety is due to another disorder, such as *Obsessive Compulsive Disorder, Major Depression, Schizophrenia, or Pervasive Developmental Disorder* [p. 56].

Viewed within this context, it can be readily observed that specific diagnosis and classification is a difficult and challenging task.

Finally, it should be emphasized that the task of establishing a classification scheme for children is usually more difficult than that faced by those classifying adult disorders (Phillips & Draguns, 1971). This is particularly so since classification of childhood problems is frequently based on externally judged social transgressions or deficiencies in intellectual and social performance (Phillips et al., 1975). Particularly with childhood fears and phobias, problems are interwoven with "normal" developmental phenomena.

There have been several attempts to develop specific classification systems for childhood fears. These studies can generally be grouped into those that employed a broad-based homogenous category system (e.g., Angelino, Dollins, & Mech, 1956; Bandura & Menlove, 1968; Hagman, 1932; Kennedy,

1965; Lapouse & Monk, 1959). A derivation of this procedure has focused on various feared object categories, but has employed factor analytic procedures to group responses (e.g., Miller, Barrett, Hampe, & Noble, 1972 b; Poznanski, 1973; Scherer & Nakamura, 1968). Another approach, integrating statistical techniques that isolate patterns of behavior which are interrelated, has also been employed (cf. Quay, 1979). Usually factor analysis is employed in this approach also. This procedure enables the researcher to isolate clusters of variables (e.g., behaviors) that are interrelated among themselves. Factor analysis provides information about the nature and organization of individual characteristics and helps clarify what a given test measures (Cronbach, 1960).

Specific Fear Classification Schemes

An early effort to classify childhood fears was reported by Angelino et al. (1956). These authors classified the fears of 1,100 students ranging in age from 9 to 18 years. The following general categories were reported: safety, school, personal appearance, natural phenomena, economical and political, health, animals, social relations, personal conduct, and supernatural. Bandura and Menlove (1968) gathered parental ratings from a 45-item fear schedule for preschoolers and developed the following three categories: animal fears, interpersonal fears (e.g., separation), and fear of inanimate objects or events (heights, thunder). It should be noted that these categories were determined *a priori* and were not devised on the basis of factor analysis. However, two studies did report the dimensions of children's fears through a factor analysis procedure. In the first, Scherer and Nakamura (1968) developed an 80-item Fear Survey Schedule for Children. The scale was administered to 99 ten-year-old children. The authors identified the ten most salient fears: being hit by a car or truck, bombing attacks/being invaded, fire/getting burned, getting a serious illness, not being able to breathe, death, getting poor grades, failing a test, being sent to the principal, and having parents argue. After determining the factor structure for the fears, the following eight factors emerged: fear of failure or criticism, major fears (primarily social), minor fears (small animals), medical fears, fear of death, fear of the dark, house–school fears, and several miscellaneous fears unrelated to the former seven factors. Interestingly, the classification of fears arrived at through this factor analysis procedure was quite similar to that developed by Angelino et al. (1956) through less formal statistical procedures.

Another fear survey schedule called the Louisville Fear Survey for Children (see Chapter 3) was developed by Miller et al. (1972 b) and administered by parents who rated 179 children between the ages of 6 and 16. Following a factor analysis of the data, the following three primary factors emerged: fear of physical injury (e.g., wars, food poisoning, surgery), natural and supernatural dangers (e.g., storm, the dark, animals), and interpersonal–social (e.g., examinations, making mistakes, criticism). A formal effort to provide a classification scheme has been presented by Miller, Barrett, and Hampe (1974). Their classification system is reported in Table 2.2. The authors note that this is a tentative classification scheme and admit that little research has been done to support the categories. Miller et al. (1974) do suggest that the first task in classification is to determine whether the phobia is a primary problem or secondary to a more pervasive one. When the phobia is the primary problem, the authors label it a *phobic trait*. When phobias are secondary to another problem the term *phobic state* is used.

The classification scheme reported in Table 2.2 is, in part, based on the Scherer and Nakamura (1968) and Miller et al. (1972 b) studies. Thus, after comparing the Scherer and Nakamura (1968) results with their work, the eight factors were reduced to three. Also, further consideration of the Lapouse and Monk (1959) data showed differences between child and parent report of fears and led the authors to advance the hypothesis that:

> phobic objects do not occur randomly, but many are interrelated. For a given patient, treatment of one phobia within a dimension should reduce the aversiveness connected with other stimuli within that dimension. In addition, if factor analysis yields anything more than just phenotypes, the same treatment should be applicable to all phobics within a given dimension. For these reasons, we decided to use the three primary factors of physical injury, natural events, and social anxiety as the major categories of child phobia [Miller et al., 1974, p. 93].

Miller et al. (1974) incorporated the school phobia classification under the category of social anxiety. The Type I and II School Phobics refer to a distinction first made by Coolidge, Hahn, and Peck (1957) and further developed by Kennedy (1965). Based upon data of 50 cases from the Human Development Clinic of Florida State University, Kennedy (1965) proposed that a differential diagnosis between two types of school phobia can be made on the basis of any seven of ten differential symptoms. Kennedy's (1965) classification scheme is presented in Table 2.3.

Kennedy (1965) employed a grade distinction in his classification system. Miller et al. (1974) dropped the grade distinction, finding that age is the more important variable, and suggested that six of nine items are sufficient to make a differential diagnosis. Marine (1968–69) has also proposed diagnostic categories for children displaying the behavioral symptom of separation anxiety and three other, more severe types of "school refusal" ("mild school refusal"; "chronic severe school refusal"; "childhood psychosis with school refusals"). These diagnostic categories are matched with four treatment modalities as well as some potential change agents.

Table 2.2. Proposed Nosology for Child Phobia

I. Physical injury	II. Natural events	III. Social anxiety	IV. Miscellaneous

A. Abstract
  1. War
  2. Riots
  3. Poisoned food
  4. Specific foods
  5. Dying
  6. Someone in family dying
  7. Seeing someone wounded
  8. Being wounded
  9. Someone in family getting ill
 10. Becoming ill
 11. Germs
 12. Choking
 13. Having an operation
 14. Hospitals
 15. Hell
 16. The devil
 17. Breaking a religious law
 18. Being kidnapped
 19. Getting lost
 20. Being adopted
 21. Parents getting a divorce
 22. Going crazy
	A. Storms
	  1. Tornadoes, floods, earthquakes
	  2. Lightning
	  3. Thunder
	B. Dark
	C. Enclosed places
	  1. Bathrooms
	  2. Closets
	  3. Elevators
	  4. Confined or locked up
	  5. Strange rooms
	D. Animals
	  1. Snakes
	  2. Insects, spiders
	  3. Rats or mice
	  4. Frogs or lizards
	  5. Dogs or cats
	  6. Horses or cows
		A. School
		  1. Young (ages 3–10)
		    (a) Type I
		    (b) Type II
		  2. Old (ages 11–22)
		    (a) Type I
		    (b) Type II
		B. Separation
		  1. Separation from parents
		  2. Parts of house
		  3. Going to sleep at night
		C. Performance
		  1. Tests or examinations
		  2. Being criticized
		  3. Making mistakes
		  4. Reciting in class
		D. Social interactions
		  1. Attending social events
		  2. Making another person angry
		  3. Crowds
		  4. Being touched by others
			1. Dirt
			2. Furry toys
			3. Sirens
			4. People who are old
			5. Crossing a street
			6. People who are ugly
			7. Loud sounds, as caps, firecrackers, explosions
			8. People in uniforms, a policeman, mailmen, etc.
			9. People of the opposite sex
			10. Having bowel movements
			11. Members of another race

B. Concrete
1. Flying in airplane
2. High places
3. Deep water
4. Strangers
5. Being seen naked

E. Other
1. Fire
2. Frightening thoughts or daydreams
3. Ghosts
4. Being alone
5. Nightmares
6. Space creatures or monsters
7. Faces at window
8. Masks or puppets
9. Sight of blood
10. People with deformities
11. Toilets

E. Medical procedures
1. Doctors or dentists
2. Getting a shot
F. Other
1. Riding in a car or bus

Source: Miller, Barrett, and Hampe (1974, Table 1). Copyright 1974 by John Wiley & Sons, Inc.; reprinted by permission.

Table 2.3. Ten Differential School Phobia Symptoms

1. The present illness is the first episode.	1. Second, third, or fourth episode.
2. Monday onset, following an illness the previous Thursday or Friday.	2. Monday onset following minor illness not a prevalent antecedent.
3. An acute onset.	3. Incipient onset.
4. Lower grades most prevalent.	4. Upper grades most prevalent.
5. Expressed concern about death.	5. Death theme not present.
6. Mother's physical health in question: actually ill or child thinks so.	6. Health of mother not an issue.
7. Good communication between parents.	7. Poor communication between parents.
8. Mother and father well adjusted in most areas.	8. Mother shows neurotic behavior; father, a character disorder.
9. Father competitive with mother in household management.	9. Father shows little interest in household or children.
10. Parents achieve understanding of dynamics easily.	10. Parents very difficult to work with.

Source: Kennedy, W. A. School phobia: Rapid treatment of fifty cases. *Journal of Abnormal Psychology*, 1965, **70**, 285–289. Reproduced by permission.

Considerations.   What can be concluded from the several attempts to diagnose and classify children's fears and phobias? After reviewing the literature on types and classification of children's fears, Ollendick (1979) suggested that an underlying dimensionality can be identified which has etiologic and treatment significance. If fears do generalize it is possible that treatment within one factor class should affect other phobias within the same class. This has obvious cost/benefit and treatment advantages as well as importance in research. Yet in our view extreme caution must be exercised in drawing firm conclusions from the above literature. This is based on the following considerations. First of all, there is a paucity of data bearing on these classification schemes. For example, Miller et al. (1974) note that their system is a tentative one and may be subject to revision based upon future work. Yet the extensive empirical base has not been forthcoming.

A second concern is the nature of the data obtained. The classification literature (and as we shall see below, the incidence data) are based on self-report from parents and children, and such self-report data are subject to considerable distortion and bias (Graziano et al., 1979). Employing sophisticated factor analysis with these data does not eliminate the problem. As we shall argue in Chapter 3, self-report data must be validated independently for their true credibility to be known. Certainly, this is necessary if faith is to be placed in a classification system.

Finally, like other survey work in the literature on children's fears and phobias, there has been an almost exclusive reliance on the feared object as a focus of classification attempts (Graziano et al., 1979). Such a classification approach carries with it the assumption that there is subject homogeneity within a particular fear category (Magrath, 1982). Thus, children who display a fear of school might be called "school phobic" or further subdivided into Type I and II following Kennedy's (1965) scheme. Yet, the category might well mask the considerable variability in what children actually fear and the circumstances maintaining the fear or phobic responses.

Even if these considerations could be minimized, there is still the issue that some components of the current classification schemes are somewhat arbitrary. For example, Miller et al. (1974b) noted that placing school under Social Anxiety was arbitrary, since females loaded significantly on this factor ($r = .63$) while males did not ($r = .07$) (p. 94). Keeping in mind these issues, we now turn to a discussion of studies that have identified deviant behaviors through multivariate statistical procedures, such as factor analysis. These studies have focused on a more general range of behaviors with several different factors emerging.

General Behavior Disorder Studies

A rather sizable literature has developed using rating scales and checklists to sample problem behavior (Achenbach, 1974; Achenbach & Edelbrock, 1978; Quay, 1979; Ross, 1980; Yule, 1981). In nearly all of these studies, multivariate statistical procedures, usually factor analysis or cluster analysis, have been employed for development of the factors identified. This literature reviewed by Quay (1979) suggests that there are a number of dimensions of behavior that occur regardless of the data used and child sample employed, namely, *conduct disorder, anxiety withdrawal, immaturity,* and *socialized aggression.* Of interest is the anxiety-withdrawal pattern of behavior. The characteristics associated with this pattern of behavior are reported in Table 2.4. Quay (1979) reports that this pattern has been found in all settings in which these children have been studied. Also, it has emerged from such assessment procedures as behavior ratings, analyses of life histories, and responses to questionnaires. Specifically, the anxiety-withdrawal dimension is characterized as:

> withdrawal rather than attack, of isolation rather than active enjoyment and of subjectively experienced anxiety and distress rather than the apparent freedom from anxiety characterizing conduct disorder [Quay, 1979].

Presumably these children are less aversive to adults and peers than those experiencing conduct disorders and the socialized aggressive disorder. Such children may also have social skill deficits, which is implied in some of the social skill training programs focused on this population (e.g., Cartledge &

**Table 2.4. Frequently Found Characteristics Defining
Anxiety-Withdrawal**

Characteristic	Total Number of Published Studies
Anxious, fearful, tense	21
Shy, timid, bashful	19
Withdrawn, seclusive, friendless	19
Depressed, sad, disturbed	16
Hypersensitive, easily hurt	15
Self-conscious, easily embarrassed	13
Feels inferior, worthless	12
Lacks self-confidence	10
Easily flustered	10
Aloof	8
Cries frequently	7
Reticent, secretive	7

Source: Adapted from Quay (1979).

Milburn, 1980; Conger & Keane, 1981; Goldstein, Sprafkin, Gershaw, & Klein, 1980; Oden, 1980).

Other authors (e.g., Achenbach & Edelbrock, 1978; Ross, 1980) have found two broad dimensions of child behavior: undercontrolled (aggressive, conduct disorder) and overcontrolled (e.g., inhibited, shy-anxious). Work in the same general mode appears to support two general dimensions that maladaptive behavior can take: toward or away from the environment (Kohn, 1969, 1973; Kohn & Rosman, 1972 a, b, 1973). For example, Kohn and Rosman (1973) administered a 90-item Social Competence Scale (SCS) (e.g., "cooperates with rules and regulations"), and a 58-item Symptom Checklist (SC) ("keeps to himself, remains aloof and distant") to 407 children ranging in age from three to six years. Two teachers rated each child. The resulting factor analysis yielded two bipolar factors on the SCS (i.e., *interest-participation versus apathy-withdrawal* and *cooperation-compliance* versus *anger-defiance*) and SC (i.e., *apathy-withdrawal* and *anger-defiance*).

Considerations.   Some positive features of the statistical approach to classification have been identified (Quay, 1979; Ross, 1980). In contrast to the clinical approach such as DSM-III, empirical evidence is gathered to support the dimensions as they exist on an observable constellation of behavior. Moreover, the more objective nature of the data permits estimation of the reliability of each dimension of behavior. Quay (1979) argues that multivariate statistical approaches are the methods of choice for development of classification systems. The proposed advantages of this approach also extend beyond methodological issues. Ross (1980) notes:

Aggression and withdrawal appear to be behavioral characteristics that permit a reliable and predictively valid mode of classifying the behavior of children whether they are found in special treatment clinics or in the general population. This, in turn, confirms that the behavior of disturbed children is not qualitatively different from the behavior of so-called normal children; the behavior lies on the same continuum, and only a judgment of magnitude (too much or too little), which is a function of tolerance level of the people who make the judgment, separates the child in the clinic from the child in the school [p. 28].

Such a conclusion has also been reached by others (e.g., Miller et al., 1971) and is in accordance with developing behavioral classification schemes (see discussion below).

However, these classification schemes have a number of limitations. The problems relate to the samples employed and the methodology used to establish the behavior dimensions. First, the dimensions identified may reflect the type of subjects employed in the studies (Ciminero & Drabman, 1977). It may be that if certain populations (e.g., mentally retarded) were employed in the studies, different results would be found (Ross, 1980). Thus, one cannot assume that these factors generalize across certain populations of subjects.

Other concerns have been expressed over the factor analysis methodology itself. Like any statistical procedure, human judgment is called upon in factor analysis strategies (Yule, 1981). In the case of factor analysis certain clusters of behavior may be labeled differently by different investigators (Ross, 1980). Relatedly, a dimension of behavior that is not represented by its constituent behavior traits in the analysis cannot be expected to appear (Quay, 1979). Moreover, since certain samples of behaviors are not represented in the assessment scale, certain behavior dimensions do not appear. Quay (1979) suggests that future research can address this issue by including a broader range of deviant behaviors and including a variety of samples of children.

Another concern involves what is being classified. The multivariate approach reviewed by Quay (1979) describes behavior dimensions and not "types" of individuals. While some writers might object to this approach, we believe that attempts to classify behaviors may best advance empirical work in this area (see Fiske, 1979). Yet, questions might still be raised over the *methods* of gathering data. Quay (1979) notes:

A somewhat more serious and more complex problem for the establishment of descriptive factor-analytic based systems has been the degree to which the methods of data collection (e.g., ratings and questionnaires) and the settings in which the data are collected influence the results. Are the behavioral dimensions that result from different methods really the same? Categories arising from the analysis of behavior ratings may or may not be the same as those arising from the analysis of life history data even though they look the same. There is always some possibility that the method may produce the result [p. 12].

Despite these problems in the approach, Quay (1979) is optimistic about the future value of classification efforts. These approaches are, after all, based on empirical studies. We are more skeptical and would argue that until such measures are supported with direct measures in various environments, a good deal of caution should be exercised. As will be emphasized in Chapter 3, self-report data, whether from the child or careprovider (teacher, parent) is characterized by methodological shortcomings.

Behavioral Classification Systems

Some behavior classification systems have been proposed as alternatives to those described above. However, in the past specific and concrete systems of behavioral diagnosis have not been generally followed in the behavior therapy field (Kazdin, 1978b). The typical practice of behavior therapists has been to discuss general classes of behavioral problems in terms of deficits, excesses, inappropriate stimulus control, and aversive response repertoires (e.g., Bandura, 1968; Bijou & Grimm, 1975; Bijou & Peterson, 1971; Bijou & Redd, 1975; Kratochwill, 1982; Marholin & Bijou, 1978). Marholin and Bijou (1978) have characterized this approach as follows: "Diagnosis or assessment is instead, oriented toward attaining the kinds of information or data that can be directly used to *develop and guide a treatment program*" (p. 15). The behavioral approach to diagnosis was developed in reaction to traditional intrapsychic models. A number of behavioral writers have specifically suggested that there is a lack of functional fit between conventional diagnostic categories and various treatment techniques within the behavioral framework (e.g., Kanfer & Saslow, 1969; Ullmann & Krasner, 1969; Yates, 1970). Within the behavioral perspective, underlying dynamics do not hold a central view in the diagnostic process. Rather, a behavioral diagnosis generally focuses on specific target behaviors and situations in which behaviors are analyzed. Nevertheless, behavioral writers have increasingly embraced some type of classification system and typically use labels characteristic of the traditional clinical literature to describe various fears, phobias, and anxieties in children.

It is becoming increasingly evident that many behavioral writers consider some sort of formal classification scheme useful in research and practice, and because of this we have witnessed a move toward the development of more formal systems of behavioral classification (e.g., Adams et al., 1977; Cautela & Upper, 1973; Kanfer & Saslow, 1969; McLemore & Benjamin, 1979; McReynolds, 1978). One of the earliest attempts at behavioral classification, which has in turn been used for both diagnostic and assessment processes, is the model proposed by Kanfer and Saslow (1969). This model (outlined in detail in Chapter 3) provides information on targets for the modification of behavior and a conceptual framework for organizing a client's behavior during assessment and treatment. Nevertheless, it has been noted that while it provides a procedure for gathering data, it does not suggest a specific way to combine the data (Dickson, 1975).

Another system called the Psychological Response Classification System (PRCS) is designed to classify responses rather than people (Adams et al., 1977). In this way, the PRCS is similar to many of the multivariate statistical techniques described above which are involved in behavioral classification rather than specific definition of trait classification schemes. The PRCS system has some specific aims that are described as follows:

> One is to take arbitrary assumptions regarding the distinctions between normal and abnormal responses out of the alpha level of classification.[2] Unless it is empirically demonstrated to be otherwise, abnormal behavior is considered to be an extension of normal behavior and similar in kind. Many difficulties have arisen from attempts to classify symptoms as distinct from nonsymptomatic behavior. It is not the proper role of the alpha level classification scheme to make value statements about what is normal and abnormal. Abnormal behavior can be defined only in the context of what is normal, which is an empirical question [p. 67].

Thus, like some of the advantages that have been proposed for the multivariate classification schemes discussed above (see Ross, 1980), the PRCS conceptualizes deviant behavior falling on a continuum with normal behavior.

In development of the PRCS system, Adams et al. (1977) have conceptualized a motor perceptual, biological, cognitive, and emotional response system format. According to these authors, the PRCS is useful in clinical practice because it provides the therapist an opportunity to empirically determine the popular data language of psychology. Second, it provides a basis for determining whether or not psychological terms or concepts must be defined further so as not to obscure diagnostic differences or produce ambiguous communications. Third, the system makes the presence or absence of the relationships among response syndromes a clinical decision based on direct observation of the client. This is advantageous because various theoretical assumptions characteristic of traditional systems are not employed. Fourth, the system provides the therapist with a conceptual model to organize and evaluate assessment devices and treatments that are employed for each response system and subsystem. Finally, the system reflects the progress of psychology with respect to information that can be generated pertinent to response systems and subsystems (pp. 75–76). However, there are at least two major limitations of the PRCS system at this time. One is that it does not specify the clinical implications of various combinations of responses from the six categories (McLemore & Benjamin, 1979). Second, there is a paucity of empirical data on the system. Nevertheless, the approach does appear useful if it can be empirically demonstrated to work in both research and practice.

Another system proposed by McReynolds (1979) is a "social-behavioral classification system" of behavioral disturbance. The approach incorporates a social-psychological perspective in that individuals are identified for psychological assessment and treatment because their behavior is presumed to be disturbing to themselves or others. In this context, one individual presents a behavioral disturbance to another in two ways. First, "The first person(s) actions disturb the second since it is the presence of responses or behavior patterns that is disturbing." Second, "There is an absence of specific responses or response patterns, and the failure of the designated deviant to engage in certain behaviors poses the disturbance" (McReynolds, 1979, p. 120). Within this system, behavior is classified as excess or deficit and so shares common characteristics with other behavioral diagnostic systems that focus on behavioral assets and deficits. As can be seen from Table 2.5, two broad categories of behavioral disturbance are described in five behavioral dimensions in terms of frequency, duration, magnitude, latency, and context. Moreover, behavior is divided into cognitive, affective, motor, and somatic actions. The 2 x 5 x 4 classes allow identification of 40 behavioral events that can be used to identify deviant behavior. It can be seen that such a system could be used in the classification of fear behaviors. For example, a child experiencing a particular pattern of fear behavior may be identified by a complaint relative to a family member and teacher who may in turn suggest partial or total removal of the problem. The nature of the behavior could then be described in terms of a deficit in the frequency of some particular behavior in several different action systems. In the latter case, the action systems are quite consistent with the previously described three-mode response assessment that should be employed in description of fears, phobias, and anxieties in children. Even though little current empirical work has been done on this system, it appears to be quite useful in the fear and phobia literature.

Another system described by McLemore and Benjamin (1979) has been conceptualized within an interpersonal behavior approach. This approach is designed to translate traditional diagnostic categories into psychosocial terms and is based on Benjamin's (1974) work in which she used both clinical and nonclinical studies to develop a model of social behavior labeled *Structure Analysis of Social Behavior* (SASB).

Considerations.   The aforementioned behavioral classification systems provide some interesting alternatives for classification of children's fears, phobias, and anxieties. It must be emphasized that each of these systems has generally grown out of a dissatisfaction with some of the traditional schemes that have been employed in the clinical literature, such as the DSM systems. Despite some possible conceptual advantages these systems may have, the

Table 2.5. Sociobehavioral Classification of Residual Behavioral Disturbance

I. Social conditions of residual disturbance
    A. Identity of complainant relative to designated deviant
        1. Self
        2. Family or family member
        3. Community agency
        4. Civil or criminal authority
        5. Helping professional
        6. Employer
        7. Friend
        8. Other
    B. Complainant request for designated deviant
        1. Behavior change
        2. Behavior control
        3. Partial removal
        4. Total removal
II. Behavioral nature of residual disturbance
    A. Behavioral complaint
        1. Excess
        2. Deficit
    B. Response dimension
        1. Frequency
        2. Duration
        3. Magnitude
        4. Latency
        5. Context
    C. Action system
        1. Cognitive
        2. Affective
        3. Motor
        4. Somatic

Source: McReynolds, W. P. DSM-III and the future of applied social science. *Professional Psychology*, 1979, **10**, 123–132. Reprinted with permission.

major limitations they share is the paucity of research to support their use in both research and practice. In almost all cases we do not have information on reliability and validity of these approaches (Hersen, 1976; Nathan, 1981; Salzinger, 1978). Specifically, there is a lack of information on their use with the clinical populations we describe in this text. Yet behavior therapists may wish to consider focusing more research on the DSM-III system. For example, after reviewing two example cases in which DSM-III and behavioral diagnoses were employed, Nathan (1981) concluded that:

> the new revision of the [DSM] has yielded a document that enables the diagnostician to do almost as well as the well-trained, conscientious behavior therapist

in recording discrete units of maladaptive behavior—symptoms—and very likely a good deal better than when called upon to put forth a summary statement (a
DSM-III diagnosis on the one hand, a behavioral analysis on the other) [p. 7].

Yet we have taken time to review them in the hopes that researchers and
others working with children experiencing fears, phobias, and related problems will undertake the task of employing them and determine their utility in
future research and practice in the area.

NORMATIVE AND DEVELOPMENTAL RESEARCH

As suggested in Chapter 1, a considerable amount of research has focused on
normative and developmental trends in the child fear and phobia area. There
are many reviews of select portions of this literature (e.g., Barrios et al.,
1981; Graziano et al., 1979; Johnson & Melamed, 1979; L. C. Miller et al,
1971; Ollendick, 1979; Rachman, 1968; Smith, 1979), but not all authors
focus on the same topics and issues. Several specific characteristics of this
literature are noteworthy. First, there has been a heavy concentration of
research on infants and preschool children. Work in this area has been
conducted in laboratory/clinic settings and in the natural environment many
times with good measures (Smith, 1979). In older school-age samples, the
methods have generally not been as good since questionnaires, rather than
direct observation procedures, have been employed.

Second, the normative and developmental data are fraught with the same
definitional problems as the clinical treatment literature. Particularly in infant research, a variety of terms have been used to describe emotional response, some of which are arbitrarily labeled fear (e.g., "distress", "tension," "stress"). But terminology is also problematic with studies focusing
on older samples of children, as is evident in research on "fear of strangers,"
"separation anxiety," and "stranger distress." For example, Bowlby (1969,
1973) has made a distinction between *anxiety* (the desire for closer proximity
to an attachment figure) and *alarm* (the desire to withdraw or avoid danger).
Both of these are regarded as examples of fear. Some authors, preferring to
use the term "wariness," refer to this as an inhibition of approach or manipulation when the infant is alerted, which may or may not result in a fear
response (e.g., Schaffer, Greenwood, & Parry, 1972), whereas others (Sroufe,
1977) use the same term to refer to an inferred low intensity fear, possibly
reflected in gaze avoidance (cf. Smith, 1979).

Third, developmental and incidence data have been measured in different
response channels and systems over different ages. Thus, while it may be
possible to monitor infant heart rate in a laboratory setting as one index of
fear, the researcher usually has employed self-report questionnaire data for
older samples of children.

Fourth, normative research, particularly with older samples of children, has focused on identification of fear stimuli (Graziano et al., 1979). Determination of what children fear is then related to certain characteristics that serve as conceptual organization schemes (e.g., age, sex, SES, etc.). The *intensity* of various fears has many times taken a back seat to the number and type of fears.

Realizing that there are a number of methodological and conceptual issues that remain to be resolved in this literature, we will venture to present some highlights of findings. We stress that our statements are tentative, and the reader is advised to make generalizations with a good deal of caution. We have somewhat arbitrarily divided our section into subheadings that correspond to previous reviews of this literature.

Sex Differences in Fears and Related Emotional States

Different conclusions are sometimes reached by authors who have discussed sex differences in fears and related emotional states. One perspective has been that, generally, girls have higher fear measures than boys (e.g., Angelino et al. 1956; Bamber, 1974; Bowlby, 1973; Croake, 1969; Croake & Knox, 1973; Cummings, 1944; Gray, 1971b; Lapouse & Monk, 1959; Pratt, 1945; Russell, 1967; Scherer & Nakamura, 1968; Spiegler & Liebert, 1970). Yet several issues must be considered in making this general statement. First, there are exceptions to this in that the method by which this phenomenon is studied leads researchers to different conclusions. For example, Maccoby and Jacklin (1974) noted that while observational studies typically do not show significant sex differences in fears, studies based on self-reports or teacher ratings do show differences. Second, some studies do not find sex differences (e.g., L. C. Miller et al., 1971; Nalven, 1970).

Sex differences also appear to vary with the type of fear being considered and its intensity (cf. Graziano et al., 1979; Smith, 1979). Lapouse and Monk (1959) found some significant sex differences in fear content (i.e., fear of certain objects), but Pratt (1945) found no fear content sex differences. Tennes and Lample (1964) reported that separation anxiety was higher in boys, but that stranger fear was greater in girls. After considering Corter's (1976) review of sex differences in separation anxiety and Lewis and Brook's (1974) review of sex differences in fear of strangers, Smith (1979) concluded that even significant findings of sex differences are difficult to replicate. Smith speculated that it is possible that sex differences interact with who initiates the separation, with boys being more distressed if *mother* leaves, but more exploratory if *they* leave the mother.

Although there are few data on the intensity of fears, some studies have reported that girls report a greater fear intensity than boys (e.g., Bamber, 1974; Russell, 1967; Scherer & Nakamura, 1968). From this literature one might conclude that there is a tendency for girls to report a greater number of fears (Graziano et al., 1979). However, we could not accept this as a reliable finding. Yet we do concur with Graziano and his associates that interpretation of the literature is difficult. These authors note:

> One cannot tell from these data if the girls' higher scores reflect greater fear reactivity or if other factors, such as sex role expectations, operated. Consistent with a general role model of feminine behavior, girls may be more willing than boys to admit their fears. Similarly, in those studies using parents' reports, the adults may incorrectly, but nevertheless reliably, attribute greater fear to girls than to boys [pp. 808–809].

However, two considerations must be advanced. As Graziano et al. (1979) suggest, some of the findings may show evolving changes in sex stereotyping. Second, when different methodologies are employed, as in the case of differences between infant and older fear research, different findings are inevitable due to the methodology itself.

Temporal Factors in Fears and Related Emotional States

After reviewing the infant literature, Smith (1979) noted that few studies have examined whether consistencies in individual fear differences vary across time, and those that have show only moderate correlations (e.g., Robson, Pedersen, & Moss, 1969). Also, when there are age relationships, these may differ on sex dimensions. As an example, Kagan (1971) reported that whereas boys who were irritable and fearful at four or eight months displayed quiet and inhibited behavior as two year olds, girls fearful at earlier ages were restless, active, and talkative as two year olds. Other studies also show sex differences (Bronson, 1969a, 1969b, 1970). For example, Bronson (1970) reported data on the development of fear over the first 8½ years. The subjects participating were part of the Berkeley Growth Study, a longitudinal investigation of children's mental and physical development. Bronson used average shyness ratings during 10 and 15 months as an index of fearfulness in infancy. Correlations between ratings of shyness during infancy with ratings made at later ages showed differences between boys and girls. Whereas the level of fearfulness for boys remains relatively stable over the first eight and one-half years, little consistency in girl's fear reactions are reported during this time. Sex differences also appeared in the predictability of fear onset with later fears, with boys exhibiting early fears remaining more fearful later, but no such trend emerged with girls.

From their review of the literature, Granziano et al. (1979) have concluded that there is a general decline from young childhood to late adolescent in the percentage of child reports of one or more specific fears (e.g., Cummings, 1944; 1946; MacFarlane et al. 1954). This finding also occurs in the number of fears reported (e.g., Angelino & Shedd, 1953; MacFarlane et al., 1954;

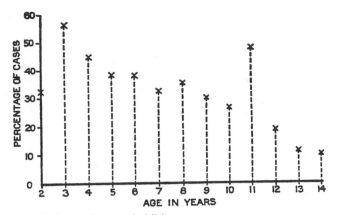

Figure 2.1. The fears of normal children.
Source: Adapted from MacFarlane, J. W., Allen, L., & Honzik, M. P. A developmental study of the behavior problems of normal children between twenty-one months and fourteen years. Berkeley: University of California Press, 1954.

Nalven, 1970; Scherer & Nakamura, 1968). Nevertheless, some studies have shown an increase in the number of reported fears around the age of 9–11 (e.g., Angelino & Shedd, 1953; MacFarlane et al., 1954) and a peak at age 11 (e.g., Chazan, 1962; MacFarlane et al., 1954; Morgan, 1959). For example, MacFarlane et al. (1954) reported the percentage frequencies of various types of fear in children (see Figure 2.1). As shown in the figure, there is a general decline in the number of fears between the ages of 3 and 10, but there is a peak at age 11.

Some studies have found that a specific type of fear is related to age (e.g., Angelino & Shedd, 1953; Angelino, Dollins, & Mech, 1956; Jersild & Holmes, 1935a; Nalven, 1970; Scherer & Nakamara, 1968). For example, in a study involving 228 7–12-year-old girls, Barnett (1969) found that fear did not differ with age, but several specific categories of fear changed with age (see Figure 2.2). As can be seen from the figure, fears of imaginary creatures and personal safety show a decline with age, while school and other social concerns increase in adolescence. Similarly, Jersild and Homes (1935a) found that fears change over time. Figure 2.3 shows the relative frequency of fear responses in children of different ages. With increasing age, the number of fears declines, but children also fear imaginary situations. Thus, many fears appear to change over time, with corresponding changes in cognitive capacity. Some findings suggest that there is with age a general decline in the fear of animals (e.g., Angelino et al., 1956; Bauer, 1976; Lapouse & Monk, 1959; Shepherd, Oppernheim, & Mitchel, 1972), the dark and imaginary creatures (e.g., Bauer, 1976; Holmes, 1936; Mowrer, 1965; Shepherd et al., 1972), but an increase with age in school and social fears (e.g., Angelino et al., 1956; Lapouse & Monk, 1959).

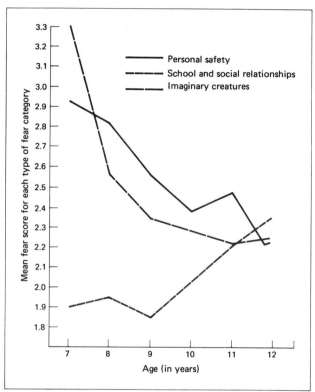

Figure 2.2. Variation in children's fears with age for imaginary creatures, school and social relationships, and personal safety.

Source: Barnett, J. T. Development of children's fears: The relationship between three systems of fear measurement. Unpublished M. A. thesis, University of Wisconsin, 1969. Reproduced by permission.

It should again be emphasized that these are general trends, and that there are exceptions. Some studies have reported no significant relationships of the number of fears and age (e.g., Croake, 1969; Croake & Knox, 1973; Lapouse & Monk, 1959; Russell, 1967). Second, even when considering the type of fear, some studies (e.g., L. C. Miller et al., 1972 b) have shown that fear of animals declines with age.

There is little information on the relationship between age and intensity of fears. Miller et al. (1974) reported the incidence of fears in a sample of 249 children aged 7–12 years. The authors used the Louisville Fear Survey Schedule and reported the rating at three intensity levels: no fear, normal or expected fear, and excessive or unrealistic fear (see Table 2.6). A general finding was that the stimuli evoked extreme fear in less than 5% of the sample. The authors noted that "the most typical response pattern approximates a J-curve in which 84% or more of the children show no fear of the stimuli, while 5 to 15% and 0 to 5% show excessive fears" (p. 104). Somewhat similar results are found in a study by Agras, Sylvester, and Oliveau (1969) who examined the epidemiology of fears and phobias. Data gathered from interviews, test questionnaires, and observations on the fears of 325 children and adults were classified as common fears, intense fears, and phobias. The authors reported that incidence of common fears was high, rate of intensive fears was low (8%), and the rate of phobias was even lower (2.2%).

From the data on temporal factors in children's fears, we can conclude that their responses to certain stimuli change with age. This relationship does not appear to be linear.

Socioeconomic Class in Fears and Related Emotional States

Graziano et al. (1979) noted that socioeconomic class (SEC) has a potentially important role in children's fears. An interesting question here is whether fears vary as a function of the SEC to which the child belongs. Some

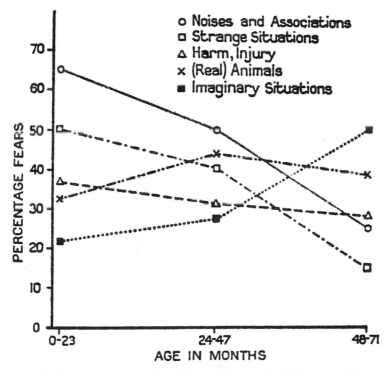

Figure 2.3. The relative frequency of fear responses in children of different ages. Source: Jersild, A. T., & Holmes, F. B. Children's fears. *Child Development Monograph*, No. 20, 1935 (a). Reproduced by permission.

Table 2.6. Frequency of Fears at Three Intensity Levels[a] in a General Population of 123 Boys and 126 Girls Between the Ages of Seven to 12

Fears	Male			Female		
	1	2	3	1	2	3
1. Dirt	93	7	0	86	14	0
2. Furry toys	98	2	0	98	2	0
3. Masks/puppets	95	5	0	90	10	0
4. Sirens	87	13	0	69	30	1
5. Insects or spiders	53	45	2	14	81	5
6. Frogs or lizards	72	28	0	24	71	5
7. Horses/cows	85	15	0	71	29	0
8. Dogs/cats	86	12	2	79	20	1
9. Snakes	28	66	6	5	82	13
10. Rats/mice	46	52	2	11	78	11
11. Storms	53	44	3	33	63	4
12. Lightning	46	51	3	24	73	3
13. Thunder	55	43	2	30	66	4
14. Fire	39	59	2	17	79	4
15. Old people	95	5	0	87	12	1
16. Crossing street	84	16	0	71	29	0
17. Sight of blood	57	41	2	40	57	3
18. People who are ugly	84	16	0	82	17	1
19. Faces at windows	56	42	2	38	57	5
20. Being kidnapped	55	43	2	38	54	8
21. Specific foods	90	10	0	79	20	1
22. Being alone	63	36	1	40	56	4
23. Being criticized	51	42	7	39	57	4

Fears	Male			Female		
	1	2	3	1	2	3
24. Being in the dark	51	46	3	34	58	8
25. Crowds	89	11	0	83	17	0
26. Strangers	60	39	1	45	53	2
27. Hospitals	57	41	2	60	39	1
28. Bathrooms	95	5	0	91	9	0
29. Closets	94	6	0	77	22	1
30. Toilets	96	4	0	91	9	0
31. Ghosts	51	46	3	38	59	3
32. The devil	54	44	2	34	63	3
33. Hell	53	45	2	39	56	5
34. School	93	6	1	90	10	0
35. Germs	77	22	1	67	32	1
36. Choking	67	32	2	61	37	2
37. Nightmares	63	35	2	54	40	6
38. Riots	63	36	1	54	44	2
39. Dying	54	45	1	48	49	3
40. Deep water	56	39	5	40	53	7
41. Tornadoes, floods, earthquakes	40	56	4	29	65	6
42. Space creatures, monsters	57	39	4	41	54	5
43. Food that might be poisoned	56	42	2	49	47	4
44. Riding in bus or car	93	7	0	87	13	0

No.	Item						
45.	Flying in airplane	73	26	1	60	38	2
46.	Loud sounds, as caps, firecrackers, explosions	76	24	0	50	48	2
47.	Being separated from parents	67	32	1	44	52	4
48.	Parents getting divorce	76	21	3	62	33	5
49.	Reciting in class	58	41	1	45	52	3
50.	Attending social events due to worries of rejection embarrassment	76	23	1	71	29	0
51.	Breaking religious law (sin)	57	41	2	51	48	1
52.	War, enemy invasion, bombing	52	45	3	51	41	8
53.	Making another person angry	52	46	2	53	47	0
54.	Entering a strange room	65	34	1	56	43	1
55.	Being confined or locked up	49	50	1	37	56	7
56.	Going to sleep at night	88	11	1	84	14	2
57.	Being touched by others	89	11	0	78	22	0
58.	People with deformities	74	26	0	59	40	1
59.	Uniformed people police-men, etc.	90	10	0	83	15	2
60.	High places	61	35	4	53	44	3
61.	Opposite sex	90	9	1	85	15	0
62.	Enclosed places	77	23	0	63	35	2
63.	Elevators	89	11	0	78	20	2
64.	Certain part of house (attic, etc.)	83	15	2	68	31	1
65.	Being ill	67	32	1	63	36	1
66.	Family member becoming ill	61	37	2	55	44	1
67.	Going crazy (insane)	80	18	2	79	20	1
68.	Getting lost	57	41	2	51	47	2
69.	Seeing someone wounded	29	67	4	24	72	4
70.	Being wounded	29	68	3	29	67	4
71.	Being seen naked	38	59	3	26	66	8
72.	Having bowel movements	92	7	1	89	10	1
73.	Receiving shots	36	57	7	33	64	3
74.	Doctors or dentists	49	48	3	38	60	2
75.	Having operation	38	60	2	39	56	5
76.	Family member dying	45	51	4	37	56	7
77.	Members of another race	85	15	0	76	22	2
78.	Making mistakes, doing something wrong	44	53	3	37	60	3
79.	Frightening thoughts or daydreams	76	24	0	69	29	2
80.	Tests, examinations	58	41	1	41	57	2
81.	Being adopted	84	14	2	73	23	4

[a] Intensity levels: 1. no fear observed; 2. normal or reasonable fear; 3. unreasonable or excessive fear.
Source: Miller, L. C., Barrett, C. L., & Hampe, E. Phobias of childhood in a prescientific era. In A. Davids (Ed.), *Child personality and psychopathology: Current Topics*. New York: Wiley, 1974.

studies have reported differences on this dimension in either type or number of reported fears (e.g., Angelino et al., 1956; Bamber, 1974; Jersild & Holmes, 1935a; Nalven, 1970; Newstattler, 1938). Others have reported that lower SEC children tend to have more fears than upper SEC children (Angelino et al., 1956; Bamber, 1974; Croake, 1969; Croake & Knox, 1973; Lapouse & Monk, 1959; Jersild & Holmes, 1935a; Jersild et al., 1933). It is also reported that lower SEC children have more fears of specific events (e.g., rats, drunks, cockroaches), whereas higher SEC children tended to fear a different set of factors, such as car accidents and train wrecks (e.g., Angelino et al., 1956; Nalven, 1970).

Lapouse and Monk (1959) reported that lower SEC children showed a larger percentage of fears and worries than the upper SEC children on school marks, what happens in the world (e.g., wars, murders), people different in nationality or race, and using other people's glasses, dishes, silver, and towels.

Any conclusions drawn from this literature must take into account the finding that lower SEC children may list specific fear items rather than more generic groupings (Nalven, 1970). As Graziano et al. (1979) have noted, this finding raises the potential that an artifact has been introduced into fear assessment over different SEC groups.

Another concern with work in trying to find differences between SEC groups relates to the nature of the SEC variable. Since different studies typically define this variable in nonsimilar ways, making comparisons across studies is difficult.

Seriousness of Fears and Related Emotional States

In some respects information on the seriousness of fears and related emotional states comes from intensity data. As noted above, many studies have not provided this type of information and so firm conclusions cannot be drawn on available data on this dimension. However, there are data on what might be characterized as more serious fears. Some authors have noted that more severe phobic disorders account for only 3 to 4% of all referrals to child psychiatrists (e.g., Marks, 1969; Poznanski, 1973). Even earlier, Graham (1964) reported only 10 phobias in 239 consecutive cases referred to the Maudsly Children's Department. Similarly, Graziano and DeGiovanni (1979) found only 7 to 8% of children were referred for specific fear related problems. The incidence of the so-called "school phobia" problem is also low, with composition being only 1–6% of child cases in psychiatric clinics (Chazan, 1962; Eisenberg, 1958). Barrios et al. (1981) speculated that although behavior therapists spend the largest percentage of their time treating fearful and anxious disorders (cf. Wade, Baker, & Hartmann, 1979; Swan & McDonald, 1978), most of these clients are not children.

As noted above, some studies have shown that the incidence of common fears is quite high, but severe phobias accounted for a rather small percentage (i.e., 5% in the Miller et al., 1974 study, and 2.2% in the Agras et al., 1969 study). Similar results were reported by Rutter, Tizard, and Whitmore (1970) who found the prevalence rate for serious fears of only 7 per 1,000 in a total population of 10- and 11-year-olds on the Isle of Wight. Even when the more severe "school phobia" pattern is examined, Leton (1972) found that it occurred at a rate of 5 per 1,000 students. Based on available data, it appears that Miller et al.'s (1974) suggestion that "the most typical response pattern approximates a J curve in which 84% or more of the children show no fear of the stimuli, while 5 to 15% show what parents consider to be normal fear and 0 to 5% show excessive fear. Stimuli eliciting the J-curve pattern include dirt, furry toys, masks or puppets, old people, and toilets, as well as many others" (pp. 104–105) is generally accurate. However, as Barrios et al. (1981) note, not all data from other studies fit this pattern.

Another way in which we can characterize information on the seriousness of children's fears is to examine the relation of fears and other related emotional states to other deviant or pathological behavior. Reviews of this aspect of the literature (e.g., Graziano et al., 1979; L. C. Miller et al., 1974) suggest that there is either insufficient data to make conclusions or that available work offers no specific answers in this area. In the case of such behavior patterns as those described by Quay (1979) used in development of a classification scheme, the various behavior patterns tend to emerge as independent factors. However, Quay (1979) notes that researchers have often failed to specify the nature of their subjects in other than very general terms (e.g., "emotionally disturbed"). Such a tactic makes it difficult to identify related problems. If such problems as "anxiety withdrawal" emerge as independent factors, there may not be a relationship to other behaviors (e.g., aggression). As noted by Miller et al. (1974), a number of investigators have found no correlation between child fears and other forms of deviant behavior (e.g., Lapouse & Monk, 1959). L. C. Miller et al. (1971) found no correlation between "school phobia" and other deviant behaviors. Also, Lapouse and Monk (1959) found no significant correlation between fears and other problematic behaviors (see Table 2.7). The authors also isolated children with ten or more fears and worries and looked for a relationship with the highest values of the combined score, but again found none. Furthermore, when a subsample of children were interviewed to determine if their reports would correspond to parent's reports, no significant relationship between fear and other pathological behavior was found. These studies seem to indicate that fears may not be strongly related to other forms of deviant behavior, yet we really have a paucity of data in this area. As Graziano et al. (1979) note, it may be that a relationship can be found when intensity is used rather than the number of fears.

Table 2.7. Relation of Number of Children's Fears and Worries to Certain Other Behavior Phenomena in a Weighted Representative Sample of 482 Children Aged 6 to 12, as Reported by Mothers.

| Other Behavior* | Percent of Children with Specified Number of Fears and Worries | | | |
	0–6	7 or more	total	(No.)
Bed-wetting				
No	60	40	100	605
Yes	59	41	100	128
Nightmares				
No	60	40	100	530
Yes	49	51	100	203
7 tension phenomena**				
0–1	61	39	100	476
2 or more	51	49	100	257
Combined score***				
0–3	58	42	100	600
4 or more	50	50	100	133

* None of the observed differences are significant at or below the 5 percent level.
** Nail-biting, grinding teeth, thumb-sucking, biting or sucking clothing, picking nose, picking sores, chewing lips or tongue.
*** The 7 tension phenomena plus bed-wetting, nightmares, stuttering, temper loss and tics.
Source: Lapouse, R., & Monk, M. A. Fears and worries in a representative sample of children. *American Journal of Orthopsychiatry*, 1959, **29**, 803–818.

A third way in which the seriousness of children's fears and related emotional states can be studied is to examine the natural course of the fear without intervention (Specific follow-up data on treatment reports will be presented in Chapter 6). There is evidence suggesting that many childhood fears are somewhat transient (e.g., Hagman, 1932; MacFarlane et al., 1954; Marks, 1969). For example, Hagman (1932) reported that 6% of the fears found in his study disappeared within one week, 54% were absent in three months, and 100% were gone in three years. Slater (1939) also reported that various fearful and anxious behaviors in two- and three-year-old children had almost completely disappeared after four weeks, and Cummings (1944, 1946) reported that fears were transitory in two- through seven-year-olds. Kraus (1973) followed 165 children (black, white, Hispanic, and Oriental) from the day they entered kindergarten through high school and some into adulthood. Some of the children displayed anxiety and fear when starting school. Yet in the total group, "separation anxiety" was relatively short-lived.

However, it is possible that more severe and persistent fears remain longer (Poznanski, 1973). Nevertheless, Agras, Chapin and Oliveau (1972) reported that 100% of untreated phobic children improved over a 5-year-period.

Data on the natural course of fears and phobias has important implications for treatment (Barrios et al., 1981). If certain fears dissipate quickly and without intervention, important questions are raised regarding initiation of formal intervention. This might imply, for example, the childhood fears should be targeted for intervention less often than other childhood problems. In support of this notion, Wilson and Evans (in press) found that therapists who were members of the Association for Advancement of Be-Behavior Therapy (AABT) made a decision that no treatment was necessary for a case of childhood fear, but that treatment was appropriate for a case of conduct disorder or social withdrawal. Apparently, the therapists noted that the behaviors exhibited by the fearful child were within "normal limits" or suggested that the parents had unrealistic expectations for the child.

The question of whether or not one should intervene with children experiencing fears and related problems depends on several considerations. As is evident from data reviewed in this chapter, it is difficult to provide empirical evidence for the negative long-term effects of fears, phobias, and related problems. This issue has similarly been raised in the treatment literature with isolated or withdrawn children (e.g., Conger & Keane, 1981). However, as noted throughout this chapter, basic questions can be raised regarding the *absence* of data in this area. We simply do not have enough data to draw firm conclusions regarding when to intervene. Aside from the absence of data, the quality of existing data also keeps us from drawing premature conclusions.

The decision, however, to intervene with children experiencing extreme fears and phobias cannot be made solely from long-term follow-up studies or developmental incidence data. Selection of a particular fear or phobia for intervention depends on several considerations that have been raised in the behavior therapy literature. For example, according to Mash and Terdall (1981), criteria for selecting a behavior problem should depend on the following:

1. Behaviors that are consistent with some developmental or local norms for performance.
2. Behaviors that have been shown, as a result of careful task analysis, to be critical components for successful performance. . . .
3. Behaviors that are subjectively rated as positive by recognized community standards. . . .
4. Behaviors that effectively discriminate between "skilled" and "nonskilled" performers.
5. Behaviors whose natural history is known to have a poor long term prognosis [p. 36].

As Mash and Terdall (1981) note, these guidelines represent tentative decision-making rules. Other guidelines might be invoked as well, such as giving priority to problems that are most aversive to parents (Bijou & Peterson,

1971) or other care providers (Tharp & Wetzel, 1969). Unfortunately, there is little empirical evidence to support the validity of target behavior selection on most childhood behavior problems (Nelson & Hayes, 1979; Voeltz & Evans, 1982; Wilson & Evans, in press). Indeed, the reliability of target behavior selection may set a lower limit on the validity that can be obtained. For example, Wilson and Evans (in press) found that in a sample of AABT members who were asked to provide written responses to brief profiles of three types of common childhood problems (fearfulness, conduct disorder, and social withdrawal), target selection was quite unreliable.

Given the paucity of empirical data in this area, we would recommend that if a child's fear is found to (1) be excessive, (2) last over a relatively long period of time, and (3) create problems in living for the parent(s) and/or child, then therapeutic intervention should be considered.

Additional Considerations

Virtually all reviews of the fear, phobia, and anxiety literature on incidence have pointed to rather severe methodological limitations in this data base. Graziano et al. (1979) captured the essence of these problems in the following statement:

> In summary, the basic subjective-report methods have obvious shortcomings: some studies interviewed children, some parents; some required lists, some ratings; the ages of children are not comparable across studies; random samplings from normal childhood populations were seldom taken; reliability and validity data were not reported [p. 812].

Generally, the problems in this area can be conceptualized on the following dimensions: type of data gathered, nature of the questions asked, who was asked, and sampling issues.

Type of Data Gathered.   The assessment strategies in the developmental and normative studies reviewed above have generally employed indirect measures including interview, rating scales, and checklists. There are, of course, exceptions to this as in the case of some well-controlled laboratory studies of infant and toddler stranger distress and separation anxiety (cf., Smith, 1979), and a few studies examining the incidence of children's fears and phobias (e.g., Agras et al., 1969; Jersild & Holmes, 1935a) that obtained data through direct observation methods.

Obviously, not all of these procedures are equally bad on methodological grounds. Some studies are not particularly trustworthy, although they certainly provide interesting data. Abe (1972) compared self-report fears of 242 mothers with their childhood fears as recollected and reported by their mothers. Other studies have asked adults to recall the onset of these child-hood fears. Such approaches are typically unable to provide the quality data needed to make firm conclusions regarding incidence because they are retro-spective and lack reliability and validity information.

Several other variations in data collection have been reported. In some studies, children and/or parents were requested to write out or verbally report things they were afraid of (e.g., Maurer, 1965; Pratt, 1945). In other studies individuals were to list the fears of other children in their own age group (e.g., Angelino et al., 1956; Nalven, 1970).

In many of these procedures, a list and rank technique was employed (e.g., Lapouse & Monk, 1959). Graziano et al. (1979) identified two major short-comings of this approach: the researcher cannot be sure whether such lists of fear stimuli are complete, and such a listing procedure provides little or no information on the intensity dimension.

Like many of the studies that have been done in the classification area, studies on incidence have generally used rating scales or checklists for both parents (e.g., L. C. Miller, 1967; L. C. Miller et al., 1971; 1972b) and child (e.g., Bamber, 1974; Russell, 1967; Scherer & Nakamura, 1968). Typically the standardized nature of the response format provides an advantage over the earlier methods based on lists and rankings. Nevertheless, these methods (e.g., the Louisville Fear Survey) have problems of reliability and validity and may create a false sense of trust in the data, unless supplemented by other direct measures [rating scales and checklists are discussed in detail in Chapter 3].

Who Is Asked. An important methodological issue in fear incidence research is who is asked about the fears. In some research, children have been asked directly (e.g., Angelino et al., 1956; Croake, 1969; Maurer, 1965; Nalven, 1970; Pratt, 1945), while other studies have used parents (usually the mother) as a data source (e.g., Hagman, 1932; Lapouse & Monk, 1959). On the face of it, asking the child appears to be a good strategy, but questions might be raised regarding the child's verbal abilities as well as his/her awareness of certain fears. However, it does appear that children are aware of various fears and anxieties, even though attempts might be made to mask the con-cerns, such as in the dying child's awareness of death (Spinetta, 1974). Use of parents or other providers might be considered more valid, but discrepan-cies in reported fears do occur. In incidence research it appears important to compare parent and child report (e.g., Lapouse & Monk, 1959) as well as supplementing verbal report through other direct measures (e.g., Agras et al., 1969; Lapouse & Monk, 1959).

Sampling Issues. When one considers normative research the issues of representativeness and generalizability immediately emerge. Yet in the fear incidence research, results do not appear generalizable because random sampling from a population is not used in most studies (Graziano et al., 1979). There are, of course, some exceptions (e.g., Lapouse & Monk, 1959; L. C. Miller et al., 1971). For example, Lapouse and Monk (1959) used the Buffalo, New York City Directory to draw a random sample. Nevertheless, this sample would hardly be representative of the total population of the United States. Moreover, the study is dated and may not generalize to contemporary fears.

Generally, it is difficult to establish a normative base because studies have not taken random samples from a representative normal population. It is also difficult to generalize because studies vary in so many different dimensions of methodology (e.g., who does the rating, the method used, quality of the data).

Nature of the Questions Asked. Graziano et al. (1979) identified the major limitation of normative research, asking the proverbial "What are the common fears of children?" Basic questions can then be raised about the desirability of continuing with research that is conducted in this fashion. These authors' essential message is that fear development and expression is a complex process influenced greatly by the learning process. We would concur wholeheartedly and in consideration of their issues and our own review of this literature, advance the following questions:

1. What are the cognitions involved in children's fears?
2. How do children naturally deal with various fears?
3. What is the adaptive value of certain fears?
4. What strategies do children and parents use to overcome certain fears?
5. To what degree are fears self-generated and maintained?
6. To what degree are fears externally generated and maintained?
7. What is the role of social skills in dealing with fear arousing situations?
8. What are the relationships of various fear types to other forms of deviant behavior?
9. What are the relationships of various fear intensities to other forms of deviant behavior?
10. What is the developmental course of children's fears, both adaptive and maladaptive?

Answers to questions like those listed above will help us to understand children's fears, phobias, and related problems.

SUMMARY AND CONCLUSION

In this chapter we have provided an overview of some issues in diagnosis, classification, and incidence. We noted that there is considerable variation in definition of fears and related emotional states. Many of the variations are presumably due to different theoretical accounts of the nature of fear, phobia, and anxiety. Despite problems with the approach, we recommended a multiple response component approach to definition of fears and related emotional states. Such a triple mode approach would take into account cognitive (e.g., thoughts, feelings), physiological (e.g., GSR, heart rate), and motor (e.g., trembling, avoidance behaviors) systems. Such an approach allows an operational definition of the problem and has utility in research, theory, and practice.

Like the area of definition, the work in diagnosis and classification is characterized by considerable diversity. The newest approach to diagnosis is represented in the DSM-III which includes a section on anxiety disorders in childhood and adolescence. Included within this system are separation anxiety disorder, avoidant disorder of childhood or adolescence, and overanxious disorder. We also discussed the sleep terror disorder within this system. Like its predecessor, DSM-II, the DSM III represents a clinical diagnostic system. Currently, there is little information available on the reliability and validity of the general DSM-III system and the anxiety disorders of children and adolescents in particular. Other diagnostic and classification systems included those based on multivariate statistical approaches, specific ones developed for children's fears and phobias and behavioral systems. The multivariate approach appears promising in that an anxiety/withdrawal pattern has been identified with some consistency. Yet the methods used to gather data (e.g., rating scales, questionnaires) limit the validity of these approaches. The specific classification schemes for fears and phobias as well as the behavioral systems appear lacking in empirical support at this time. Nevertheless, emerging behavioral systems do offer promise in classification, particularly those employing a three-system response component approach. Considerable research has been focused on the normative and developmental aspects of children's fears and related emotional states. Unfortunately, this research has not been particularly illuminating in offering clear statements about the role of sex, temporal factors, SEC, and seriousness of these problems. Methodological problems also plague this area of empirical investigation. Particularly problematic has been the nature of the data obtained (as through rating scales, interviews, checklists) and the type of questions that have been asked (i.e., what do children fear). Little data are available on the intensity of children's fears.

NOTES

1. For an overview of the WHO, ICD-9, GAP, and California I-Level system, the reader is referred to Quay (1979).

2. Adams et al. (1977) suggest that development of a classification system is initiated with the construction of lower-order categories called an "alpha taxonomy." In this stage the basic terminology or operational definition of science are constructed. This further requires a thorough description of the observable attributes of a phenomenon (see also, Brunner, Goodnow, & Austin, 1965).

CHAPTER 3

Assessment of Children's Fears and Phobias

Major advances have occurred in the development of behavioral approaches to assessment. These advances have been well documented in numerous books (e.g., Barlow, 1981; Ciminero, Calhoun, & Adams, 1977; Cone & Hawkins, 1977; Haynes, 1978, Hersen & Bellack, 1976, 1981; Mash & Terdall, 1981a; Wiggins, 1973) devoted to the topic of behavioral assessment. However, with the exception of a few books (e.g., Mash & Terdall, 1976a, 1981) and several chapters (e.g., Ciminero & Drabman, 1977; Evans & Nelson, 1977; Kratochwill, 1982), little of this work has been devoted to assessment of children. Fortunately, there have been several reviews devoted to assessment of children's fears and related problems (e.g., Barrios & Shigetomi, in press; Barrios, Hartmann, & Shigetomi, 1981; Miller, Barrett, & Hampe, 1974). We will build upon these efforts as well as establish several new issues and directions.

It must also be emphasized that the numerous issues raised in the behavioral assessment of adult disorders have a great deal of relevance for assessment of child disorders in general and for the assessment of fears and related problems specifically. Indeed, many sources on assessment of adult fears and related problems (e.g., Agras & Jacob, 1981; Bernstein, 1973; Borkovec, Weerts, & Bernstein, 1977; Emmelkamp, 1979; Lang, 1977b) have created an important foundation for work in the area of child assessment.

In this chapter we present an overview of the various behavioral assessment strategies that have been employed with children experiencing fears and related problems. The chapter presents some ways child behavioral assessment can be used within contemporary behavior therapy, models of behavioral assessment, and a conceptual framework for behavioral assessment of children's fears. Thereafter, specific methods of behavioral assessment are presented along with illustrations of their use in research and practice. Finally, some conceptual issues in child behavioral assessment are presented as a context for future work in the field.

CHILD BEHAVIORAL ASSESSMENT: GENERAL ISSUES

Behavioral Assessment Applications

Behavioral assessment of children's fears and related problems has been used in three areas: selection or classification, treatment program development and monitoring, and research. As we observed in Chapter 2, behavioral assessment strategies are being used to select clients for treatment programs and to assign them to various diagnostic categories (e.g., DSM-III). Conceptual and methodological work in this area is really in its infancy compared to other developments in the field. Moreover, numerous issues regarding the utility of behavioral classification systems and how these systems articulate to more traditional schemes already engrained in research and practice remain unresolved.

The second use of behavioral assessment is more established conceptually, although much empirical work needs to be devoted to determining how assessment leads to *development* of treatment programs. At the conceptual level, behavioral assessment has usually been characterized as being specific to a client's problem, linked to treatment plan development, and continuous throughout treatment. Yet questions have been raised over the degree to which assessment is actually linked to treatment plan development (Hartmann et al., 1979), as well as the extent to which behavioral assessment is continuous in actual practice (Barlow, 1981). Solutions to these issues will likely come from empirical work (in the former case) and development of practical and standardized measures (see Kratochwill, 1982; Nelson, 1981).

The applications of behavioral assessment in clinical research is perhaps the area where major advances have been made. Indeed, assessment and design methodology have been a major characteristic of behavior therapy and its scientific focus (Deitz, 1978; Kazdin & Wilson, 1978). Definite advances have been made in the systematic evaluation of clinical interventions (Bellack & Hersen, 1978). Behavioral assessment strategies have been used in both group (Kazdin, 1980e) and single case or time series research (Hersen & Barlow, 1976; Kazdin, 1978b; Kratochwill, 1978). Assessment has been helpful in elucidating which treatments are effective with clients and the components that are active in package treatment programs. More detailed contributions of behavioral methodology are presented in Chapter 6.

Behavioral Versus Traditional Assessment

A major issue in the field of child behavior assessment is defining what is included in the area on terms of procedures and techniques. To suggest that the field is remarkably diverse is somewhat of an understatement. Behavioral assessment is part of the larger domain of behavior therapy or behavior modification which is growing increasingly diverse in research and practice (Kazdin, 1979a). As noted in Chapter 1, contemporary behavior therapy consists of several areas including applied behavior analysis, mediational S-R approaches, social learning theory, and cognitive behavior modification (Kazdin & Wilson, 1978). Somewhat different assessment techniques tend to be associated with these subdomains of the field.

Generally, behavioral assessment has embraced a conceptual approach that involves a problem-solving strategy rather than a set of specific techniques and procedures (Evans & Nelson, 1977; Mash & Terdall, 1981). This perspective provides some consistency in defining what behavioral assessment is, but it also expands the range of techniques and procedures that might be employed in the area. As will become evident in subsequent sections of this chapter, a number of different techniques have been used to assess children's fears and related problems. In many cases, devices developed for more traditional assessment models are employed in child behavioral assessment (e.g., self-report measures, checklists and rating scales).

Attempts to define behavioral assessment have typically focused on several conceptual and theoretical dimensions that contrast it with traditional assessment approaches (Hartmann et al., 1979). Usually the major differences between behavioral and traditional assessment emanate from the assumptions that each approach adheres to in explaining human behavior (Nelson & Hayes, 1979). Individuals working within the traditional approach typically focus assessment toward identifying underlying causes. In contrast, behavioral assessors typically focus on environmental or person-environmental events as they have relevance to developing a treatment program. Actually behavioral assessment can be distinguished from more traditional forms of assessment on several dimensions. A summary of these differences has been compiled by Hartmann et al. (1979) and is displayed in Table 3.1. Within the context of childhood fears, and related problems, traditional assessment approaches have tended to emphasize intraorganismic variables to account for these disorders. In such assessment, traditional approaches focus more heavily on constructs where overt behavior (e.g., behavioral avoidance) is considered a *sign* of underlying pathology and the *situation* in which the client is assessed is of less or little importance.

Yet it is important to recognize that traditional assessment is not a uniform approach with consistent models and techniques. For example, traditional approaches include both psychodynamic and trait models (Korchin & Schuldberg, 1981). The psychodynamic model is characterized by the following:

(a) uses a number of procedures,
(b) intended to tap various areas of psychological functioning,

Table 3.1. Differences Between Behavioral and Traditional Approaches to Assessment

	Behavioral	Traditional
I. Assumptions		
1. Conception of personality	Personality constructs mainly employed to summarize specific behavior patterns, if at all	Personality as a reflection of enduring underlying states or traits
2. Causes of behavior	Maintaining conditions sought in current environment	Intrapsychic or within the individual
II. Implications		
1. Role of behavior	Important as a sample of person's repertoire in specific situation	Behavior assumes importance only insofar as it indexes underlying causes
2. Role of history	Relatively unimportant, except, for example, to provide a retrospective baseline	Crucial in that present conditions seen as a product of the past
3. Consistency of behavior	Behavior thought to be specific to the situation	Behavior expected to be consistent across time and settings
III. Uses of data	To describe target behaviors and maintaining conditions To select the appropriate treatment To evaluate and revise treatment	To describe personality functioning and etiology To diagnose or classify To make prognosis; to predict
IV. Other characteristics		
1. Level of inferences	Low	Medium to high
2. Comparisons	More emphasis on intraindividual or idiographic	More emphasis on interindividual or nomothetic
3. Methods of assessment	More emphasis on direct methods (e.g., observations of behavior in natural environment)	More emphasis on indirect methods (e.g., interviews and self-report)
4. Timing of assessment	More ongoing; prior, during, and after treatment	Pre- and perhaps posttreatment, or strictly to diagnose
5. Scope of assessment	Specific measures and of more variables (e.g., of target behaviors in various situations, of side effects, context, strengths as well as deficiencies)	More global measures (e.g., of cure, or improvement) but only of the individual

Source: Hartmann, D. P., Roper, B. L., & Bradford, D.C. Some relationships between behavioral and traditional assessment. *Journal of Behavioral Assessment*, 1979, **1**, 3–21.

(c) both at a conscious and unconscious level,

(d) using projective techniques as well as more objective and standardized tests,

(e) in both cases, interpretations may rest on symbolic signs as well as scorable responses,

(f) with the goal of describing individuals in personalogical rather than normative terms [Korchin & Schuldberg, 1981, p. 1147].

Generally, the psychodynamic approach is aimed at providing a multifaceted description of the child which in turn promotes a unique and individual approach to assessment.

Another traditional model, called the psychometric approach, is characterized by the use of a variety of individual and group tests to compare individuals along various trait-dimensions. Within this approach, various personality structures are given major emphasis in accounting for behavior disorders (Mischel, 1968; 1974), as the following description suggests:

> The modern approach (to personality testing) says let's find out what personality structure we should be measuring first and then find devices to measure them. . . . In my own work we started with a list of all the personality traits that existed in the English language. We have available new, powerful techniques like factor analysis for analyzing the interrelationships among these traits empirically and finding the factors of major importance which explained the relationships among the literally thousands of traits people use to describe personality. It has taken us 30 or 40 years to bring the personality area to the same precision as people like Spearman and Thurstone did in the ability area, but we now have a number of modern questionnaires which measure well replicated personality dimensions [Cattell cited in Krug, 1978, p. 29].

Although trait theorists disagree on what traits explain certain patterns of behavior, there is general agreement that traits explain why certain behavior patterns are consistent across time and settings, and that various behavior patterns are expressions of traits.

In contrast to these psychodynamic and traditional assessment approaches, the behavioral model generally places heavy emphasis on the direct measurement of a *sample* of a child's problematic behavior in the situation in which it occurs and the client-situation interactions (Bandura, 1977; Kazdin, 1979a; Mischel, 1968, 1973). The focus on behavior as a sample in situations is considered important because it provides information on factors that are currently responsible for maintaining fears and related problems. Generally, the fear-related behaviors are assessed without a reliance on underlying causes.

Models of Behavioral Assessment

The development of different models of behavioral assessment is reflective of the evolution of behavior therapy in general as well as its diversity. Initially, the S-R model was used to conceptualize assessment, but this was expanded to include stimulus (S), response (R), contingency (K), and consequence (C) (Lindsley, 1964). A model that has been popular within the more applied behavior analytic area was proposed by Stuart (1970) and involves an A (antecedent), B (behaviors), and C (consequences) formulation. Another model, taking into account organistic variables, was introduced by Kanfer and Saslow (1969) and involves a S-O-R-K-C framework.

Accompanying the Kanfer and Saslow (1969) approach are seven specific components that have been used to guide assessment across many areas of the field:

1. An *initial analysis of the problem situation*, in which the various behaviors that brought the client to treatment are specified.
2. A *clarification of the problem situation*, in which various environmental variables are specified.
3. A *motivational analysis*, in which reinforcing and punishing stimuli are identified.
4. A *developmental analysis*, in which biological, sociological, and behavioral changes of potential relevance to treatment are identified.
5. An *analysis of self-control*, in which the situations and behaviors the client can control are identified.
6. An *analysis of social situations*, in which the intrapersonal relationships of individuals in the client's environment and their various aversive and reinforcing qualities are specified.
7. An *analysis of the socio-cultural physical environment*, in which normative standards of behavior and the client's opportunities for support are evaluated [pp. 433–437].

Within the context of assessing children's fears and related problems, several positive features of this approach can be identified. First, the S-O-R-K-C model includes components that might not be focused on in other approaches. The model would promote a three-mode response assessment, a focus that more adequately reflects the complex nature of fears and related disorders. The model promotes assessment of behavioral assets as well as deficits. In children experiencing phobic reactions this is important because identification of behavioral assets may help predict the success of treatment as well as identify areas where treatment might be focused. For example, children who have mental imagery skills might become candidates for coping skills treatment (e.g., Peterson & Shigetomi, 1981). Also, children who are able to use verbal controlling responses may be trained to cope with feared situations (Kanfer, Karoly, & Newman, 1975).

It should be noted that while the Kanfer and Saslow (1969) model provides a framework for gathering data, specific methods and techniques remain the choice of the therapist. Moreover, data interpretation from this approach remains subjective (Dickson, 1975) as does selection of a specific treatment strategy (Ciminero, 1977), and the model or method of monitoring the treatment program (Ciminero & Drabman, 1977). Despite these potential shortcomings, the model is extremely useful in content and focus for child fear assessment.

Another model specifically focusing on anxiety assessment is the functional analytic strategy proposed by Borkovec et al. (1977). Their approach involves five major questions that must be answered in assessment:

1. *What is the nature of the stimulus classes that elicit and/or signal anxiety response components of this presenting problem?*
2. *What response components are functionally relevant to the presenting problem?*
3. *Does the client display an anticipatory anxiety reaction and, if so, what is its component structure and spatial/temporal, thematic, and semantic relationship to feared stimuli?*
4. *Does the client's anxiety response pattern represent an inappropriately conditioned response to an objectively nonthreatening situation, or is it an appropriate reaction to situations that, for a variety of reasons, are harmful, dangerous, or punishing?*
5. *What are the immediate and/or long-term consequences of each anxiety response component* [pp. 374–378]?

This functional behavioral model appears useful for conceptualizing assessment of children's fears and related problems for several reasons. To begin with, the model is relatively comprehensive in areas in which fear assessment should take place. For example, because the model takes into account "anticipatory anxiety" it would be relevant in assessing children's avoidance behavior as fearful situations are approached (e.g., school-related fears or phobias). In addition, the approach promotes implementation of the three-mode response assessment (see discussion below), and so provides a more comprehensive picture of the fear problem in terms of the areas sampled. Another positive feature of the model is that it can be linked to treatment planning and monitoring. As noted by Borkovec et al. (1977), determination of stimuli that trigger anticipatory anxiety can help develop measures to implement gradual exposure procedures (e.g., participant modeling, systematic desensitization).

The major consideration with this model and the others reviewed in this section is the paucity of research explicating how they might be applied with children experiencing fears, phobias, and related problems. Until we know more about the efficacy of these approaches from empirical work, each of them must be used with caution, although we believe that they can provide an extremely useful model for behavioral assessment.

A Conceptual Framework for Behavioral Fear Assessment

Because assessment of children's fears and related problems represents a diverse set of procedures and techniques, we will present a conceptual framework to assist researchers and practitioners in selection and use of a particular assessment approach. The present conceptual framework is based on the simultaneous consideration of several aspects of the assessment process outlined by Cone and his associates (Cone, 1978, 1979; Cone & Hawkins, 1977). Within this conceptual framework, called the Behavioral Assessment Grid (BAG), three aspects of the assessment process are considered (see Figure 3.1) (1) the behavioral contents assessed, (2) the methods used to assess them, and (3) the types of generalization (i.e., reliability and validity) established for the scores on the measure being classified.[1]

Contents. As noted in Chapter 2, assessment in the area of fears and related problems usually focuses on three content areas, systems (Lang, 1968, 1971, 1977a), or channels (Paul & Bernstein, 1973). The response channels are not always perfectly correlated, although they are usually related to some extent (Hodgson & Rachman, 1974; Rachman & Hodgson, 1974). Therefore, data obtained from one response channel may have important implications for data that one might obtain from another channel.

In any assessment conducted within the context of the three channel approach, it is important to make a distinction between mode of the measurement strategy and the content area it is designed to assess (Cone, 1978). Thus, the three behavioral content areas can be measured by a technique or device whose mode may be behavioral, self-report, or physiological. For example, the behavior therapist might obtain information on the motor component of dog fear through an interview in which questions are asked regarding the degree to which s/he is able to approach a particular dog. Thus, the interview assesses motor response via the interview mode. Similarly, motor responses could be measured through an analogue BAT. In making distinctions among various assessment strategies, it is also important to emphasize that some measurement strategies are only theoretical possibilities (i.e., cognitive activities cannot be measured using ratings or direct observation by others).

Methods. The methods used to gather data can be ordered along a continuum of directness representing the extent to which they:

1. Measure the target response of clinical relevance (i.e., the clinical fear).
2. Measure the target response at the time and place of its natural occurrence (i.e., in the presence of the feared stimulus).

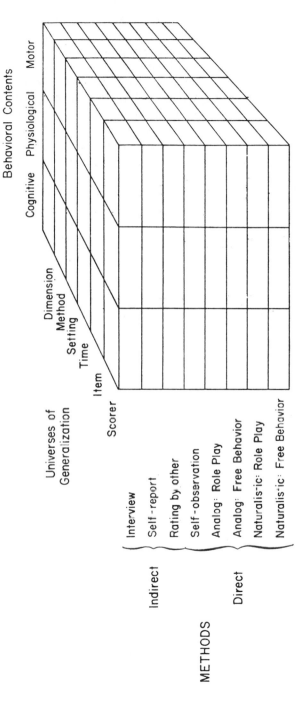

Figure 3.1. The Behavioral Assessment Grid (BAG), a taxonomy of behavioral assessment integrating contents, methods, and universes of generalization.

Source: Cone, J. D. The Behavioral Assessment Grid (BAG): A Conceptual framework and a taxonomy. *Behavior Therapy,* 1978, **9**, 882–888. Reprinted by permission.

Several different methods of assessment are usually employed that can be conceptualized as either direct or indirect. Interviews, self-report measures, and checklists and rating scales can be conceptualized as indirect measures because they are a verbal representation of more clinically relevant activities that occur at some other time and place. For example, in the interview the child client or careprovider typically report events that occurred at some other time and place (i.e., other than in the interview setting at the time the interview occurs). The indirect methods have an important place within behavioral assessment, but until recently have not had a formal rationale for their use. However, in addition to the Cone (1978) conceptualization, a theoretical perspective based on social behaviorism psychometrics has been offered as a rationale for indirect measures (Burns, 1980). This framework is part of the larger paradigm of social behaviorism (Staats, 1975).

Several procedures are included within the domain of direct assessment methods. These include self-observation or monitoring, direct observation by others (in either analogue or natural settings), and psychophysiological measures. In the self-monitoring form of assessment, the observer and observee are the same. The self-observation form of assessment generally differs from self-report in that observation of the behavior occurs at the time of its natural occurrence in self-monitoring, whereas responses refer to past events in self-report. In direct observation, an observer provides data on a client's behavior (clinical target) in either a naturalistic or analogue setting. It should be emphasized that the analogue nature of assessment can vary on a number of dimensions, such as the setting in which the assessment occurs, nature of the response required, person doing the assessment, and instructions given the client (see Chapter 6). Thus, although the Cone (1978) analogue conceptualization is quite useful, we prefer an approach that takes into account a number of analogue dimensions in direct observational assessment. Finally, various physiological assessment procedures are used to obtain information on fears and related problems in the physiological channel.

Several issues are important to consider in the Cone (1978) formulation. To begin with, some assessment methods or devices actually measure more than one channel within the same instrument. For example, a self-report questionnaire may include items that provide a measure of the motoric response channel, but could also include items that refer to cognitions or physiological responses. Second, when measures within the three content areas are monitored, it cannot be assumed that they are highly correlated (Cone, 1979; Bellack & Hersen, 1977a, 1977b). Possible reasons for low correlations among the three response systems include problems in determining what is meant by each mode, concern as to whether modes or channels should be conceptualized at all, and methodological problems in research investigating the relations (see a discussion of these issues in Chapter 6).

Finally, the finding that the three systems do not correlate highly may have implications for treatment. Treatment can be focused on the areas where problems occur. We now explore a number of different assessment strategies that have been used with children experiencing fears and related problems.

SPECIFIC ASSESSMENT TECHNIQUES
AND STRATEGIES

A considerably large number of behavioral assessment devices and procedures have been used with children experiencing fears and related problems. We have grouped the many devices and procedures into the following categories: Interviews, Self-Report Inventories, Checklist and Rating Scales, Self-Monitoring, Direct Observation and Unobtrusive Measures, and Psychophysiological techniques. There are many strategies that are subsumed under these general assessment domains. Although other conceptual groupings could easily be established, this framework is employed so that various methodological issues can be raised in the use of particular assessment procedures. However, it will become obvious to the reader that there is considerable overlap among the various categories at times, especially with regard to the response channel being assessed.

Interview Assessment

The interview assessment format perhaps represents one of the most frequent and common assessment strategies used with children experiencing fears and related problems. Indeed, the clinical interview is likely the most often used assessment strategy for gathering data across all therapeutic orientations. There is a rather extensive literature reviewing conceptual and methodological aspects of clinical interviewing (e.g., Burke & DeMers, 1979; Cormier & Cormier, 1979; Maloney & Ward, 1976) and a number of sources reviewing this topic in the behavioral literature (e.g., Ciminero, 1977; Ciminero & Drabman, 1977; Haynes & Jensen, 1979; Linehan, 1977; Meyer, Liddel, & Lyons, 1977; Morganstern, 1976).

To provide the reader with a framework for the use of interview assessment with children's fears and related problems, we have found the approach of Burke and DeMers (1979) useful. The authors have described three dimensions (i.e., predetermination of questions, interviewer response options, and breadth of content explored) that can be combined into a conceptual model making 27 different interview assessment formats. Each of these are discussed within the context of their application to assessing children's fears and related disorders.

Predetermination of Questions

Interview Types.   One dimension on which the interview can vary is the degree to which interviewer questions are predetermined. Somewhat arbitrarily, these categories include a standardized interview, the moderately standardized interview, and the unstandardized interview. In the standardized interview, a list of questions or statements are followed during the actual interview. Relatively few standardized formats are available for assessment of children's fears. Table 3.2 shows an example of a standardized format for an initial interview developed by Morris (1980) that can be used with the child and/or parents where there are concerns over fears and related problems. Less standardized interview assessment procedures can be employed as well. For example, a number of semistandardized formats have been developed for conducting a behavioral assessment interview (e.g., Bergan, 1977; Bersoff & Grieger, 1971; Holland, 1970; Wahler & Cormier, 1970). In such strategies a greater degree of flexibility could be expected since exact wording and phrasing are not specified. In the behavioral consultation model developed by Bergan (1977) and his associates, some structure is apparent in the specific categories that are used. Another less structured format is the Behavioral Analysis System developed by Kanfer and Grimm (1977). An outline of this system is presented in Table 3.3. The system provides less structure than the approaches that employ relatively standardized script responses for the therapist/interviewer. However, because both the Bergan (1977) and Kanfer and Grimm (1977) approaches provide an ordering of the questions or areas to be discussed, they have important structures within the assessment.

Table 3.2. Suggested Guide For The Conduct Of The Initial Interview

---

A. What is the problem behavior? What seems to be troubling you? What is the fear you have?
   1. How long have you had this difficulty?
   2. When does this fear or thought usually come into your mind? When does this problem seem to occur the most? In what types of situations or circumstances does the problem occur? Are there any reasons you can think of for its occurrence? When does the problem/fear *not* occur?
   3. Has the problem been the same all along—or has it gotten better or worse?
      (a) Is there any situation that you can associate with it getting better or worse?
B. General Background
   1. When born? Where?
   2. How many brothers and sisters do you have?
      (a) Where are you in the birth order?
      (b) How much older is your eldest or youngest same sex sibling?
      (c) How did(do) you get along with him(her)?
   3. Parents—are they still alive? When did each die?

Table 3.2. (*continued*)

C. Father
1. What kind of person is(was) he—especially during your early years (4–8 years)? How does he now act towards you? Please explain/elaborate.
2. Is(was) he interested in you? Are(were) you interested in what he had to say?
3. Has(did) he ever punish(ed) you? Please elaborate.
4. Has(did) he play favorites with the children? How do(did) you feel about this? Please elaborate.
5. Does(did) he have any fears that you knew of?

D. Mother
Same questions asked about the father

E. Parents
1. Do(did) they like each other? Did they like you?
2. Do(did) they behave toward you as if they liked you?
3. Do(did) they get along together?
   (a) Fight much? Divorce threats?
   (b) Was there hollering and yelling at each other?
4. Do(did) they show outward signs of affection towards each other. Please elaborate.

F. Significant others
1. Any other adults who played an important part of your life?
2. Describe what they are(were) like and how they play an important role in your life.

G. Additional/Related fears
1. Any additional fears
2. When did they occur?
3. Do you still have some of these? When did they stop?

H. School/Friends
1. What grade(year) are you in? Name of school.
2. Like school?
3. Best liked subjects? Worse liked subjects?
4. Sports—Do you participate in them or watch them?
   (a) How are(were) you in them?
5. Friends
   (a) Have you made any friends at school?
   (b) Any real close ones?
   (c) What do you usually do with your friends? Where do you usually go?
   (d) What do your friends like about you? What do they dislike about you?
   (e) How often do you see your friends outside of school? Where do you see them?
6. Anyone at school that you are(were) afraid of? Is the person the same sex as you?
7. Are (were) you afraid of any teachers? Why?
8. What do you do after school?

I. Job
1. Do you have a part-time job?
2. What kind of work do you do?
3. Do you like your job? What do you like the best/least about your job?
4. Any thoughts about quitting?
5. What other types of jobs have you had? Why did you leave them?

Table 3.2 continued on p. 84.

Table 3.2. (*continued*)

J. Dating
   1. At what age did you begin dating?
   2. Would you describe where you usually go on dates?
      (a) Do you go to parties?
      (b) Do you go to movies?
      (c) Do you go out to eat?
   3. Do you usually go out with other couples on dates or alone?
   4. Do you usually date more than one guy/girl at a time?
   5. Do you see someone now in a steady/regular fashion?
   6. Where do you usually go on your dates? Do you (your date) drive? Do you (your date's) parents drive? Do you take the bus?
K. Environment
   1. Do you like the area of the city where you are now living?
   2. Anything that you are not satisfied with?
   3. What's your religion?
      (a) Is it important to you? In what way?
      (b) How religious are you (not at all, mildly, moderately, or extremely)?
      (c) Do you spend a lot of time in church/temple-related activities?

Source: Adapted from Morris, R. J. Fear reduction methods. In F. H. Kanfer & A. P. Goldstein (Eds.), *Helping people change*. (2nd ed.) New York: Pergamon Press, 1980. Reproduced with permission.

At the other end of the continuum are those interview assessment strategies that have no predetermined questions or format. Such formats typically provide a good deal of flexibility in exploration of the problem.

Considerations. Associated with each type of interview format are several methodological and conceptual issues. In the case of the unstandardized interview, clinicians are usually free to pursue many different directions, thereby allowing exploration of some issues in greater depth than would occur in a more structured format. However, there are some important information losses with this format. First of all, different individuals, even with the same theoretical persuasion, are unlikely to obtain the same information from the same client with the same problem. When this occurs, it is difficult to assume that the same treatment would be applied. In short, both the reliability and validity of the assessment procedure may be compromised. Data bearing on this issue come from a study by Hay, Hay, Angle, and Nelson (1979) in which four interviewers conducted comprehensive behavioral interviews with the same four clients. The results of the study suggested that it was possible to generalize across interviewers on the overall number of problem areas for a client. Yet, inter-interviewer agreement on specific problem areas and items demonstrated low levels of reliability. Various factors including input variables (e.g., differences in questions asked), output

Table 3.3. A Behavioral Analysis System

I. Behavioral Deficits
   A. Inadequate base of knowledge for guiding behavior
   B. Failure to engage in acceptable social behaviors due to skills deficits
   C. Inability to supplement or counter immediate environmental influences and regulate one's behavior through self-directing response
   D. Deficiencies in self-reinforcement for performance
   E. Deficits in monitoring one's own behavior
   F. Inability to alter responses in conflict situations
   G. Limited behavior repertoire due to restricted range of reinforcers
   H. Deficits in cognitive and/or motor behaviors necessary to meet the demands of daily living
II. Behavioral Excesses
   A. Conditional inappropriate anxiety to objects of events
   B. Excessive self-observational activity
III. Problems in Environmental Stimulus Control
   A. Affective responses to stimulus objects or events leading to subjective distress or unacceptable behavior
   B. Failure to offer support or opportunities for behaviors appropriate in a different milieu
   C. Failure to meet environmental demands or responsibilities arising from inefficient organization of time
IV. Inappropriate Self-Generated Stimulus Control
   A. Self-descriptions serving as cues for behaviors leading to negative outcomes
   B. Verbal/symbolic activity serving to cue inappropriate behavior
   C. Faulty labeling of internal cues
V. Inappropriate Contingency Arrangement
   A. Failure of the environment to support appropriate behavior
   B. Environmental maintenance of undesirable behavior
   C. Excessive use of positive reinforcement for desirable behaviors
   D. Delivery of reinforcement independent of responding

Source: Kanfer, F. H., & Grimm, L. G. Behavioral analysis: Selecting target behaviors in the interview. *Behavior Modification*, 1977, **1**, 7–28.

variables (e.g., method of recording the data), and consistency of client responses (e.g., inconsistent client responses) were identified as factors that can reduce the reliability of a problem identification interview. Actually, according to Haynes and Jensen (1979) several potential sources of error can occur in the interview:

1. Differences in race, sex, or social class between interviewer and client.
2. The retrospective nature of the interview process and error associated with retrospective data.
3. Interviewer knowledge of hypotheses or classification of clients.
4. The social sensitivity and type of information elicited.
5. The age of the client.
6. The population being interviewed.

7. The content, format and structure of the interview.
8. Bias in the reports of mediator-clients.
9. Bias presumed to be inherent in all self-report measures [p. 103].

These types of problems can occur across any type of structured or unstructured interview. Yet when a relatively standardized format is employed, several positive features can be identified (Wiens, 1976): (a) the data are quantifiable, (b) reliability is improved, and (c) inexperienced personnel can be used.

Response Options

Available Options.   The interview can also vary along the lines of the response options allowed of the interviewee. Three general categories can be described (Burke & DeMers, 1979):

- *Closed-response-option*—the assessment interview contains more than two-thirds of predetermined questions.
- *Open-response-option*—the assessment interview contains more than two-thirds of open-ended response options.
- *Mixed-response option*—the assessment interview contains more than one-third of the questions that are closed ended and more than one-third that are open ended.

Considerations.   There are both advantages and disadvantages to various response options outlined above. For example, close-ended questions tend to elicit more clear and structured responses (e.g., yes or no). Such responses should be easily scored and will likely increase the reliability of the interview. On the other hand, more open-ended response options could promote a more flexible approach to elucidating aspects of the problem. The therapist would have the option of exploring areas that might otherwise be ruled out.

Content Areas Explored

Breadth of Areas.   The interview represents an assessment approach in which various models of assessment (discussed above) can guide the content explored. For example, the Kanfer and Saslow (1969) model can serve as a guideline for exploration of the fear problem. Such an approach would represent a broad basis for analysis of the problem, in contrast to the adoption of a more A-B-C approach, which would tend to focus the efforts of the therapist on a more narrow aspect of the problem.

Considerations.   Within the context of the current knowledge base in behavioral interview assessment, there is little formal data that can guide assessment interview efforts with children's fears and related problems. In practice it is likely that the content areas explored will be determined by the theoretical persuasion of the individual conducting the interview.

General Considerations

After reviewing the behavioral assessment interview literature, Ciminero and Drabman (1977) noted that "the data available at this time suggest that one must be very cautious, if not skeptical, of interview data for children and parents" (p. 56). Unfortunately, we must make the same conclusions in the area of interview assessment of children's fears and related problems. However, empirical work on the behavioral interview is beginning to appear, particularly in the area of teaching these strategies to clinical pharmacists (Keane, Black, Collins, & Vinson, 1982) and school psychology students (Brown, Kratochwill, & Bergan, 1982).

Despite caution in the use of interview assessment, a number of positive features of this approach should encourage its use within behavioral assessment of children's fears and related problems. Specifically, some advantages gleaned from the behavioral literature are apparent (Kratochwill, 1982; Linehan, 1977). As is evident from the dimensions described above, the therapist has a number of options in structuring questions, response options, and content explored. Many other assessment formats do not allow this degree of flexibility in the assessment process. These options allow therapists working in the fear and phobia area to assess a number of dimensions of the problem. Second, the interview is an assessment approach that promotes the development of a relationship with the client, in contrast to other approaches (e.g., direct observation) that may not promote a formal personal contact. Of course, the relationship established depends upon the individual with whom the therapist comes into contact. In some cases this may be the child and in others the child's careprovider. The importance of the relationship in assessment cannot be overstressed, particularly when the therapist is dealing with the client experiencing the fear or related problematic emotion. A third advantage of the assessment interview is that it is possible to obtain data that might otherwise be left untapped. Generally, the interview is useful with other assessment approaches. Information gained during the interview may prompt other forms of assessment, since statements made by the client or careprovider may form the basis for pursuing other techniques that further elucidate the fear.

SELF-REPORT MEASURES

As noted earlier in the chapter, we categorize self-report measures as indirect samples of behavior because the assessment involves a verbal representation of more clinically relevant behavior occurring at another time and place. In the past, self-report measures have sometimes been avoided in behavioral assessment. This is due to perceived problems inherent in verbal reports when considered as anything other than verbal behavior, and the sometimes subjective formats (or lack of formats) that have been employed in work in this area.

Recently there has been more emphasis placed on this form of assessment for several reasons. The growing emphasis on cognitive behavior therapy has given self-reported verbalizations increased credibility (e.g., Kendall, 1981; Kendall & Finch, 1979; Kendall & Hollon, 1979). Also, there has been more recognition for the notion that the operational criteria for the existence of a problem lies with the client's self-reported verbalizations (Tasto, 1977). Recognition of this rather straightforward issue has been apparent in the literature for some time, yet formal attempts to measure these aspects of self-report have only occurred recently. In addition, self-report measures have become more acceptable as assessment has focused on three response channels, including measures of motoric responses, physiological activity, and cognitions.

Many different self-report measures have been used in assessment of children's fears and related problems. In a great many cases, instruments developed for more traditional assessment purposes (i.e., within the psychometric model) have been adopted for behavioral assessment. Several excellent reviews of self-report measures in the area of childhood fears, phobias, and related problems have been published (e.g., Barrios et al., 1981; Johnson & Melamed, 1979; Miller, Barrett, & Hampe, 1974).

Children's Manifest Anxiety Scale

Castaneda, McCandless, and Palermo (1956) developed the Children's Manifest Anxiety Scales (CMAS) as a measure of a child's chronic state of anxiety. The scale consists of 42 items with an additional 11 items composing the lie scale. There are over 100 published studies in the literature on this scale (see Reynolds, 1977 for a review). Also, Johnson and Melamed (1979) have presented a brief review of the CMAS. Reynolds and Richmond (1978) revised the scale by reordering items, adding and deleting items and developing new norms. The scale was also renamed "What I Think and Feel." The scale has also been standardized for kindergarten children (Reynolds, Bradly, & Steel, 1980).

Work has been done on the Revised Children's Manifest Anxiety Scale (RCMAS) in the areas of content (Reynolds & Richmond, 1978), concurrent (Reynolds, 1980b), construct (Reynolds, 1980a; Reynolds & Richman, 1978, and predictive validity (Reynolds, 1981). Recently, Reynolds and Page (1982) have presented national normative and reliability data for the revised CMAS. Items for the RCMAS are reported in Table 3.4. In their work on the scale,

Table 3.4. Items for the Revised Children's Manifest Anxiety Scale

1. I have trouble making up my mind.
2. I get nervous when things do not go the right way for me.
3. Others seem to do things easier than I can.
4. I like everyone I know.
5. Often I have trouble getting my breath.
6. I worry a lot of the time.
7. I am afraid of a lot of things.
8. I am always kind.
9. I get mad easily.
10. I worry about what my parents will say to me.
11. I feel that others do not like the way I do things.
12. I always have good manners.
13. It is hard for me to get to sleep at night.
14. I worry about what other people think about me.
15. I feel alone even when there are people with me.
16. I am always good.
17. Often I feel sick in my stomach.
18. My feelings get hurt easily.
19. My hands feel sweaty.
20. I am always nice to everyone.
21. I am tired a lot.
22. I worry about what is going to happen.
23. Other children are happier than I.
24. I tell the truth every single time.
25. I have bad dreams.
26. My feelings get hurt easily when I am fussed at.
27. I feel someone will tell me I do things the wrong way.
28. I never get angry.
29. I wake up scared some of the time.
30. I worry when I go to bed at night.
31. It is hard for me to keep my mind on my school work.
32. I never say things I shouldn't.
33. I wiggle in my seat a lot.
34. I am nervous.
35. A lot of people are against me.
36. I never lie.
37. I often worry about something bad happening to me.

Source: Reynolds, C. R., & Paget, K. D. Factor analysis of the Revised Children's Manifest Anxiety Scale for Blacks, Whites, males, and females with a national normative sample. *Journal of Consulting and Clinical Psychology*, 1981, **49**, 352–359. Copyright 1981, the American Psychological Association. Reproduced by permission.

Reynolds and Richmond (1979) found three anxiety factors: "physiological," "worry/oversensitivity," and "concentration." These factors showed a close relationship to an earlier factor-analytic study (N = 245) reported by Finch, Kendall, and Montgomery (1974) on the CMAS, namely, worry and oversensitivity (e.g., I worry most of the time), physiological (e.g., often I feel sick to my stomach), and concentration (e.g., I have trouble making up my mind).

Recently, Reynolds and Paget (1981) raised questions over the earlier Reynolds and Richmond (1979) study, both in terms of certain anomolies in the data (certain items loaded higher than would logically be expected in the factor analysis), and the ratio of sample size (N = 329) to variables (28). To deal with these issues Reynolds and Paget (1981) involved 4,972 children between the ages of 6 and 19 years in a national standardization. The authors found that three anxiety factors emerged: the physiological factor (items 1, 5, 9, 13, 17, 19, 21, 25, 29, and 33); the worry/oversensitivity factor (items 2, 6, 7, 10, 14, 18, 22, 26, 30, 34, and 37); and the concentration factor (items 3, 11, 15, 23, 27, 31, and 35). The authors also found a large general anxiety (Ag) factor. The authors also reported that the lie scale separated into two distinct factors. When the three anxiety and two lie factors were separately applied to males, females, whites, and blacks, the solution was appropriate for all groups. Also, the factor structure of the RCMAS is generally invariant with respect to race and sex.

Test Anxiety Scale for Children

The Test Anxiety Scale for Children (TASC) is a 30-item instrument developed by Sarason, Davidson, Lighthall, Waite, and Ruebush (1960). According to the authors, items for the TASC were chosen based on the following criteria:

1. A "yes" answer to a question should, on the face of it, be admission of behavior which is experienced as unpleasant. Put in another way, a "yes" answer should not indicate behavior which a child would regard as desirable or reflecting a happy state of affairs.
2. A question should contain the element of anticipation of dangerous or painful consequences.
3. There should be questions involving bodily reactions in test and testing situations.
4. There should be a sampling of reactions to a variety of test-like situations [p. 90].

Sarason et al. (1960) were also interested in the relationship between anxiety in test-like situations and anxiety in other situations. To examine this relationship, the General Anxiety Scale for Children (GASC) was developed. In their original work, Sarason et al. (1960) administered the TASC and GASC in one setting and interspersed between them instructions to draw a man, a woman, and a child of the same sex as the subject. The GASC has a series of questions that serve as a lie scale.

There are a number of considerations accompanying administration of these tests as well as information on reliability and validity (see Sarason et al., 1960 for an overview). Generally, the split-half reliability of the TASC ranges between $r = .88$ to $r = .90$ (e.g., Mann, Taylor, Proger, & Marrell, 1968; Sarason, Davidson, Lighthall, & Warte, 1958). The test-retest reliability is somewhat lower, $r = .67$ (Sarason et al., 1960).

In the validity area, initial relationships between teacher ratings of children's classroom anxieties and their TASC scores were quite low ($r = .20$) (see Sarason et al., 1960). Some studies have been done on the concurrent or predictive validity of the TASC. In these studies intelligence and achievement tests are usually correlated with the TASC. Johnson and Melamed (1979) noted that both types of tests are low to moderately related to TASC scores, but with high-anxious children scoring more poorly (e.g., Cotler & Palmer, 1970; Hill & Sarason, 1966; Kestenbaum, & Seiner, 1970; Mann et al., 1968; Milgram & Milgram, 1977; Sarason et al., 1960; Young & Brown, 1973). After reviewing their initial validity studies, Sarason et al. (1960) noted that the following hypotheses were explicitly or implicitly supported:

1. In conventional tests of mental ability the performance of the test anxious child is interfered with primarily because such tests contain many cues which, so to speak, tell the child that he is in a situation of danger in that he is being evaluated by authority figures whose response to his failure will reduce the possibility of need gratification and arouse in him impulses toward these figures, the expression of which will create a still more dangerous situation for him.
2. In testing situations where such cues are minimal, the performance of the test anxious child will be interfered with little or not at all.
3. The greater the degree of anxiety experienced in test and test-like situations, the greater the number of non-test situations in which the anxiety will be experienced [pp. 157–158].

The TASC is generally recognized as a multidimensional scale (e.g., Dunn, 1965; Feld & Lewis, 1967). For example, Feld and Lewis (1967) conducted a factor analysis on nearly 7,500 second grade children. The four factors that emerged included Test Anxiety, Remote School Concern, Poor Self-evaluation, and Somatic Signs of Anxiety. These factors are essentially the same for males and females.

Children's School Questionnaire

The Children's School Questionnaire (CSQ) consists of 198 questions read orally to the child. The CSQ, developed by Phillips (1966a, 1978), contains items obtained from the TASC (Sarason et al., 1960), the Achievement

Anxiety Scale (Stanford, Deniber, & Stanford, 1963), the Avoidance Anxiety Scale (Paivio, Baldwin, & Berger, 1961), the Defensiveness Scale for Children (Lighthall, 1963), and the Children's Personality Questionnaire (Porter & Cattell, 1963). Also, Phillips prepared a number of items to measure aspects of achievement, social stress, and coping style. The items representing each of these categories were split into thirds, and Forms 1, 2, and 3 were developed, each consisting of 66 items.

Phillips (1978) reports information on reliability and validity of the test. When the *KR 21* formula was applied to the school anxiety items, values of .95 or higher were obtained. The stability of school anxiety ranged from $r = .50$ to $r = .67$, with stabilities declining as the length between testing periods increased.

The 74 items constituting school anxiety were analyzed and four factors emerged: Factor 1 was labeled Fear of Assertiveness and Self-Expression; Factor 2 as Test Anxiety (which included items from the TASC), Factor 3 as Lack of Confidence in Meeting Expectations of Others; Factor 4 as Physiologic Reactivity Associated with Low Tolerance of Stress (Phillips, 1978). Phillips (1978) also reports that 26 of the 30 items of the TASC were among the 74 items constituting school anxiety. Correlations computed for the four factors over time periods up to two years yielded reliabilities in the .40's and .50's. Phillips (1978) argues that, "if it is assumed that there are four major components in school anxiety, as our series of factor analytic studies indicates, then it appears that our school anxiety scale (SAS) more adequately represents these components than does the TASC" (p. 29).

Fear Survey Schedule for Children

Scherer and Nakamura (1968) developed a Fear Survey Schedule for Children (FSS-FC). The 80-item scale was modeled after the Wolpe-Lang Scale used in adult fear assessment, with several items identical to the adult scale. The items included were developed under the following categories: School, Home, Social, Physical, Animal, Travel, Classical Phobia, and Miscellaneous.

The FSS-FC and the CMAS were administered to 59 boys and 40 girls ages 9 through 12. A factor analysis of the data yielded the factors described in Table 3.5, which are similar to those reported by Miller et al. (1972b).

The split-half reliability of the FSS-FC is $r = .94$ (Scherer & Nakamura, 1968), and an overall correlation of $r = .49$ was found between the FSS-FC and the CMAS.

Johnson and Melamed (1979) report that the instrument shows some sensitivity to treatment manipulations (e.g., Melamed, Hawes, Heiby, & Glick, 1975; Melamed, Weinstein, Hawes, & Katin-Barland, 1975; Melamed, Yurcheson, Fleece, Hutcheson, & Hawes, 1978), yet statistically significant dif-

Table 3.5. Fear Survey Schedule for Children

Item

Factor I. "Fear of failure or criticism"
  28. Being called on unexpectedly by the teacher
  31. My parents criticizing me
  35. Getting a cut or injury
  36. Being in a big crowd
  46. Having to perform or play at a recital
  48. Being criticized by others
  52. Strange or mean looking dogs
  57. Nightmares
  63. Having to wear clothes different from others
  69. Doing something new
  71. Closed places
  74. Elevators
  80. Taking a test
Factor II. "Major fears"
  5. Looking foolish
  15. Being sent to the principal
  20. Bombing attacks—being invaded
  34. Fire—getting burned
  41. Being hit by a car or truck
  50. The sight of blood
  58. Falling from high places
  59. Getting a shock from electricity
  64. Getting punished by my father
  65. Having to stay after school
  66. Making mistakes
  70. Germs or getting a serious illness
  72. Earthquakes
  73. Russia
  76. Not being able to breathe
Factor IV. "Minor fears—travel"
  2. Riding in the car or on the bus
  4. Lizards
  6. Ghosts or spooky things
  7. Sharp objects
  11. Snakes
  12. Talking on the telephone
  13. Roller coasters or carnival rides
  16. Riding on the train
  23. High places like on mountains
  25. Spiders
  27. Flying in a plane
  43. Playing rough games during physical education
  49. Strange-looking people
  53. Cemeteries
  67. Mystery movie
  78. Worms or snails

Table 3.5 continued on p. 94.

Table 3.5. (*continued*)

Item

Factor V. "Medical fears"
- 7. Sharp objects
- 8. Having to go to the hospital
- 21. Getting a shot from the nurse or doctor
- 22. Going to the dentist
- 51. Going to the doctor
- 55. Getting a haircut
- 56. Deep water or the ocean
- 61. Getting car sick
- 98. My feelings get hurt easily
- 103. My feelings get hurt easily when I am scolded
- 112. I get tired easily

Factor VII. "Fear of death"
- 7. Sharp objects
- 9. Death or dead people
- 10. Getting lost in a strange place
- 14. Getting sick at school
- 18. Bears or wolves
- 20. Bombing attacks—being invaded
- 26. A burglar breaking into our house
- 32. Guns
- 33. Being in a fight
- 77. Getting a bee sting
- 84. I notice my heart beats very fast sometimes

Factor VIII. "Fear of the dark"
- 6. Ghosts or spooky things
- 17. Being left at home with a sitter
- 45. Dark rooms or closets
- 60. Going to bed in the dark
- 62. Being alone
- 75. Dark places
- 105. I am afraid of the dark

Factor IX. "Home-school fears"
- 3. Getting punished by my mother
- 24. Being teased
- 29. Getting poor grades
- 31. My parents criticizing me
- 38. Having to eat some food I don't like
- 40. Failing a test
- 42. Having to go to school
- 44. Having my parents argue
- 64. Getting punished by my father
- 66. Making mistakes

Factor X. "Miscellaneous fears"
- 30. Bats or birds
- 37. Thunderstorms
- 39. Cats
- 47. Ants or beetles

Table 3.5. (*continued*)

Item
57. Nightmares
68. Loud sirens
79. Rats or mice
83. I blush easily

Source: Scherer, M. W., & Nakamura, C. Y. A fear survey schedule for children (FSS-FC): A factor analytic comparison with manifest anxiety (CMAS). *Behavior Research & Therapy*, 1968, **6**, 173–182.

ferences were found on only one of these studies (Melamed et al., 1978).

Scherer and Nakamura (1968) speculate that the scale could be used for the following purposes:

(1) An assessment of fear in psychological test batteries in order to be able to specify specific sources of fear arousal;
(2) A pre- and post-measure of therapeutic effects in anxiety reduction;
(3) A means of specifying individual differences in research 'arousal' studies;
(4) A means of selecting subjects for desensitization studies [p. 182].

Whether or not the FSS-FC will be able to serve in these roles will be determined by future research.

More recently, Ryall and Dietiker (1979) developed a modified version of the FSS-FC. This scale consists of 48 specific fear items and two blanks (for atypical fear stimuli) that children from kindergarten through sixth grade rate on a three point scale ("not scared or nervous or afraid," "a little scared," "very scared") The authors report test-retest reliabilities from .79 to .91. A unique characteristic of the scale is a procedure that allows the child to select his/her own word to denote a fear.

State-Trait Anxiety Inventory for Children

The *State-Trait Anxiety Inventory for Children* (S-TAIC) was developed by Speilberger (1973) and includes two 20-item self-report scales. The scales measure both anxiety that is purported to vary over time and across situations (A-State) and a more stable anxiety (A-Trait). Information on norming, reliability, and validity data are available in the manual and/or published literature. Johnson and Melamed (1979) noted that the norming involved no careful assessment of stability across various geographical regions.

Split-half reliability is high ($r = .89$ for A-State and $r = .88$ for A-Trait), but considerably lower for test-retest over 3 months ($r = .63$ for A-State and $r = .44$ for A-Trait; Finch, Montgomery, & Deardoff, 1974b), and over the same day retest ($r = .72$ for A-State and $r = .65$ for A-Trait; Finch, Kendall, Montgomery, & Morris, 1975). Some studies have reported higher reliabilities ($r = .94$) for the A-Trait (Bedell & Roitzsch, 1976).

Validity data on the STAIC have not been particularly promising, especially in supporting the state-trait distinction (Johnson & Melamed, 1979). For example, the A-Trait measures have not always correlated higher with the CMAS than the A-State measures (e.g., Finch & Nelson, 1974; Montgomery & Finch, 1974). One would expect such consistent high correlations with the CMAS which is assumed to be a measure of A-Trait. Other validity data suggest that the STAIC has been useful in distinguishing emotionally disturbed children from normals and that A-State scores increase in response to situational stress, but mixed results in a number of studies have been characteristic (see Johnson & Melamed, 1980 for a brief review).

Finch, Kendall, and Montgomery (1976) conducted a factor-analytic study on the STAIC with 120 emotionally disturbed and 126 normal children. The authors found the A-State factors to be bipolar: one dimension included worry, feelings of tension, and nervousness, while the other included pleasantness, relaxation, and happiness. The two A-trait factors to emerge were worry and indecisiveness and rumination. In the normal group an additional factor emerged: difficulty sleeping and sweaty hands. The authors also found that for emotionally disturbed children, the A-State factors accounted for most of the variance, whereas for normals, an approximately equal proportion of the variance was accounted for both A-State and A-Trait factors.

Louisville Fear Survey for Children

The *Louisville Fear Survey for Children* (Miller, Barrett, Hampe, & Noble, 1972b) is an 81-item scale for children, ages 4–18. The LFSC can be completed by children or adults for both self-ratings and ratings by others (e.g., parents, teachers, peers). A rating is conducted on a three-point scale: no fear, normal or reasonable fear, or unrealistic fear (excessive). Each item in the LFSC refers to one fear object. Miller et al. (1972) reported a factor analysis on parent ratings which will be discussed in a later section. No reliability or validity data on child ratings are available. There is some evidence to suggest that child and parent ratings may not correspond highly (Miller, Barrett, Hampe, & Noble, 1971).

Miscellaneous Self-Report Measures

Several other general self-report inventories have been employed to assess children's fears and related problems. For example, Walker, Hedberg, Clement, and Wright (1981) presented a fear survey that is currently under development. The authors indicate that the instrument is used to help identify general stimuli that produce anxiety or fear. Once this information is obtained, the therapist conducts more intensive interviewing to determine the extent of the problem and what the focus of treatment might be.

Several specific self-report instruments have been employed in assessment of children's fears and related problems. Some instruments have been used to assess specific objects or events of fear. For example, the *Hospital Fears Rating Scale* (Melamed & Siegel, 1975) consists of eight items from the medical fears subscale of the *Fear Survey Schedule for Children*, eight items related to assessing hospital fears, and some miscellaneous items.

The *Snake Attitude Measure* (Kornhaber & Schroeder, 1974) is comprised of 16 sets of three pictures (sets include a snake and two other reptiles, amphibians, mammals, insects, or birds) and is designed to assess avoidance (fear). Children are requested to indicate which creature they like the most and which animal they dislike most. The number of snake pictures liked minus the number of snake pictures disliked represents the child's snake attitude score.

When considering cognitive components of fear and related problems, behavior therapists have employed a number of more traditional formats for obtaining information. For example, Melamed and Siegel (1975) used the *Human Figure Drawing Test* (Koppitz, 1968). Projective instruments have also been used, as in the case of Vernon (1973) who employed a modified projective (Dorkey & Amen, 1947).

In sampling self-reported fears of specific situations or objects, Kelley's (1976) version of the *Fear Thermometer* (Walk, 1956) has been used in assessment of children. The apparatus can be manipulated by the child to indicate one of five levels of fear. The levels are differentiated by color.

Barrios et al. (1981) describe a variation of the fear thermometer procedure called the "faces test." In such a procedure the child is requested to choose a face that best corresponds to how he/she felt during a specific situation. The advantage that the authors identify with this approach is that the rating task may be simplified, and language skills are minimized in the rating. Unfortunately, adequate reliability and validity have not been established for the procedure (e.g., Glennon & Weisz, 1978; Peterson & Shigetomi, 1978).

General Considerations

Self-report measures used to assess children's fears and related problems will likely continue to be a popular measurement strategy. With the increased emphasis on three-mode response assessment, self-report measures will allow the therapist to assess aspects of fear that would otherwise not be addressed. Simply stated, some data are only available through this form of assessment. Perhaps the major reason for their use in research and practice is that they are easy and convenient to administer. The clinician can usually obtain a great deal of information in a relatively small amount of time. Some of the inventories described above might be used for general screening purposes. In such cases large numbers of children could be assessed for less time and cost than through other methods (e.g., direct observation). Aside from these benefits, self-report measures promote the use of a personal criterion for distress. Presumably, children might report personal distress and still not display physiological or overt behavioral avoidance of a problem. In some respects, this represents a humanistic concern in the assessment of more than one response channel within the same instrument (e.g., cognitive and motor).

In considering the use of self-report measures it also is important to recognize that they vary on a number of dimensions (Kazdin, 1980e).

1. *Specific* vs. *Global*. Many of the above described scales are used to identify very specific fear stimuli (e.g., fear of snakes), whereas others are more global (e.g., general classes of fear stimuli). Scales should be selected for the purposes for which they are intended. Selection of a global instrument for identification of a specific fear would be inappropriate.

2. *Publically observable* vs. *Private events*. Depending on the type of questions asked, some responses are more publically verifiable (Bellack & Hersen, 1977b). For example, consider these questions to a child regarding a particular fear: "Do your palms sweat when you approach school?" "Are you afraid of moths?" The former question has more potential to be objectively verified than does the latter question, which is more personal.

3. *Relatively Permanent Characteristics* vs. *More Transient Aspects of Performance*. A child may be asked to self report a fear in the cognitive domain immediately after being exposed to a fear stimulus. This differs considerably from an instrument designed to tap "trait" dimensions where anxiety is presumed to be a more permanent aspect of behavior or personality.

4. *Direct* vs. *Indirect*. In some self-report measures, the child may know the direct purpose for the assessment (e.g., an anxiety scale) whereas in other types of self-report assessment, the purpose may be indirect or obscured from him/her (as in projective testing). Differential awareness may influence the type of data obtained.

5. *Format*. As is evident in our review of the various self-report measures for children's fears, a variety of formats are in common use. These vary from Likert-type items to more open-ended response options. Generally, it is unknown which type of response type will be most useful in a particular case [pp. 228–229].

The limitations of self-report measures have been generally well articulated in research (Kazdin, 1980e) and practice, both in the general use of these techniques (e.g., Bellack & Hersen, 1977b; Haynes, 1978; Kratochwill, 1982; Tasto, 1977) and for children's fear assessment in particular (e.g., Barrios et al., 1981; Johnson & Melamed, 1979). A major concern that can be raised is the degree to which the data are an accurate reflection of the actual fear. Children's reports are not always consistent, may not correspond to other measures of the fear (via the three response modes), and are subject to distortions. Moreover, children's responses to various items on self-report scales may not correspond to parent or teacher report of these "fears."

Some of the instruments described above (e.g., CMAS) include lie scales for this very reason. Yet whether this scale measures "lies" is subject to some debate. It is possible that items, format, and situational factors account for variability in responses even within the same scale. In addition, a range of factors including *social desirability* may influence responses (Kazdin, 1980e).

A second concern with many of the more traditional self-report scales is that they were designed for purposes other than those typically falling within the general domain of behavioral assessment. As Barrios et al. (1981) note, inventories that attempt to assess cross-situational cognitive aspects of fear typically fail to describe individual situations adequately. Indeed, such scales do not usually include items that would allow the specific situational analysis characteristic of behavioral assessment. Moreover, such traditional instruments often fail to identify the specific nature of the cognitive problem.

Another major limitation of some existing self-report scales is the overall paucity of data on norming, reliability, and validity. This is particularly worrisome because many of the previously discussed scales are being widely used in research and practice. Normative data are especially important in view of the developmental nature of fears and related problems (Barrios et al., 1981).

A fourth limitation of many of the self-report scales is the lack of descriptive detail in the items children are asked to respond to (Barrios et al., 1981). For example, it is unclear if children's responses reflect a fear of spiders and snakes in general or a fear of specific types of spiders and snakes. Such information is usually not available from most scales, necessitating further inquiry as suggested by Walker et al. (1981) in use of their scale. Also related to the types of items is the concern over the kind of questions asked on many scales. As Graziano et al. (1979) noted, most fear survey studies have used scales that ask the question "What are the common fears of children?" (p. 812). Such fear assessment could probably be continued indefinitely, but ultimately only embraces a small part of the fear process. Most surveys do not tap elements of other factors related to fears. Graziano et al. (1979) note:

> Remaining unasked are questions concerning the operation of mediating cognitions in children's fear experiences, the degree to which fears are self- or externally generated and maintained, and the effects of fear behavior on the child's

social environment and the effects of feedback influence on the child. One must investigate how children in their natural environments typically deal with fearful events and how their strategies vary with developmental level, sex, and so on. One must study the conditions under which natural coping processes fail and fear processes become debilitating, and one must determine the optimum conditions for fear-reduction intervention [p. 813].

Certainly, it is impossible for self-report assessment strategies to independently bear the brunt of addressing these issues. Other assessment strategies would need to be considered as well. Nevertheless, some areas can be developed that will have utility for improving self-report measures, particularly in assessment of the child's cognitions (Barrios et al., 1981). For example, modifications in performance tests might be made so that cognitions could be examined through self-report strategies. Such strategies as having a child "think out loud" during role-play tasks, while in the presence of the fear stimulus, or even through imaginal approaches could be useful (Smith & Sharpe, 1970).

BEHAVIOR CHECKLISTS AND RATING SCALES

Behavior checklists and rating scales are similar in format to many self-report measures described in the previous section. However in these indirect assessment strategies, an individual is asked to rate the client (child) based on past observations of that child's behavior. Thus, the identifying features of these measures is that the rating occurs subsequent to the actual behavior of interest, rather than at the time of occurrence (Cone, 1978; Wiggins, 1973). The scales to be described in this section are of two general kinds. First are those of a general nature that do not focus exclusively on fears and related problems (e.g., social withdrawal). Such scales usually include items within several general domains in addition to a fear or anxiety plus withdrawal subdomain (e.g., aggression, conduct disorder). Second, there are scales that focus more specifically on fears and related problems. The content of these scales is related to fears, at least on a face validity basis.

General Rating Scales and Checklists

As noted in Chapter 2, rating scales and checklists have been one of the major assessment strategies in diagnosis and classification efforts (see Quay, 1979). It is beyond the scope of this section to review all the scales that include components relevant to assessment of children's fears or "anxiety-withdrawal." Thus, only a discussion of some of the methodological and conceptual assessment considerations will be reviewed. Typically, each rating scale is completed by an individual who has some familiarity with the child. The formats for conducting such a rating vary across scales as does the time span within which the rating is to be conducted. Usually, rating scales have been used to form an overall index of the level of child adjustment. The scales vary considerably in their norming, reliability, and validity features. Unlike some of the other behavior fear assessment strategies, there is a rather large body of literature available on norming, reliability, and validity (e.g., Kendall, Pellegrini, & Urban, 1981; O'Leary & Johnson, 1979).

Specific Fear Rating Scales and Checklists

There are relatively few formalized fear rating scales and checklists. One instrument that is to be used along with the TASC is the *Teacher Rating Scale* (Sarason et al., 1960). This scale consists of 17 items and is used to assess the motor components of a child's anxiety or fear. Some reliability and validity data for the teacher rating (TA) scale are reported by Sarason et al. (1960). Correlations between the TASC and the TR are generally of a small magnitude (e.g., $r = .31$).

As noted in the section on self-report measures, the LFSC can be used for fear assessment within the general domain of rating scales. The LFSC (Miller et al., 1972) can be completed by the child or adult (parent, teacher). According to Miller et al. (1972) a factor analysis of parent ratings on the LFSC revealed three primary dimensions: fear of physical injury, natural events, and psychic stress. Parents made ratings on 179 children (N = 88 males and 91 females) ranging in age from 6 to 16 years. The authors found results similar to the child ratings reported by Scherer and Nakamura (1968). However, the authors were careful to point out that it was premature to suggest that parents and children will report the same general fears. To begin with, research would need to be conducted wherein the parent and children are in the same setting when the ratings are made. Also in some past work, there has been little congruence between parent and child reporting (e.g., Miller, Marrett, Hampe, & Noble, 1971).

Using a slightly different approach, Vernon (1973) reported the use of the *Global Mood Scale* (Vernon, Foley, & Schulman, 1967) and the *Posthospital Behavior Questionnaire* (Vernon, Schulman, & Foley, 1966). In the *Global Mood Scale* the child's general mood is rated on a 7-interval scale. The *Posthospital Behavior Questionnaire* contains 27 items that describe a specific behavior such as refusal to leave home or enter the dark. Five response alternatives ranging from "much less than before" to "much more than before" are used by mothers to compare their children's behavior in the past week with his/her behavior prior to hospitalization.

To supplement their direct observation measure, Glennon and Weisz (1978) used the *Parent Anxiety Rating Scale* and the *Teacher's Separation*

Anxiety Scale (Doris, McIntyre, Kelsey, & Lehman, 1971). The *Parent Anxiety Rating Scale* consists of 25 items, some of which are concerned with the child's separation anxiety. In the *Teacher's Separation Anxiety Scale* the teacher rates the child's reaction to separation from mother or father when left at the nursery school.

Graziano and Mooney (1980) asked parents to complete a 120-item fear strength questionnaire on several dimensions of their children's fears: frequency, intensity, duration, seriousness, degree of disruption, degree of school interference, and disruption to social adjustment. Thus, the measure includes many dimensions of fear and goes beyond the more typical assessment of what children fear.

General Considerations

Behavior checklists and rating scales have been a popular assessment strategy among behavior therapists (Kratochwill, 1982). Yet with the exception of the general scales, very few have been developed for assessment of children's fears and related problems. Recently, the advantages and limitations of these types of assessment strategies have been articulated (e.g., Ciminero & Drabman, 1977; O'Leary & Johnson, 1979; Saal, Downey, Lahey, 1980; Walls, Werner, Bacon, & Zane, 1977) and several positive features have been noted. Compared with some of the other assessment strategies reviewed in this chapter, rating scales and checklists are usually economical in therapist time and cost. In many cases the child or careprovider can obtain data that would be difficult to obtain through other means. It should be emphasized that it is our *opinion* that these devices are time and cost efficient in the general sense. However, to our knowledge there are no empirical comparisons of these methods with other behavioral assessment strategies to determine their relative cost effectiveness. Moreover, they do not always provide *specific* information on treatment and so their efficiency may waver when this dimension is considered in comparisons.

Second, many of the checklists and rating scales are designed in a way that allows a relatively comprehensive picture of the problem. For example, in the case of the general scales the therapist may be able to identify items that are related to the fear problem. In the more specific fear schedules, a large variety of fear stimuli can usually be identified. This may be useful in developing the treatment program, as in constructing a fear-hierarchy for desensitization.

The third advantage, related to the second, is being able to identify problems that may be missed through other assessment techniques. It is possible that children experiencing fears and related problems may have difficulties in the area of social and academic functioning. Too narrow a focus on the fear problem may exclude an area also in need of intervention. More empirical work needs to be focused on this area, since it will have implications for intervention programs and their scope and content.

A further advantage of checklists and rating scales is that data from these devices have generally been easy to quantify, relative to other behavioral assessment methods. The methods of data quantification have occurred through many strategies, including factor analysis and multidimensional scaling. Indeed, these methods have been applied to rating scale data to develop classification schemes which have included anxiety-withdrawal (see Quay, 1979 and Chapter 2 of this book).

Aside from their role in identification of problems, these measures have been used to monitor program success in a pre-post fashion. In this context, rating scales and checklists could be added to other outcome measures to help clarify treatment program effects.

These scales also can serve as a measure of social validation (Kazdin, 1977b; Wolf, 1978). As traditionally conceived, social validation refers to the external validation of the goals, procedures, and results of therapeutic outcome. For example, a researcher may use a general fear rating scale to measure the outcome and generalization of treatment. To the degree that the scale demonstrates a successful outcome, (e.g., reduced number of fears, better adjustment) beyond that of the specific focus of the intervention, the results would likely be deemed important by careproviders. Moreover, many checklists and rating scales have normative data.

Despite these potential advantages of checklists and rating scales, many issues can be raised over their use in research and practice (e.g., Anastasi, 1976; Evans & Nelson, 1977; Kratochwill, 1982; Saal et al., 1980; Severson, 1971; Spivack & Swift, 1973). Within the conceptual framework presented here (see also Cone, 1978), these procedures represent an indirect measure of behavior; that is, data are gathered retrospectively so their relation to the actual occurrence of the fear behavior is usually unknown. There is some evidence that teachers can make reasonable predictions of behavior (e.g., Strain, Cooke, & Apolloni, 1976), but we have virtually no data regarding the relation of ratings to actual fear behaviors exhibited in various environments. This is a serious validity issue, and until the information is available, conclusions regarding the existence of the problem must remain very tenuous.

A second major issue related to use of these measures is the rationale for item selection. Most of the scales contain items that remained from the factor analysis (or other techniques) which validated that the measure contributed to a cluster of "behaviors" (e.g., anxiety/withdrawal). However, many of the items within a particular cluster (factor) can vary widely on specificity and type of fear or anxiety. For example, an item such as "worries a lot" is quite different from one such as "is afraid of the dark." The latter item is more specific and would likely provide the therapist with more of a lead on what situations to explore for further assessment. Yet, the objects and situations are a part of the picture, but for the behavior analyst, a large part of the picture is still missing in the use of these devices.

A third and related problem is that even the more specific scales for assessing fears provide little information on the situations in which the problem occurs. In the most general sense, one could infer that a teacher would rate behaviors occurring in the school setting and a parent those behaviors occurring in the home. But this type of situational analysis remains primitive until the specific conditions are known (e.g., where in the home/school, who is present, what are the reinforcing contingencies).

Fourth, scale instructions have not always been clear in specifying the conditions under which the scale should be administered. In part, this type of information is relevant to conducting an analysis of the problem described above. Yet many scales fail to specify even the time period the child is to be observed before making the rating.

A fifth issue relates to the factors that are known to influence the quality of the actual ratings. Traditional issues that have been raised regarding the quality of ratings include halo, leniency or severity, central tendency and restriction of range, and inter-rater reliability or agreement (Saal et al., 1980). Unfortunately, as Saal et al. (1980) point out, the research on these concerns has added more heat than light due to (a) lack of agreement regarding conceptual definitions for the above criteria for quality ratings, (b) a lack of agreement regarding the operational definitions (statistical criteria), and (c) the variety of research designs for drawing conclusions from the rating data. The suggestions offered by these authors can certainly be of benefit to behavioral researchers working in this area. Greater specificity in the use of various terms and consideration of a multivariate approach to evaluating the characteristics of ratings can be most useful.

Sixth, virtually every scale used for assessment of children's fears is constructed for detection of negative behaviors; that is, things that children may fear or find stressful. As noted in Chapter 1, with the exception of a few writers (e.g., Rachman, 1978), individuals have focused primary attention on fear rather than "courage" or prosocial behaviors. There are several reasons for focusing on positive or prosocial behaviors in future work on developing fear survey schedules. To begin with, information obtained on assets is important for establishing a treatment program. Assessment of behavioral assets is a component of some assessment models and is quite important for a thorough fear assessment. This suggests that fearful children might profit from social skill training. The positive skills within the child's repertoire can be identified during assessment of behavioral assets.

A final concern with the behavioral rating scales focused specifically on children's fears is the overall lack of data on reliability, validity, and norming. To some extent, the general rating scales represent among the best instruments on psychometric dimensions. However, this has not been the course of development for the more specific fear instruments. While establishing the psychometric credibility of instruments seems imperative, attention must also be focused on developing instruments that are of more relevance to behavioral assessors. Whether or not the traditional psychometric criteria will apply to these devices remains subject to some debate (Cone, 1981).

SELF-MONITORING

Self-monitoring (SM) has been used relatively infrequently in the assessment of children's fears and related problems. It requires the child to discriminate and record the occurrence of his/her own behavior at the time it actually occurs. It is in this regard that SM is distinguished from self-report assessment, which involves report of behavior that occurred at some other time and place. SM has been a popular topic in the behavioral assessment literature, and the reader is referred to several sources for an overview (e.g., Ciminero, Nelson, & Lipinski, 1977; Haynes, 1978; Chapter 9, Kazdin, 1974b; Mahoney, 1977; McFall, 1977b; Nelson, 1977).

SM is typically used for assessment purposes in gathering data to develop an intervention program. However, it has also been shown to be reactive. When SM is reactive it can change the target response that is being recorded. When the change is in a positive direction, therapeutic benefits from the procedure are said to occur. Although self-monitoring has not been used as an independent fear treatment, it has been used as part of a self-control program by Graziano and his associates (Graziano et al., 1979; 1980). In both these studies (described in detail in Chaper 5), children and parents participated in self-control training programs. In the studies children were given a booklet which contained both written instructions for daily practice of a self-control program and space to record the number of tokens earned each night. This allowed a self-monitoring record of progress. Self-monitoring has frequently been used as part of a more total self-control program (Thoresen & Mahoney, 1974).

Self-Monitoring Assessment

Assessment has been the usual purpose for asking children to engage in SM. In fear assessment, SM may be beneficial in several areas. First, it represents one major method for gathering data on private events or cognitions. Generally, the direct method of SM is preferred over other self-report strategies. Second, SM may be very useful during the initial stages of assessment when the therapist is attempting to determine the types of things the child fears and the situations in which this usually occurs. A behavioral diary in which self-monitored data can be recorded may be very useful in pinpointing the problem. Figure 3.2 shows a behavioral diary of a 12-year-old boy who

Self-Monitoring Assessment Diary

Date: November 10, 1981

Client's Name: James Miller

Clinician: Paul Harris, Ph.D., School Psychologist

Target Behavior(s): Fear of tests in math class

| | | | | | *Dimensions* | | | | |
Time	Loca-tion	Persons Present	Preceding Thoughts	Other Preced-ing Actions or Events	Target Behavior	Subsequent Thoughts	Other Subsequent Actions & Events
10:00 AM	Rm 216	Mrs. Anderson, Math Teacher	"I hate math" "I'm going to fail another test"	Mrs. Anderson says we are going to have a test today	Fear of test Staying in test room	"I can't pass this test"	I get up to go to the bathroom be-cause I have to vomit
10:20 AM	Rm 216	Teacher	"I can't pass the test with the time left"	Mrs. Anderson says I should do the best I can	Same	"I feel like crying"	I sit in the chair and look at the blue book

Figure 3.2. Example of a self-monitoring diary of a child who self-recorded his fear of tests at school.

self-recorded his fear of taking a test in school. As can be observed in the figure, the data obtained are quite revealing. Most of the material obtained from this SM activity is directly relevant to treatment program planning.

Aside from obtaining data for development of a treatment program, the same information can typically be used for monitoring the effectiveness of an intervention. Although the scope of application of SM to fears and related problems remains to be determined, this assessment strategy is gaining an impressive range of applications (see Nelson, 1977).

A variety of recording devices and formats can be used for SM and are usually tailored for the specific target problem. Common methods include record booklets, checklists, forms (as in Figure 3.1), counters, meters, timers, measures, scales, residual records, archival records, among others. An example of a SM device is Walk's (1956) fear thermometer which was originally developed for use with adults. Kelley (1976) has developed a version suitable for children. It consists of a device that can be manipulated by the child to indicate one of five fear levels which are differentiated by color.

Another SM procedure is the *in vivo* thought-sampling technique reported by Klinger (1978) that could be used with children in fearful situations. The child would carry a portable beeper and record his/her cognitions or feelings at variable beeper intervals. Such procedures appear to hold promise in assessment of fearful children (Barrios et al., 1981).

Other forms that could be used for SM have been reported by Cautela (1977) and Cautela and Groden (1978). For example, Cautela and Groden (1978) report a *Relaxation Data Sheet for Adults and Older Children* and a *Cues for Tension and Anxiety Survey Schedule* (CTASS) that can be used during relaxation training and desensitization treatment (see Chapter 4). However, empirical data regarding the use of these procedures with children experiencing fears and related problems has not occurred.

General Considerations

The application of SM is not a routine assessment strategy, but rather is influenced by a number of factors. When SM is used primarily for assessment, variables have been identified that influence the accuracy and reactivity of this method. Table 3.6 shows some variables that have been identified as influencing both accuracy and reactivity (see McFall, 1977; Nelson, 1977).

Generally, during assessment the therapist attempts to maximize the accuracy of the data obtained. Accurate data present a better picture of the problem and are a primary objective during assessment. In such assessment the therapist will try to reduce or not actively enhance reactivity. However, reactivity sometimes, but not consistently, occurs and changes the target behavior. It has been occasionally difficult to predict when SM will be reactive. In fact, different theoretical explanations have been offered for why SM

Table 3.6. Factors Influencing Self-Monitoring

Accuracy	Reactivity
1. TRAINING: Clients should be trained in the use of SM. Training the 12-year-old boy in SM will result in better accuracy (see Mahoney, 1977, for an example of training).	1. MOTIVATION: Clients who are motivated to change their behavior prior to engaging in SM are more likely to demonstrate reactive effects.
2. SYSTEMATIC METHODS: Systematic SM methods, such as using the record form in Figure 3.2, will typically result in more reliable and accurate outcomes than those methods that are more informal and nonsystematic.	2. VALENCE: Depending on how clients value a particular SM behavior, it may or may not change. Generally, positively valued behaviors are likely to increase, negatively valued behaviors are likely to decrease, and neutral behaviors may not change.
3. CHARACTERISTICS OF THE SM DEVICE: A SM device, which is easy to use, allows simple data collection, and does not depend on the client's memory, will usually provide more accurate data than when such a form is not employed.	3. TARGET BEHAVIORS: The nature of the target behavior chosen for SM may influence reactivity.
4. TIMING: Generally, the closer in time the actual SM act is to the occurrence of the target behavior, the more likely the data will be accurate.	4. GOALS, REINFORCEMENT, AND FEEDBACK: Specific performance goals, feedback, and reinforcement scheduled as part of SM could increase reactivity.
5. RESPONSE COMPETITION: When a client is required to monitor concurrent responses, his or her attention is divided. This may cause interference and thereby reduce the accuracy of the SM data.	5. TIMING: Reactivity may vary as a function of the timing of SM. For example, recording prior to a behavior act may be more reactive than recording subsequent to its occurrence.

6. RESPONSE EFFORT: The more time and energy the client must spend on the SM activity, the less accurate the data may be. Thus, aspects of "time" and "energy" may prove to be aversive.

7. REINFORCEMENT: Contingent positive reinforcement for accurate recording tends to increase accuracy. Some external criterion is usually established for accuracy.

8. AWARENESS OF ACCURACY ASSESSMENT: The clinician should monitor the client's data and make him or her aware that accuracy is being monitored. Such client awareness will typically increase accuracy.

9. SELECTION OF TARGET BEHAVIORS: Since some behaviors are more salient, more easily discriminated, or more memorable, variations in accuracy will occur from differences in these dimensions. Generally, higher levels of accuracy have been established on motor behaviors (e.g., number of times the person says "ah"), and positively valued behaviors are more accurately recorded than those that are negatively valued.

10. CHARACTERISTICS OF CLIENTS: Some clients are more accurate recorders than others. One would generally expect young children to be less accurate than older children, adolescents, and adults. However, individual variations will occur within ages.

6. SELF-MONITORING DEVICES: Generally, the more obtrusive the recording device, the more reactive it tends to be (e.g., hand-held timer is more reactive than one that is out of sight and "awareness").

7. NUMBER OF TARGET BEHAVIORS: As the number of target behaviors being monitored increases, reactivity may decrease.

8. SCHEDULE OF SELF-MONITORING: Continuous SM may be more reactive than intermittent SM.

Source: Adapted from McFall, R. M. Parameters of self-monitoring. In R. B. Stuart (Ed.), *Behavioral strategies, techniques, and outcomes.* New York: Brunner/Mazel, 1977; and Nelson, R. O. Assessment and therapeutic functions of self-monitoring. In M. Hersen, R. M. Eisler, & P. M. Miller (Eds.), *Progress in behavior modification* (vol. 5). New York: Academic Press, 1977.

is reactive, including Kanfer's position (1975, 1977) that the SM response leads to self-evaluation and self-administered consequences which change the actual response. Another view has been advanced by Rachlin (1974) who suggests that the SM response cues the various environmental consequences that control behavior. Recently, Nelson and Hayes (1981; see also Hayes & Nelson, 1977) have argued that the entire SM process prompts the external consequences that control behavior. This SM process includes some of the variables listed in Table 3.6, among others. Presently, this broad-based view building on Rachlin's work holds promise for explaining reactivity at the theoretical level as well as generating procedures to predict and control its effect.

Generally, SM deserves a more central role in both assessment and treatment in the area of children's fears. SM has been used as part of a more complete self-control program (e.g., Glynn, Thomas, & Shee, 1973; Thoresen & Mahoney, 1974) and will likely make major contributions to treatment in the fear and phobia area.

DIRECT OBSERVATION ASSESSMENT

Much of the behavior therapy research on children's fears and related problems has employed direct observation of behavior in either naturalistic (e.g., home, school), contrived, or analogue settings (clinic, hospital). Direct observational strategies have three major characteristics, including the "recording of behavioral events in their natural settings at the time they occur, not retrospectively, the use of trained observer-coders, and descriptions of behaviors which require little if any inference by observers to code the events" (Jones, Reid, & Patterson, 1975, p. 46). Several different classes of direct observational assessment strategies have been used. These include Behavioral Avoidance Tests, global behavioral ratings, and direct observation in naturalistic settings.

Behavioral Avoidance Tests

One of the most common direct observational assessment strategies is the Behavioral Avoidance Test (BAT). The technique has a long history (e.g., Jersild & Holmes, 1935a) with the Lang and Lazovik (1963) technique serving as a prototype for most work in the field (Barrios et al., 1981). Although there are many variations of the procedure, the strategy usually consists of presenting a child with various phobic stimuli, and requesting that he/she make approach responses toward the object. Observers record the approach responses on a predetermined form. An example of a relatively straight-

Table 3.7. Behavioral Avoidance Test for Dog Fearful Clients

Steps	Step Completed?	
	Yes	No
1. Walk around the corner to the yellow line.		
2. Walk to the white line on the floor.		
3. Walk to the red line on the floor.		
4. Walk to the yellow line by the door.		
5. Walk all the way up to Corey's playpen.		
6. Sit on that chair next to the playpen.		
7. Stand up and touch Corey's fur.		
8. Pet Corey now and keep petting him while I slowly count to 9.		
9. Go over to the white market where the door is and open the door.		
10. Now pick up Corey's leash.		
11. Take Corey out of the playpen and stay there while I slowly count to 9.		
12. Walk Corey over to the green rug.		
13. Sit down there with Corey.		
14. Pet him while I slowly count to 9.		
15. Give Corey the dog biscuit.		
16. Brush Corey's fur with the brush.		
17. Get up and walk Corey back to the playpen.		
18. Get in the playpen with him.		
19. Sit down next to Corey.		
20. Give Corey another dog biscuit.		
21. Pet Corey again while I count to 9.		
22. Put your arm around Corey.		
23. Get up now, come out of the playpen, and close the door.		

Source: Morisano, E. R. *A comparison of the effects of contact desensitization and symbolic modeling in the treatment of dog avoidant retarded persons.* Unpublished doctoral dissertation Syracuse University, 1981. Reprinted with permission.

forward form is that used by Morisano (1981) in the treatment of dog avoidant retarded persons (see Table 3.7).

We have found that BATs have been used quite frequently in children's fear research. Barrios et al. (1981) and Barrios and Shigetomi (in preparation) presented some studies and characteristics of BATs in children's fear assessment and these sources should be consulted for a comprehensive review. It should be emphasized that the BAT *does not* represent one standard approach, but rather is tailored for the particular fear or problem targeted for intervention. BATs provide a number of avoidance measures, including response latency, number of tasks completed, and distance from the feared object. In addition, a passive BAT can be employed, where the therapist moves the feared object toward the child (e.g., Murphy & Bootzin, 1973).

The non-standardized feature of these procedures may be considered a disadvantage (Barrios et al., 1981). The lack of standardized measurers makes comparison across studies somewhat difficult. BATs can actually vary across several dimensions—first, the number of steps may vary widely across studies [e.g., from 3 (Kuroda, 1969) to 29 (Ritter, 1968)]. The variation in number of steps is not in itself problematic, but when evidence suggests that segmentation of the BAT into increasingly smaller steps produces greater approach behavior (e.g., Nawas, 1971), questions can be raised about the external validity of the results (i.e., implementation of the same treatment with a different subject with the same or different fear).

Second, the instructions provided before and during the BAT may differ across studies. For example, a child might be told that the type of snake he/she is to approach is not harmful versus being told nothing about the fear stimulus. It is possible that the child could show avoidant behavior due to the lack of information or knowledge about the stimulus (Bernstein & Paul, 1971). This may not be a validity concern within a particular study where each treatment condition has the same instructions, but variation *across* studies that use the BAT will cause interpretive difficulties.

A third and related problem is the actual "threat" posed by the stimulus. Some authors have noted that reduction of uncertainty with the BAT results in greater approach behavior and less physiological arousal (Lick, Unger, & Condiante, 1978). For example, knowing that a spider or snake will remain in a cage will likely reduce anxiety over approach toward the feared object.

Fourth, instructions for terminating the approach performance may influence performance on the BAT. Sometimes children are instructed to "do your best" or "try as hard as you can," which can result in approach behavior greater than that provided under the lack of such goal statements (Kelly, 1976). Children may also be allowed to verbally indicate when they want to terminate approach toward the fear stimulus, which in turn can influence performance.

Fifth, as has been discussed in the adult fear research literature (e.g., Bernstein & Nietzel, 1973, 1974), the nature of the instructions (i.e., high versus low demand instructions) presented to clients may influence their performance on the BAT. However, the degree to which this factor biases the outcome data has not yet been systematically studied.

Sixth, the BATs may vary from study to study in the manner in which the actual instructions are given. If a therapist is present in the assessment room or a model is giving sequential instructions, results will likely differ from those cases where the therapist presents instructions prior to the actual test and remains outside the room. As Barrios et al. (1981) note, adult phobic research suggests that exposure to a live model presenting sequential instructions generally facilitates approach toward the stimulus (Bernstein & Nietzel, 1973).

A seventh major concern with BATs for child fear assessment is the general lack of both reliability and validity data on these measures (Barrios et al., 1981; Johnson & Melamed, 1979). In the absence of this information, one does not know how useful these strategies will be when applied in future work.

One final, and perhaps most central concern regarding many BATs is that they are an analogue to fear assessment in the natural environment, requiring the child to respond to stimuli that simulate those found in the natural environment (e.g., a snake or spider in the cage). Not all BATs are conducted under strict analogue conditions, but many are, as our review of the literature has indicated. Indeed, BATs are but one dimension of the analogue nature of much behavior therapy research in this area (see Chapter 6).

Despite these concerns, when BATs are conducted under experimental research conditions, their analogue nature can promote several advantages (cf. Haynes, 1978; McFall, 1977; Nay, 1977). To begin with, BATs used in an analogue context permit a greater degree of control than might be obtained in more unstructured settings. Analogue assessment may also allow measurement of behavior that would be impossible to develop under naturalistic conditions. For example, it is not always easy to find a friendly rattlesnake so that a BAT can be constructed. In addition, many BATs may prove less costly than going into the natural environment to observe the behaviors directly. Finally, many of the factors that could contaminate assessment efforts in the natural environment are quite possibly avoided by analogue formats.

Aside from the positive features associated with the analogue characteristics of BATs, these measures can be recommended for future research and practice. First, the BATs allow a practical means of assessing the motoric responses. As noted above, assessment of the motoric channel through BATs is not limited to approach behaviors. A variety of measures can be taken including facial expressions, trembling, time needed to complete various steps, and latency, among others (cf. Barrios & Shigetomi, in preparation). Such an assessment format with multiple dimensions will also facilitate research on the three systems. Finally, the BATs have direct implications for treatment. As noted by Barrios and Shigetomi (in preparation), the BATs are invaluable within the context of directly addressing the idiosyncratic nature of a child's fear. Thus, BATs represent one of the few strategies in which the treatment process is directly related to assessing progress.

Despite these advantages, we would recommend that BATs be used in conjunction with other assessment information obtained from settings in which the fear usually occurs. This could be accomplished through direct observation of the problem in addition to other measures described in this chapter.

Global Behavior Ratings

Another direct measure of behavior can be obtained through a variety of procedures sometimes referred to as Global Behavioral Ratings. These procedures involve the recording of the behavior at the time of its occurrence, but usually on a dimensional scale (e.g., seldom to always, definitely negative to definitely positive). In some respects, global ratings simplify the measurement process, but there is usually a corresponding loss of information depending on the actual rating format. Several positive features of these scales can be identified (Kazdin, 1980e). First, these methods represent a flexible assessment method in that many dimensions of behavior can be rated. Second, they usually provide a summary evaluation of the child's status on some problem before, during, and after treatment. Third, global ratings provide a standardized format for soliciting the judgments of therapists or others (parents, teachers) involved with the client. Some of the most common scales in the fear area have been recently reviewed (e.g., Barrios et al., 1981; Johnson & Melamed, 1979).

Peterson and Shigetomi (1981), for example, report the use of the *Medical Laboratory Observation Scale*, the *Child Behavioral Observational Rating*, and the *Child Behavior Checklist* in a study evaluating the efficacy of various modeling and self-control procedures in the prevention of anxiety associated with hospitalization and surgery.[2] In the *Medical Laboratory Observation* format, a laboratory technician who drew blood from the child rated the child on three 5-point Likert-type scales "measuring how anxious the child seemed, how cooperative he or she was, and how well he or she tolerated the procedure" (p. 6). The *Child Behavior Checklist* is completed by the parent, nurse, and observer on 16 maladaptive behaviors typical of anxious hospitalized children. The *Child Behavior Observational Rating* is completed by parents, nurses, and an independent observer on a 5-point Likert-type scale of anxiety and cooperation.

Global ratings, even when used to rate behavior at the time of its natural occurrence have several disadvantages in both research and practice. Kazdin (1980e) elucidated several of these problems. A major concern is that it is not always clear what these ratings measure. The "global" in the rating sometimes makes the data obtained ambiguous, particularly when no operational definitions specify the dimension of the rating. Second, due to the lack of specificity in the ratings, responses are likely to change over time. Such changes may occur independent of the actual change in the fear problem.

Third, when different global ratings are used across different studies, comparisons of the treatment are difficult, if not impossible to make. This problem would be reduced somewhat by employing an existing scale, such as the BPRS (e.g., Melamed et al.). Fourth, global ratings may be insensitive to certain types of behavioral changes. An overall rating of anxiety is usually not as sensitive as a direct measure of the construct on some overt motor dimension. Finally, such measures are subject to a number of biases because specific criteria for conducting the rating are usually absent.

Direct Observation in Naturalistic Settings

In addition to the aforementioned direct observational assessment methods, researchers working in the area of children's fear and related problems have observed their clients directly in natural settings (e.g., Ayllon et al., 1970; Kuroda, 1969; Lewis, 1974; Miller & Kratochwill, 1979; Pomerantz, Peterson, Marholin, & Stern, 1977). In this type of assessment, the therapist typically develops a code specific to the target behaviors identified for treatment (e.g., crying, behavioral avoidance). For example, Neisworth, Madle, and Goeke (1975) measured "separation anxiety" by recording the duration of crying, screaming, and sobbing during daily preschool activities. Unfortunately, few authors have developed standardized observational manuals and recording formats that can be implemented in naturalistic settings.

Many of the fear observational measures have been used in health-related settings. For example, Melamed and Siegel (1975) report the use of an *Observer Rating Scale of Anxiety* (ORSA) that was developed to assess the motor component of children's anxiety who were waiting for surgery. The scale is completed by an observer who rates the presence or absence of each of the 29 responses during certain time intervals. Interrater agreement has been as high as 94%. Melamed and her associates also report the use of a *Behavior Profile Rating Scale* (BPRS) designed for measuring child behaviors that disrupt dental treatment (Melamed, Hawes, Heiby, & Glick, 1975; Melamed, Weinstein, Hawes, & Katin-Borland, 1975). The scale, reproduced in Table 3.8 has 27 items and is completed by a dentist. Measures of cooperativeness and anxiety have occurred with intercorrelations between observers of .75 or above (Johnson & Melamed, 1979). Johnson and Melamed (1979) also report that dentists' ratings of a child's fear of dentistry are positively correlated with the child's subsequent BPRS scores (Klorman, Ratner, Arata, King, & Sveen, 1977), and that both the ORSA and the BPRS have differentiated treated from untreated children (e.g., Melamed, Hawes, Heiby, & Glick, 1975; Melamed & Siegel, 1975; Melamed, Weinstein, Hawes, & Katin-Borlin, 1975).

Also focusing on the dental setting is a scale reported by Frankl, Shiere, and Fogels (1962). In this procedure the observer rates the child's behavior

Table 3.8. Behavior Profile Rating Scale

	Successive 3-minute observation periods									
	1	2	3	4	5	6	7	8	9	10
Separation from mother										
(3) Cries										
(4) Clings to mother										
(4) Refuses to leave mother										
(5) Bodily carried in										
Office behavior										
(1) Inappropriate mouth closing										
(1) Choking										
(2) Won't sit back										
(2) Attempts to dislodge instruments										
(2) Verbal complaints										
(2) Overreaction to pain										
(2) White knuckles										
(2) Negativism										
(2) Eyes closed										
(3) Cries at injection										
(3) Verbal message to terminate										
(3) Refuses to open mouth										
(3) Rigid posture										
(3) Crying										
(3) Dentist uses loud voice										
(4) Restraints used										
(4) Kicks										
(4) Stands up										
(4) Rolls over										

Table 3.8. (*continued*)

	Successive 3-minute observation periods									
	1	2	3	4	5	6	7	8	9	10
(5) Dislodges instruments										
(5) Refuses to sit in chair										
(5) Faints										
(5) Leaves chair										

Source: From B. G. Melamed, D. Weinstein, R. Hawes, and M. Katin-Borland, Reduction of fear-related dental management problems using filmed modeling. *Journal of the American Dental Association*, 1975, **90**, 822–826. Copyright © 1975 by the American Dental Association. Reprinted by permission.

ranging from definitely negative to definitely positive during various points of the dental examination and actual treatment of the child (such as separation from the mother, exposure to the dental settings, administration of medication). Johnson and Melamed (1979) report that interrater agreement is at least 90% (e.g., Johnson, 1971; Johnson & Macheu, 1973; Koenigsberg & Johnson, 1972; Wright & Alpern, 1971; Wright, Alpern, & Leake, 1973). Such measures have also been sensitive to treatment manipulations (e.g., Johnson & Machen, 1973; Melamed, Hawes, Heiby, & Glick, 1975; Melamed, Weinstein, Hawes & Katin-Borland, 1975). Another scale is the *Preschool Observation Scale of Anxiety* (POSA) reported by Glennon and Weisz (1978). The observer rates the occurrence of 30 indicators of anxiety while the children perform tasks in the presence and absence of their mothers (e.g., rigid posture, trembling voice, and trembling lips).

Katz, Kellerman, and Siegel (1980) report the development of an observational behavior scale to measure anxiety responses to bone marrow aspirations in children with cancer. In the study, 115 children were observed by five observers in the clinic treatment setting. Katz and his associates constructed a list of behaviors thought to be indicative of anxiety in the treatment setting. Twenty-five behavioral measures were collected and operationally defined (see Table 3.9). These items were placed in random order in scale form and the scale was called the *Procedure Behavioral Rating Scale* (PBRS).

In the study, the bone marrow aspiration procedure was divided into four phases (p. 358):

Phase 1: Child is called from waiting room.   Child reaches door of treatment room.

Phase 2: Child enters treatment room.   Clothes are removed.

Phase 3: Site is cleansed, local anesthetic is   Needle is withdrawn.
          administered, BMA procedure is
          done.
Phase 4: Band-aid is placed.   Child leaves room.

Table 3.9. PBRS Behavioral Items and Operational Definitions

Item	Operational definition
Cry	Tears in eyes or running down face
Cling	Physically holds on to parent, significant other, or nurse
Fear verbal	Says "I'm scared," "I'm afraid," etc.
Pain verbal	Says "Ow," "Ouch," "It hurts," "You're hurting me," etc.
Groan[a]	Nonverbal, vocal expression of pain or discomfort
Scream	No tears, raises voice, verbal or nonverbal
Laugh[a]	Smiling with a chuckling sound
Stall	Verbal expression of delay ("Wait a minute," "I'm not ready yet," etc.) or behavioral delay (ignores nurse's instructions)
Stoic silence[a]	Child does not respond to questions or remarks of others, may appear "trancelike"
Carry	Has to be physically carried into or out of room or placed on table, not because of physical inability to do so on his or her own
Flail	Random gross movements of arms or legs, without intention to make aggressive contact
Nausea verbal[a]	Says "I'm sick," "I feel nauseous," "My stomach feels like I'm going to throw up"
Vomit[a]	Includes retching, dry heaves
Urinate/defecate[a]	Soils or wets self
Kick[a]	Intentional movement of leg(s) to make aggressive physical contact
Hit[a]	Intentional movement of arm(s) or hand(s) to make aggressive physical contact
Bite[a]	Intentional closing of jaw to make aggressive physical contact

Table 3.9. (*continued*)

Item	Operational definition
Verbal hostility[a]	Says "I hate you," "You're mean," etc.
Refusal position	Does not follow instructions with regard to body placement on treatment table
Restrain	Has to be held down because of lack of cooperativeness
Curse[a]	Verbally utters profanity
Muscular rigidity	Any of following behaviors: clenched fists, white knuckles, gritted teeth, clenched jaw, wrinkled brow, eyes clenched shut, contracted limbs, body stiffness
Questions[a]	Nondelay, information-seeking verbal behavior ("What are you doing now?" "Is it over yet?" etc.)
Emotional support	Verbal or nonverbal solicitation of hugs, physical comfort, or expression of empathy from parent, significant other, or nurse
Requests termination	Verbally asks/pleads that procedure be stopped

Note. PBRS = Procedure Behavioral Rating Scale.
[a] These items were subsequently eliminated.
Source: E. R. Katz, J. Kellerman, & S. E. Siegel. Behavioral distress in children with cancer undergoing medical procedures. Developmental considerations. Journal of Consulting and Clinical Psychology, 1980, **48**, 356–365. Copyright 1980 by The American Psychological Association. Reproduced by permission.

To supplement the behavioral observations, a nurse performing the BMA rated the child's anxiety using a 5-point Likert-type scale (1 = not at all anxious to 5 = extremely anxious). The authors reported that they were able to reliably measure distress in the children (i.e., Pearson correlations between observers were. Phase 1, $r. = 94$, Phase 2, $r = .88$, Phase 3, $r = .91$, Phase 4, $r = .92$; the PBRS total score $r = .94$). Originally, 25 items were used, but subsequent statistical analysis made possible a scale of 13 items. The authors also report that the PBRS was effective in identifying anxious children. The authors also reported a significant relationship between age and both quantity and type of anxious behavior, with the younger children tending to exhibit a greater variety of anxious behaviors over a longer period of time than older children. Also, a developmental trend toward behavioral withdrawal and increased muscle tension with increased age was found. Consistent with some previous work, sex differences were also found: females tended to display higher levels of anxiety than males (e.g., Melamed & Siegel, 1975; Reynolds & Richmond, 1978).

Although the Katz et al. (1980) scale appears promising, questions have been raised over what the scale actually measures. Shachan and Dant (1981) argued that the scale actually measures anxiety and pain. Katz, Kellerman, and Siegel (1981) appear to agree with this interpretation and note that the scale should be considered a measure of *behavioral distress* with components of anxiety, fear, and pain. However, Katz et al. (1981) note that subsequent research incorporating self-report measures of fear and pain have suggested that fear self-report correlates higher with the scale and independent nurse ratings than pain self-report.

Wine (1979) reports an observational procedure in which children varying in test anxiety were observed during a period preceding an examination and when no examinations were scheduled. Behavior categories included attending behaviors, task-related behaviors, activity, communication, and various interpersonal behaviors.

General Considerations

Direct observation of children through one of the strategies described in this section is generally a preferred method in behavioral assessment of children's fears. When direct observational assessment is employed, a number of methodological factors must be considered and attempts made to adhere to current standards in this area. The literature addressing these concerns is rather extensive, and the reader is referred to some of the major sources in this area (e.g., Foster & Cone, 1980; Haynes, 1978; Haynes & Horn, in press; Haynes & Wilson, 1979; Johnson & Bolstad, 1973; Jones et al., 1974; Kazdin, 1981b; Kent & Foster, 1977; Wasik & Loven, 1980; Wildman & Erickson, 1977). A first consideration relates to the use of an existing code or development of a new code specific to a particular problem or fear. As noted above, there are relatively few codes that would cover a range of children's fears. In fact, many of the BATs have been developed for specific fear assessment. Nevertheless, it appears important to continue development of some relatively standardized direct fear assessment formats. Some of the direct observational rating scales are perhaps closest to this more standardized approach. Yet the field could profit from more standardized measures for use in both naturalistic and analogue settings.

A second concern in use of direct observational methods relates to the definition of behavior that is developed. Generally, behavior therapists have avoided a more construct-oriented approach in favor of specific behavioral descriptions. In the future this process must also involve verifying the accuracy of the instrument developed (Cone, 1981; Foster & Cone, 1980). In direct observational assessment, data should be compared to some standard (objective criterion) to establish accuracy. Once initial accuracy is established subsequent applications can be compared to the standard. This is not going to be an easy process in fear research, but is possible to accomplish. For example, a mechanical distance recorder could be used during the initial baseline sessions and serve as an accuracy standard over the course of the study for the direct observational measures (see Foster & Cone, 1980 for more details).

A third and similar factor that must be considered is the relation between the target problem and the dependent measures chosen to represent the fear "construct." Researchers must continue efforts to examine the degree of correspondence that exists among the various devices. The measures chosen for observation must be representative of the problem (e.g., through social validation, global ratings), related to the right property of the behavior (e.g., frequency, intensity, duration, magnitude, qualitative features), and occur in the right settings (e.g., where the problem occurs) (Foster & Cone, 1980).

Fourth, the researcher and practitioner must ensure that the observers are well trained. Observers should be trained under conditions that approximate those under which the study will be conducted. Retraining during the study to again establish accuracy should be done because observers have been known to "drift" from the original criteria established (e.g., Kazdin, 1977a; Kent & Foster, 1977).

Fifth, two or more observers should be used so that measures of interobserver agreement can be established. The choice of an interobserver agreement measure is a complex issue in its own right. It is beyond the scope of our presentation to review each of the considerations surrounding gathering and calculating measures of interobserver agreement in observational research, and the interested reader is referred to several sources for a review of issues (e.g., Haynes, 1978; Haynes & Wilson, 1979; Kent & Foster, 1977; Wasik & Loven, 1980).

A final consideration in observation methods is the obtrusiveness of the measurement procedures used (Kazdin, 1979). When data recording is obtrusive, the client may become aware that measurement is taking place and this may invoke reactivity in the assessment process. Reactive effects are said to occur when the process of recording alters behavior, either permanently or temporarily (Haynes & Horn, in press). To the degree that the data are influenced by the reactivity of recording, both the internal and external validity of the results can be influenced. Thus, an attempt to reduce or minimize reactivity has been proposed (Haynes & Horn, in press; Kazdin, 1979c). Haynes and Horn (in press) propose the following strategies:

(a) participant observers can be used,
(b) alternative measures can be used to supplement the regular measures,
(c) covert observation can be implemented,
(d) procedures can be implemented to reduce or minimize the obtrusive ness of observation,
(e) various technologies can be used (e.g., telemetry, video-cameras, tape recorders),

(f) the therapist can minimize subject-observation and other discriminative properties of the observation,

(g) the therapist can train and instruct observers to act naturally,

(h) during data collection, the therapist should allow sufficient time for dissipation of reactive slope and variability in observations,

(i) the therapist can use a number of observers and observation procedures to help cancel out differential effects.

Direct observation procedures represent a promising assessment strategy for children's fears, phobias, and related problems. By addressing the above methodological issues, the researcher/practitioner can obtain quality data for treatment planning and monitoring.

PSYCHOPHYSIOLOGICAL ASSESSMENT

The use of psychophysiological assessment has increased in behavior therapy research on fears and related problems because of the growing recognition of the complexity of the fear and anxiety construct. Focus on a narrow range of measures appears to be an unacceptable standard for current research and practice in the fear area. Also, with a corresponding emphasis on three-mode response assessment, a focus on the physiological dimension is more likely to be considered than it otherwise would have in the past. As a result of these issues, there has been a growing literature in psychophysiological assessment within the field in general (e.g., Haynes, 1978; Hersen & Barlow, 1976; Kallman & Feuerstein, 1977; Ray & Kimmel, 1979) and in anxiety or fear assessment specifically (e.g., Agras & Jacob, 1981; Borkovec, Weertz, & Bernstein, 1977; Nietzel & Bernstein, 1981; Taylor & Agras, 1981). However, there have been relatively few discussions of psychophysiological assessment with children experiencing fears and related problems (see Barrios et al., 1981; Johnson & Melamed, 1979; Melamed & Siegel, 1980 for exceptions), and there have been relatively few empirical treatment studies where psychophysiological measures have been monitored in the applied research literature.

In this section we review those psychophysiological methods that have been the most commonly used for fear and anxiety measurement. These include strategies within the domain of electromyographic, cardiovascular, and electrodermal measures (Nietzel & Bernstein, 1981).

Electromyography

Electromyography or EMG refers to the measurement of the electrical activity generated when the skeletal muscles contract. Muscular tension is inferred from the measurement of the muscle contraction (Haynes, 1978). In the usual assessment strategy, EMG is recorded by attaching electrodes to the subject's skin at several sites.

Generally, EMG measures have not been used often with children. However, they could have a range of applications during therapy research and practice. For example, such measures could be used when children are presented with the fear stimulus. Measurements could then be taken pre-post or repeatedly over the course of therapy. Such measures could also be used to supplement other psychophysiological and behavior assessment strategies.

Generally, EMG levels have been found sensitive to general arousal, but such measures demonstrate low correlations with other physiological measures, and, at least in adult clients, frontal EMG levels do not always correlate with EMG measures from other sites (Nietzel & Bernstein, 1981). However, it must be stressed that literature addressing this issue with children experiencing fears and related problems is generally sparse.

Cardiovascular Measures

The most common measures of cardiovascular activity have been heart rate, blood pressure, and peripheral blood flow. According to Neitzel and Bernstein (1981) heart rate is one of the most common measures, possibly because such measures are less sensitive to measurement artifacts and are typically monitored relatively easily. Systolic and diastolic blood pressure have also been used, with systolic being considered a better measure because it is typically more sensitive to short-term environmental measures. Measures of blood flow through peripheral arterioles usually include strain gauges and pletysmography. In addition, surface temperature can also be assessed.

Like EMG, none of these cardiovascular measures have been used extensively with children. In some early studies, heart rate measures were found to increase when the children were asked their most fearful experiences (Tal & Miklich, 1976) and when given "test" versus "game" instructions. However, as Johnson and Melamed (1979) note, such heart rate responses also occur when other emotions are imagined, as occurred in the Tal and Miklich (1976) study when children were asked to imagine angry experiences.

Some evidence also suggests that heart rate measures may not correlate with other measures of anxiety. Kutina and Fischer (1977) gathered heart rate data on children who were exposed to a dental examination and had to read a difficult text in public. Measures were also gathered on teacher, observer, and sociometric ratings of anxiety. Only in the case of reading the text in public did a score on the CMAS correlate with heart rate, but even these were in the opposite direction. This sometimes occurs since subjects show a heart rate deceleration in response to certain fear stimuli (Nietzel & Bernstein, 1981). In yet another study, Sternbach (1962) recorded heart rate, among a number of physiological responses (skin resistance, gastric motility, respiration rate, eyeblink rate, finger pulse volume) on ten children as they viewed Walt Disney's *Bambi*. Children were then asked to report what segments were the most scary. However, low correlations were found between the self-report "fear" at the scary segment and the physiological measures.

Several more clinical studies have also monitored cardiovascular functioning. For example, in the Van Hasset et al. (1979) study, the 11-year-old multi-phobic child was assessed using motoric (ladder climb, blood BAT, and test taking), cognitive (*Target Complaint Scale*) and physiological measures. Physiological arousal on the ladder climb task was assessed by measuring the child's pulse rate five minutes after arrival for a probe and again immediately prior to ascending the ladder. The authors calculated change scores by subtracting the second reading from the first. Also, heart rate and finger pulse volume were monitored throughout the BAT and test taking task (the reader is referred to their methods section for a detailed description of scoring). The outcome of this measurement across the study is reported in Figure 3.3. It can be observed that there was a decrease in heart rate for the ladder climb task under the relaxation treatment, followed by a further decrease with the implementation of desensitization. However, no change occurred on finger pulse volume or heart rate changes for the BAT and test taking tasks.

In another study, Shapiro (1975) studied children's responses to injections by monitoring heart rate, behavioral, and self-reports of fear. He found an increase in self-reported needle avoidance on the day children were to receive their injections and a corresponding increase in heart rate. Also, the lower the preinjection heart rate, the less avoidance behavior was emitted during actual injections.

Melamed, Yurcheson, Fleece, Hutchinson, and Hawes (1978) studied the influence of film preparation on 80 children undergoing dental treatment. Measures were taken on the CFSS, including 15 specific dental items, self-report on a five-point fear thermometer, the Palmer Sweat Index, the BRPS, other observer ratings, and GSR and cardiac responses. The latter two measures were taken during film viewing and treatment by means of a Grass polygraph. The authors found that heart rate reflected a difference according to type of film seen. Also, no correlations among the various measures (self-report and behavioral) and heart rate were reported during the film viewing.

In the past, heart rate has been the measure of choice among cardiovascular indexes, possibly due to the relative ease with which these measures are taken and its accuracy (Nietzel & Bernstein, 1981). However, Nietzel and Bernstein (1981) point out two cautions with these measures. First of all, heart rate has been known to be sensitive to motor and perceptual activities which are in turn easily confounded with stress. A second consideration is

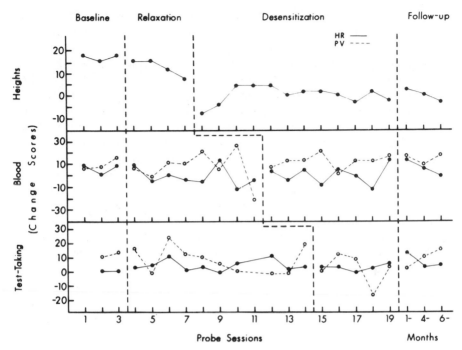

Figure 3.3. Physiological responses (heart rate = HR; pulse volume = PV) in probe sessions during baseline, relaxation training, systematic desensitization, and follow-up. A multiple baseline analysis of treatment for phobias of heights, blood, and test taking.

Source: Van Hasselt, V. B., Hersen, M., Bellack, A., Rosenblum, N. D., & Lamparski, D. Tripartite assessment of the effects of systematic desensitization in a multi-phobic child: An experimental analysis. *Journal of Behavior Therapy & Experimental Psychiatry*, 1979, **10**, 51–55. Reproduced by permission

that heart rate can be idiosyncratic with individual clients. As previously noted, heart rate can actually decrease or not change at all in response to anxiety. Perhaps the major consideration with these measures is that they have not been used extensively with children, making knowledge in this area limited.

Electrodermal Measures

The most common electrodermal measures used in fear assessment are skin conductance and skin resistance. These measures are taken by placing electrodes on the skin and passing an electric current between them with the results displayed on a polygraph or meter. While these measures have been used extensively in laboratory studies of adult desensitization (Melamed et al., 1975) they have not been used extensively with children (Barrios et al., 1981; Johnson & Melamed, 1980).

Several studies have, however, reported the use of electrodermal measures (Melamed et al., 1975, 1978; Melamed & Siegel, 1975; Shapiro, 1975). For example, Shapiro (1975) used tape bands applied to the child's left hand index finger for three minutes. The darkness of finger print was judged on a ten-point scale by two observers. Shapiro (1975) found that finger sweat and ambient temperature were highly correlated. In fact, temperature accounted for a high proportion of variance in finger sweat measures.

Melamed and her associates have used palmar sweat prints (PSP) in a series of studies for measuring intervention effects. Such procedures have demonstrated a test-retest reliability of $r = .64$ over a one-day test-retest interval and $r = .60$ over a 15-day interval (Lare, 1966). Johnson and Melamed (1979) report that the PSP measures have been sensitive to stresses associated with such activities as surgery (e.g., Johnson & Stockdale, 1975; Melamed, Hawes, Heiby, & Glick, 1975; Melamed & Siegel, 1975; Venham, Bengston, & Cipes, 1977). For example, in the Melamed and Siegel (1975) study, 60 children who were to undergo elective surgery for hernias, tonsillectomies, or urinary-genital tract difficulties were shown on hospital admission either a peer modeling film of a child being hospitalized and receiving surgery or an unrelated control film (see discussion of this study in Chapter 5). The authors gathered state (or situational) measures of anxiety, including self-report, behavioral observation, and PSP. The PSP was recorded from the index finger of the child's left hand. Interobserver agreement on the print resulted in a Pearson-product-moment correlation of .93. Melamed and Siegel (1975) reported that the PSP, along with the self-report and direct observational measures showed a reduction of preoperative and postoperative fear arousal in the experimental as compared to the control condition.

Generally, electrodermal measures represent a useful psychophysiological assessment technique. However, such measures are influenced by both procedural variations (e.g., change in measurement strategy) and environmental intrusions (e.g., introducing stressors other than the fear stimulus; Nietzel & Bernstein, 1981). Barrios et al. (1981) have also suggested that electrodermal measures are sensitive to novel and interesting stimuli (cf. Raskin, 1973; Sokolov, 1963). More information on these measures can be found in several sources (e.g., Edelberg, 1972; Prokasy & Raskin, 1973).

General Considerations

The use of psychophysiological measures with children experiencing fear and related problems raises a number of issues (Barrios et al., 1981; Hersen & Barlow, 1976; Kallman & Fuerstein, 1977; Ray & Raczynski, 1981). First of all, psychophysiological assessment is quite expensive in research and practice. Due to the complexity and expense of implementing these measures, they should provide data that cannot be obtained as reliably and efficiently by other procedures. Unfortunately, at this time it is difficult to offer data to make an informed response to this issue, particularly in work with children. It is possible that alternatives to psychophysiological monitoring equipment could be used to tap the physiological content area. Barrios et al. (1981) have suggested several strategies that might be employed. For example, they note such devices as the Autonomic Perception Questionnaire (Mandler, Mandler, & Uviller, 1958) could be modified for self-report assessment with children. Also, various telemetry devices might be used because they permit unobtrusive assessment options. Finally, self-monitoring strategies in which the child is taught to take his/her own pulse could be used. However, many of these options remain unexplored in clinical settings.

A second consideration in the use of these measures is that psychophysiological assessment should provide the therapist with information about the selection and monitoring of the treatment. This aspect of psychophysiological recording is perhaps one of the most challenging aspects. As noted from our review of the research literature, these measures have application in this role, but the psychophysiological recording may not always correlate with other assessment strategies such as self-report or direct observational measures. Also, in some cases we simply do not know what the relationship will be because these data have not been available.

A third concern with all users of the psychophysiological measures is that they should possess adequate reliability and validity. Ray and Kimmel (1979) have pointed to a number of methodological issues in this domain, many of which are complex and require sophisticated statistical applications. For example, the authors note that change scores may be correlated with baselines, requiring the use of regression methods. Also, since individuals may have different ranges for various measures used, corrections will have to be made. A variety of statistical procedures will be necessary, including multivariate approaches (e.g., discriminate analysis, multiple regression, multivariate ANOVA), cross-validation techniques, and factor and cluster analysis.

Finally, when psychophysiological measures are used in applied or clinical research, a class of variables may influence the quality of the data. These factors have implications for the actual quality of the data that are obtained in practice as well. A very practical concern with these methods is that the equipment is often sensitive and may fail mechanically. Another concern with this form of assessment is that especially young children may resist wearing the equipment. Also, children who are especially active may through their activity influence the quality of recordings that are obtained.

Another concern with psychophysiological monitoring is that the therapist must allow time for the child to adapt to the equipment. Both the reactivity and the length of the adaptation phase will vary depending on the individual child. Related to this are the habituation effects that will occur with repeated measurement. It will be important to distinguish the effect of treatment from both habituation and adaptation.

Psychophysiological measures are also quite sensitive to a number of therapist variables, contextual variables, stimulus and situational demands, response stereotypy and stimulus complexity, novelty, and cognitive factors (Barrios et al., 1981).

A major consideration in the use of psychophysiological recording is deciding which system to choose in monitoring the fear. At this time it is not at all clear what is the *measure of choice* for a specific fear. Until we are able to empirically determine what are the best measures, researchers and practitioners should use more than one within and across the three domains discussed above. A related concern is that when various psychophysiological measures are employed in the fear area, the fear "construct" cannot be assumed to exist independent of other assessment methods such as self-report and direct recordings.

SUMMARY AND CONCLUSIONS

In this chapter we have provided an overview of some general issues involved in the application of behavioral assessment to children's fears and related problems, including a contrast of behavioral and traditional assessment, and a conceptual framework for behavioral assessment. We noted that in behavioral assessment, there is more emphasis on the environment and conditions maintaining fear responses in the environment than in traditional approaches. Because fears and related problems are considered to be a function of the person and the person-environmental interaction in the behavioral approach, they are not consistent across time in the same way that a more trait-oriented approach to traditional assessment would suggest. In addition, we provided a behavioral framework for conducting assessment organized along dimensions of direct and indirect assessment. The indirect approaches generally do not measure the target behavior of clinical relevance at the time and places of its natural occurrence. Direct methods measure the target behavior at the time of its natural occurrence.

Behavioral assessment methods include interview, self-report, behavior checklist and rating scales, self-monitoring, and direct observational assessment procedures. We reviewed a number of interview assessment formats, noting that these must be organized around the framework of predetermination of questions, response options, and the breadth of contents explored. Generally, there are few standardized interview approaches for use with fears and phobias; however, there are a number of existing formats described in the literature which can be used, such as the Kanfer and Saslow (1969) framework and the consultation approach developed by Bergan (1977) and his colleagues.

A number of self-report measures have been developed in the area of children's fears and related problems, including, for example, the *Children's Manifest Anxiety Scale*, the *Test Anxiety Scale for Children*, the *Children's School Questionnaire*, the *Fear Survey Schedule for Children*, the *Louisville Fear Survey Schedule for Children*, as well as a number of miscellaneous scales. Most of these scales have been developed in areas outside of behavioral psychology for purposes other than behavioral assessment, such as identifying variables that contribute to developing, implementing, and monitoring a treatment program. In this regard, many of the scales lack the specificity required by the behavioral assessment approach. Because many of these scales also lack norming, reliability, and validity, they must be used with caution in the behavioral assessment field.

A number of behavioral checklists and rating scales were reviewed as they relate to assessment of children's fears. Some of these scales are quite general and provide little information on identifying specific types of fears and phobias. Several specific checklists and rating scales can be completed by parents and teachers, and these were discussed in the context of a number of methodological and conceptual features. Generally, these scales can be quite useful in behavioral assessment, but we recommend that they be supplemented by more direct observational measures.

With regard to direct assessment measures in the fear area, we believe that self-monitoring, direct observational assessment, and psychophysiological assessment should be used with greater frequency in fear assessment. In this regard we concur with Barlow and Wolfe (1981), who noted that there was a general consensus among fear and phobia researchers that global measures tend to obscure differences in treatments and that the specific measurement of specific problems is an important direction in the future. Self-monitoring approaches show some promise in this area, but we have very little empirical evaluation with this type of assessment procedure. Nevertheless, a number of related theoretical papers and research reports have appeared in the literature, and we would recommend use of these procedures in the future.

Direct observational strategies appear to be extremely useful for assessing fears and related problems, and a number of BATs have been developed in this area. These measures show a great deal of promise, but need to be standardized. Information on norming reliability and validity also needs to be established, and it has been suggested that BATs need to be more focused on clinical problems in clinical settings. In addition to BATs, researchers and practitioners in the area of children's fears and related problems could use a number of available checklists and direct observational assessment formats in the natural environment. These strategies appear useful, but behavioral researchers must get on with the task of developing standardized formats.

Finally, a number of psychophysiological assessment strategies were reviewed including electromyography, cardiovascular measures, and electrodermal measures. These procedures appear appropriate for assessment of fears and related problems, particularly when considering a three-mode response assessment; nevertheless questions can be raised regarding the usefulness of psychophysiological data (Barlow & Wolfe, 1981). As noted by some of the participants at the National Institute of Mental Health conference, it may be that psychophysiological indices do not need to be gathered in a routine or automatic way. Perhaps these measures should reflect the precise aspects of behavior when a physiological system and theoretical issue are raised as important. However, their cost and technical requirements militate against their use in many research and clinical settings.

We believe that many advances have been made in the assessment of children's fears and related problems, some of them outside of behavioral psychology as traditionally conceived. Yet many of these areas appear primarily the focus of future research before they can be routinely accepted in clinical practice. A major future priority should be to provide research on the accuracy, reliability, and norming of various methods for assessing fears and related problems in children. This should be done using the three-mode response system as a framework for developing measures. Future fear research should involve the work of individual investigators as well as major research programs with a federal funding base.

NOTES

1. We do not discuss the generalizability issue in detail here. Generally, behavioral assessment can be generalized across six major universes: (1) scorer, (2) item, (3) time, (4) setting, (5) method, (6) dimension. More detailed discussion of this issue can be found in Cone (1977).
2. These scales were named by Barrios and Shigetomi (in preparation), but are not listed under these names in the original article.

CHAPTER 4

Desensitization and Flooding Therapies

In recent years there has been a rapid proliferation of behaviorally-oriented research on the development and application of fear reduction methods with children (see, for example, reviews by Gelfand, 1978; Graziano, DeGiovanni, & Garcia, 1979; Hatzenbuehler & Schroeder, 1978; Johnson, 1979; Miller, Barrett & Hampe, 1974; Ollendick, 1979). The assumptions underlying these approaches follow the behavioral position discussed in Chapter 1. There are currently five major behavioral therapy methods of fear reduction in children: systematic desensitization (including variations of this procedure); flooding methods; contingency management procedures; modeling procedures; and self-control procedures.

In this chapter, we discuss systematic desensitization and the variants of this approach as well as the flooding therapies. We will also review single case time series experiments, uncontrolled case studies, and between group experiments that have been used to investigate the efficacy of these methods.

SYSTEMATIC DESENSITIZATION

Systematic desensitization was developed in the early 1950s by Joseph Wolpe. It is reported to be the most frequently used behavior therapy procedure for reducing children's fears and phobias (Ollendick, 1979). The basic assumption of this technique is that a fear response can be inhibited by substituting an activity which is antagonistic to the fear response. The response which is most typically inhibited by this treatment process is anxiety, and the response frequently substituted for the anxiety is relaxation and calmness. For example, if an 11-year-old boy has a fear of riding in a car and feels very anxious and nauseous each time he rides or sits in one, we would help him inhibit his anxiety and discomfort by teaching him to relax and feel calm. Thus, we would *desensitize* him or *counter-condition* his fear of riding in cars.

The desensitization process is accomplished by exposing the child, in small, graduated steps, to the feared situation or event as he/she is performing an activity antagonistic to anxiety. The gradual exposure to the fear stimulus can take place through fantasy—where the child is asked to imagine being in various fear-related situations or pretends he/she is a popular superhero who approaches the feared event while performing usual superhero-related activities—or in real life (i.e., in vivo). Wolpe (1958) termed the principle that underlies the desensitization process as *reciprocal inhibition*. He described this principle in the following way: "If a response inhibitory to anxiety can be made to occur in the presence of anxiety-evoking stimuli, it will weaken the connection between these stimuli and the anxiety responses" (Wolpe, 1962, p. 562).

Before initiating the desensitization procedure, or any other behavior therapy fear reduction method, the therapist must first identify the child's fear as well as the circumstances under which the fear occurs. This is usually accomplished within the framework of the assessment strategies discussed in Chapter 3.

The goal of the initial assessment period is *not* to identify the causal factors that are responsible for a child's fear. It is generally accepted by behavior therapists that children have very complex learning histories, and that it is fallacious to assume that a retrospective (and, at times, highly impressionistic) account of a child's development and present activities over two or three initial assessment sessions will uncover *the* factor(s) that caused his/her fear. The initial assessment period can only provide the therapist with a picture of who the child is, what type of environment s/he comes from, and the possible exigencies that not only contribute to his/her fear but also to his/her general repertoire of behaviors. This period will also help the therapist support or refute various hypotheses about the nature of the child's fears and related problems, assist in specifying the goals of therapy, determine the behavior therapy procedure that is most appropriate for the child, and provide the therapist with sufficient information to determine if treatment can be carried out within the limitations set by the child, his/her parents, and other events in his/her life situation.

The Desensitization Procedure

Following the initial assessment period, the therapist typically outlines for the child (and where appropriate the parents) what will take place next. For example, the therapist might say the following to a high school student (or adapt it for a younger child):

> The emotional reactions that you experience come from your past experiences with others your age, older people, and different situations. These reactions

oftentimes lead to feelings of anxiety or tenseness which are not appropriate. Since these feelings of tenseness and anxiety occur within ourselves, it is possible to work with your feelings and reactions right here in the office by having you imagine those activities or events which cause your emotional reactions [adapted from Paul, 1966].

The behavior therapist might add that the type of fear the child is experiencing was learned just as many other complex and involved behaviors/activities have been learned over the years at home and school and can be unlearned by using a procedure called systematic desensitization. The procedure would then be outlined briefly (adapting the following statement to the child's developmental level):

The first stage consists of relaxation training where I am going to teach you how to become very relaxed. Once you have learned to relax, we will then use this relaxed state to counter the anxiety and tenseness that you feel whenever you are in the feared situation(s). We will do this by having you imagine—while you are still very relaxed—a series of progressively more tension or anxiety provoking scenes which you and I will develop . . . and which are directly related to fear. In other words, we will countercondition or counter your fear and tenseness in the feared situation(s). This procedure has been found to be very effective in the treatment of many types of fears, and we have used it successfully in the past with others/other children who have fears like yours. We will start the procedure by first teaching you how to become more relaxed and then asking you to practice the procedure at home.[1]

Following this introduction, the therapist should then answer any questions that the child and/or parents might have about the procedure.

There are essentially three phases to systematic desensitization: (1) relaxation training; (2) development of the anxiety hierarchy; and (3) systematic desensitization proper.[2]

Relaxation Training

The first step in relaxation training is to have the child become very comfortable. This can be accomplished by having the child, for example, lean back in a recliner chair or lie down on a couch located in a quiet, softly lighted room. The room should be in a quiet area away from any appreciable outside noise. Taking the child's developmental level into consideration, the therapist says something like the following:

I am going to teach you how to become very relaxed. In doing this I am going to ask you to tense up and relax opposing sets of muscles—proceeding through a series of these. That is, I am going to ask you to tense up and relax different sets of muscles so that there is a cumulative effect of relaxation over your whole body. (Pause) Okay, now, I would like you to. . . .

The relaxation steps presented in Table 4.1 are then initiated. These steps represent a modified version of a technique developed by Jacobson (1938) for inducing deep muscle relaxation. The whole procedure usually takes about 20-25 minutes to administer—each step taking about 10 seconds with a 10-15 second pause between each step. During the first few relaxation training sessions, it is often helpful for the therapist to practice the relaxation procedure with the child so that he/she can observe how to correctly perform a particular step. Before training begins it may also be helpful for the therapist to explain to the child the physical and emotional changes that they will begin to experience during relaxation training. This becomes especially important for those children whom the therapist feels have never (or rarely) experienced a waking "relaxed state." For example, the therapist might say:

In teaching you how to relax, you will begin to feel, at times, your muscles becoming heavy or loose and even maybe limp. You'll probably especially notice this relaxed feeling after you have tensed your muscles and then relaxed them. This is perfectly normal and don't be the least concerned. This is the natural result of you learning to relax your body. You may also feel, at times, self-conscious or embarrassed during the relaxation training. This is also perfectly natural, and this feeling will go away as you become more skilled in teaching yourself to relax.

At first the therapist may also have to physically guide the child in performing some of the steps, gradually fading out the assistance. Also, the therapist should make sure that the presentation of each step is paced to the child's ease of performing each step. It might be found, for example, that certain steps will need to be presented and practiced many times by a child before they are mastered. It should be noted, however, that there is no well-established method of determining whether a child has achieved mastery in teaching himself/herself to relax other than through (1) his/her self-report, (2) the therapist's inference or rating concerning the child's level of tension, and/or (3) through the monitoring of the child's heart rate and respiration (see, for example, reviews by Luiselli, 1980; Luiselli, Marholin, Steinman, & Steinman, 1979). One rating method which has received some empirical support involves the use of the *Relaxation Checklist* (Luiselli, 1980).

Once the child has gained a medium level of proficiency at relaxation training (usually after three sessions) the therapist should encourage him/her to practice the relaxation method at home or during a quiet time period at school (e.g., Bergland & Chal, 1972). The practice sessions should last 10-15 minutes per session and take place at least twice per day. In order to enhance the child's practice, some therapists record the relaxation procedure on cas-

**Table 4.1. An Introduction To The Relaxation Training Steps
Of Systematic Desensitization**

Steps in Relaxation

1. Take a deep breath and hold it (for about 10 seconds). Hold it. Okay, let it out.
2. Raise both of your hands about half way above the couch (or arms of the chair) and breath normally. Now, drop your hands to the couch (or down).
3. Now hold your arms out and make a tight fist. Really tight. Feel the tension in your hands. I am going to count to three and when I say "three" I want you to drop your hands. One . . . Two . . . Three.
4. Raise your arms again, and bend your fingers back the other way (toward your body). Now drop your hands and relax.
5. Raise your arms. Now drop them and relax.
6. Now raise your arms again, but this time "flap" your hands around. Okay, relax again.
7. Raise your arms again. Now relax.
8. Raise your arms above the couch (chair) again and tense your biceps until they shake. Breathe normally, and keep your hands loose. Relax your hands. (Notice how you have a warm feeling of relaxation).
9. Now hold your arms out to your side and tense your biceps. Make sure that you breathe normally. Relax your arms.
10. Now arch your shoulders back. Hold it. Make sure that your arms are relaxed. Now relax.
11. Hunch your shoulders forward. Hold it, and make sure that you breathe normally and keep your arms relaxed. Okay, relax. (Notice the feeling of relief from tensing and relaxing your muscles.)
12. Now turn your head to the right and tense your neck. Relax and bring your head back again to its natural position.
13. Turn your head to the left and tense your neck. Relax and bring your head back again to its natural position.
14. Now bend you head back slightly toward the chair. Hold it. Okay, now bring your head back slowly to its natural position.[3]
15. This time bring your head down almost to your chest. Hold it. Now relax and let your head come back to its natural resting position.
16. Now, open your mouth as much as possible. A little wider, okay, relax. (Mouth must be partly open at end.)
17. Now tense your lips by closing your mouth. Okay, relax.
18. Put your tongue at the roof of your mouth. Press hard. (Pause) Relax and allow your tongue to come to a comfortable position in your mouth.
19. Now put your tongue at the bottom of your mouth. Press down hard. Relax and let your tongue come to a comfortable position in your mouth.
20. Now just lie (sit) there and relax. Try not to think of anything.
21. To control self-verbalization, I want you to go through the motions of singing a high note—not aloud! Okay, start singing to yourself. Hold that note. Now relax. (You are becoming more and more relaxed.)
22. Now sing a medium tone and make your vocal cords tense again. Relax.
23. Now sing a low note and make your vocal cords tense again. Relax (Your vocal apparatus should be relaxed now. Relax your mouth.)
24. Now close your eyes. Squeeze them tight and breathe naturally. Notice the tension. Now relax. (Notice how the pain goes away when you relax.)
25. Now let your eyes relax and keep your mouth open slightly.

Table 4.1. (*continued*)

Steps in Relaxation

26. Open your eyes as much as possible. Hold it. Now relax your eyes.
27. Now wrinkle your forehead as much as possible. Hold it. Okay, relax.
28. Now take a deep breath and hold it. Relax.
29. Now exhale. Breathe all the air out . . . all of it out. Relax. (Notice the wondrous feeling of breathing again.)
30. Imagine that there are weights pulling on all your muscles making them flaccid and relaxed . . . pulling your arms and body into the couch.
31. Pull your stomach muscles together. Tighter. Okay, relax.
32. Now extend your muscles as if you were a prize fighter. Make your stomach hard. Relax. (You are becoming more and more relaxed.)
33. Now tense your buttocks. Tighter. Hold it. Now relax.
34. Now search the upper part of your body and relax any part that is tense. First the facial muscles. (Pause 3–5 sec.) Then the vocal muscles. (Pause 3–5 sec.) The neck region. (Pause 3–5 sec.) Your shoulder . . . relax any part which is tense (Pause) Now the arms and fingers. Relax these. Becoming very relaxed.
35. Maintaining this relaxation, raise both of your legs (about a 45° angle). Now relax. (Notice that this further relaxes you.)
36. Now bend your feet back so that your toes point toward your face. Relax your mouth. Bend them hard. Relax.
37. Bend your feet the other way . . . away from your body. Not far. Notice the tension. Okay, relax.
38. Relax. (Pause) Now curl your toes together as hard as you can. Tighter. Okay, relax. (Quiet . . . silence for about 30 seconds.)
39. This completes the formal relaxation procedure. Now explore your body from your feet up. Make sure that every muscle is relaxed. (Say slowly)—first your toes, your feet, your legs, buttocks, stomach, shoulder, neck, eyes, and finally your forehead—all should be relaxed now. (Quiet—silence for about 10 seconds). Just lie there and feel very relaxed, noticing the warmness of the relaxation. (Pause) I would like you to stay this way for about one more minute, and then I am going to count to five. When I reach five, I want you to open your eyes feeling very calm and refreshed. (Quiet—silence for about one minute.) Okay, when I count to five I want you to open your eyes feeling very calm and refreshed. One . . . feeling very calm; two . . . very calm, very refreshed; three . . . very refreshed; four . . . and five.

Source: Adapted in part from Jacobson (1938), Rimm (1967, personal communication), and Wolpe and Lazarus (1966); reprinted from Morris (1980).

sette tapes and have the child or parents play the tape while he/she is practicing each day. Others provide the child, where it seems appropriate, with a list of the muscle groups and encourage the child's parents and/or teachers to practice the relaxation procedure with the child.

In most cases, relaxation training will last for about three or four sessions. Throughout this training phase, it is often helpful to point out to children the changes that they will be experiencing in their bodily sensations (making sure the therapist uses words that they understand). For example, the therapist might say:

"Notice the warm, soft feeling of relaxation."
"Notice how your _____ (a particular muscle group) now feels . . . they are warm, heavy, and relaxed."
"Notice the difference in your body between tensing and relaxing your muscles."
"Notice how good it feels to relax your muscles."
"Notice how you are becoming more and more relaxed—feeling relaxation throughout your body . . . becoming more and more relaxed."

The therapist should also reiterate at various times such phrases as: "Breathe normally"; "Smooth, even breathing"; "Keep your _____ (a previously relaxed series of muscle groupings) relaxed"; "As you relax more muscles, you are becoming more and more relaxed."

Some children cannot relax using this training method. No matter how motivated they are, they simply find it difficult to respond or find the training instructions too complex to comprehend and/or carry-out.[4] A few children are even fearful to engage in relaxation training. In an attempt to deal with a person's difficulty in learning to relax, Morris (1973) proposed a shaping procedure to teach children and adults to close their eyes for increasingly longer periods of time during the relaxation training session. Similarly, Cautela and Groden (1978) discuss the use of shaping to assist children in learning how to tense and then relax particular muscle groupings. They also suggest using various squeeze toys to help children, especially those with special needs, in learning how to tense their arms and hands, as well as the use of certain air flow toys (e.g., whistle, party horn, harmonica, bubble pipes, etc.) to teach the breathing steps portions of the relaxation training program. Other adjunctive methods such as biofeedback-assisted relaxation (e.g., Tarler-Benlolo, 1978; Javel & Denholtz, 1975; Reeves & Maelica, 1975), the use of hypnosis or carbon dioxide-oxygen (Wolpe & Lazarus, 1966; Wolpe, 1973), and the administering of such drugs as Brevital (Brady, 1966, 1972; Friedman, 1966) have been recommended by some writers to assist adult clients in achieving relaxation, but there is currently no organized body of literature which supports their use with children.

In some cases, the child's difficulty in learning to relax is due to the fact that he/she is *not ready* to learn how to relax, i.e., may not have the requisite skills necessary for profiting from exposure to the relaxation procedure. Since it is not always clear which children are ready, Cautela and Groden (1978) suggest that each child who is to be exposed to relaxation training first be given the relaxation readiness pretest presented in Table 4.2. If the child successfully completes each of the three phases across all three trials, then the child is ready for relaxation training. If, on the other hand, the child does not pass a particular phase, then he/she should be trained in that readiness skill area before initiating relaxation training.

Table 4.2. Relaxation Readiness Pretest

The following pretest should be administered to the child. Give three trials for each response.

Name of Child: _____ CODE: ✓ = Correct
Date:_____   X = Incorrect
                                            NR = No Response

PHASE I. BASIC SKILLS	Trial 1	Trial 2	Trial 3
1. Ask the child to sit quietly in a chair for 5 seconds, feet still, back straight, head up, without moving or vocalizing. Repeat 2 more times.			
2. Say "Look at me," and ask the child to maintain eye contact for 3 seconds. Child must respond within 5 seconds. Repeat 2 more times.			
PHASE II. IMITATIVE SKILLS 3. Say "Do this," and raise your hand above your head. Child should imitate this response correctly within 5 seconds. Repeat 2 more times.			
4. Say "Do this," and you tap the table. Child should be able to imitate this response correctly by tapping the table. Repeat 2 more times.			
5. Say "Do this," and you tap your chest. Child should be able to imitate correctly by tapping his chest. Repeat 2 more times.			
PHASE III. FOLLOWING SIMPLE INSTRUCTIONS 6. Say "Stand up." Child should stand up in front of his chair within 5 seconds. Repeat this instruction 2 more times.			
7. Say "Sit down." Child should sit down in his chair within 5 seconds. Repeat this instruction 2 more times.			
8. Stand 6 feet from the child and say "Come here." Child should stand up and walk toward you without inappropriate movements or vocalizations. Repeat 2 more times.			

Source: Cautela, J. R., & Groden, J. *Relaxation. A comprehensive manual for adults, children, and children with special needs.* Champaign, Illinois: Research Press, 1978. Reprinted with permission.

Development of the Anxiety Hierarchy

Following the initial interview and during the relaxation phase, the therapist should begin planning an anxiety hierarchy with the child (and where appropriate, his/her parents) for each of the fears identified in the interview as needing reduction. A hierarchy is usually constructed on only the fear(s) that the child and therapist agree upon as in need of change during or immediately following the assessment period. The therapist should not impose treatment on a child for a fear which he/she has not agreed is in need of being reduced.

Typically, the client is given ten 3 × 5 inch index cards and asked to write down on each card (with or without parent assistance) a brief description of different situations regarding his/her fear which produce certain levels of anxiety or tension. Specifically, the child is asked to describe on the cards those situations that are related to his/her fear and that produce increasing amounts of anxiety, tension, uneasiness, and/or discomfort. Each of the ten cards is assigned a number which is a multiple of 10, and the child is asked to assign a brief description regarding his/her fear to each card, with the card having the value of 100 containing a description of the most anxiety-provoking situation, and the 10 card having a description of a very low anxiety provoking situation. Examples of some initial hierarchies are listed in Table 4.3.[5]

When the child returns with the prepared hierarchy, the therapist goes through it with him/her and adds intermediary items whenever it seems appropriate.[6] Children's hierarchies often differ markedly from each other, even those having to do with the same type of fear. Hierarchies vary on such factors as the child's unique interpretation of the events occurring in the feared situation(s), the number and type of people present in the feared situation(s), temporal and/or spatial considerations, type of environment in which the fear might occur, level of embarrassment which the child might feel if placed in or exposed to the feared situation, and degree to which the child feels he/she can escape from or leave the feared situation without being noticed by others. For example, a 13 year-old girl who had a fear of balloons (specifically, balloons popping) would avoid anyone who was holding a balloon, but would approach a person who was holding a balloon and even talk and stand close to him/her if necessary if she was with her girlfriends. She felt that her fear was quite "silly" and did not want her girlfriends to know about it. Her hierarchy dealt with the number of balloons present at any one time, who was holding the balloon(s), and the surprise and non-escape element of entering a room or visiting a place with and without friends and suddenly seeing a balloon.

The final hierarchy usually takes at least part of two or three sessions to develop and should represent a slow and smooth gradation of anxiety-provoking situations, each of which the child can easily imagine. Most hierarchies contain 20-25 items. It is not unusual, however, for those hierarchies that represent a very specific fear (e.g., fear of becoming sick while riding in a car, being alone in the house, or entering a swimming pool) to contain fewer items, while those representing a more complex fear (e.g., fear of being

Table 4.3. Examples of Initial Hierarchies

Fear of being alone
10. Being with a group of people at night or during the day.
20. Being alone in a room with another female.
30. Thinking about the possibility of being alone in my house during the day.
40. Walking to class early in the morning when there are few people outside.
50. At home alone in my bedroom during the day.
60. Driving a car alone at night and feeling a man is following me.
70. Walking alone on a city street downtown at night with a girlfriend.
80. Being alone at night in a house with a young child for whom I am babysitting.
90. Thinking about being at home alone at night a few hours before I will actually be alone.
100. Sitting alone in the living room of my house at night with the doors closed.

Fear of riding on a school bus
10. Wake up at 7:00 a.m. and think about taking the bus in an hour.
20. At home and look out front window and see a bus (not my bus) pass by.
30. At home at 8:15 a.m. and know I have to meet the bus in five minutes.
40. Outside of house and see bus coming down the street.
50. Bus stops in front of my house.
60. Bus driver opens doors of bus and other kids start climbing up the stairs.
70. I board the bus.
80. Sitting in the bus and the doors close.
90. On the bus for five minutes.
100. On the bus with kids yelling and laughing and the bus is stopped at a long red light.

Fear of evaluation
10. Sitting in my living room talking to my girlfriend about what we will do after we graduate from high school.
20. Studying at my desk at night.
30. Talking with a boy I just met at lunch.
40. Practicing volleyball after school for important league game that night.
50. Raising my hand in class to ask a question.
60. Not starting on first team for league game.
70. Not being asked out on a date by a boy I like.
80. Going to front of class to pick up an exam paper that teacher is handing out.
90. Receiving a low grade on an exam.
100. Telling parents that I received a low grade on an exam.

Fear of being away from home
10. Reading about people going to far away places.
20. Playing with my dog in front of house.
30. Seeing a scary movie about people going to strange or unknown places.
40. Being at next door neighbor's house after school.
50. Having to stay late after school to finish some work.
60. Traveling by car across town with parents.
70. Traveling by car with parents to another city.
80. Traveling by car across town with a neighbor.
90. Traveling in bus with other kids from church to another city.
100. Spending a night in a motel with other kids from church in another city.

evaluated, fear of school, of losing control, or using a public toilet) to contain more items. In Table 4.4, we have listed an example of a final hierarchy.

While developing the final hierarchy, the therapist should also determine what the child considers to be a very relaxing situation—one that the child can easily imagine and which he/she would rate as a zero on the hierarchy. This situation should be unrelated to the child's fear and promote a high level of comfort and happiness. Some examples of "zero-level" scenes are:

- Reading a good novel in bed before going to sleep.
- Watching the Muppets (television program).
- Having parent read to child before going to bed at night.
- Playing in a swimming pool.
- Riding bicycle in the neighborhood.
- Hiking in the woods.
- Playing with electric train set.

Table 4.4. Example of Final Hierarchy for Test Anxiety

You are attending a regular class session.
You hear about someone else who has a test.
You are studying at home. You are reading a normal assignment.
You are in class. The teacher announces a major exam in two weeks.
You are at home studying. You are beginning to review and study for a test that is a week away.
You are at home studying, and you are studying for the important test. It is now Tuesday and three days before the test on Friday.
You are at home studying and preparing for the upcoming exam. It is now Wednesday, two days before the test on Friday.
It's Thursday night, the night before the exam on Friday. You are talking with another student about the exam tomorrow.
It's the night before the exam, and you are home studying for it.
It's the day of the exam, and you have one hour left to study.
It's the day of the exam. You have been studying. You are now walking on your way to the test.
You are standing outside the test room talking with other students about the upcoming test.
You are sitting in the testing room waiting for the test to be passed out.
You are leaving the exam room, and you are talking with other students about the test. Many of their answers do not agree with yours.
You are sitting in the classroom waiting for the graded test to be passed back by the teacher.
It's right before the test, and you hear a student ask a possible test question which you cannot answer.
You are taking the important test. While trying to think of an answer, you notice everyone around you writing rapidly.
While taking the test, you come to a question you are unable to answer. You draw a blank.

Table 4.4 continued on p. 142.

Table 4.4. (*continued*)

You are in the important exam. The teacher announces 30 minutes remaining but
you have an hour's work left.
You are in the important exam. The teacher announces 15 minutes remaining but
you have an hour's work left.

Source: Deffenbacher, J. L., & Kemper, C. C. Systematic desensitization of test
anxiety in junior high students. *The School Counselor*, 1974, **12**, 216–222. Reproduced with permission.

Systematic Desensitization Proper

By the time the therapist is ready to begin the desensitization proper sessions, the child should have had sufficient time to practice relaxation and be
proficient at relaxing himself/herself on command. If the child has developed several hierarchies, the therapist should first work on the one that is
most distressing. Then, if time allows, the therapist can work on other hierarchies, but probably should not go beyond exposing the child to two or
three different hierarchies in a given therapy hour.

The first desensitization session starts with having the child spend about
three to five minutes relaxing himself/herself on the couch or in the recliner
chair. During this time the therapist suggests to the child that he/she is becoming increasingly more relaxed and is achieving a deeper and deeper level of
relaxation. The therapist might add the following comments during this
phase:

> Your whole body is becoming heavier . . . all your muscles are relaxing more
> and more. Your arms are becoming very relaxed. (Pause) Your shoulders. (Pause)
> and your eyes . . . very relaxed. Your forehead . . . very relaxed . . . noticing
> that as you become more relaxed you're feeling more and more calm. (Pause)
> Very relaxed . . . relaxing any part of your face which feels the least bit tense.
> (Pause) Now, back down to your neck, your shoulders, your chest, your but-
> tocks, your thighs, your legs, your feet . . . very, very relaxed. (Pause) Feeling
> very at ease and very comfortable.

The child is also asked by the therapist to indicate, by raising his right index
finger, when a very relaxed and comfortable state has been achieved.

After the child signals, the therapist asks him/her to visualize a number of
scenes from the hierarchy that the two of them developed over the past few
sessions. The therapist asks the child to imagine each scene as clearly and as
vividly as possible while still maintaining a very relaxed state. If the child
feels the least bit of anxiety or tension imagining a particular scene, he/she
is told to signal immediately with the right finger.

At this point, the therapist asks the child to indicate with his/her index finger if he/she is still feeling very calm and relaxed. If the child signals, the therapist presents the zero level scene. If the child does not signal, the therapist reviews with the child the earlier relaxation sequence until he/she no longer indicates feeling tense.

The zero level scene is presented for approximately 15 seconds. Each hierarchy scene is presented three to four times with a maximum exposure time of five seconds for the first presentation, and a gradual increase up to 10 seconds for subsequent presentations. The hierarchy items are presented first in ascending order, starting with the lowest feared item first, with relaxation periods between each scene varying from 10 to 15 seconds. In most cases, three to four different scenes are presented per session. This means that a particular desensitization session will last between 15 and 20 minutes. The remainder of the hour can be devoted to discussing issues related to the child's fear (e.g., what happened during the week regarding the fear), to the desensitization of another fear hierarchy, or to working on some other problem area with the child.

After the last scene is presented for a particular session, and if the decision is to not go onto another hierarchy, the therapist usually asks the child to relax for a short period of time. The therapist then starts the *ending phase* of the session by saying the following.

Just relax . . . feeling very comfortable and at ease, I would like you to stay this way until I count to five. When I reach five, I want you to open your eyes feeling very calm and refreshed. (Pause) One, feeling very calm; two, very calm and refreshed; three, very refreshed; four and five.

The same general format is followed for all subsequent desensitization sessions. The scenes should not be presented in a rapid manner, but in a conversational way that conveys both understanding and concern for the child. Each scene should be presented until the child has three consecutive successes. If, however, the child has two consecutive failures (indications of anxiety), the therapist should go back to the previous successfully passed scene and work back up the hierarchy again. If failure occurs again, the previously successful scene should be repeated so that the client ends the session with a positive experience. The ending phase (described above) should then be initiated. It is often helpful to then review with the child the problems he/she was having with the difficult scene. Modifications in the hierarchy or in other aspects of the desensitization procedure should then occur. For example, if the child feels he/she is having to make too much of a change from one scene to the next, the therapist may choose to intersperse one or two scenes between these scenes to make the change more gradual. Typically, the added scenes would differ from the previously passed and the next failed scenes along some spatial and/or temporal dimension, incorporating the contents of the failed scene but making it *less* fearful. An example of this follows:

> Marsha was a 10-year-old girl who feared standing in line in the school cafeteria, as well as in line to enter school at the beginning of the school day. Her fear often resulted in her refusing to go to school to avoid the "embarrassment of other kids looking at me." Systematic desensitization was used and treatment proceeded smoothly through the hierarchy until she reached item #65—"Walking into the cafeteria and seeing five or ten other kids waiting in line." Marsha repeatedly failed this item but passed the previous item (#60—"Walking down the hallway towards the cafeteria and seeing the open doors of the cafeteria ahead of me"). Following a discussion with her, two additional items were added: (1) #62—"Walking into the cafeteria and seeing no one waiting in line yet," and (2) #64—"Walking into the cafeteria and seeing two or three other kids waiting in line."

Additional Considerations

Although there has been a substantial amount of clinical and analogue research conducted with adults on those factors which contribute to the effectiveness of systematic desensitization, very little controlled research of this nature has been performed with children (see for example, Graziano et al., 1978; Hatzenbuehler & Schroeder, 1978; Ollendick, 1979). This is especially surprising given the relatively large number of uncontrolled case studies reported in the literature and the fact that this method is often reported to be the most frequently used behavior therapy procedure for reducing children's fears.

Some client factors that might contribute to the effectiveness of systematic desensitization therapy with children—and which therapists should be aware of prior to and/or during therapy—are the following: age of child receiving treatment, child's level of visual imagery, his/her ability to relax, ability to follow instructions, level of acquiescence, and threshold for fatigue (see, for example, Kissel, 1972). Regarding the age factor, very few studies report the successful use of systematic desensitization with children under nine years of age.

Imagery level is theoretically (and in practice) an important factor in Wolpean desensitization. Some evidence suggests (e.g., Levin, 1976; Pressley, 1977) that children can form visual images by approximately the age of nine; however, this work has not been conducted in the area of systematic desensitization. For example, one research question which needs to be answered is what level of visual imagery is needed by children in order for systematic desensitization to be successful? Since few guidelines are available in this regard, we suggest that the therapist conduct an informal imagery test during the hierarchy construction phase on those children for whom systematic desensitization therapy is planned. For example, the therapist might show a picture to a child for 20 seconds, like the one presented in Figure 4.1, preceded by the instructions, "I am going to show you a picture for a while. I want you to concentrate on what you see in the picture. After I take it away, I want you to tell me exactly where you saw certain parts of the picture." After the 20 seconds, the therapist would then give the child a blank 8 × 10 inch sheet of paper and ask him/her to indicate by check mark and the corresponding number of the item referred to, where 15 of the objects were situated on the paper. The therapist would then ask where the first of the 15 objects was situated and wait for the child to respond on the paper before proceeding to the next item on the list, and so forth.[7] The therapist could also create a number of incongruous pictorial descriptions (e.g., a fish smoking a cigar; a tree talking to a little boy; or two rabbits playing checkers). Then, the therapist asks the child to close his/her eyes and says: "I am going to describe a few pictures to you one at a time. I want you to imagine each picture as quickly as you can. After you have a picture clearly and vividly in view in your imagination, I want you to raise your hand." The speed (reaction time) with which the child raises his/her hand to report visualizing the scenes and/or the percentage of correct placements of the recalled objects in Figure 4.1 might provide the therapist with information concerning a child's imagery level.

A more formal method of assessing imagery could involve the use of the Betts (1969) *Vividness of Mental Imagery Scale.* This scale has been used as a measure of imagery ability by Hiscock and Cohen (1973) and McLemore (1972). In essence, the person is asked to rate the vividness of certain images which are described to him/her along the following dimension:

1. [Image is] perfectly clear and as vivid as the actual experience.
2. Very clear and comparable in vividness to the actual experience.
3. Moderately clear and vivid.
4. Not clear or vivid, but recognizable.
5. Vague and dim.
6. So vague and dim as to be hardly discernible.
7. Not present at all; you only know that you are thinking of the object [Suckerman, 1977].

For example, he/she would be asked to think of a relative or friend who is seen frequently, considering carefully the picture that comes before the mind's eye. Then the degree of clearness and vividness of the person's exact contour of face, head, shoulders, and body should be rated. Similarly, the person would be asked to rate such scenes as: the sun setting below the horizon, the whistle of a locomotive train, the honk of an automobile, the feel of sand, the

Figure 4.1. Sample photograph which might be used in conducting an informal assessment of a child's level of imagery (Suckerman, 1977).
  Source: Heiman, A. W. *The new phonics we use, readiness/introducing the alphabet.* Chicago: Lyons & Carnahan, 1972. Reprinted by permission.

prick of a pine cone, and so forth. Given the paucity of research in this area, our suggestion is that if the therapist suspects a low level of visual imagery in a child, it might be best to use other desensitization methods or behavior therapy approaches.

With regard to relaxation level, a therapist might find a few children having difficulty achieving a relaxed state—no matter how long they practice relaxation training. Some behavioral indicies of children *not* being relaxed while practicing (or following the completion of) the relaxation steps are the following: giggling or smiling, rapid movement of their eyelids, frequent yawning, unsolicited comments, rapid and/or uneven breathing, repeatedly opening eyes and/or squeezing eyes closed, moving their bodies around in the recliner chair or on the couch to find a comfortable position, hands clenching chair or tapping, and/or muscular tightness around the lips or the facial muscles (e.g., Luiselli, 1980). Also, as we discussed earlier, some children may not achieve a relaxed state because they cannot follow the therapist's instructions or cannot perform a particular step in the relaxation program. In the latter case, as suggested by Cautela and Groden (1978), the therapist may have to shape the correct behavior. In the former case, the therapist may need to simplify the instructions and/or model the particular step and use shaping to develop the correct behavior. The therapist might also consider using some of the other methods discussed in the "Relaxation Training" section. Lastly, it might be helpful to use in the background the favorite musical tape(s) or record(s) that the child finds very soothing or quieting. If, however, none of these methods is successful in helping the child become relaxed, the therapist should consider using other desensitization methods or behavior therapy approaches. Similarly, if it is found that a particular child has difficulty following single and multi-stage commands, then other fear reduction methods should also be tried.

To assess whether a child is having difficulty following commands, the Cautela and Groden (1978) pretest presented in Table 4.2 could be used. To this list the therapist might add more complex two-, three-, and four-stage commands. For example, the following commands might be added (Morris, 1976):

Stand up and sit down.
Stand up and twirl around, sit down.
Stand up, jump up and down, sit down.
Stand up, walk to door, touch door with one hand, come back and sit down in the chair.
Stand up, move chair back and forth, twirl around twice, walk to the door and touch it three times, hop back on one foot, sit down in chair.

Acquiescence and fatigue are two other client variables that the therapist should be aware of during the conduct of systematic desensitization. Some children may never signal anxiety while imagining various scenes and may never indicate that they are experiencing difficulty relaxing by themselves. In some cases, this is good because it suggests that desensitization is proceeding smoothly. In other cases, however, this suggests that the child is attempting to behave in a socially desirable manner—i.e., the child is reluctant to express himself/herself directly regarding the progress of therapy in favor of attempting to create an impression that desensitization is progressing smoothly. To reduce this possibility during the desensitization sessions, the therapist should mention at various times throughout the session: "Remember to signal whenever you feel the slightest amount of anxiety." The therapist should also make every effort neither to convey dissatisfaction with a child's signaling of anxiety nor satisfaction that the child did not signal anxiety during a particular session. In both instances, the child may surmise that the therapist does not really want any signaling of anxiety.

Similarly, if the therapist is not responsive to a child's fatigue in therapy, steady progress might also be effected. It may be helpful, therefore, for the therapist to ask the child after some of the sessions (1) whether too many scenes or hierarchies were being presented in the session, (2) whether he/she was able to vividly imagine and be "completely involved" in the scenes, or found himself/herself "drifting-off" towards other thoughts and images, or (3) if he/she tended to fall asleep at times finding it difficult to maintain the awake and relaxed state.

As in the case of client variables, little research has been conducted with children on the contribution of therapist or setting variables on the outcome of systematic desensitization. Some research has been conducted with adults (see, for example, Morris & Magrath, 1982; Morris & Suckerman, 1974 a,b, 1976), but it is not clear whether these findings can be transferred to the conduct of systematic desensitization with children. In light of the paucity of research on these variables, we agree with other writers (e.g., Goldfried & Davison, 1976; Wilson & Evans, 1977) that desensitization should be conducted within a context of a sound therapist-client relationship.

Finally, during the initial stages of systematic desensitization, the therapist should encourage both the child and parents to avoid whenever possible the temptation of entering the actual feared situation. If the child must enter the situation, he/she should avoid doing so at "full throttle." As desensitization progresses, however, the child should be encouraged to enter aspects of the feared situation which correspond to the lower hierarchy items that have been successfully passed and for which he/she now feels little, if any, tension or anxiety. The therapist should also discuss with the child what the results were of his/her entering these previous tension-provoking situations, and determine whether any review sessions are needed on the earlier aspects of the hierarchy.

SUPPORTIVE RESEARCH

Compared to the adult phobia literature, relatively little systematic research has been conducted on the effectiveness of systematic desensitization therapy on children's fears, and yet from all indications in the clinical literature, this treatment approach is the one which is most frequently used in reducing children's fears (see, for example, Graziano et al., 1978; Hatzenbuehler & Schroeder, 1978; Ollendick, 1979; Tryon, 1980). Mann and Rosenthal (1969), for example, compared direct (systematic) and vicarious (children observing other children receiving treatment) desensitization in individual and group treatment settings with a no-treatment control group. The children in the treatment groups consisted of 50 seventh graders, while the children in the control group were 21 eighth graders. Compared to the control group, the treatment groups showed a significantly greater reduction on their respective self-report test anxiety scores and a significant improvement in their performance on a reading test. No significant differences, however, were found between the individual or group, direct or vicarious desensitization methods.

With regard to other school-related fears, Taylor (1972) reported the successful use of systematic desensitization with a 15-year-old female "school phobic." The case was especially interesting since the girl engaged in excessive urination during school and in school-related activities which contributed to her avoiding school and withdrawing from social relationships. Her anxiety hierarchies involved three themes: riding in the school bus, being in school, and participating in class activities. A four month follow-up evaluation indicated that she was no longer experiencing frequent urination and that she was experiencing satisfactory relationships in school.

Miller (1972) treated a 10-year-old male who was reluctant to go to school and experienced "extreme fear" of being separated from his mother as well as a fear of his own death. Using systematic desensitization, Miller found that the child's fear of separating from his mother decreased gradually over the 11 treatment weeks. Systematic desensitization was also effective in reducing the boy's school phobia, but was not successful in decreasing his fear of his own death. Lazarus (1960) also treated a school phobic child with systematic desensitization. Following her ninth birthday, the girl became enuretic, afraid of the dark, and developed at school "violent" abdominal pains which eventually resulted in her being excused from class and her mother having to come to school. It was determined that her multiple fears were the result of her fear of being separated from her mother. Desensitization took five sessions over a 10-day period. A 15-month follow-up revealed a "very occasional" enuretic incident with no reported school-related problems.

In another case study, Kushner (1965) used systematic desensitization to reduce the fears of a 17-year-old male who feared driving his car, being driven by others, and being around cars. After three treatment sessions, the client reported feeling better. At the sixth and last session, the client felt 90% improved. At the three-month follow-up, there was further improvement and no recurrence of his fears. MacDonald (1975) also reported the successful use of systematic desensitization with an 11-year-old boy who had a dog phobia which had lasted for eight years. By the sixth session, the boy reported staying outdoors without worrying about dogs, and at the fourteenth session, his parents reported that he was engaging in appropriate interactions in both benign and threatening dog encounters. In addition to the use of desensitization, MacDonald added some adjuncts to treatment, for example, dog pictures in his room, writing a happy story about himself and a dog, audio tape recording of barking dogs, skill training regarding interacting with dogs and programmed outdoor activity. The results were maintained at a two-year follow-up period.

An adjunct to systematic desensitization was also used in a study by Saunders (1976) involving a 13-year-old boy who developed motion sickness and vomiting during trips in cars or buses. In addition to the standard desensitization method, Saunders added an *in vivo* relaxation component, where the boy approached and was sitting in a vehicle. Treatment was completed in 11 sessions over a four-month period. At the 19-month follow-up period, the child reported no nausea, and was able to take a long trip with his family and ride the bus to school.

Each of the case studies described above, as well as others (e.g., O'Farrell & Hedlund, in press), can best be described as clinical/descriptive case studies. Only a very few controlled single subject experiments have been published. For example, Van Hasselt, Hersen, Bellack, and Rosenblum (1979) used systematic desensitization with an 11-year-old boy who had fears of blood, heights, and taking tests. The authors measured the boy's motoric, cognitive, and physiological responses to each fear. Treatment lasted for four relaxation sessions and four to six desensitization sessions for each fear. Although relaxation training did not appreciably change any of the dependent measures, systematic desensitization was found to effect "impressive" changes on all but the physiological measure. A second controlled study by Ollendick (1979) also demonstrated the effectiveness of systematic desensitization. Using a withdrawal design, Ollendick treated a 16-year-old anorexic male who feared gaining weight and the subsequent peer criticism he felt would be directed at him. While the desensitization procedure was in effect the adolescent gained weight, and when the procedure was withdrawn he began to lose weight. Upon reinstating desensitization, he began gaining weight again, thereby demonstrating experimental control of the desensitization procedure. Following the completion of the use of desensitization an adjunctive weight maintenance-enhancing procedure was introduced. At the 18-month follow-up, the adolescent's weight gain was maintained, while at the two-year follow-up a slight drop in weight was found.

With respect to research comparing systematic desensitization to other psychotherapy approaches, only one study has been reported. Miller, Barrett, Hampe, and Noble (1972) compared the relative effectiveness of systematic desensitization and conventional psychotherapy to a waiting list control condition with children having various phobias. The desensitization condition lasted 24 sessions and included at times assertive training, presence of parents in the desensitization sessions, and assistance of parents in developing alternative responses for children to fear and anxiety. This method therefore included elements which were additional to standard systematic desensitization. The conventional psychotherapy condition also lasted 24 sessions and included having the child talk out his/her feelings and conflicts where the emphasis was on affective expression of and subsequent cognitive awareness of preconditions for fear. As in the desensitization condition, parents were also seen and worked with to alter the child's home environment and to remove any potential contributing factors to the child's fear. It thus appeared that the two treatment approaches contained many common elements. Outcome was assessed in terms of the clinician's ratings of the intensity and extensity of each child's fear and by the ratings of parents on the *Louisville Behavior Checklist* and the *Louisville Fear Survey for Children*. No children's actual fear responses were systematically observed by the researchers.

The overall results for the clinicians' ratings showed that neither treatment method was superior to the waiting list control condition. However, when age was considered, it was found that children between six and ten years of age in both therapy groups significantly improved over the waiting list control children. No differences were found between the desensitization and psychotherapy conditions for the 6-10 year olds or the 11-15 year olds. In addition, the level of experience of the clinician (20 years experience versus a recent graduate with minimal child therapy experience) did not have a significant effect on the outcome of the study, nor did such factors as sex of child, IQ, or chronicity of fears. With respect to parent ratings, parents of children in both treatment groups, across age groups, reported significantly greater improvement in their children than did parents of children in the waiting list control condition. No significant differences, however, were found between the two treatment groups. The results on each of the dependent measures were maintained at a six-week follow-up. A two-year follow-up (Hampe, Noble, Miller, & Barrett, 1973) showed that the improvement in the children had been maintained. It was also found that most of those children who were in the waiting list control group or who did not respond to treatment, also improved over the two-year period. In some cases, however, this improvement was due to additional therapy these children received.

Given the "impure" nature of the systematic desensitization group, the fact that no overt children's fears were observed, and that this study has not been replicated, it is difficult to interpret the meaningfulness of these findings, especially in light of the uncontrolled case study and controlled research literature discussed earlier which supports the use of systematic desensitization. Thus, in combining the results of all of the experiments and case studies reported, these findings suggest that systematic desensitization is a potentially effective treatment method for reducing a variety of fears and phobias in children from 9-17 years of age. It should be noted, however, that this conclusion is quite tentative, given the limited number of controlled investigations using this treatment procedure and the apparently contradictory findings reported in the only comparative clinical outcome study. In addition, since few studies have been reported using this procedure with children less than nine years of age, it is not clear what conclusions can be made except that supportive research findings with this age group are quite sparse.

Variations of Systematic Desensitization

Some alternatives to individual systematic desensitization have been proposed by researchers, each of which involve variations of the desensitization procedure discussed above. Six of these variations are discussed here.

Group Systematic Desensitization.   This method involves the same basic phases as individual systematic desensitization, but the phases are adapted for group administration. Typically, groups of five to eight persons are included in this group procedure. Relaxation training is conducted in a medium to large size room, using adjustable patio chaise lounges or foam rubber mats on the floor. Hierarchy construction is conducted in the group with the group rank ordering the hierarchy items. An alternative approach is for the therapist to bring to the group a listing of potential hierarchy items like the ones presented in Table 4.5. The group would decide which ones were appropriate, make any necessary modifications in the items, and then rank order them.

Desensitization proper is conducted in a slightly different manner from the individual approach. The general rule is that desensitization is geared to the slowest progressing person in the group. If, for example, only one child is experiencing anxiety over a particular imagined scene, the others in the group are told to continue relaxing or, in some cases, to imagine their neutral scene. The therapist would then go through repeated presentations of that particular scene and/or other previous successfully passed scenes, until the child passed the difficult scene.

Table 4.5. Possible Items for a Text Anxiety Hierarchy

You hear about a friend who has a test soon.

On the first day of class, the teacher announces the number of tests she will be giving during the first grading period.

Your teacher announces that there will be a test in one week.

It's a couple of days before the test and you still have a lot to study. You know that you will be able to prepare adequately for the exam only if you work steadily and efficiently.

You start studying for the test.

You are studying and wondering how you will remember everything for the test.

It's the night before the exam and you're reviewing everything.

You get all ready for your class and it's a few minutes before you have to leave for school.

You're at school and you walk to your class where you have to take the test, and you're thinking about the test.

You enter the classroom where the exam is given.

You take your seat and wait for the teacher to come to you with the test.

Others around you are talking about the material being covered on the test and you're trying to answer their questions to yourself.

You see the teacher handing out the exams and you watch others get their copy of the test.

You get your copy of the exam and look it over.

You see a lot of questions you think you should know, but you can't remember the answers to them.

You start the test and wonder how well you are doing compared to the others in your class.

You get to your class expecting a routine discussion or lecture and the teacher passes out a surprise quiz.

You come to an ambiguous question. You think you know the answer but the question can be interpreted in more than one way.

While answering an essay question, you realize that what you are writing is incorrect and that you will have to cross out what you have written and being again.

The teacher has just told the class that only half the time remains for you to complete the exam. You have completed less than half of the test and realize that you will have to work more rapidly in order to finish the exam.

You see others finish the test and hand in their papers and you aren't finished yet.

There are two minutes remaining in the test. If you work very quickly, you will be able to answer all the questions.

You turn in the exam and hear others talking about the test. You didn't answer the questions the same way they did.

Source: Adapted, in part, from Martinez, L. *A comparison of self-control desensitization with systematic desensitization in the reduction of test anxiety.* Unpublished dissertation. Syracuse University, 1978.

In terms of supportive research, we again find a disproportionate amount of research being conducted on group desensitization with adults than with children, and in both instances the majority of research is on school-related problems (e.g., test anxiety, speech anxiety, reading difficulties). For example, Kondas (1967) used group systematic desensitization with test-anxious (oral examination) 11–15-year-old students. Compared to the relaxation or hierarchy only groups, the desensitization group showed significant decreases on their self-reported fears and palmar perspiration measures. Barabasz (1973) also studied the relative effectiveness of group desensitization with test-anxious students. Working with fifth and sixth graders, he divided students into high and low test-anxious subjects on the basis of their galvanic skin reaction to a series of stimuli including imagined test-taking scenes. Half of the subjects in each condition were then assigned to either a desensitization or no treatment condition. Desensitization treatment lasted for five consecutive school days. The results showed that high anxious desensitization subjects showed significant reductions on autonomic measures of anxiety and higher performance on a group test than did high anxious no-treatment control subjects. In addition, no differences were found on either dependent measure for the experimental and control low anxious subjects. No follow-up assessment period was reported. Other studies on test anxiety (e.g., Deffenbacher & Kemper, 1974 a,b; Laxer, Quarter, Kooman, & Walker, 1969) have also reported group systematic desensitization treatment to be effective. In one set of studies (e.g., Deffenbacher & Kemper, 1974 a,b), however, student grade point average was the only outcome variable used to measure treatment success, while in another study (e.g., Laxer et al., 1969) only a few self-report anxiety outcome measures were found to significantly decrease as a result of treatment, and no significant improvement was found in subjects' academic work.

Miller and Madsen (1970) worked with "anxious" seventh graders who had reading problems. Subjects were assigned to either a group systematic desensitization condition, a reading (practice) placebo condition, or a no-treatment control group. Each treatment condition took place twice per week, 30 minutes per session for 10 weeks. Compared with the no-treatment controls, the desensitization and placebo conditions showed significant changes on self-report measures of anxiety and no appreciable changes on reading achievement or teacher ratings. No follow-up evaluation, however, occurred. Johnson, Tyler, Thompson, and Jones (1971) also found that group systematic desensitization was as effective as a speech practice/rehearsal condition in significantly reducing the self-report speech anxiety scores of speech anxious middle school children.

In Vivo Desensitization.   In this method, the child is exposed to the items on the hierarchy in the real or actual situation rather than through his/her imagination. Relaxation training is not used as the counterconditioned response to the feared situation. Instead, those feelings of comfort, security, and trust that the child has developed for the therapist, which have emerged from the therapeutic relationship, are used as the counterconditioning agent.

The therapist goes into the real-life situation with the child and encourages him/her to go through each item on the hierarchy. An example of this procedure, used with a 10-year-old "school phobic" boy, is the following:

The desensitization procedure in this case was carried out in the school environment. The school officials were informed of the procedure and they cooperated fully with the therapist. Jimmy was told that each day the therapist would accompany him to school and that together they would approach the school gradually. Since it was known that he could tolerate going by the school in a car, the first step consisted of Jimmy and the therapist sitting in the car in front of the school. The other steps were as follows: (2) getting out of the car and approaching the curb, (3) going to the sidewalk, (4) going to the bottom of the steps of the school, (5) going to the top of the steps, (6) going to the door, (7) entering the school, (8) approaching the classroom a certain distance each day down the hall, (9) entering the classroom, (10) being present in the classroom with the teacher, (11) being present in the classroom with the teacher and one or two classmates, and (12) being present in the classroom with a full class. This procedure was carried out over 20 consecutive days, including Saturdays and Sundays. The amount of time spent each day ranged between 20 and 40 minutes and involved about 10 to 12 hours of the therapist's time.

The therapist and Jimmy began by coming to school early in the morning when no one else was present. Jimmy was told to report any uncomfortable feeling he was experiencing, and when he reported that he was feeling afraid, the therapist immediately indicated that it was time to return to the car and generously praised Jimmy for what he had accomplished. On several days the patient did not go beyond the previous day's achievement and was asked to remain at that point for a longer period of time. When Jimmy finally entered the classroom he reported that he was very anxious when the children began to come into the schoolyard. On the following days, the teacher and one or two students came into the classroom while Jimmy was there (deliberately arranged), but when it came time for school to start officially, he reported that he felt more anxious so that it was necessary to leave before the children came to the classroom. On the 19th day, after Jimmy had been in the classroom with the teacher and two students for several days, the therapist pointed out to Jimmy that he was no longer afraid of school, since he was now able to immerse himself completely in the school environment. The therapist added that he was going to withdraw from the situation. On the next day, the 20th in the desensitization procedure, it was arranged for the father to take the patient to school and talk with the principal. This was done with ease, and the principal decided that it would be sufficient for Jimmy to do his schoolwork in the principal's office. Later that same day, mistakenly thinking that the patient's classroom was empty, the principal brought him to the classroom. Through the class window Jimmy could see that the students were in the room. When he saw that another youngster was occupying the desk to which he had been assigned, the patient politely told the youngster that he was in his seat. Since that time Jimmy has remained in school, and a 2-year follow-up had indicated that there have been no subsequent manifestations of the phobia [Garvey & Hegrenes, 1966, p. 149. Reprinted with permission].

In terms of corroborating research, a number of studies have been published over the past 15-20 years that have used *in vivo* desensitization either alone or in combination with some other procedure to reduce fears in children (e.g., Bentler, 1962; Craghan & Musante, 1975; Eikeland, 1973; Freeman, Roy, & Hemmick, 1976; Garvey & Hegrenes, 1966; Kuroda, 1969; O'Reilly, 1971; Phillips & Wolpe, 1981; Pomerantz, Peterson, Marholin, & Stern, 1977; Tasto, 1969; Van der Ploeg, 1975). Few of these studies, however, are well controlled and none has systematically examined the relative effectiveness of only *in vivo* desensitization. Freeman et al. (1976) presented a case study of a seven and one-half-year-old boy who had a fear of having a physical examination. The therapist was a nurse who had a good relationship with the child. The nurse took the child to the examining room and gradually exposed him to the 11-step physical examination hierarchy. Treatment lasted over a seven session period, with the child permitting in the last session an examination of his entire body. Physicians were then gradually introduced, and after three additional sessions the boy permitted the physician to examine him entirely. Craghan and Musante (1975) used this method with a seven-year-old boy who had a fear of high buildings. Treatment lasted six sessions and involved both *in vivo* desensitization and game playing with the therapist (e.g., jumping over sidewalk cracks, kicking buildings, and throwing snowballs at buildings). Following treatment and at the three-month and one-year follow-up, the child showed no indication of being afraid of high buildings. O'Reilly (1971) combined *in vivo* desensitization with an alternative competing response notion with a six-year-old girl who refused to go to school because she was afraid of the school fire bell. A tape of children's stories and songs was played in the girl's classroom combined with the gradual introduction (from barely audible to normal volume) of a five-second tape recording of the school's fire bell. Upon completion of the 10-week treatment period, the girl demonstrated a "rapid" and "apparent nonreversible" reduction in her fear response and no longer refused to go to school. This procedure is similar to Jones' (1924a) approach with a three-year-old child, Peter, who was afraid of a rabbit. Jones paired the boy's eating of food with gradually introducing the rabbit closer and closer to the child. Furthermore, like the O'Reilly procedure this treatment was conducted within a setting where there were other fearless children. This approach was also used by Kuroda (1969) in eliminating the fears of frogs and earthworms in three- and four-year-old children.

In vivo desensitization approaches have also been used by parents of phobic children under the supervision of a therapist (e.g., Bentler, 1962; Pomerantz et al., 1977; Stableford, 1979; Tasto, 1969). For example, Bentler (1962) reports a case involving an 11½-month-old girl who was afraid of water. He established a hierarchy with the mother involving increasing exposure to water (for example, from toys being placed in an empty bathtub, to the child being placed near the kitchen sink which was filled with water with toys floating in it, to washing the child in the bathtub). This graduated approach was combined with the child's "affective responses toward toys," body contact with the mother and "other mother-related stimuli." By age 12¾ months, the child "was thoroughly recovered," with no additional fears reported at either 13 months or 18 months of age. Similarly, Pomerantz et al. (1977) taught the mother of a four-year-old boy, to use *in vivo* desensitization, participant modeling, and contingent reinforcement to reduce her son's fear. After developing a bath water hierarchy, a home assistant trained the mother in the implementation of the treatment procedures, modeling the procedures and coaching her. The child's fear of water was eliminated in 11 days and was maintained at this level at one- and six-month follow-up periods.

In summary, although a number of case/descriptive studies have reported successful use of *in vivo* desensitization, no well-controlled research has been published on this method. Because most of the case studies in the literature have used this method in combination with other procedures, the relative effectiveness of this procedure remains questionable.

Automated Systematic Desensitization.   In this procedure, the client goes through the desensitization process by listening to a series of tape-recorded scene presentations prepared by the therapist with the client's assistance. Developed by Lang (Wolpe, 1969) this procedure allows the client to pace himself/herself through the desensitization process. A variation of this automated procedure is called *self-directed desensitization* (e.g., Baker, Cohen, & Saunders, 1973, Rosen, 1976). In this procedure, the person uses instructional materials typically provided by the therapist and conducts the treatment at his/her own pace at home. The major difference between these methods is that the automated method is structured by the therapist and uses recording devices and/or computers in the therapist's office to present treatment, whereas in self-directed treatment the person develops the treatment package by himself/herself at home with minimal therapist control. Both procedures have been used mainly with adults, but a few studies have been conducted with children. For example, Wish, Hasazi, and Jurgela (1973) report the use of this type of procedure with an 11-year-old male who had a fear of loud noises. Following the construction of the hierarchy and relaxation training, a tape of the child's favorite music was made with sounds from the fear hierarchy superimposed. The child was instructed to relax in a dark room at home and listen to the tape with the volume gradually increased over the eight-day, three-session per day period. By the end of treatment, the child could listen comfortably to the sounds he feared most at a loud intensity. In addition, the child did not show any fear responses to other noises (e.g., balloon pop or firecracker). The child's behavior was maintained at a 9-month follow-up period. Although other automated and self-directed desensitization studies have been published (e.g., Baker et al., 1973; Biglan, Villowck, & Wick, 1979; Rosen, Glasgow, & Barrera, 1976), the Wish et al. (1973) study appears to be one of the few involving the use of children. This is an interesting treatment approach and one in need of a good deal more research before any definitive statement can be made about its relative effectiveness in reducing children's fears.

Emotive Imagery.   This method was first used by Lazarus and Abramovitz (1962) to adapt the desensitization proper phase to children. It involves the use of those anxiety-inhibiting images in children which arouse feelings of excitement associated with adventure, as well as feelings of pride, mirth, etc., and consists of the following steps:

(a)   As in the usual method of systematic desensitization, a gradual hierarchy is drawn up.

(b)   By sympathetic conversation and inquiry, the clinician establishes the nature of the child's hero images and the wish fulfillments and identifications which accompany them.

(c)   The child is asked to close his eyes and imagine a sequence of events which is close enough to his everyday life to be credible, but within which is woven a story concerning his favorite hero or alter ego.

(d)   When the clinician judges that these emotions have been maximally aroused, he introduces, as a natural part of the narrative, the lowest item in the hierarchy. If there is evidence that anxiety is being inhibited, the procedure is repeated as in ordinary systematic desensitization until the highest item in the hierarchy is tolerated without distress [Wolpe & Lazarus, 1966, p. 143].

Only a few studies that have used this procedure have been published. For example, Boyd (1980) used this method with a 16-year-old "school phobic" male who was mildly retarded. After two weeks of therapy, the boy was able to attend school for the full day and, in fact, finished the school year with no recurrence of the school phobia. He did, however, miss a few days occasionally. Jackson and King (1981) used this procedure successfully with a 5½-year-old boy who was afraid of the dark. The hero image that the boy chose in this case was the fictional character, Batman, and during treatment the boy was asked to imagine that he and Batman had joined forces and that he was a special agent. In addition, Lazarus and Abramovitz (1962) report in a series of case/descriptive studies the successful use of the procedure with a dog phobic 14 year old, a 10 year old who was afraid of the dark, and an 8 year old who was enuretic and afraid of going to school. In each case, the procedural steps outlined above were followed to effect a reduction in each child's fears. Although this approach is quite innovative and has some clinical support, well-controlled research has not yet been published to support its effectiveness.

Contact Desensitization.   Developed by Ritter (1968, 1969 a, b), this method has been used with both children and adults and combines elements of desensitization and modeling approaches. The desensitization process is carried out by exposing the child to each step on the fear hierarchy only after each step has first been demonstrated/modeled by the therapist. Upon modeling a particular step, the therapist helps the child perform that step, touching the child to help guide him/her, encouraging the child with various motivating statements, and praising the child for making progress. The therapist then gradually removes his/her prompts until the child can perform each step alone. In summary, this procedure consists of three major components: modeling the desired behavior, use of physical and verbal prompts, and gradual withdrawal of therapist assistance/contact. Rimm and Masters (1974) and Morris (1976) have suggested a fourth component of this procedure—the therapist's presence/relationship with the client—although the relative contribution of one aspect of this factor (therapist warmth) in contact desensitization treatment with adult acrophobic persons has been questioned by Morris and Magrath (1979). An example of a hierarchy used with children who were afraid to enter a swimming pool is presented in Table 4.6. Each step was first performed fearlessly by the therapist/experimenter, followed by the therapist physically guiding the children through the steps and encouraging and praising them. As each child practiced a particular step, the therapist's prompts were gradually withdrawn until s/he could perform that step without assistance.

In terms of supportive research, Ritter (1968) assigned 44 snake avoidant children to one of three groups: contact desensitization, live modeling, and a no-treatment control condition. The children in the two treatment groups received two 35-minute small group sessions. The results showed that both treatment conditions were superior to the no-treatment group on a behavior avoidance test, and that the children in the contact desensitization group showed more improvement than the children in the modeling group. In a second study with snake avoidant children, Ritter (1969) found that contact desensitization was superior to a contact desensitization treatment without a touch condition. Murphy and Bootzin (1973) discovered that the active versus passive participation of children in contact desensitization did not seem to matter. That is, whether the children in the experiment approached the feared snake in the standard contact desensitization manner (active condition) or the experimenter/therapist gradually approached the children with the snake (passive condition) did not influence the outcome of the study. Both treatment conditions were superior to the no-treatment control condition.

Table 4.6. Hierarchy for Children Afraid to Enter a Swimming Pool

1. Let's begin by walking into the pool room to the white marker (one-quarter of the way to the pool).
2. Walk to the yellow marker on the floor (half of the way).
3. Walk to the red marker on the floor (three-quarters of the way).
4. Walk to the green marker by the edge of the pool.
5. Sit down right there (by the edge of the pool).
6. Let's see you put your feet in the water, while I slowly count to 9. 1 . . . 2 . . . 3
7. . . . 4 . . . 5 . . . 6
8. . . . 7 . . . 8 . . . 9
9. Get up and walk into the water to the red marker and stay there until I count to 6. 1 . . . 2 . . . 3
10. . . . 4 . . . 5 . . . 6
11. Walk to the green marker (halfway down ramp) and stay there until I count to 6. 1 . . . 2 . . . 3
12. . . . 4 . . . 5 . . . 6
13. Walk to the yellow marker (bottom of ramp: 2'6" deep) and stay there until I count to 9. You can hold onto the edge. 1 . . . 2 . . . 3
14. . . . 4 . . . 5 . . . 6
15. . . . 7 . . . 8 . . . 9
16. Let's see if you can stand there without holding on (only if person held on in previous step).
17. Walk out to the red marker (3' from edge) and then come back to me.
18. Splash some water on yourself; hold on to edge if you like.
19. Do that without holding on (only if person held on in previous step).
20. Splash some water on your face; you may hold on to the edge if you like.
21. Do that without holding on (only if person held on in previous step).
22. Squat down and blow some bubbles in the water. You can hold on if you like.
23. Blow bubbles without holding on (only if person held on in previous step).
24. Put you whole face in the water. You may hold on if you like.
25. Do that again without holding on (only if person held on in previous step).
26. Put your whole body under water. You can hold on if you like.
27. Do that again without holding on (only if person held on in previous step).
28. Walk out in the water up to your chin (if pool depth permits).
29. Hold onto the kickboard and put your face in the water.
30. Hold onto the kickboard and take one foot off the ground.
31. Hold onto the kickboard and take both feet off the ground.
32. Put your face in the water again and take your feet off the bottom.
33. Let's go down to the deep end of the pool. Sit on the edge and put your feet in the water.
34. O.K. Now climb down the ladder.
35. Now hold onto the edge right here by the green marker.
36. While still holding on, put your whole body under water.
37. Hold onto the kickboard.
38. While still holding on put your face in the water.
39. Do that again, but now put your whole head under water.
40. O.K. Now climb out of the pool and come over to the blue marker. Jump in the water right here (at pool depth of 3'6" or 5' depending on person's height).

Source: Morris, R. J. *Behavior modification with children: A systematic guide*. Cambridge, Mass.: Winthrop, 1976. Reprinted with permission.

Morris and Dolker (in press) studied the relative contribution of various components of contact desensitization with snake avoidant 4- and 5-year-old children. Specifically, they assigned children to one of five experimental conditions: contact desensitization, contact desensitization without therapist touch, verbal input (information about snake) plus therapist modeling, verbal input alone, and no treatment control. The results showed that all groups improved significantly from pretest to posttest on the behavior avoidance test. In addition, contact desensitization was found to be as effective in reducing childrens' avoidance behavior as contact desensitization without therapist touch, and both groups were found to be significantly more effective than the no-treatment control condition. No other significant differences were found. The finding regarding the apparently noncritical contribution of therapist touch to contact desensitization is in contradiction to Ritter's (1969) study. Her research, however, was conducted within a group procedure with adult acrophobic persons. The finding regarding the apparent practice effect shown by subjects in all five conditions from pretest to posttest also supports other studies (e.g., Lewis, 1974; Murphy & Bootzin, 1973).

Self-control Desensitization.   The last variation to be discussed is self-control desensitization (Goldfried, 1971; Meichenbaum, 1974, 1980). In this approach the desensitization procedure is construed as training the client in coping skills, i.e., desensitization treatment is viewed as teaching the client to cope with anxiety. Clients are told, for example, to apply relaxation training whenever they become aware of an increase in their feelings of anxiety and tension. During the desensitization proper phase they are also encouraged to continue imagining a scene which produces anxiety and to "relax away" the anxiety and/or to imagine themselves becoming fearful and then seeing themselves coping with the anxiety and tenseness that they feel. This variation is based on the view that clients will not always be in a position where they can readily leave a fearful and tension arousing situation and that they must learn to cope with the situation on their own. Rehearsal for this possibility, therefore, should take place in therapy. In this regard, it is not important for the anxiety hierarchy to be theme-oriented as in standard systematic desensitization (Goldfried & Goldfried, 1977). The hierarchy need only be composed of situations arousing increasing amounts of anxiety, independent of theme. The following rationale for clients has been suggested by Goldfried (1971):

There are various situations where, on the basis of your past experience, you have learned to react by becoming tense (anxious, nervous, fearful). What I plan to do is help you to learn how to cope with these situations more successfully, so that they do not make you as upset. This will be done by taking note of a number of those situations which upset you to varying degrees, and then having you learn to cope with the less stressful situations before moving on to the more difficult ones. Part of the treatment involves learning how to relax, so that in situations where you feel yourself getting nervous you will be better able to eliminate this tenseness. Learning to relax is much like learning any other skill. When a person learns to drive, he initially has difficulty in coordinating everything, and often finds himself very much aware of what he is doing. With more and more practice, however, the procedures involved in driving become easier and more automatic. You may find the same thing occurring to you when you try to relax in those situations where you feel yourself starting to become tense. You will find that as you persist, however, it will become easier and easier [p. 231].

In terms of corroborating research, there is a paucity of literature which supports this approach with children (e.g., Bornstein & Knapp, 1981; Di Nardo & Di Nardo, 1981). Bornstein and Knapp (1981), for example, used this procedure with a 12-year-old boy who had fears of separation, travel, and illness. Treatment effects were assessed using a multiple baseline design across these fears. The authors report that the child's fear-related verbal comments, as well as the ratings on the *Fear Survey Schedule*, for each fear showed "marked reductions" following treatment. In addition, these changes were maintained at the one-year follow-up period. It should be noted, however, that no behavioral avoidance observations or physiological measures were taken on the child. Although Bornstein and Knapp (1981) conclude that their findings provide "experimental support for the clinical merit of self-control desensitization" (p. 281), our position is that such findings are highly speculative in terms of providing such "experimental support," especially given the lack of behavioral observations in the natural environment and the absence of physiological measures (see Chapter 6).

Commentary.   From this review of the variations in the use of systematic desensitization it becomes quite apparent that the one procedure which has the most controlled research to support its effectiveness is contact desensitization. Interestingly, however, this procedure is also the *only* method discussed in this section which has the least number of clinical/descriptive case studies to support its efficacy. It would therefore seem reasonable to state that additional research with long-term follow-up is needed on contact desensitization therapy with clinically-relevant fears and phobias before any clear statement can be made about its external validity.

FLOODING THERAPIES

Like systematic desensitization, flooding fear reduction methods make use of the imaginal presentation of anxiety-provoking material. Unlike systematic desensitization, however, these methods from the very beginning have the child imagine a very fearful and threatening scene. In addition, the fearful scene is not presented for a short period of time while the child is relaxed; rather, the scene is presented for a prolonged period without having the child undergo any previous relaxation training. The purpose, therefore, of these methods is to produce a frightening imaginal experience in the child of such magnitude that it will actually result in a reduction in his/her fear of a particular event, object, or situation, rather than heighten it. Two major types of flooding therapy have been discussed in the literature: implosive therapy and flooding. These two procedures have more in common than noticeable differences.

Implosive Therapy

Developed by Thomas G. Stampfl and associates (Stampfl, 1961; Stampfl & Levis, 1967), this method utilizes principles from both learning theory and psychodynamic theory. Though Stampfl maintains that fears and their associated anxiety are learned, he does not assume that such fears can be most effectively reduced by a counterconditioning approach. Rather, he believes that a person can best unlearn a fear by using a procedure based on an *extinction model*. Here, extinction refers to the gradual reduction in the occurrence of an anxiety response as a result of the continuous presentation of the fear producing stimulus in the absence of the reinforcement which perpetuates the fear. In therapy, this extinction process is accomplished by having the therapist "represent, reinstate, or symbolically reproduce the stimuli (cues) to which the anxiety response has been conditioned" without presenting the concomitant reinforcement which maintains the response (Stampfl & Levis, 1967, p. 499).[8]

Development of the Avoidance Serial Cue Hierarchy

From information obtained during the initial intake assessment, the therapist develops hypotheses concerning the important cues in the child's fear. The therapist also develops these hypotheses from interviews with the child's parents and, when it seems appropriate, from the child's teacher(s) and principal (Ollendick & Gruen, 1972; Smith & Sharpe, 1970). In many cases, the hypothesized cues that are contributing to the child's fear or phobia are situational events in his/her life that can be readily identified. For example, in the case of a child who is "school phobic," the situational events may be the sight of the child's school building, teacher(s), and classmates, particular noises in school, being called on in class to answer a question, or having people comment on the child's appearance and/or athletic ability.

The remaining cues are formulated by the therapist and are based on psychodynamic theory and on the therapist's knowledge of common reactions by children who have similar problems. They are derived from the child's nonverbal behavior and comments by his/her parents, school authorities, and others, and represent those psychodynamic areas which the therapist believes are relevant to the child's fear. According to Stampfl and Levis (1967), these cues are usually related to themes of aggression and hostility, oral and anal activity, sexual activity, punishment, rejection, bodily injury, loss of impulse control, and guilt. They describe four of the hypothesized dynamic cues in the following manner:

Aggression. Scenes presented in this area usually center around the expression of anger, hostility, and aggression by the patient toward parental, sibling, spouse, or other significant figures in his life. Various degrees of bodily injury are described including complete body mutilation and death of the victim.

Punishment. The patient is instructed to visualize himself as the recipient of the anger, hostility, and aggression of the various significant individuals in his life. The punishment inflicted in the scene is frequently a result of the patient's engaging in some forbidden act.

Sexual material. In this area a wide variety of hypothesized cues related to sex are presented. For example, primal and Oedipal scenes and scenes of castration, fellatio, and homosexuality are presented.

Loss of Control. Scenes are presented where the patient is encouraged to imagine himself losing impulse control to such an extent that he acts out avoided sexual or aggressive impulses. These scenes usually are followed by scenes where the individual is directed to visualize himself hospitalized for the rest of his life in a back ward of a mental hospital as a result of his loss of impulse control. This area is tapped primarily with patients who express fear of "becoming insane" or concern about being hopeless and incurable. [From Stampfl, T. G., and Levis, D. J. Essentials of implosive therapy: A learning-based-psychodynamic behavioral therapy. *Journal of Abnormal Psychology,* 1967, **72**, 501. Reprinted by permission.]

Those cues which are lowest on the hierarchy are assumed to be the situations and events which the child can associate with his/her fear. The highest cues are those internal dynamic cues that the therapist believes are closely associated with the child's basic psychological problem. The particular dynamic themes emphasized in the hierarchy will depend on the child's problem and the information obtained in the initial assessment.

The hierarchy scenes are developed by the therapist after the initial assessment is completed. They are typically not developed jointly by the client and the therapist, as in systematic desensitization. Furthermore, the hierarchy is quite different from the one developed in systematic desensitization. For example, the Avoidance Serial Cue Hierarchy only contains items which are thought to be capable of producing a maximum level of anxiety in the client. This is not the case for the desensitization hierarchy. The latter hierarchy is developed for a different reason—to proceed gradually up the hierarchy in order to minimize the possibility that the client will experience any anxiety. The Avoidance Serial Cue Hierarchy on the other hand starts with items that produce anxiety in the person and proceeds from external stimuli that evoke anxiety to hypothesized internal stimuli which also produce maximum levels of anxiety.

An example of this type of hierarchy for an 8-year-old boy whose main pervasive fear was of bleeding to death from bodily injury is presented below.

> You are alone walking through a forest going to a lake to fish and you hear weird noises and see strange things. . . . The wind begins blowing very hard and you trip and hit your head on a rock. . . . When you get up, blood trickles down your forehead into your eyes, nose, and mouth. . . . You feel dizzy and lost. You cry and no one is there to help you. You feel all alone and the blood continues to trickle. . . . You fall down again and when you open your eyes you see brown, hairy rats all around you. There are hundreds of them and they are coming after you . . . to eat you. . . . They begin nibbling at your feet, biting your toes, and pulling them off. They are scratching and showing their teeth. It is getting very dark now and it is raining. . . . Now they are over your whole body, running across it, and biting you all over. Blood runs from all parts of your body and you hear the thunder and there is lightning. . . . They pierce your neck. You wish someone would come, even an ambulance, but it doesn't. You scream and a big, hairy rat jumps in your mouth. You feel him biting your tongue and scratching you. . . . Finally, the rats that feed on your blood grow and become man-size. They tear off your arms and just keep attacking you. They tear out your eyes and you can't get away from them [Ollendick & Gruen, 1972, p. 391].

Implosive Therapy Proper

After the hierarchy has been developed, the therapist describes implosive therapy to the child and his/her parents.[9] The child is told that a number of scenes will be presented and that every effort should be made to become "lost" in the scenes, vividly imagining them to the fullest extent possible as if "really there." The child is also encouraged to "live" the scenes with genuine emotion and feeling. The goal, therefore, of this phase of implosive therapy is for the person "to reproduce in the absence of physical pain, as good as an approximation as possible, the sights, sounds, and tactual experiences originally present in the primary . . ." situation in which the fear was learned (Stampfl & Levis, 1968, p. 33).

The person undergoing implosive therapy is neither asked to accept the accuracy of what is imagined nor to agree that the scenes are representative of his/her fear. The scenes are presented by the therapist and elaborated on in vivid detail. Often the scenes are also presented in a dramatic fashion. According to Stampfl and Levis (1967):

An attempt is made by the therapist to attain a maximal level of anxiety evocation from the patient. When a high level of anxiety is achieved, the patient is held on this level until some sign of spontaneous reduction in the anxiety-inducing value of the cues appears . . . the process is repeated, and again, at the first sign of spontaneous reduction of fear, new variations are introduced to elicit an intense anxiety response. This procedure is repeated until a significant diminution in anxiety has resulted [p. 500].

One way of determining if the scenes are producing anxiety to observe if the child is flushing, sweating, grimacing, moving his/her head from side to side, or increasing motoric activity in the chair. In addition, both Ollendick and Gruen (1972) and Smith and Sharpe (1970) suggest that the child be asked how he/she is feeling while a particular scene is being presented.

The implosion procedure is continued for 30-40 minutes per session. The person is encouraged to practice imagining the implosive scenes at home about once a day. This practice not only extends treatment outside the therapist's office, and therefore aids generalization, it also helps the child realize that fears can be effectively dealt with by using implosive therapy.

Flooding

Flooding therapy is a variant of implosive therapy. Like implosive therapy, it involves the prolonged exposure through imagination of an intensive fearful situation. The major difference between these two methods is typically in the type of scenes to which people are exposed. Instead of exposing children to horrifying scenes in which certain aversive consequences occur (e.g., eating flesh, death, destruction, etc.), scenes are described in which the feared external stimuli are presented for an extended period of time.[10] An example of a flooding scene is the following:

While studying at your desk in the laboratory you suddenly become aware of a large rat crawling up your leg. You jump up and try to shake it off, but it runs up your side . . . across your face . . . into your hair and is caught there. In an attempt to get loose, its tail falls down onto your face and touches your lips. You try to get him off your head, but you fail . . . etc. [Adapted from Rachman, 1966, p. 3].

Thus, psychodynamic cues and/or interpretations are not used in the formulation of the scenes; rather, the therapist uses only the external cues and vividly describes the scenes in a way similar to implosive therapy. Scenes are presented for about the same period of time as in implosive therapy, and an attempt is also made to maintain the person's anxiety arousal at a maximum level throughout the session.

An interesting alternative to imaginal flooding is *in vivo* flooding (e.g., Kandel, Ayllon, & Rosenbaum, 1977; Yule, Sacks, & Hersov, 1974). Here the child is systematically exposed to an overexaggerated version of the feared object or event. For example, Yule et al. (1974) placed a 9-year-old boy with a noise phobia (specifically, the noise of the bursting of balloons) in a small room filled with 50 balloons. The therapist began popping some of the balloons, and the child did the same thing. In the next session, the child was surrounded by 100–150 balloons and encouraged to pop them with prompting by the therapist. After two sessions there were no signs of a balloon phobia, and at a 25 month follow-up period there was no indication of any recurrence of the phobia.

Additional Considerations

With regard to implosive therapy, Stampfl and Levis (1967) state that "the more accurate the hypothesized cues and the more realistically they are presented the greater the extinction effect . . . will be" (p. 499). This statement suggests that the therapist should be quite knowledgeable in psychodynamic theory, especially psychoanalytic theory. If not, the therapist should probably refrain from using this procedure and instead consider using the flooding method or some other intervention procedure. Another issue regarding implosive therapy is Gelfand's (1978) concern that many clinicians would be reluctant to expose young children to this type of stress-enhancing procedure "if effective, alternative treatment methods are available" (p. 338). In addition, she notes that there is the risk that the treatment setting will be so aversive that the child will refuse to cooperate or to return for subsequent sessions. Some writers (e.g., Marshall, Gauthier, Christie, Currie, & Gordon, 1977; Redd, Porterfield, & Anderson, 1979) have even suggested that imaginal exposure to horrifying situations may, under certain conditions, strengthen a person's fear. It is our contention, therefore, that flooding therapies should be used with caution by the therapist. The therapist needs to be sensitive to the person receiving treatment and the person needs to have sufficient trust and confidence in the therapist so that he/she associates the anxiety-provoking experience with the feared object or event and not with the therapist (Ullman & Krasner, 1969, 1975). The therapist must also be capable of dealing with a child who might have a very negative experience to the anxiety-provoking scenes that are presented.

Another consideration has to do with those factors that contribute to the effectiveness of flooding therapies with children. We are not aware of any published research that has systematically investigated such client factors as: age of child receiving treatment, child's level of visual imagery, his/her ability to follow instructions, and the child's level of acquiescence and threshold for fatigue. With regard to the age factor, no imaginal flooding or implosive therapy study has been published with children under seven years of age; however, *in vivo* flooding studies have been reported with children as young as four years of age.

Since imagery is such an important factor in imaginal flooding therapies, it would seem that research needs to be conducted on what level of visual imagery is needed by children in order to undergo an imaginal flooding therapy procedure.[11] As in the case of systematic desensitization, we suggest that the therapist conduct an informal or formal imagery test during the hierarchy construction phase or following the interview on those children for whom implosive therapy or imaginal flooding is planned. The same imagery assessment procedures discussed for systematic desensitization (pp. 144–147) could also be used for these therapies, or the therapist may wish to construct his/her own assessment instrument which would be more consistent with the nature of the scenes presented in these therapies. For example, Levis (1980) suggests that the therapist set aside approximately 20 minutes at the end of the intake interview "to train the client in imagining 'neutral' scenes." The purpose of this training, according to Levis (1980) is "to establish a crude baseline for the ability of the client to imagine various stimuli and to establish the therapist as the essential director of the scenes" (p. 110). The neutral scenes may be walking on a street, watching television, or eating a meal, with the client being asked to focus on details in the scenes. In addition, the therapist may need to examine the level at which a child can follow instructions, as well as his/her ability to transfer these instructions into rather complex and involved imagery. Again, the types of tests discussed in this regard in the systematic desensitization section of this chapter may be of assistance to the therapist.

With respect to acquiescence and fatigue, it would seem important for the therapist to be able to differentiate these two factors from a child's demonstration of, for example, "a significant diminution in anxiety" as a result of the implosive therapy procedure. As in the case of systematic desensitization, little or no research has been published on the relative contribution of these factors to the successful outcome of the flooding therapies. It may therefore be helpful for the therapist to discuss with the child following a particular session how the child felt during the session—for example, whether it was possible to "really experience" the various aspects of the scene or whether he/she felt tense and fearful or just tired and was waiting for the scene to stop. As an alternative, the therapist may wish to incorporate Smith and Sharpe's (1970) procedure during each session, where the child is asked to describe some aspect of the scene and to describe his/her feelings at that point in time. This procedure not only provides the therapist with information concerning fatigue and the desire to do what the child considers to be socially desirable, but it may also aid the child in focusing on the presented scene.

With respect to therapist or setting variables, little information has been published on these topics. Levis (1980), however, reports that implosive therapy requires that the therapist have extensive knowledge in both learning theory and psychodynamic theory, "as well as being comfortable with the anxiety generated from scene presentations" (p. 146). In addition, he states:

> Experience indicates the technique can be successfully used by a wide variety of different therapeutic personalities. Individuals who are sensitive and empathetic clinicians seem to make the best implosive therapists [Levis, 1980, p. 146].

In light of the paucity of research on therapist and setting variables, we feel that these flooding therapies should only be conducted within the framework of a sound client-therapist relationship, where the client has developed trust and confidence in the therapist's ability to help the client.

Finally, for both implosive therapy as well as imaginal and *in vivo* flooding, it is often helpful for the client to present an anxiety-provoking scene to himself/herself or engage in the feared activity *after* these have been presented a few times by the therapist. Under the therapist's supervision, the child is encouraged to act out the scene or *in vivo* experience fully. In addition, sometimes the client will mention to the therapist additional situations or events that produce his/her fear. Wherever possible, these should be noted by the therapist and included in the next therapy session.

Supportive Research

As in the case of the desensitization literature, although a fair amount of research has been published on the effectiveness of flooding therapies with adult phobics, little has been published on the effectiveness of these procedures with children (e.g., Handler, 1972; Hersen, 1968; Kandel et al., 1977; Ollendick & Gruen, 1972; Smith & Sharpe, 1970; Yule et al., 1974), and most of the studies published have been uncontrolled and descriptive case studies. For example, Smith and Sharpe (1970) used implosive therapy to treat a 13-year-old boy who was "school phobic." Therapy lasted six consecutive days during which time the child was asked to imagine various anxiety-arousing scenes regarding school attendance. The results showed that after the first session, the child was able to attend his math class with moderate anxiety, by the end of the fourth session he returned to school full time with some anxiety, and by the end of the fifth and sixth sessions, he felt positive about school and reported no anxiety. At the 13-week follow-up period he continued his regular school attendance. Teachers reported that he displayed a decreased achievement anxiety, increased relaxation, and decreased compulsivity. Following Smith and Sharpe's (1970) approach, Ollendick and Gruen

(1972) used this procedure to treat an 8-year-old boy who exhibited "an excessive and persistent phobia of bodily injury." his fear was expressed through sleepless nights, hives, and asthmatic bronchitis. Following two therapy sessions, the number of sleepless nights dropped down appreciably to two per week. In addition, no recurrence of his hives or bronchitis was reported at the six-month follow-up period, and he had not experienced any sleepless nights for two consecutive months. Handler (1972) and Hersen (1968) also report in descriptive case studies the successful use of implosive therapy.

With respect to flooding, Yule et al. (1974) successfully applied *in vivo* flooding to a nine-year-old boy who had a noise phobia (specifically the bursting of balloons). An interesting aspect of this case was that previous to this treatment Yule et al. were able to successfully reduce all other aspects of the child's noise phobia with *in vivo* desensitization, except for that aspect having to do with balloons bursting. This set of circumstances then necessitated the use of the flooding procedure described earlier. Kandel et al. (1977) also report successfully using *in vivo* flooding with two children who had extreme social withdrawal. Interestingly, one child was four years of age and diagnosed as having minimal brain disorder (MBD) with hyperactivity and emotional problems, and the other child was eight years old and diagnosed as autistic and MBD. The procedure showed that both children could learn how to interact and respond to others following treatment in their natural school environment. Few additional studies have been published on the use of flooding with children.

SUMMARY AND CONCLUSIONS

Two major fear reduction methods have been discussed in this chapter: systematic desensitization and flooding therapies. In addition, variants of each of these therapies have been reviewed, namely, group systematic desensitization, *in vivo* desensitization, automated and self-directed desensitization, emotive imagery, contact desensitization, self-control desensitization, and *in vivo* flooding. Research supporting the relative effectiveness of all of these procedures has also been reviewed.

Without doubt, the most heavily researched fear reduction method discussed in this chapter involves systematic desensitization treatment. The majority of studies, however, are of the descriptive or uncontrolled case study variety, limiting any conclusions which can be drawn regarding the relative effectiveness of this treatment. On the other hand, a variation of this procedure, called contact desensitization, appears to have a fair amount of empirical support in the literature. In many studies it has been shown to be very effective in reducing children's fears, although the number of clinical fears in which this procedure has been used is somewhat limited.

Given the paucity of controlled research on the flooding therapies, as well as only a few case studies, there presently is very limited empirical support for the use of these fear reduction methods with children. It is clear that extensive research is necessary on this form of treatment before any definitive statement can be made on its relative effectiveness. Discussion of the type of research that may be necessary is discussed in Chapter 6.

Major empirical questions still remain for both the desensitization and flooding therapies. Researchers, for example, have not even approached answering the question, "Which fear reduction method should be used, under what conditions, for which age group, and for which type of fear?" In order to answer this question, there is a need for outcome research on these therapies and studies designed to identify the critical components of each therapy, as well as research which investigates the relative contribution of therapist, client, and setting variables.

NOTES

1. Adapted from Paul (1966).
2. Since therapists differ in regard to some of the details of systematic desensitization, what is described in this section is the manner in which one of us (RJM) conducts this therapy with children.
3. The child should not be encouraged to bend his neck either all the way back or forward.
4. Some children cannot relax because they cannot physically perform many of the steps in the relaxation program due to a diagnosed (or, in some cases, undiagnosed) physical disability or auditory-based learning difficulty (i.e., the child has difficulty following instructions presented orally). Wherever possible, the therapist should adapt the relaxation procedure to a child's disability (see, for example, Cautela & Groden, 1978), but also recognize that there is a paucity of literature supporting or questioning the use of relaxation training in systematic desensitization with physical or learning handicaps (e.g., Ince, 1976).
5. Throughout this chapter the unquoted hierarchies have been modified to protect the anonymity of the children involved.
6. In some cases, it might be appropriate for the therapist to review the initial hierarchy with both the child and his/her parents. The decision to do this should be based on such factors as the child's age, level of verbal skills, nature of his/her relationship with the parents, and the parents' level of knowledge and involvement with the child's fear.
7. This imagery test is based on Suckerman (1977).
8. In this statement, Stampfl and Levis (1967) are using the term "reinforcement" in the classical conditioning sense of the word, i.e., the procedure of following a conditioned stimulus (CS) with an unconditioned stimulus (UCS).
9. The therapist may find it helpful to not only explain the treatment to parents but

also the rationale underlying the procedure. Smith and Sharpe (1970) also report providing parents with reading material concerning this treatment approach.

10. This distinction between flooding and implosive therapy has been questioned by Levis (1974).

11. According to Levis (1980), research has not yet been conducted on whether implosive therapy is less effective with persons who have difficulty imagining scenes. He states: "Clinically, the problem is handled by simply asking the client to do the best they can. . . . If imagery is still reported to be unclear [after extra time is taken by the therapist to develop scenes which include background cues and, at least initially, actual events the client can recall], proceed with the scene without worrying about the matter" [Levis, 1980, p. 144].

CHAPTER 5

Contingency Management, Modeling, and Self-Control Therapies

As noted in Chapter 4, there has been a rapid proliferation of research articles on the application of fear reduction methods derived from theories of learning (see, for example, reviews by Gelfand, 1978; Graziano et al., 1979; Hatzenbuehler & Schroeder, 1978; Ollendick, 1979; Richards & Siegel, 1978). These methods together with other learning theory-based intervention procedures for the treatment of maladaptive behavior(s) in children and adults generally follow the assumptions of the behavioral position (see Chapter 1) In the previous chapter, we discussed the application of systematic desensitization and the flooding therapies for reducing fears in children. In this chapter, we will discuss three additional behavioral methods of fear reduction: contingency management, modeling, and self-control procedures. We will also review various uncontrolled and/or descriptive case studies that have used these procedures as well as controlled experiments.

CONTINGENCY MANAGEMENT

The systematic use of contingency management procedures for the reduction of fears and phobias in children has its origins in the writing of Ivan Pavlov (e.g., Pavlov, 1927), B. F. Skinner (e.g., Skinner, 1938, 1953, 1961, 1969) and John B. Watson (e.g., Watson, 1913, 1919; Watson & Rayner, 1920). Each stressed the importance of the causal relationship between stimuli and behavior. In this section, we describe the most frequently used contingency management procedures for treating children's fears, phobias, and related problems. Specifically, the following methods are discussed: positive reinforcement, shaping, extinction, and stimulus fading.

Positive Reinforcement

Positive reinforcement is typically defined as an event or activity that immediately follows a behavior and results in an increase in the frequency of performance of that behavior.[1] Thus, a positive reinforcer is something that *follows* a particular behavior and *strengthens* the number of times it occurs. A reinforcer is therefore defined here in terms of its effects on a child's approach behavior toward the feared stimulus.

Positive reinforcement has been used both alone and in combination with other behavior therapy procedures in reducing various fears and fear-related behaviors in children. For example, Williamson, Jewell, Sanders, Haney, and White (1977) used reinforcement to treat the reluctant speech of two young boys. Although each child spoke to family members, they each avoided speaking to anyone outside the home, except for one child who would talk to adults in whispers. Williamson et al. used a token reinforcement system for each child. For one child, the tokens were used contingent on the frequency of verbalizations toward peers during recess at school. The reinforcers that the child could exchange for the tokens included a 45-minute class party (for 45 verbalizations during recess) and various privileges (such as being first in the lunch line). The program for the second child was carried out at his home and in the clinic. He received tokens for either prompted or spontaneous speech in either setting with his brother or a "stranger" (cohort therapist). In each of the cases which Williamson et al. presented, the speech of the children increased and was maintained for the first child at a one-year follow-up and for the second child at a two-month follow-up.

In a case study, Sluckin and Jehu (1969) used reinforcement to treat a selectively mute four-year, eleven-month girl who was extremely fearful of strangers. In the treatment program, a psychiatric social worker first consulted with the mother on the development of the intervention plan. The child was seen in the home by the social worker, where a procedure using tangible reinforcement was employed. Gradually, the mother was faded out of the home while the child's talking was reinforced. The child eventually began to speak to adults and children. Other cases have also been reported of the successful use of positive reinforcement in the reduction of selective mutism in children (e.g., Austad, 1979; Bauermeister & Jemail, 1975; Bednar, 1974; Reid, Hawkins, Keutzer, McNeal, Phelps, Reid & Meas, 1967). These studies are only illustrative of the literature on this behavior. A more comprehensive review of this literature can be found in Kratochwill (1981).

Social withdrawal is another behavior that has been treated successfully using positive reinforcement.[2] For example, Kirby and Toler (1970) report a case study where reinforcement was used to decrease the isolated behavior of a five-year-old preschool boy. He was reinforced by his teacher after he passed out candy to his classmates. The results showed that he spent a larger percentage of his time with his classmates during the reinforcement period, and that the number of activities he initiated with other children rose steadily. Allen, Hart, Buell, Harris, and Wolf (1964) also concluded that the systematic use of social reinforcement (teacher attention) with a four-year-old preschool girl was sufficient for the development and maintenance of interactive play with her peers.

Similarly, Simkins (1971) was able to increase the level of peer interaction of eight girls using positive reinforcement. Specifically, he assigned points to the girls contingent on their interacting with their peers. He found that when points were combined with social reinforcement (e.g., praise and attention), special incentive, and instructions, there was a significantly larger increase in the duration of peer interaction than when only the point system was used. Strain and Timm (1974), however, did find that contingent adult attention was effective in increasing the level of social interaction in an emotionally disturbed child, and that this method produced higher rates of positive interactions by the child than by reinforcing peers for interacting with the child. The successful use of positive reinforcement in modifying the level of social interaction and prosocial behavior in children has also been reported, for example, by Hart, Reynolds, Baer, Brawley and Harris (1968) and Romanczyk, Diament, Goren, Trunell and Harris (1975). These studies are again only illustrative of the literature on this behavior. A more comprehensive review of this literature can be found in Conger and Keane (1981).

Reinforcement was also used in an experiment by Leitenberg and Callahan (1973) to reduce children's darkness fears. Fourteen children were each assigned to the experimental treatment and control (pretest and posttest only) conditions with four females and three males in each group. The average age for the experimental group was six years and for the control group was five years, four months. The experimental group received a treatment procedure which Leitenberg called "reinforced practice." This procedure involved providing the children in the experimental group with feedback regarding the exact time they spent in the darkened room plus praise, reinforcement, repeated practice during each session and instructions. The results showed that the reinforced practice procedure produced significant improvement over the control condition in the length of time that the children remained in both the partially and completely darkened test rooms.

A reinforcement contingency contracting system was used by Vaal (1973) to reduce the "school phobia" of a 13-year-old boy who was absent from school on 94% of the school days over the first six months of the school year. After a meeting with the child, school personnel, and his parents, the following criterion/target behaviors were established for him as part of his contingency contract:

(1) coming to school on time without any tantrum behavior;
(2) attending all classes on the schedule. . . .
(3) remaining in school until dismissal time each day [Vaal, 1973, p. 372].

If he met these criteria each day, he was then allowed to engage in various privileges/activities of his choice when he returned home. Some of these activities included: (1) attending a professional basketball game, (2) going bowling on Saturdays, and (3) playing basketball with friends after school. If he did not meet the criteria, these activities were withheld. The contingency contract started on the first school day of the seventh month of the school year and lasted for six weeks. Vaal (1973) reported that for the next three months the boy "did not miss a single day of school . . . he came on time every day, came without any inappropriate tantrum behavior, attended all his classes, and was late for none" (p. 372). Following a two and one-half month summer vacation, and over a four-month period during the subsequent school year, Vaal reported that the boy only missed one and one-half days of school. Vaal (1973) accounts for the child's drastic change in attending school in the following manner:

> The contingency contracting procedures now created a school attendance situation which was more reinforcing to the subject than it was for him to remain at home. A feature of this particular contract was that the reinforcers used were the same privileges which the parents previously had granted the subject regardless of his behavior during the school day. Thus, by simply making existing privileges contingent upon certain behaviors, the subject was returned to the school situation after a 6-month absence [p. 373].

Variations of Positive Reinforcement

Reinforcement has often been used with other contingency management procedures for reducing fears in children. For example, Ayllon, Smith and Rogers (1970) used positive reinforcement, shaping-prompting, and withdrawal of social consequences to reduce the "school phobia" of an eight-year-old girl.[3] After conducting an extensive behavior analysis to determine the contributing factors to the child's school phobia, Ayllon et al. established a five phase treatment procedure. The five treatment phases, including the initial baseline and behavioral assessment periods, are outlined in Table 5.1. The first phase consisted of prompting and shaping the child's school attendance. This was accomplished by having an assistant take the child to school toward the end of the school day and sit near her in the classroom until the school day was over. She was also given candy to distribute to her siblings at the end of school and was encouraged to walk home with them. The amount of time that the child attended school in the afternoon gradually increased and the length of time that the assistant stayed with the child gradually decreased. On the eighth day the child attended school by herself with her siblings, but this voluntary attendance behavior was not maintained the next day or for the next six school days. The second treatment phase was then initiated where the child's mother was asked to leave for work at the same time that the child and her siblings were to leave for school. Ayllon et al. reasoned that this approach might remove any of the mother's possible positive social consequences (reinforcement) for the child not attending school. The procedure did not result in any increase in the child's school attendance.

The third phase of treatment was then begun involving a home-based contingent reinforcement and token economy-like procedure for school attendance combined with the prompting-shaping procedure of phase one (this time involving the mother rather than an assistant). This procedure again resulted in the child attending school with assistance, but it did not contribute to her voluntarily attending school. The fourth phase was therefore instituted where the mother met the child and her siblings at school and provided them with tangible reinforcers and social consequences. The home-based contingent reinforcement and token economy procedure for school attendance was also continued. If the child did not voluntarily go to the school with her siblings and meet her mother, her mother went home and on one occasion "firmly proceeded to take Val by the hand and with hardly any words between them, they rushed back to school," and on another occasion "scolded Val and pushed her out of the house and literally all the way to school" (Ayllon et al., 1970, pp. 134–135). This procedure contributed to the child voluntarily attending school with her siblings.

During the fifth phase of treatment, the mother first discontinued meeting the child and her siblings at school and subsequently withdrew the home-based positive reinforcement program. This fading procedure did not produce any disruption in the child's voluntary school attendance. Her voluntary attendance was also found to be maintained at a six- and nine-month follow-up period.

A second variation involving positive reinforcement is described by Luiselli (1977). He combined reinforcement with a time-out procedure in the treatment of a toilet phobic 15-year-old severely mentally retarded boy. Although the boy was previously completely toilet trained, he began to avoid the use of the bathroom and plugged his ears and hyperventilated whenever the toilet was mentioned to him. Following the baseline period, he received token reinforcement and praise for appropriate use of the toilet and was reinforced for increased approach behavior toward the toilet. The reinforcement he received was gradually changed to increasing intermittent schedules. He was also encouraged to self-record his use of the toilet. In addition to the reinforcement aspects of the treatment procedure, he was also exposed to the use of a 40-minute exclusion time-out procedure whenever he wet his pants.

Table 5.1. Procedural and Behavioral Progression During the Treatment of a School Phobic Child

Temporal Sequence	Procedure	Valerie's Behavior
Baseline observations Day 1–10	Observations taken at home and at the neighbor's apartment where Val spent her day	Valerie stayed at home when siblings left for school. Mother took Val to neighbor's apartment as she left for work.
Behavioral assessment Day 11–13	Assistant showed school materials to Val and prompted academic work.	Val reacted well to books; she colored pictures and copied numbers and letters.
Behavioral assessment Day 13	Assistant invited Val for a car ride after completing academic work at neighbor's apartment.	Val readily accepted car ride and on way back to neighbor's apartment she also accepted hamburger offered her.
Procedure I Days 14–20	Taken by assistant to school. Assistant stayed with her in classroom. Attendance made progressively earlier while assistant's stay in classroom progressively lessens.	Val attended school with assistant. Performed school work. Left school with siblings at closing time.
Day 21	Assistant did not take Val to school.	Val and siblings attended school on their own.
Procedure I Day 22	Val taken by assistant to school.	Val attended school with assistant. Performed school work. Left with siblings at school closing time.
Return to baseline observations Days 23–27	Observations taken at home.	Val stayed at home when siblings left for school. Mother took Val to neighbor's apartment as she left for work
Procedure 2 Day 28–29	Mother left for work when children left for school.	Val stayed at home when children left for school. Mother took her to neighbor's apartment as she left for work.

Procedure 3 Day 40–49	Taken by mother to school. Home-based motivational system.	Val stayed at home when siblings left for school. Followed mother quietly when taken to school.
Procedure 4 Day 50–59	On Day 50, mother left for school before children left home. Home-based motivational system.	Siblings met mother at school door. Val stayed at home.
	After 15 minutes of waiting in school, mother returned home and took Val to school.	Val meekly followed her mother.
	On Day 51, mother left for school before children left home.	Val and siblings met mother at school door.
	On Day 52, mother left for school before children left home.	Siblings met mother at school door. Val stayed at home.
	After 15 minutes of waiting in school, mother returned home and physically hit and dragged Valerie to school.	Valerie cried and pleaded with her mother not to hit her. Cried all the way to school.
	On Day 53–59, mother left for school before children left home.	Val and siblings met mother at school door.
Fading Procedure(s) Day 60–69	Mother discontinued going to school before children. Mother maintained home-based motivational system.	Val and siblings attended school on their own.
Fading Procedure(s) Day 70	Mother discontinued home-based motivational system.	Val and siblings attended school on their own.

Source: Ayllon, T., Smith, D., & Rogers, M. Behavioral management of school phobia. *Journal of Behavior Therapy and Experimental Psychiatry*, 1970, **1**, 125–138. Reprinted with permission.

Results over the 28-week treatment period showed that his frequency of pants wetting per week dropped appreciably over time, from an average of 15.6 incidents per week during baseline to 2.6 times per week during the use of intermittent reinforcement. At the four-month follow-up one incident had been recorded, and at the six-month and one-year follow-up periods, no incidents had been recorded.

Another variation in the use of positive reinforcement has been described by Patterson (1965). He used a doll play situation plus tangible reinforcers (candy) and social reinforcement to reduce the school phobia of a seven-year-old boy. The treatment procedure took place four days per week, 15 minutes per session for 23 sessions. Treatment consisted of the boy being reinforced in the play situation for making fearless verbal statements about the male doll and not being afraid of being separated from his mother. This was also followed up at home by the mother reinforcing the boy for being away from the mother. The content of the play situations involved: the mother leaving the male doll in a doctor's office; having the mother go shopping without the boy doll; having the boy doll involved in various graduated school-related activities while his mother remained at home; and, the boy doll receiving minor injuries while playing with his peers and not being afraid or returning home to be with his mother. An excerpt from the tenth therapy session appears in table 5.2 and illustrates the procedures used throughout the sessions.

By the ninth session, a visiting teacher began to assist the child with his reading and then within a few additional sessions the teacher accompanied him to school. The teacher then gradually left him alone in his classroom for increasing periods of time. Play treatment sessions continued during this time, and his parents were encouraged to praise him for his attendance. The child then chose to ride to school by himself and to stay for one hour. His parents again reinforced this decision, and subsequently "he then announced that he would return to school full time within the week, which he did" (Patterson, 1965, p. 283). At a three-month follow-up, the school reported "dramatic improvement" in his adjustment and "no further evidence of fearfulness."

Patterson concluded that this procedure is an effective therapy package for reducing a child's fears. He added, however, that "there is little doubt" that both the parents and teacher enhanced the generalization of the child's behavior change from the playroom to the natural environment. He further emphasized the importance in this therapy for the therapist to become a secondary reinforcer for the child—to maximize the child's responsiveness.

Another variation in the use of positive reinforcement has been discussed by Lazarus, Davison, and Polefka (1965). They combined the use of positive reinforcement (tokens and social reinforcement) with *in vivo* desensitization

Table 5.2. Excerpt From Patterson's (1965) Tenth Therapy Session With A School Phobic Child

Therapist:	What shall we have Henry do today?
Karl:	Well, we could have him go to school.
Therapist:	Yeah, I think that is a good idea, to have some work on going to school again today. That probably is the hardest thing for him to do. O.K., here he is (picking up the Henry doll). Where is mamma, oh here she is (sets up blocks and furniture). Ah, maybe we had better have Little Henry start off from home; when he does go to school, we won't have him go into the classroom today; he'll just run errands for the principal; no reading or writing this time. So Little Henry is talking to his mother and he says, "Mom, I think I'll go to school for a little while today." What does mom say?
Karl:	O.K.
Therapist:	Is he afraid when he is right there talking to mamma?
Karl:	No. (one M&M)
Therapist:	And so he gets on his bike and says bye-bye-mamma. He stops half way to school. What does he think now that mamma is not there?
Karl:	Ma-amma (laughs).
Therapist:	Yeah, but what does he do? Does he go back or go on to school?
Karl:	Goes to school. (one M&M)
Therapist:	Yeah, that's right he goes to school; Little Henry would go back and look but Big Henry would go on to school . . . and he goes to the principal's office and says, "Hi, Mr. Principal. I thought I would come back to school for a little while. Can I run some errands for you?" Henry gives the note to the teacher, then he is coming back to the principal's office. He stops. What is he thinking about now?
Karl:	Mamma is not there again.
Therapist:	Yeah, he is scaring himself again. Now, does he go back to the principal's office or does he go home?
Karl:	He goes back to the office. (one M&M)
Therapist:	Yeah, that is right, he does. At least Big Henry would do that, Little Henry would get scareder and more scareder; but Big Henry feels pretty good. "I am back Mr. Principal." The principal says, "Why don't you go down to the cafeteria and get a glass of milk. I don't have any more errands for you to run right now." So he goes and is sitting here drinking his milk. What does he think about now? Every time he is alone he thinks about this.
Karl:	Mamma again.
Therapist:	That's right, he always thinks about mamma. Does he go home?
Karl:	No. (one M&M)

Source: Patterson, G. R. A learning theory approach to the treatment of the school phobic child. In L. P. Ullmann & L. Krasner (Eds.), *Case Studies in behavior modification*. New York: Holt, 1965. Reprinted with permission.

and emotive imagery to reduce the school phobia in a nine-year-old boy who had been absent from school for three weeks. A summary of the steps used in this procedure are outlined in Table 5.3. Treatment continued over a four

Table 5.3. Summary of Steps Used in the Therapy Procedure by Lazarus et al. With a School Phobic Child

- On a Sunday afternoon, accompanied by the therapists, he walked from his house to the school. The therapists were able to allay Paul's anxiety by means of distraction and humor, so that his initial exposure was relatively pleasant.
- On the next two days at 8:30 A.M., accompanied by one of the therapists, he walked from his house into the schoolyard. Again, Paul's feelings of anxiety were reduced by means of coaxing, encouragement, relaxation, and the use of "emotive imagery" (i.e., the deliberate picturing of subjectively pleasant images such as Christmas and a visit to Disneyland, while relating them to the school situation). Approximately 15 minutes were spent roaming around the school grounds, after which Paul returned home.
- After school was over for the day, the therapist was able to persuade the boy to enter the classroom and sit down at his desk. Part of the normal school routine was then playfully enacted.
- On the following three mornings, the therapist accompanied the boy into the classroom with the other children. They chatted with the teacher, and left immediately after the opening exercises.
- A week after beginning this program, Paul spent the entire morning in class. The therapist sat in the classroom and smiled approvingly at Paul whenever he interacted with his classmates or the teacher. . . . Two days later when Paul and the therapist arrived at school, the boy lined up with the other children and allowed the therapist to wait for him beside the classroom. . . .
- Thereafter, the therapist sat in the school library adjoining the classroom.
- It was then agreed that the therapist would leave at 2:30 P.M. while Paul remained for the last hour of school.
- On the following day, Paul remained alone at school from 1:45 P.M. until 2:45 P.M. . . . Instead of fetching the boy at his home, the therapist arranged to meet him at the school gate at 8:30 A.M. Paul also agreed to remain alone at school from 10:45 A.M. until noon provided that the therapist return to eat lunch with him. At 1:45 P.M. the therapist left again with the promise that if the boy remained until school ended (3:30 P.M.) he would visit Paul that evening and play the guitar for him.
- After meeting the boy in the mornings, the therapist gradually left him alone at school for progressively longer periods of time. After six days of this procedure, the therapist was able to leave at 10 A.M.
- The boy was assured that the therapist would be in the faculty room until 10 A.M., if needed. Thus, he came to school knowing the therapist was present, but not actually seeing him.
- With Paul's consent the therapist arrived at school shortly after the boy entered the classroom at 8:40 A.M.
- School attendance independent of the therapist's presence was achieved by means of specific rewards (a comic book, and variously colored tokens which would eventually procure a baseball glove) contingent upon his entering school and remaining there alone. He was at liberty to telephone the therapist in the morning if he wanted him at school, in which event he would forfeit his rewards for that day.
- Since the therapist's presence seemed to have at least as much reward value as the comic books and tokens, it was necessary to enlist the mother's cooperation to effect the therapist's final withdrawal.

Table 5.3. (*continued*)

- Approximately 3 weeks later, Paul had accumulated enough tokens to procure his baseball glove. He then agreed with his parents that rewards of this kind were no longer necessary.

Source: Lazarus, A. A., Davison, G. C., & Polefka, D. A. Classical and operant factors in the treatment of school phobia. *Journal of Abnormal Psychology*, 1965, **70**, 225–229. Reprinted with permission.

and one-half-month period, and during this time the boy gradually returned to school with minimal anxiety. Ten months following treatment, the parents reported that the treatment gains were maintained. Lazarus et al. (1965) concluded that the boy's high anxiety during the initial stages of treatment necessitated the use of desensitization procedures to reduce anxiety, but upon reaching a reduced level of anxiety, the authors felt that a contingency management approach was then appropriate.

Kellerman (1980) also reported the use of a variation of positive reinforcement. He worked with three children who had long histories of various forms of night fears. One child was a five-year-old boy with a seven-month history of "nocturnal anxiety" and nightmares; another was an 8-year-old girl with a four-year history of fears related to darkness, sleep, kidnappers, separation, and school; and the third child was a 13-year-old girl with a five-year history of fears related to being alone at night and darkness and who also had nightmares. Kellerman had the five-year-old boy practice being angry at the object of his fear, Dracula, rather than fearful. He also instructed the parents: (1) not to protect him from fear stimuli (e.g., T.V. characters), (2) to reinforce him for appropriate sleep behavior, and (3) to praise him for assertive behavior. Similarly, the 8-year-old girl was instructed to practice being angry at the objects of her night fears, and it was also arranged that she be reinforced for appropriate sleep behavior. Treatment lasted three to four sessions for each child. Kellerman reported that within two weeks following treatment each child's night fear(s) was eliminated. Follow-up for the children ranged from 9–24 months following treatment, and in each case there was no recurrence of any night fears.

Shaping

For various reasons, some children have difficulty approaching a feared stimulus even though they have received positive reinforcement for their approach behavior. In some cases, the reason why they do not respond to positive reinforcement is because the approach behavior, or the series of responses which they emit, is too complex for them to master. The nature of the approach behavior to the feared stimulus involves so many steps that the children are unresponsive to the reinforcement contingency. An example of this situation is described below involving an 11-year-old boy.

> John was referred to a psychologist because he was afraid to leave his home except to go to school. If he had the occasion of being away from his home—with the exception of being at school—he would "become nervous . . . get dizzy . . . be scared," and try very quickly to return home. Since John was very responsive to adult attention and, seemingly enjoyed being with his parents, his parents were instructed to take John for short rides to places and reinforce him verbally for agreeing to go out and be away from the house.

> This procedure continued for 10 days with no noticeable reduction in John's avoidance to leave his house. In fact, John reported that he continued to experience his "nervous and dizzy" feelings on these trips. Attempts to reinforce him for staying at school for a short period of time after school also failed. He also refused to go to sporting events or after-school parties.

In those cases where positive reinforcement of the desired approach behavior is ineffective, the therapist might consider the use of shaping, where the child is taught the desired behavior in successive steps with each step gradually approximating the desired target behavior. For example, instead of reinforcing John, as in the above example, for taking short rides with his parents, the psychologist might reinforce him for approaching the front of the house, then for standing on the porch outside, and so forth, gradually leading to an increase in the time and distance the child is away from his house.

Other than the Ayllon et al. (1970) study discussed earlier, only a few studies have been published using the shaping procedure. For example, Luiselli (1978) used a graduated exposure/shaping procedure with a seven-year-old boy diagnosed as autistic who was afraid to ride a school bus. Initially, the child was familiarized with the bus by having him sit in it with his mother while it was parked at the school. His mother also reinforced him for this behavior. The mother and the therapist then gradually removed themselves from the bus. The child was then reinforced for riding with the mother and therapist on the bus to school. This was then followed by rides with the therapist only and then finally alone. Luiselli reports that the treatment took seven days and that one year later the boy continued to ride the bus alone.

In another study, Tahmisian and McReynolds (1971) used shaping to reduce the "school phobia" (refusal to attend school) of a 13-year-old girl. This case is striking in that the authors report that systematic desensitization was first tried with this girl, but was found ineffective in assisting her to attend school. Tahmisian and McReynolds then brought in her parents to assist in the implementation of the shaping program. The program involved having the parents spend increasing amounts of time walking around school after/before class with the child, and alternating this with having the child walk around school by herself. This gradually led to the child attending her first class alone and finally all classes alone. Within three weeks, the authors report that the child was attending school regularly and that her school attendance was maintained at the four-week follow-up period.

Shaping has also been used with selectively mute children. For example, Rosenbaum and Kellman (1973) successfully treated a third grade mute girl by involving school personnel in various procedures. The program consisted of three phases conducted by the teacher and speech therapist. During Phase I, speech with an adult in a one-to-one setting was established. A shaping procedure was used in two 20-minute sessions each week in which the girl received M&M's and praise for speaking. In Phase II a transfer of speech to the classroom through *in vivo* successive approximation to the classroom environment was accomplished. The teacher and peers gradually entered the individual room in the presence of the girl's speech. Phase III involved expansion of the group by requesting the girl to invite other children from her class to the speech session. After the entire class has been invited (and with concomitant teacher approval for verbal behavior in the classroom), the girl responded aloud when asked a question in front of the entire class. The authors report that approximately two and one-half months following the termination of treatment, the girl was participating fully in all aspects of her classwork. Other cases involving the use of shaping to reduce a child's selective mutism have also been reported by Bednar (1974), Rasbury (1974), and Semenoff, Park, and Smith (1976).

Stimulus Fading

In some instances, a fearful child can perform nonfearful behavior in *selected* settings or under certain conditions, but not in other settings. When this situation occurs, some writers have proposed the use of a *stimulus fading* procedure. Stimulus fading involves teaching the child to perform the non-fearful response in the previous setting(s). This fading process is accomplished by gradually shifting the characteristics of the setting(s). For example, Wulbert, Nyman, Snow and Owen (1973) used stimulus fading to teach a six-year-old selectively mute girl to verbalize to a stranger. She spoke to her parents but not in kindergarten, at Sunday school, or at preschool. In the experimental condition, the child received candy and social praise from her mother for making verbal and motor responses while a stranger/experimenter was slowly faded into the stimulus situation. The graded steps used by the stranger are presented in Table 5.4. Later in the sessions, if responses were made, a time-out of one-minute duration was initiated. In the control condition, the stranger reinforced the same series of verbal and motor responses

Table 5.4. Graded Steps of Stranger's Closeness Used in Stimulus Fading Experiment.

0. Stranger neither visible nor audible
   A. Neither visible nor audible
   B. Not visible but audible over radio. . . .
   C. Not visible but audible over radio and from hall
1. Stranger Visible at door
   A. Visible and audible standing in hall, turned 180° away from Emma [child's name]
   B. Visible and audible standing in doorway, turned 180°
   C. Visible and audible standing inside room, with door closed, turned 180°
   D. Visible and audible inside room, door closed, turned 135°
   E. Visible and audible inside room, door closed, turned 90°
   F. Visible and audible inside room, door closed, turned 45°
   G. Visible and audible facing with dark glasses on
   H. Inside room with door closed, facing, radio off
2. Stranger inside room halfway to chair
3. Stranger inside room standing at chair
4. Stranger inside room sitting in chair
5. Stranger reading questions in unison with person already in stimulus control setting
   A. Inside room reading task items in unison with mother and/or handing cards together
   B. Inside room reading the critical element of the task item alone and/or handing cards together except mother drops hand before Emma takes card
   C. Inside room reading the critical element of task alone, handing cards alone
6. Stranger reading questions alone while person in stimulus control setting remains seated at table
   A. Inside room reading all the directions alone, holding and handing cards
   B. Inside room mother silent, but watching
   C. Inside room mother reading at table
7. Stranger reading questions alone while person in stimulus control setting moves away from the table
   A. Inside room mother reading with chair away from table
   B. Inside room mother reading with chair beside door
   C. Inside room mother in doorway
   D. Inside room mother in hallway
8. Inside room mother absent

Source: Wulbert, M., Nyman, B. A., Snow, I., & Owen, Y. The efficacy of stimulus fading and contingency management in the treatment of elective mutism: A case study. *Journal of Applied Behavior Analysis*, 1973, **6**, 435–441. Copyright by Society for the Experimental Analysis of Behavior, Inc., reproduced by permission.

and also used a one minute time-out procedure later in the sessions when no response occurred (no fading procedure was used). Treatment took place in a clinic setting three times a week, over a three and one-half week period, with the experimental and control sessions being alternated every 10 minutes.

As Figure 5.1 shows, during the first six days of treatment, as Experimenter 1 moved closer to the girl, her motor behavior dropped off slightly from what it had been when Experimenter 1 was not present. On the other hand, her verbal responses dropped off completely as Experimenter 1 moved closer to her. When the time-out contingency was put into effect on Day 7, the child responded to all verbal and motor task items presented during the experimental sessions. This 100% level of responding continued on days 8, 9, and 10 and Experimenter 1 moved closer and acquired complete stimulus control of her behavior from her mother.

In the control sessions, with the time-out contingency in effect, the child was completely unresponsive in her motor and verbal responses without the presence of stimulus fading. Interestingly, as Figure 5.2 shows, there was a definite trend indicating that as each of seven experimenters were faded into the treatment program, while using time-out, the girl adapted to each more quickly.

The program was then successfully moved to the school with Experimenter 7 (the child's teacher) obtaining a response from her. Wulbert et al. (1973) concluded that the use of stimulus fading, combined with a time-out contin-

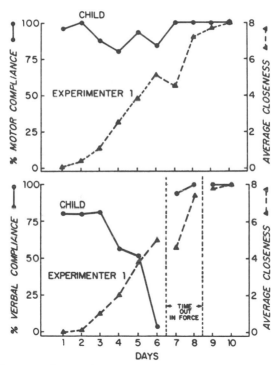

Figure 5.1. Percent of compliance to demands for verbal and motor response during experimental periods as Experimenter 1 faded in to stimulus control. A time-out contingency was in effect on Days 7 and 8.

Source: Wulbert, M., Nyman, B. A., Snow, I., & Owen, Y. The efficacy of stimulus fading and contingency management in the treatment of elective mutism: A case study. *Journal of Applied Behavior Analysis*, 1973, **6**, 435–441. Copyright by Society for the Experimental Analysis of Behavior, Inc., reproduced by permission.

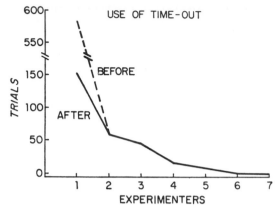

Figure 5.2. Number of trials to fade in successive experimenters to stimulus control.

Source: Wulbert, M., Nyman, B. A., Snow, I., & Owen, Y. The efficacy of stimulus fading and contingency management in the treatment of elective mutism: A case study. *Journal of Applied Behavior Analysis*, 1973, **6**, 435–441. Copyright by Society for the Experimental Analysis of Behavior, Inc., reproduced by permission.

gency for non-responding, was an effective component in the contingency management treatment of selective mutism. As Kratochwill (1981) notes, however, the authors present no evidence that complete (normal) verbal responding was achieved by the girl in school.

Stimulus fading has also been used by other researchers for the treatment of selective mutism (e.g., Clayton, 1981; Conrad, Delk, & Williams, 1974; Lipton, 1980; Reid, Hawkins, Keutzer, McNeal, Phelps, Reid & Meas, 1967). For example, Conrad et al. (1974) worked with an 11-year-old American Indian girl, who had been totally mute in school for the past five years. Parental reports and observations showed that she interacted normally with parents, siblings, and friends outside of school. Treatment began at home with the child's mother, where the child already verbalized. Gradually, through successive approximation, the researcher changed the stimulus settings until the child responded verbally to the teacher's questions in the classroom setting. Treatment took 12 sessions. Conrad et al. report that the child responded verbally once in the classroom. Although she continued to respond verbally at the one year follow-up, Conrad et al. noted that she rarely verbalized spontaneously or initiated conversations.

Lipton (1980) worked with a six-year-old girl who had a complete absence of speech in kindergarten. Treatment began with the child and therapist working together in a room away from the classroom setting. Activities consisted of structured game playing that required verbal interaction, working on an exercise book using verbal instructions, and doing picture completion tasks orally. The child's loudness of speech was shaped initially from a whisper level (a response loud enough to move a piece of string approximately five inches from the child's mouth) to increasingly louder levels. The sessions were then gradually moved from the first room to the school library and then to the classroom. Lipton reported that by the tenth session the child engaged in regular and consistent conversation, and that this behavior continued at the six-month follow-up period.

Stimulus fading was also used by Neisworth, Madle, and Goeke (1975) for the treatment of "separation anxiety" (crying, sobbing, screaming, withdrawal) in a four-year-old preschool girl. The mother was instructed to stay in the preschool for several sessions before being faded out and to reinforce the girl for nonanxious behavior. The child was also reinforced by staff for increased involvement in school activities. Treatment lasted for 18 hours, over an eight-day period. Neisworth et al. report that the procedure produced almost an immediate cessation of anxious behavior on the part of the child, and that this behavior was maintained at the two-, four-, and six-month follow-up periods.

Since only a few fear-related behaviors have been treated using the stimulus fading method, any generalization about the relative effectiveness of this procedure with other children's fears and phobias must be made with caution.

Extinction

Because some children exhibit fears and/or fear-related responses because they are (or have been) reinforced for performing them, it is possible to reduce this behavior by making certain that a child is not reinforced. *Extinction* refers to the removal of those reinforcing consequences which follow a child's avoidance response. For this procedure to be effective, the therapist *must* be able to identify those consequences that are reinforcing the child's fear response and be in a position to determine (1) when those consequences will occur, (2) the relative contribution of those consequences to the frequency of the child's fear behavior, and (3) whether he/she can modify the occurrence of the consequences. For example, one of the most common reinforcing consequences for a child's fear behavior is his/her parents' attention. If after a series of observations and discussions with parents, the therapist hypothesizes parental attention as a major contributing/causal factor to the child's fear behavior, he/she must then determine the frequency and conditions under which that attention occurs and whether the parents are willing to modify their reaction(s) to their child.

A number of studies have used the extinction procedure with fearful or phobic children (Boer & Sipprelle, 1970; Gresham & Nagle, 1981; Hersen, 1970; Piersal & Kratochwill, 1981; Stableford, 1979; Waye, 1979). Many of these studies, however, have combined the extinction procedure with rein-forcement for appropriate/nonfearful behavior(s). For example, Hersen (1970) worked with a 12 ½-year-old boy who had a school phobia. The child's case was striking in that his five other siblings also had a history of school phobic responses. Hersen also determined in the introductory intake sessions that his parents inadvertently reinforced him each morning by coaxing and cajol-ing him for approximately two hours to go to school. A three-part procedure was therefore initiated over the 15 weeks of treatment. First, the child's mother was seen by the therapist and instructed over a number of sessions to (1) be "deaf and dumb" to the child's crying and firm about him attending school, (2) reward the child with praise for his school-related coping behav-iors, such as his success in extracurricular activities, and (3) be aware that the child might show other school-related avoidant behavior and that these should also be placed on extinction.

Next, Hersen speculated from the initial intake interview that a guidance counselor at school had also been a contributing reinforcing agent to the child's phobia by providing attention to the boy's crying and anxiety. The therapist then visited with the counselor at school and instructed him to see the boy for only five minutes per visit and to firmly insist that the child return to classes. The third part of the treatment consisted of the therapist seeing the boy in therapy to (1) give the therapist the opportunity to verbally reinforce him for demonstrating pro-school coping responses, (2) extinguish through nonattention inappropriate school-related responses, and (3) pro-vide the child with an opportunity to express his views regarding such issues as the treatment program at home. Hersen reported that following treatment the boy was attending school normally and that his academic performance had returned to its pre-phobia level (above average academic performance). A six-month follow-up evaluation showed that the post-treatment behavior was being maintained.

A case study reported by Waye (1979) also used an extinction procedure as part of the treatment package for a five-year-old girl who had a fear that her thumbs were shrinking. Waye determined that her fear resulted from four factors: (1) memory work at Sunday school (e.g., "Neglect Bible, refuse to pray and you will shrink") where the girl associated shrinking parts with bad behavior, (2) the child's belief in hand shrinking mediated through comic-book models, (3) the anatomy of the hand and the relative position and size of the thumb to the other fingers, and (4) parental attention to the child's intense fear. The treatment package consisted of the parents ignoring all outbursts by the child regarding the nature of her hands, as well as all hand shrinkage reports. The parents were also instructed to pay attention to her when she was involved in appropriate play behaviors. Two strangers were also utilized to dispel her belief that her thumbs were shrinking. This was achieved by requiring the child to compare her hands with a cardboard model that had been traced of her hands. The comparison occurred in a matter-of-fact fashion with the strangers making sure that they did not reinforce her reports of shrinkage or her associated outbursts.

Waye reported that following one week of treatment, the girl reported that her ears were shrinking, and after ten days of treatment the frequency of her hand shrinking reports dropped to zero. At a six-month follow-up, the girl's behavior was maintained. At 24 months, however, the child indicated that her mouth was shrinking. This was then treated by the mother in a matter-of-fact, nonreinforcing manner. Twenty-six months post-treatment, there were no reports of body parts shrinking by the girl.

Variations of Extinction

As we mentioned earlier, most studies that have used the extinction procedure have also included the use of positive reinforcement for appropriate and/or nonfearful behaviors. Combining the use of extinction and reinforcement in this manner is consistent with the general behavior modification approach to reducing those maladaptive behaviors that have been theorized or observed to be maintained by reinforcing consequences (see, for example, Kazdin, 1980c; Kratochwill, 1981; Morris, 1976).

One additional variation involving the use of extinction has been reported by Boer and Sipprelle (1970). They worked with a four-year-old girl who avoided foods requiring chewing. Prior to treatment, she had lived on liquids for six months. The authors reported that her behavior apparently developed following a trip to a doctor's office for a sore throat, as well as the earlier ingestion of an overdose of aspirin. It appeared, Boer and Sipprelle concluded, that she had developed a strong conditioned anxiety response to doctors. Treatment lasted seven sessions and consisted of extinguishing her avoidance of doctors and reinforcing incompatible and appropriate behavior. The mother was also asked to discontinue attending to the child's non-eating activities. In addition, shaping and positive reinforcement for appropriate eating took place, as well as generalization training to the home with her mother as therapy agent.

Boer and Sipprelle reported that after the fourth clinic session, the girl was eating solid foods in the clinic, and after the fifth session, a "normal" eating pattern was found at home. At follow-up 13 months later, she ate solid foods at home without any restrictions.

Another study by Stableford (1979) combined the use of extinction with *in vivo* deconditioning. The author worked with a three-year-old girl who had a noise phobia. Treatment was carried out by her parents and involved: (1) minimizing any parental attention to her fear reactions to noises and (2) exposing her to gradually increasing levels of noise at home and in the car. Telephone contact with the parents revealed that after two weeks the child responded favorably to most noises, but after five weeks of treatment she still could not tolerate sounds from the car radio. The parents were again instructed to ignore the child's complaints/fear reactions and to distract her with toys, etc. One month later, the child's behavior improved, and six months later the child had no signs of her noise phobia in any situation.

Additional Considerations

Earlier in this chapter, we stressed that a contingency management approach to children's fears and phobias emphasized the causal relationship between a child's observable behavior (phobic response) and various environmental stimuli. The specific goal of treatment, therefore, is to increase the rate or frequency of the child's behavior and to maintain it at that level over time. Treatment first involves an analysis of those factors that contribute to the low rate of behavior, followed by the manipulation of those factors in order to increase the frequency of the behavior and finally the provision of pleasant consequences to maintain the level of the behavior.

Interestingly, few controlled experiments have been published on contingency management procedures that support the efficacy of this approach. The vast majority of studies are descriptive and/or uncontrolled case studies. Furthermore, most studies combine many contingency management procedures into one treatment package, making it difficult to discern which procedure(s) is responsible for the reduction of the child's fear response. Because of this, it is difficult to know which contingency management procedure should be used with children who have similar fears or phobias.

In surveying the literature, it also becomes clear that only a narrow range of children's fears and phobias have been investigated using a contingency management approach. The overriding majority of published studies involving contingency management procedures have been limited to only *three* categories of behaviors: school phobia, social withdrawal, and selective mutism—with only 5–10 additional case studies investigating a few other children's fears or phobias. An immediate issue is the generalizability of this approach to other clinical fears and phobias (see, for example, Ross, 1981). At best, given the restrictive nature of the literature in this area, it would appear that a therapist should proceed with caution in the use of any contingency management procedure on behaviors other than those related to school phobia, social withdrawal, and selective mutism.

In addition, no research has been reported in the contingency management literature on the relative contribution of therapist and/or client variables on the outcome of therapy. For example, would we have the same treatment outcome using positive reinforcement for a school phobic child, whether the therapist was male or female, young or old, experienced or inexperienced in the use of the procedure, and so forth? Would the treatment outcome be influenced by the age of the child receiving treatment, the sex of the child, the chronicity of the fear or phobia, or by the number of other fears that the child has?

Finally, it appears that researchers in this treatment area have concentrated mainly on only the avoidance behavior of the child who has a fear, not considering in their respective research studies the notion of the triple mode response system which was discussed in Chapter 3. It would seem that a fruitful line of research, for example, would be to determine if contingency management methods not only reduce a child's school avoidant behavior, but also his/her attitude and/or feelings about school, as well as the child's physiological responsiveness to the school situation.

MODELING

Behavior change that results from the observation of another person has been typically referred to as *modeling* (e.g., Bandura, 1969; Kazdin & Wilson, 1978). Although the concept of modeling or imitation learning has been studied for almost 100 years, it has only been within the past 20 years that it has been applied to the treatment and understanding of clinical problems in children and, specifically, to the treatment of children's fears and phobias (see, for example, Bandura, 1969, 1971; Bandura & Walters, 1963). Generally speaking, the person who is most often associated with introducing this concept into the fear reduction methods literature is Albert Bandura. Bandura's social learning theory position regarding the development of fears in children is reviewed briefly in Chapter 1. With respect to treatment, Rimm and Masters (1979) summarize the functions of modeling procedures in the following manner:

[A person] may learn new, appropriate behavior patterns, and modeling may thus serve an *acquisition* function. More likely, the observation of a model's behavior in various situations may provide social *facilitation* of appropriate behaviors by inducing the client to perform these behaviors, of which he was previously capable, at more appropriate times, in more appropriate ways, or toward more appropriate people. Modeling may lead to the *disinhibition* of behaviors that the client had avoided because of fear or anxiety. And, while disinhibiting behaviors, modeling may promote the *vicarious* and *direct extinction* of the fear associated with the person, animal, or object toward which the behavior was directed [pp. 103–104].

In this section, we first describe the general aspects of the modeling procedure, and then discuss the two major categories of modeling: *live modeling* and *symbolic modeling*.

Modeling Proper

Although there are two distinct categories of modeling (and several variations within each category), we tend to find certain factors that are common
to both categories. As Bandura (1969) states:

> [Through modeling] one can acquire intricate response patterns merely by ob-
> serving the performance of appropriate models; emotional responses can be
> conditioned observationally by witnessing the affective reactions of others un-
> dergoing painful or pleasurable experiences; *fearful and avoidant behavior can be
> extinguished vicariously through observation of modeled approach behavior toward
> feared objects without any adverse consequences accruing to the performer*; . . .
> and, finally, the expression of well-learned responses can be enhanced and
> socially regulated through the actions of influential models [p. 118, italics added].

Therefore, modeling involves learning through the observation of others and
the imitative changes in a person's behavior(s) that may occur as a result of
the observing activities (Rimm & Masters, 1979).

The modeling procedure consists of an individual called the *model* (e.g., a
therapist, parent, teacher, peer, or sibling) and a person called the *observer*
(i.e., the phobic child). The observer typically observes the model perform a
behavior that the observer has a history of avoiding. The behavior is performed within a stimulus setting that is familiar to the observer and involves
approaching a feared object, event, or activity which is the same (or similar)
to the one the observer fears. Thus, if a child is fearful of very active large
dogs who are not chained or on a leash, it would not be an appropriate
modeling situation to have a model touch and play with a small, quiet,
leashed dog, unless, of course, the latter dog was only one in a series of
gradually more active and larger dogs with which the model was planning to
touch and play.

One aspect of the modeling situation that seems to be important for
effecting positive behavior change in the observer is to have the child observe
the model experience positive and/or safe consequences during his/her presence in or involvement with the feared situation, event, or object (Perry &
Furukawa, 1980). In addition, as Figure 5.3 summarizes, Bandura (1969,
1977) has delineated four component processes which he theorizes contribute to the effectiveness of (and, in fact, govern) modeling. Although these
four processes represent a theoretical statement by Bandura regarding the
components of modeling, they can, as Rimm and Masters (1979) suggest,
relate to any direct application of the modeling procedure to such areas as
the treatment of children's fears and phobias. The therapist should therefore
be certain that the child can (1) *attend* to the various aspects of the modeling
situation (e.g., the child can sit and watch the modeling event throughout its

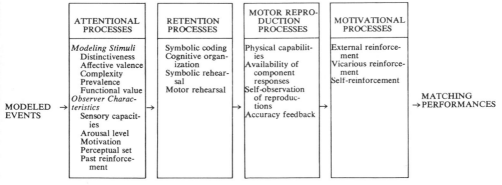

ATTENTIONAL PROCESSES	RETENTION PROCESSES	MOTOR REPRO-DUCTION PROCESSES	MOTIVATIONAL PROCESSES
Modeling Stimuli Distinctiveness Affective valence Complexity Prevalence Functional value *Observer Charac-teristics* Sensory capacit-ies Arousal level Motivation Perceptual set Past reinforce-ment	Symbolic coding Cognitive organ-ization Symbolic rehear-sal Motor rehearsal	Physical capabilit-ies Availability of component responses Self-observation of reproduc-tions Accuracy feedback	External reinforce-ment Vicarious reinforce-ment Self-reinforcement

MODELED →   →   →   →   MATCHING
EVENTS   → PERFORMANCES

Figure 5.3. Component processes proposed by Bandura as governing observation-al learning in the social learning analysis.
Source: Bandura, A. *Social learning theory*. Englewood Cliffs, N.J.: Prentice-Hall, 1977. Reprinted with permission.

duration, the child can note the relevant contextual aspects of the event, etc.); (2) *retain* what has been learned from observing the modeling situation; (3) *motorically reproduce* or match what has been observed in the modeling situation; and (4) when necessary, has the *motivation* to perform the behav-ior observed.

Finally, with respect to the nature of the model's approach behavior towards the feared stimulus, object or event, most writers agree with Ban-dura (1971) that the model should perform his/her approach behavior in a graduated fashion. That is, as in the case of the anxiety hierarchy in *in vivo* desensitization, the model should approach the feared stimulus gradually and in a confident manner—in increasing bold steps with each being per-ceived by the client as more and more threatening. As Gelfand (1978) states with regard to children's animal fears:

> Observation of a competent and fearless model may be particularly important in the instruction of young children who most probably lack handling skills, and who might otherwise elicit barking, hissing, and pursuit by the very animal they fear as a result of their panicky attempts at escape. . . . Also, the child may reject the possibility of emulating models who are so obviously successful and thus dissimilar to himself [pp. 334–335].

Live Modeling

This form of modeling involves the actual or live demonstraton of the grad-uated approach behavior of the model toward the feared situation. For example, Bandura, Grusec, and Menlove (1967) studied the effect of live modeling on the fear of dogs of 48 children who ranged in age from three to five years. In addition to live modeling, Bandura et al. studied the contribution of the modeling context (positive versus neutral) on approach behavior of the children. Specifically, children were assigned to one of four groups: (1) *modeling, positive context*, where the children watched a peer model fearlessly interact with a dog within the context of a party atmosphere; (2) *modeling, neutral context*, where the children also observed the model approach the dog, but they did so while seated at a table; (3) *exposure, positive context*, where the children were having a party and the dog was present, but no modeling with the dog occurred; and (4) *positive context*, where the children were having a party with no dog present. Each group of children was exposed to eight 10-minute sessions held over four consecutive days. Follow-up evaluation took place one month later. As Figure 5.4. shows regarding the mean approach behavior for each group at pretest, posttest, and follow-up, the live modeling conditions were superior to the other two conditions. The children in the two modeling groups demonstrated significantly more approach behavior than the children in the dog exposure or positive context only conditions. In looking at the performance of the most fearful children at pretest, Bandura et al. found that 55% of those children in the modeling group ended up performing the terminal setup in a Behavior Avoidance Test, whereas only 13% did so from the remaining two groups.

White and Davis (1974) studied the relative effectiveness of live modeling, observation/exposure only, and a no-treatment control condition on the dental treatment avoidance behavior of eight girls ranging from four to eight years of age. The live modeling condition consisted of having each of the five children sit behind a one-way screen with a dental student and observe a patient/confederate (an eight-year-old girl) undergo dental treatment. In the observation/exposure condition, the five children each sat behind the one-way screen and the dentist and his assistant merely named and manipulated the equipment used in the modeling condition. No model was present. The children in both conditions were each exposed to six sessions over a three-week period. The results showed that both the live modeling condition and the exposure condition were significantly more effective than the no-treatment condition in reducing the dental treatment avoidance behavior of the children. In addition, White and Davis (1974) stated, "The behavior of the children under the Modeling condition was far more adaptive and mature. . . . These subjects never required direct support from a significant other" (p. 31).

Mann and Rosenthal (1969) report a study involving seventh and eighth graders who were referred by a counselor for test anxiety. They compared direct systematic desensitization and modeled desensitization in both individual and group situations. For example, some children were desensitized individually while they were observed by a peer, while others were desensitized in a group and also observed by a group of peers. There was also a

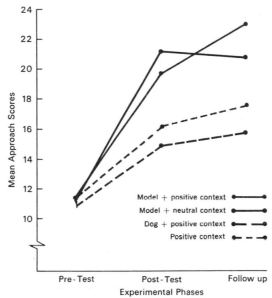

Figure 5.4. Mean dog-approach scores achieved by children in each of the treatment conditions on the three different periods of assessment.

Source: Bandura, A., Grusec, J. E. & Menlove, F. L. Vicarious extinction of avoidance behavior. *Journal of Personality and Social Psychology*, 1967, **5**, 16–23. Reprinted with permission.

condition where a group of children observed a peer model being desensitized. The results showed that all of the treatment procedures produced significantly better self-report scores and performance on test-taking samples than the no-treatment control condition.

Ritter (1968) compared live group modeling, contact desensitization (participant modeling), and a no-treatment control condition on the snake avoidant behavior of 44 children who ranged from five to eleven years of age. Children in the live modeling condition observed several peers exhibit progressively more intimate interactions with a snake. The participant modeling group received Ritter's standard contact desensitization (see Chapter 4). Children were seen for two 35-minute sessions over a two-week period. The results showed that both live modeling and contact desensitization were more effective in reducing children's avoidance behavior than the no-treatment condition. Further analyses, however, revealed that 53% of the children in the modeling condition completed the terminal item on a Behavior Avoidance Test, whereas 80% of the children in the participant modeling group completed the terminal item. No follow-up information was provided. More recently, Matson (1981) reported the successful use of participant modeling with mentally retarded children who had a fear of adult strangers. The results were also maintained at a six-month follow-up period.

Commentary. As the reader will note, few studies have been published on live modeling with children. A few more have been published involving both children and adults (e.g., Bandura, Blanchard, & Ritter, 1968; Blanchard, 1970; Ritter, 1969), but it is not clear what generalizations can be drawn from these latter studies to children. It should be noted further that the types of fears that have been studied with the live modeling only procedure have been limited mostly to animals, test anxiety, and dental treatments. Consequently, any use of this procedure with other very intense clinical fears and phobias in children should be viewed as speculative, and the therapist should proceed with caution.

Symbolic Modeling

This form of modeling typically involves the presentation of the model either through film, videotape, or imagination. For example, Bandura and Menlove (1968) studied the effects of filmed modeling on the dog avoidant behavior of 48 children ranging in age from three to five years. One group observed a fearless five-year-old male engage in increasingly more fear provoking contact with a dog. For example, the initial film sequences showed the model looking at the dog in the playpen and occasionally petting the dog, while subsequent sequences displayed the model inside the playpen, feeding and petting the dog.

The second experimental group observed several male and female models interacting with a number of dogs of varying sizes. The third group was a control condition, where the children observed a film of equivalent length to the others on Disneyland (no dogs present in the film). The children all viewed eight different movies, three minutes per movie, twice per day, over four consecutive days. The results, presented in Figure 5.5, showed that children in both film modeling conditions significantly increased their approach scores at posttest and follow-up periods on the Behavior Avoidance Test over that of the control condition children. No significant differences were found between the approach scores of the two modeling groups. The authors report, however, that when the incidence of terminal performances (i.e., being alone with the dog in the playpen) as compared between the two modeling groups, the multiple models condition was slightly better at posttest and significantly better at the one-month follow-up than either the single model or control conditions. Other studies supporting the effectiveness of symbolic modeling include Hill, Liebert, and Mott (1968), Kornhaber and Schroeder (1974), Vernon and Bailey, (1974), and Weissbrod and Bryan (1973).

A second illustrative experiment involving symbolic modeling was conducted by Melamed and Siegel (1975). They studied the relative effectiveness of symbolic modeling on reducing the anxiety level of children who were

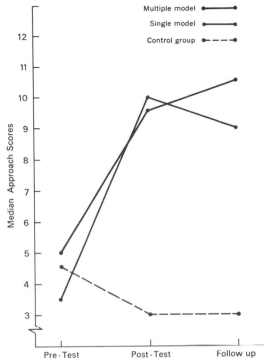

Figure 5.5. Median dog approach scores achieved by children receiving either single model or multiple model treatments or who participated in a control condition.

Source: Bandura, A. and Menlove, F. Factors determining vicarious extinction of avoidance behavior through symbolic modeling. *Journal of Personality and Social Psychology*, 1968, **8**, 99–108. Reprinted with permission.

facing hospitalization and surgery. Sixty children were used in this study, ranging from 4 to 12 years of age. The children were all being hospitalized for the first time and scheduled to have elective surgery for either hernia, tonsillectomy, or urinary-genital tract problems. Thirty children in the modeling condition arrived at the hospital one hour prior to admission time and saw a 16-minute film, *Ethan Has An Operation*. Melamed and Siegel (1975) describe the film in the following manner:

> [The film] depicts a 7 year-old white male who has been hospitalized for a hernia operation. . . . [It] consists of 15 scenes showing various events that most children encounter when hospitalized for elective surgery from the time of admission to time of discharge including the child's orientation to the hospital ward and medical personnel such as the surgeon and anesthesiologist; having a blood test and exposure to standard hospital equipment; separation from the mother; and scenes in the operating and recovery rooms. In addition to explana-

tions of the hospital procedure provided by the medical staff, various scenes are narrated by the child, who describes his feelings and concerns . . . at each stage of the hospital experience. Both the child's behavior and verbal remarks exemplify some anxiety and apprehension, he is able to overcome his initial fears [coping model] and complete each event in a successful and nonanxious manner [p. 514].

The 30 control condition children also arrived early at the hospital and saw a 12 minute film, *Living Things Are Everywhere*, about a child on a nature walk. Following the films, all children were given the hospital's standard preoperative instructions. Six measures were used in the study: three indices of trait anxiety (the Anxiety scale of the *Personality Inventory for Children, Children's Manifest Anxiety Scale*, and the *Human Figure Drawing Test*) and situational/state anxiety (*Palmar Sweat Index, Hospital Fears Rating Scale*, and an *Observer Rating Scale of Anxiety*). The trait measures were obtained prior to the children observing the films and at a 26-day postoperative follow-up period. The situational anxiety measures were taken pre-film, the evening before the surgery, and at the 26-day follow-up period.

The results showed that the filmed modeling condition significantly reduced all measures of situational anxiety in the children compared to the control condition, and that these significant differences were maintained at the follow-up period. No differences, however, were found between the modeling and control conditions on the trait anxiety measures.

Melamed and her colleagues (e.g., Melamed, Hawes, Hieby, & Glick, 1975; Melamed, Weinstein, Hawes, & Katin-Borland, 1975; Melamed, Yurcheson, Fleece, Hutcherson, & Hawes, 1978) and Klorman, Hilpert, Michael, LaGana, & Sveen (1980) have also shown symbolic modeling to be effective in reducing children's fears and uncooperative behavior during dental treatment. Similarly, Vernon and Bailey (1974) studied the relative effectiveness of a modeling film on the induction of anesthesia in children, while Geidel and Gulbrandsen (as reported in Melamed & Siegel, 1980) investigated the use of a modeling videotape for preschool children coping with a physical examination.

A third illustrative example of the use of symbolic modeling is a study by O'Connor (1969) concerned with social withdrawal in preschool children. In this study 13 nursery school children who showed extreme social withdrawal were assigned to one of two conditions: filmed modeling group and a neutral film control group. The 23-minute modeling film showed increasing social interactions between children with positive consequences present for those interactions. The 20-minute control film was of Marineland dolphins. Each child viewed the respective film alone and then returned to the classroom. The results showed that the modeling film produced increased levels of social interaction in the experimental children, while the control film did not produce any change in the level of children's social interaction.

In a later study, O'Connor (1972) studied the effectiveness of modeling and shaping on the modification of social withdrawal in a similar group of children. Thirty-three preschoolers were assigned to one of four groups: modeling film plus shaping (reinforcement) of social interaction; modeling film only; shaping (reinforcement) only of social interaction; and a no-treatment control condition. The results showed that at posttest there were no significant differences on children's levels of social interaction between the modeling plus shaping and modeling alone conditions or between the shaping and modeling plus shaping conditions. At follow-up, however, only the modeling plus shaping and modeling conditions were found to remain stable over time in terms of the children's level of social interaction. Similarly, Evers and Schwarz (1973) found, using the O'Connor (1969) film that there was no difference in level of children's social interaction between a modeling alone and modeling plus teacher social reinforcement condition at either posttest or follow-up. Gelfand (1978), on the other hand, reports a study by Clement, Roberts and Lantz (1976) in which they did not find a reinforcement, modeling, or modeling plus reinforcement condition to add significantly to the effectiveness of the play therapy procedure being used to change the shy, withdrawn behavior of young boys. Gelfand further reports that the authors suggest that their results may be due to their film's lack of a narrative sound track or to their failure to use coping models who visibly increased in their social skills. Other studies supporting the effectiveness of symbolic modeling in reducing social withdrawal in children include Evers-Pasquale and Sherman (1975) and Keller and Carlson (1974).

Another form of modeling has involved the combined use of filmed modeling and client participation. For example, Lewis (1974) examined the relative effectiveness of client participation plus filmed modeling with a film modeling only, participation only, and a no-treatment control condition in children having a fear of swimming. There were ten black children in each group, between 5 and 12 years of age, attending a Boy's Club summer camp. In the client participation plus modeling condition, each child was shown an eight-minute film showing three children performing tasks in a swimming pool that were similar to the avoidance test items that each subject was exposed to during pretesting. Immediately following the film, a female experimenter spent ten minutes in the pool with each subject, encouraging him to practice the items on the avoidance test and physically assisting the child in trying the steps if necessary. The experimenter also gave social reinforcement for each child's attempt at or completion of an item on the avoidance test. The children in the modeling condition viewed the eight-minute film and were exposed to a ten-minute game of checkers alongside the pool. No participation in the water occurred. The children in the participation group were shown an eight-minute neutral film (three short cartoons) containing no elements of water activities plus the ten-minute checkers game described earlier. Lewis found that all three treatment procedures were more effective than the no-treatment control condition, and that the filmed modeling plus client participation condition was significantly better in reducing children's fears than any of the other procedures. Similar findings regarding the relative effectiveness of client participation plus modeling have been reported by Bandura, Jeffrey, and Wright (1974) and Ross, Ross, and Evans (1971).

Another symbolic modeling procedure is called *covert modeling*. This procedure involves the use of modeling sequences that are rehearsed in imagination and follow a designated script (Rosenthal, 1980). Although some studies have reported the use of this procedure with adults (e.g., Kazdin, 1973, 1974a), little evidence exists regarding the relative effectiveness of this procedure in changing children's fears and related problems. As Rosenthal (1980) suggests, it remains to be confirmed whether children would "have difficulty in correctly imagining the required therapy scripts" (p. 250).

Commentary.   As in the case of live modeling, the reader will note that symbolic modeling procedures have most often been used with only a small number of fears and phobias in children: dog and snake fears, social withdrawal, and impending dental or surgical care. Although there has been a fair amount of well-controlled research published on the use of this procedure with children, the nature and extent of the fears and phobias studied have been quite limited. It is therefore suggested that therapists use caution in the use of this procedure for the treatment of other intense clinical fears and phobias in children.

Additional Considerations

As mentioned earlier, Bandura (1969, 1977) maintains that for modeling to be effective, the observer must be able to reproduce the modeled behavior, and be motivated when necessary to demonstrate the behavior. Perry and Furukawa (1980) point out that the therapist can do a great deal to ensure that conditions facilitate the modeling process by attending to his/her choice of the model and the model behaviors, the characteristics of the observer, and the structuring of the manner in which the model and his/her behaviors are represented. To assist the therapist in attending to these factors, Perry and Furukawa (1980) have developed the checklist presented in Table 5.5.

Model Characteristics.   In summarizing their review of relevant factors, Perry and Furukawa (1980) report that a model who is generally similar to the observer in age, sex, race, and attitudes is more likely to be imitated. High prestige (though not extremely prestigous) models are more likely to be imitated as, in general, are coping, warm and nuturing models. Zimmerman (1977) indicates, however, that it would be erroneous to conclude that mod-

Table 5.5. Factors Which Enhance Modeling

I. Factors enhancing acquisition (learning and retention)

  A. Characteristics of the model
1. Similarity in sex, age, race, and attitudes
2. Prestige
3. Competence
4. Warmth and nurturance
5. Reward value

  B. Characteristics of the observer
1. Capacity to process and retain information
2. Uncertainty
3. Level of anxiety
4. Other personality factors

  C. Characteristics of the modeling presentation
1. Live or symbolic model
2. Multiple models
3. Slider model
4. Graduated modeling procedures
5. Instructions
6. Commentary on features and rules
7. Summarization by observer
8. Rehearsal
9. Minimization of distracting stimuli

II. Factors enhancing performance

  A. Factors providing incentive for performance
1. Vicarious reinforcement (reward to model)
2. Vicarious extinction of fear of responding (no negative consequences to model)
3. Direct reinforcement
4. Imitation of children

  B. Factors affecting quality of performance
1. Rehearsal
2. Participant modeling

  C. Transfer and generalization of performance
1. Similarity of training setting to everyday environment
2. Repeated practice affecting response hierarchy
3. Incentives for performance in natural setting
4. Learning principles governing a class of behaviors.
5. Provision of variation in training situations.

Source: Perry, M. A., & Furukawa, M. J. Modeling methods. In F. H. Kanfer & A. P. Goldstein (Eds.), *Helping people change.* (2nd ed.) New York: Pergamon Press, Inc., 1980. Reprinted with permission.

els are not effective unless they possess these characteristics. He argues that "differences in imitation that we attribute to a model's characteristics have been relatively small and often occur inconsistently" (p. 54).

Observer Characteristics. A variety of characteristics have also been examined regarding this factor. Perry and Furukawa (1980) report that the therapist should attend to the observer's intellectual strengths and weaknesses, and be able to accommodate the modeling situation to this factor. Independent of this factor, however, it seems clear that the observer must be sufficiently imitative to profit from the modeling experience. If the therapist has doubts in this regard, he/she should test the child's degree of imitativeness for both simple and multi-stage instructions and/or modeled activities.

A variety of personality "traits" have also been associated with a greater amount of imitation in children—for example, a high need for social approval, high dependency, and low personal competency. With respect to such demographic characteristics as the model's race, and sex, no clear evidence has appeared in the literature that supports the view, for example, that the observer should be of the same race and sex as the model. There is some evidence (e.g., Klorman et al., 1980; Melamed & Siegel, 1980), however, to suggest that the level of the observer's previous experience affects the outcome of modeling. Lastly, the age of the observer may also be important, with other children being influenced more by the model than younger children (Zimmerman, 1977).

Characteristics of the Modeling Presentation.　With regard to whether live or symbolic modeling should be used, the data are not clear. Perry and Furukawa (1980) suggest that a live model is more interesting to many people than a symbolic one, and that a live model can alter his/her performance if necessary for a child. Symbolic modeling situations, on the other hand, can be edited and refined whenever necessary and can be used repeatedly in clinical settings. Bandura (1969) concluded, however, that symbolic modeling was less powerful than live modeling, but "the diminished efficacy of symbolic modeling can be offset by a broader sampling of models and aversive [feared] stimulus objects" (p. 180).

Modeling may also be enhanced through the use of multiple models (Bandura & Menlove, 1968). Perry and Furukawa (1980) state that "using different models enhances the presentation by showing both the generality of the behavior as well as its appropriateness for this particular observer" (p. 138). Including different models also increases the probability of the observer identifying someone whom he/she sees as similar to him/her.

Perry and Furukawa further suggest that instructions or commentary should possibly be part of the modeling presentation. For example, introductory instructions could be included to inform the observer what will take place, and subsequent commentary during the modeling display might "prime" the observer what to look for. Similarly, Gelfand (1978) has suggested that the researcher/therapist may want to consider the narration or commentary, under certain circumstances, to be in a self-speech, first person form. Goldstein, Sprafkin, and Gershaw (1976) have also commented on methods of enhancing modeling:

> Greater modeling will occur when the modeling display shows the behaviors to be imitated: (a) in a clear and detailed manner, (b) in the order from least to most difficult behaviors, (c) with enough repetition to make overlearning likely, (d) with as little irrelevant (not to be learned) detail as possible, and (e) when several different models, rather than a single model, are used [p. 6].

Supportive Research

The vast majority of studies on the use of live and symbolic modeling to reduce children's fears and phobias have been controlled experiments (see, for example, reviews by Bandura, 1969, 1977; Bryan & Schwarz, 1971; Gelfand, 1978; Graziano et al., 1979; Melamed & Siegel, 1980; Peterson & Shigetomi, 1981; Richards & Siegel, 1978). Generally speaking, these studies fall into four categories of "fears": animals; social withdrawal; impending dental or other medical treatment or elective surgery; and test anxiety. Little or no research has been conducted on such other children's fears and phobias as speech anxiety, loud noises, heights, school, nightmares, moving vehicles, and separation from parents. One might reason, therefore, that any generalizability of the research findings on modeling to these other fears and phobias is quite limited (see, for example, Ross, 1981). In addition, as Graziano et al. (1979) suggest, we might question the extent to which the children typically used in the various modeling studies were, in fact, "severely fearful children." Graziano et al. acknowledge that some of the children in the Bandura and Menlove (1968) study and in the dental and medical fears studies were quite fearful, but point out that most of them were not chosen because of their severe and intense levels of fear and anxiety or because of the length of their duration.

Graziano et al. further state:

> Although modeling appears to be quite effective with mild to moderate fears, its usefulness in reducing phobias or severe fears has not yet been shown. In order for modeling to be effective, the child must attend to the model. Children who are highly fearful may find watching any interaction with the phobic stimulus so aversive that they look away, thus avoiding the fear stimulus [1979, p. 818].

As we pointed out in the previous section, a fair amount of research has been conducted on the relative contribution of model characteristics, client characteristics, and modeling setting factors on the outcome of modeling (see, for example, reviews by Melamed & Siegel, 1980; Perry & Furukawa, 1980). Further research, however, is needed on how such factors as the age of the client/observer, as well as the number and chronicity of client fears and phobias, impact on the findings regarding these latter three variables. It would also seem appropriate to investigate the relative contribution of the modeling facilitator (i.e., the therapist, experimenter, parent, etc., who brings the child to and away from the modeling environment) in these research studies. Specifically, to what extent does the modeling facilitator's behavior during treatment contribute to the outcome of the modeling procedure.

Modeling research has also typically concentrated only on the child's approach behavior toward the feared stimulus through the use of a Behavior Avoidance Test. Some researchers have included attitudinal and physiological measures in their studies, but apparently not with the same regularity and vigor as with the inclusion of a Behavior Avoidance Test. It therefore appears that few investigators have included the notion of the triple mode response system in their studies (see Chapter 3). A notable exception has been the research by Melamed and her colleagues where they have attempted to include both attitudinal and physiological measures, as well as behavioral observations (e.g., Melamed & Siegel, 1980).

In terms of comparative research, few modeling studies have been conducted on children's fears and phobias. Ritter (1968), for example, compared contact desensitization, "vicarious desensitization"—or what might be more appropriately labeled live modeling using multiple models—and a no-treatment control condition with snake fearful children. In the contact desensitization condition, children in small groups observed the adult experimenter handle and pet a snake after taking it from its cage. After one of the children agreed to participate and touch the snake, the experimenter first had the child put on a glove and place his hand on her hand while petting the snake. The experimenter then gradually removed her assistance and eventually encouraged the child to stroke the snake without wearing the glove. This process was continued with the other children in the group. This was then followed by the children taking turns being the therapist and working with the other children in stroking the snake. The vicarious desensitization condition involved having five peer models demonstrate tasks with the snake to a small group of children. The tasks performed were listed as part of a Behavior Avoidance Test. The children who were the experimental subjects were not encouraged to participate/interact directly with the snake. Each treatment condition lasted for two 35-minute sessions.

The results showed that 80% of the children in the contact desensitization group were able to complete the terminal behavior on the Behavior Avoidance Test, whereas only 53% of the children in the live modeling condition and none of the children in the control conditions were able to perform the terminal behavior. Both treatment groups were therefore found to produce significant reductions in children's snake avoidance behavior, with contact desensitization being superior to modeling.

Lastly, Machen and Johnson (1974) compared symbolic modeling and desensitization on the reduction of dental treatment anxiety levels in preschool children. Thirty-one children participated in the study. The children had no previous experience with a dentist. The desensitization condition was conducted on an *in vivo* basis, with children seen three at a time for one 30-minute session and gradually introduced to various dental stimuli. In the modeling group, the children were also seen three at a time and viewed an

11-minute videotape of a child exhibiting positive behavior during dental treatment, as well as being verbally reinforced by the dentist. The results showed that both treatment groups produced significantly lower dental treatment anxiety levels in the children from pretest to posttest, but that there was no significant difference between desensitization and modeling at posttest— both groups were equally effective in reducing the children's anxiety levels.

Variations in Modeling

A number of studies (e.g., Esveldt-Dawson, Wisner, Unis, Matson, & Kazdin, 1982; Ross, Ross, & Evans, 1971; Stokes & Kennedy, 1980; Whitehill, Hersen, & Bellack, 1980) have been published that represent variations on the modeling method. For example, Whitehill, Hersen, and Bellack (1980) tested the effectiveness of a social skills training package on teaching conversation behavior to socially isloated children. The training package consisted of instructions, live modeling, behavior rehearsal, performance feedback, and programmed generalization. Three boys and one girl, ranging in age from eight to ten years, participated in this study. Treatment was oriented toward teaching these children to make informative statements to peers, request shared activity, and ask open-ended questions. Treatment took three weeks, with three 20–30-minute training sessions per week. Follow-up occurred at four weeks and eight weeks posttreatment. The results showed that the treatment package improved the target behaviors in the children and their overall conversational abilities, and that these findings were maintained at the two follow-up periods. Another social skills training package has been discussed by Oden (1980) and Oden and Asher (1977).

Another example of a modeling variation is presented by Ross, Ross, and Evans (1971) in their treatment of a six-year-old boy who had extreme social withdrawal. The first four treatment sessions consisted of the male adult model establishing generalized imitative behavior in the child. This was accomplished by the model being praised with a variety of tangible and social rewards and rewarding the child for imitative responses. The second phase of treatment lasted 17 sessions and consisted of the repeated use of seven procedures: the modeling of a graduated series of social interactions between the model and other children with the target child observing; symbolic modeling involving the brief presentations of pictures, short stories, and films followed by discussions of the reward value of young children; providing information to the child regarding the nature of social interactions; role play where the model and child demonstrated appropriate social behavior within the context of prearranged arguments; a graduated series of joint participation in social activities on the part of the child and model; live modeling where the model demonstrated and then provided the child with practice in general game skills, etc.; and situational tests where the child went to a nearby park and was instructed to engage in increasingly long and close social interactions. Treatment lasted for seven weeks, with three 90-minute sessions per week. The results showed that the treatment was effective in increasing the child's level of social interaction. Other variations in modeling methods for increasing social interaction and cooperative play in socially withdrawn handicapped children have been discussed by Morris and Dolker (1974) and Strain, Shores, and Timm (1977).

As the reader will note, no one modeling variation has emerged as the predominant alternative modeling approach to reducing children's fears and related problems. What has emerged, however, is the emphasis on using modeling packages that include not only modeling, but also contingency management methods and *in vivo* desensitization-like methods to reduce children's fears and fear-related behaviors. This appears to be a fruitful area of investigation that needs many more controlled outcome and comparison studies before any definitive statement can be made regarding the relative effectiveness in these packages in reducing children's fears, phobias, and related behaviors.

SELF-CONTROL

Self-control can be conceptualized as a process through which a person becomes the primary agent in directing and regulating those aspects of his/ her behavior that lead to preplanned and specific behavioral outcomes and/ or consequences (Goldfried & Merbaum, 1973; Kanfer, 1980; Richards & Siegel, 1978). Although the notion of self-control and related self-regulation processes have been included for some time in theoretical discussions and the empirical literature on learning and conditioning (e.g., Bandura, 1969; Dollard & Miller, 1950; Homme, 1966; Kanfer & Phillips, 1970; Skinner, 1953), it has only been since the early to mid-1970s that they gained some popularity and became integrated into the behavior therapy literature, contributing substantially to the subarea called "cognitive behavior therapy" (see, for example, Goldfried & Goldfried, 1980; Mahoney, 1974; Meichenbaum & Genest, 1980). Although it appears to encompass a defined therapy approach, self-control actually encompasses numerous intervention methods, each sharing as its common base the recognition of the contribution of cognitive processes to behavior change and the view that individuals can regulate their own behavior. Another common element between these methods, according to Kanfer (1980), involves the therapist and his/her role as the "instigator and motivator" in helping the client begin a behavior change program. Self-control is therefore not so much a clearly defined treatment approach as a treatment emphasis or strategy in which the therapist teaches the client how, when, and where to use various cognitions to facilitate the learning of a new (and/or more personally satisfying) behavior pattern (Kanfer, 1980; Richards & Siegel, 1978).

In the area of fear reduction, self-control procedures focus on helping individuals develop specific thinking skills and apply them whenever they are confronted with a particular feared stimulus, event, or object. As with many self-control procedures, the therapist conducts his/her therapy sessions within a consultation/negotiation model.

> The therapist serves as a consultant and expert who negotiates with the client in how to go about change and to what end. The interactions are future oriented in that they focus on the development of general repertoires for dealing with problem situations. They deal with past experiences only as they are needed to help the client recognize inappropriateness of his current behaviors or to facilitate a behavioral analysis by providing information about the conditions under which a maladaptive behavior has developed [Kanfer, 1980, p. 336].

Interestingly, although self-control procedures have been used often (see, for example, Deffenbacher, 1976; Deffenbacher, Mathis, & Michaels, 1979; Deffenbacher & Michaels, 1980; Denney, 1980; Goldfried & Davison, 1976; Horan, Layng, & Pursell, 1976; Meichenbaum, 1974), only a small number of studies have been published on the use of this approach with fearful or phobic children (e.g., Genshaft, 1982; Graziano, Mooney, Huber, & Ignasiak, 1979; Kanfer, Karoly, & Newman, 1975; Leal, Baxter, Martin, & Marx, 1981; Peterson & Shigetomi, 1981; Siegel & Peterson, in press). Consequently, any conclusions regarding the relative effectiveness of this approach in treating children's fears and phobias must be viewed, at best, as speculative until additional research data are gathered. It is within the framework of this cautionary note that we review the general method and some of the available research on the use of self-control in the treatment of children's fears and phobias.

Self-Control Proper

In essence, the self-control approach involves, according to Meichenbaum and Genest (1980), helping the child:

> (1) become aware of the negative thinking styles that impede performance and that lead to emotional upset and inadequate performance; (2) generate, in collaboration with the trainer, a set of incompatible, specific self-statements, rules, strategies, and so on, which the trainee can then employ; and (3) learn specific adaptive, cognitive and behavior skills [p. 403].

This is not an easy assignment for either the child/client or therapist. It demands first that the child is *aware* of his/her fear or phobia to the extent that he/she can identify the various *motoric aspects* of the fear (i.e., what the child does when he/she is afraid), *cognitive components* (i.e., what the child thinks or says to himself/herself when afraid), *physiological components* (i.e., how the body reacts when the child is afraid, and which part(s) of his/her body is involved), and *conditions* under which s/he becomes fearful. Secondly, it demands that the child has the verbal capacity to generate with the therapist a series of incompatible self-statements and rules, which the child can incorporate, at least temporarily, into his/her verbal repertoire. And, third, it demands that the child be able to apply these self-statements and rules, under those conditions in which he/she experiences fear. Kanfer (1980) has outlined further the features of an effective self-control program, recognizing that the particular sequence listed below may differ from case to case:

1. A behavior analysis, including a description of specific problem behaviors, positive and negative reinforcers appropriate for the client's strengths and skills, and the resources in the client's environment that can be enlisted to aid the behavior change process.
2. Observation and self-monitoring of the target behavior.
3. Development of a plan for behavior change. Negotiation of a contract that includes clear specification of the goals to be achieved, the time allowed for the program, and the consequences for achieving it, as well as the methods for producing the behavior change.
4. A brief discussion with the client on the underlying assumptions and rationale of the techniques to be used.
5. Modeling and role play of the desired behaviors.
6. Frequent external verification of progress and of factors that have retarded progress, as well as feedback and reevaluation of the contract.
7. Recording and inspection of qualitative and quantitative data documenting the change. Extension of the desired behavior to many different situations or areas of life.
8. A self-reinforcement program that relies increasingly on the person's self-reactions, is sufficiently varied to avoid satiation, and is effective in changing the target behavior.
9. Execution of new behaviors by the client in his natural environment with discussion and correction of the behavior, as needed.
10. Frequent verbalization of the procedural effects, the means by which they are achieved and situations to which they can be applied in the future.
11. Continuing strong support by the helper for any activity in which the client assumes increasing responsibility for following the program accurately and extending it to other problematic behaviors.
12. Summarizing what has been learned in the change process and preparing the client to transfer the new knowledge and skills to future situations [pp. 383–384].

Additional Considerations

Before initiating a self-control approach, one basic issue that needs to be resolved has to do with the child's *motivation* for behavior change and his/her willingness to accept *responsibility* in treatment for changing his/her behavior (Kanfer, 1980; Thoresen & Mahoney 1974). The relative effectiveness of this approach more than any other therapy discussed in this chapter is tied not only to the effectiveness of the procedure and the competency of the therapist, but to the receptiveness and interest level of the child in receiving treatment and implementing it in the natural setting. Kanfer (1980) maintains that when a client is concerned about his/her behavior problem and "can anticipate improvement by its resolution," then self-control can be more easily used. Other factors that influence a client's commitment to carry out a self-control program appear in Table 5.6.

As we alluded to in the previous section, self-control is a very promising approach regarding the treatment of children's fears and phobias, but given the paucity of supportive research may not be the treatment of choice.

Table 5.6. Factors That May Influence the Commitment to Execute a Self-Control Program*

Commitment Easier	Commitment Difficult
1. Delayed Program Onset	1. Program begins immediately
2. History of pos. Rf. for promise-making	2. Past failure to keep promises was punished
3. Recent indulgence to satiation	
4. Guilt, discomfort and fear over action (aversive effects of response) is high	3. Problematic behavior is not perceived to be under client's control—"can't be helped"
5. Escape from social disapproval	
6. Presence of others making promises (modeling and social pressure)	4. Pos. Rf. for problem behavior is high
7. Behavior to be changed is private and cannot be easily checked	5. Criteria for change too high
8. Promise is vaguely phrased	6. Consequences of nonfulfillment are harsh
9. Promise-making leads to social approval or immediate benefits	7. Behavior is publicly observable
	8. Support for program planning is not anticipated

* Note: Expression of commitment does not guarantee execution of the program. Other factors, such as program requirements and reinforcement for execution in its early stages, determine fulfillment of a commitment after it is made.
Source: Kanfer, F. H. Self-management methods. In F. H. Kanfer & A. P. Goldstein (Eds.), *Helping people change.* (2nd ed.) New York: Pergamon Press, 1980. Reprinted with permission.

Supportive Research

In one of the first studies conducted in this area, Kanfer, Karoly, and New-man (1975) compared the effectiveness of two types of verbal controlling responses on the reduction of children's fear of the dark. Forty-five children, five to six years of age, participated in the study. Each child could not stay alone in the dark for more than 27 seconds. The children were assigned to one of three conditions: (1) a competence group where they heard and re-hearsed sentences emphasizing their respective competence and active con-trol in the fear situation, e.g., "I am a brave boy (girl). I can take care of myself in the dark"; (2) a stimulus group where they heard and rehearsed sentences emphasizing reducing the aversive qualities of the fear situation, e.g., "The dark is a fun place to be. There are many good things in the dark"; (3) a neutral group, where they rehearsed sentences related to *Mary Had A Little Lamb* (Kanfer et al., 1975, p. 253). Training took place in a well-lighted room, and testing took place in a dark one. Pretest and posttest measures consisted of duration of darkness and terminal light intensity (degree of illumination children needed to stay in room).

The results showed that from the pretest to first posttest period, the com-petence and stimulus groups remained in the darkened room significantly longer than the neutral group, and at the second posttest the competence group remained in the room significantly longer than either the stimulus or neutral groups, with no significant difference between the stimulus and neu-tral groups at the second posttest period. With regard to illumination, the competence group was also found to be superior to the other two groups. Kanfer et al. concluded that training effectiveness was related to the content of the learned sentences in the respective three groups. Placing an emphasis on the child's competence in dealing with the dark may be the salient com-ponent in teaching children to cope with stressful/feared situations.

In another study Graziano, Mooney, Huber, and Ignasiak (1979) used self-control instructions plus relaxation training and pleasant imagery to reduce "severe, clinical level" night fears of long duration in children. Five boys and two girls participated in the study, ranging in age from 8.7 to 12.8 years. The children came from six families. The families were seen for five weeks (two weeks for assessment and three weeks for instruction), with the parents and children seen in separate groups. The children were instructed to practice relaxation by imagining a pleasant scene and reciting "brave" self-statement each night with their parents.

A token economy program was also established where the children would receive tokens for doing their exercises at home and for going to bed and being brave throughout the night. The parents were instructed to initiate children's exercises at night and to use tokens and praise. The measures included parent ratings of the number of child fears, strength of fears, and behavioral criteria (e.g., ten consecutive fearless nights).

The results showed that it took from 3 to 19 weeks ($X = 8.7$ weeks) for all of the children to meet the behavioral criteria. Graziano et al. further report that each child's "fear strength" steadily decreased through posttreatment and the three-month, six-month, and one-year follow-up periods. Total number of fears also decreased with only one out of the seven children not completely free of fears at the one-year follow-up. Finally, both parents and children reported that the program improved the children's fear behavior and sleeping patterns. Graziano and Mooney (1980) used this treatment program with another set of families having children with "severe, highly disruptive, nighttime fears," comparing the treatment outcome with a matched no-treatment control condition. They found, in comparison with the control condition, that the treatment package was significantly effective in reducing the strength of fears in the children, as well as the frequency and duration of the fearful events. The experimental treatment children were also significantly less disruptive according to parent ratings. Thus, it appears that the training package significantly contributed to the parent ratings of improvement in their children. Follow-up information via the telephone also confirmed the effectiveness of the treatment package. At 12 months, for example, only one child in the experimental group did not meet the behavioral criteria discussed above. Follow-up data on the control group were not available, since they began receiving the treatment package after the experimental group completed their posttest.

In another variation on the self-control approach, Peterson and Shigetomi (1981) conducted a study with children who were to receive elective tonsillectomies. The 66 children (35 girls and 31 boys) ages 2.5 to 10.5 years ($X = 5.47$ years), were assigned to one of four conditions; (1) preoperative information, where children were invited to a "party" four days before their surgery and informed via a story and a puppet of the "typical hospital stay from admission to discharge," (2) coping procedures, where children received the preoperative information plus cue-controlled muscle relaxation (using the cue "calm"); (3) distracting mental imagery training (imagining a scene that was "quiet and made them feel happy") and comforting self-talk (the children, for example, were encouraged to think of the phrase "I will be all better in a little while); (4) filmed modeling, where the children received the preoperative information plus Melamed and Siegel's (1975) film, *Ethan Has an Operation* (discussed on pp. 199–200 of this chapter); and, (5) coping plus filmed modeling, where the children were also given a 15-minute hospital tour and spent another 15 to 20 minutes eating ice cream and cookies following the tour. Six categories of dependent measures were used, encompassing the triple mode response system notion discussed in Chapter 3.

The results showed that children receiving the two coping conditions experienced less distress during their hospital stay than the children in the modeling only or information only groups. Furthermore, children receiving the coping plus modeling procedure were more calm and cooperative during invasive procedures than the coping or modeling alone conditions. In a subsequent study, Siegel and Peterson (1981) conducted similar research with children undergoing dental treatment. They compared the coping skills condition described above with a sensory information condition (i.e., children were told what to expect and heard audio tape recordings of the dental equipment) and a no-treatment/attention condition. The results showed that there was no significant difference between the coping and sensory information conditions on any of the measures taken during or after restorative treatment, and that both treatment groups fared better on the measures than the no-treatment control children.

Commentary.   Given the paucity and conflicting nature of the research in this area, we feel that no definitive statements can be made at this point on the merits of a self-control approach in reducing children's fears and phobias. The area is a burgeoning one in need of additional well-controlled research like that of the Kanfer et al. (1975) study described above to determine first if a "pure" self-control approach is viable with fearful children and under what conditions and with which types of fears. If this approach is not shown to be a viable procedure, it seems that researchers should next do what Graziano and Mooney (1980), Peterson and Shigetomi (1981), and Siegel and Peterson (1981) have done—namely, add other procedures like contingency management, relaxation, and imagery procedures to the basic self-control approach in a systematic fashion to see if they effect behavior change.

SUMMARY AND CONCLUSIONS

In this chapter, we have reviewed three major behavior therapy methods of fear reduction in children: contingency management, modeling, and self-control therapies. In addition, variants of each of these models were discussed as well as the research supporting the relative effectiveness of these methods. Discussions concerning the use of each method with clinical populations and procedural considerations were also presented.

The least researched method involves the use of self-control, while the most researched method involves modeling. The method having the most case examples, and fewest controlled research studies is the contingency management approach. Interestingly, these methods have been used to some extent with different children's fears and phobias. For example, the contingency management literature has centered mainly on the treatment of school phobia, selective mutism, and social withdrawal, while the modeling literature has emphasized the treatment of animal fears, impending dental and surgical intervention, and social withdrawal. At this point it is too early to discern any direction in the self-control literature, although of the five studies published three were concerned with nighttime/dark fears and two with impending dental or surgical work.

As with the two other behavior therapy methods discussed in Chapter 4 (systematic desensitization and the flooding therapies), major empirical questions are still present regarding these three procedures. First, researchers have not yet substantially verified the relative effectiveness of most of these procedures in a controlled experimental fashion, with either nonclinical or clinically-relevant fears. Secondly, few researchers studying these methods have been concerned with assessing therapy outcome using the triple mode response system. The only fear reduction studies that have incorporated on more than a few occasions the triple mode response system into controlled clinical and laboratory research are those involving symbolic modeling. For example, Bandura and his colleagues examined the use of this procedure with primarily nonclinical fears (snakes or dogs), while Melamed and her colleagues studied the application of this method with children who primarily have transitory and highly situationally specific clinical fears.

A third question that has not yet been answered involves identifying those conditions under which the treatments are effective—for example, which procedures are effective for which age groups, for which fears and phobias, with which type of therapist, in which type of setting(s)? A fourth question has to do with the cost-efficient nature of treatment. For example, how realistic is it for a therapist living in Chicago to purchase videotape equipment and videotapes and then go out and make a modeling tape for a child who became tearful on a recent vacation while walking in the desert? Or, how cost-efficient is it for a therapist to purchase videotape equipment and a "canned" videotape on hospital operations and surgical procedures when he/she may only see one or two children per year who have this problem?

Finally, the vast majority of the supportive case studies and experiments reviewed in this chapter have involved working with a child who has a single phobia. Most therapists realize very quickly, however, that it is the *rare* child that they see in their practice or in a school setting who only has one fear or phobia. The question then arises as to the applicability or external validity of these research findings to clinical practice. Independent of these comments, however, some very active research is being conducted on these three methods, and each appear to be very promising fear reduction methods.

NOTES

1. For discussion purposes, we are considering the term "positive reinforcement" ("reinforcer") to be synonomous with "reinforcement" ("reinforcer").
2. The problem with treating both social withdrawal and selective mutism is that the clinician or the teacher may not be able to discern whether these two behaviors are, for example, fear-related problems (i.e., fear of interacting with peers and fear of speaking in non-family settings and/or to strangers), behavioral deficits, or non-compliant or oppositional behaviors. It would seem that *before* a fear reduction treatment regimen is initiated, the therapist should decide during the assessment period (see Chapter 3) in which of these response categories the target child's behavior falls. A behavior that falls into the behavioral deficit or noncompliant category may necessitate a different treatment approach than one that is construed as a fear or fear related behavior. The interested reader is also referred to Kratochwill (1981) for a more complete discussion of the selective mutism literature and to Conger and Keane (1981) for a review of the social withdrawal literature.
3. This variation by Ayllon et al. in the use of positive reinforcement represents an excellent description of a contingency management account of the treatment of school phobia. We therefore review this study in detail.

CHAPTER 6

Methodological and
Assessment Considerations

In previous chapters we have provided an overview of various behavioral approaches to the assessment and treatment of fears and phobias in children. A major issue that confronts anyone reading the available literature is whether the various behavior therapies achieve any success with childhood fears and related problems. That is, is the child who is troubled by fears and phobias likely to benefit from any of the various forms of therapy recommended or employed for fears and phobias? Pertinent to answering this question is a subset of conceptually related issues. First, will a particular treatment be better than the normal developmental course of the problem given no intervention? That is, would the child improve as rapidly if simply left alone? Some of the information reviewed in Chapters 1 and 2 suggests that some fears are a normal part of childhood development. Second, given that some form of psychological intervention is employed, are the improvements greater than those that would be produced by such effects as human characteristics, "placebo effects," or suggestion? This question is designed to address the issue of whether or not there are any active "ingredients" in the psychological interventions over and above the aforementioned therapeutic characteristics. Third, once a psychological intervention is implemented for various fears and phobias, what is the occurrence of spontaneous remissions? This question focuses on the reappearance of the problem once successful treatment has been established and terminated.

After reviewing the different forms of behavior therapy that have focused on childhood fears and phobias the question has frequently arisen as to whether one form of therapy is more effective than another. This issue of the relative efficacy of various therapies was in part prompted by Eysenck's (1952) classic paper on the effects of psychotherapy and has pervaded psychologic and psychiatric literature (cf. Rachman & Wilson, 1980). Indeed, there has been growing interest in comparing behavior therapy with traditional or verbal psychotherapies (see Kazdin & Wilson, 1978). Comparative outcome studies typically involve the analysis of two or more therapies to determine if one is better than the other.

Comparative outcome research, however, has some conceptual problems and may be based on questionable assumptions. Unfortunately, the relatively heavy emphasis on comparative outcome research may lead to problems in generating knowledge in an area of research. Several reasons for reducing an emphasis on comparative outcome research can be advanced (Rachman & Wilson, 1980). First of all, comparative outcome research might not be the place to initiate investigation. Comparative outcome studies (both short and long term) should usually be preceded by clinical observation and basic laboratory studies (Agras & Berkowitz, 1980). A second problem is that many comparative outcome studies in the area of children's fears and phobias have been flawed methodologically.

The literature on assessment and treatment of fears and phobias in children raises a number of methodological and conceptual issues elaborated in this chapter. These methodological and conceptual issues have important implications for both treatment and future research in the area. Generally, there are a large number of methodological and conceptual concerns that can be raised across all the therapeutic techniques reviewed in previous chapters. This chapter provides a general overview of various concerns raised in the evaluation of therapeutic interventions (e.g., Bergin & Suinn, 1975; Gaines-Schwartz, Hadley, & Strupp, 1978; Kazdin & Wilson, 1978; Rachman & Wilson, 1980; Garfield & Bergin, 1978).

The growing number of methodological and conceptual issues in therapy research have provided serious challenges to the existing treatment reports in the fear and phobia literature. More importantly, however, these issues have provided a number of directions for future empirical work in the field. In the following sections we review some major methodological and conceptual issues, including definitional concerns, criteria for evaluation of outcomes, experimental and therapeutic criteria, client-related criteria, efficiency and cost-related criteria, criteria for generalization and follow-up, and procedures for programming generalization.

DEFINITION OF FEARS, PHOBIAS, AND ANXIETIES

The Nature of the Problem

Issues involved in the definition of fears and related problems were discussed in Chapter 2. We noted that a three-mode or channel approach to assessment should be used to operationalize the definition of the problem encountered by the clinician. Generally, the same approach can be used for clinical research in the area.

Increasingly researchers within the behavioral model have recommended a three-mode approach to diagnosis, assessment, and treatment of fears, phobias, and related problems. Yet a number of considerations can be advanced that emerge as problematic within the behavioral approach. Little clinical research in this area has used the three-mode approach to assessment as our review of the literature demonstrates. One possible reason for this is that there are different approaches/models of behavior therapy and individuals working within these different positions emphasize different aspects of data in assessment. As noted in Chapters 4 and 5, behavior therapy is characterized by operant or applied behavior analysis, mediational S-R, cognitive, and social learning conceptualizations. Researchers using diverse therapeutic approaches (e.g., modeling, reinforcement, desensitization) focus on somewhat different aspects of behavior for fears, phobias, and related problems. For example, individuals operating from an operant paradigm tend to focus on specific behaviors and the environmental consequences that affect these operations. In this regard, a major focus of therapeutic efforts is to increase or decrease behavior, initially through various principles of reinforcement (cf. Mavissakalian & Barlow, 1981). For example, a number of studies reviewed in Chapter 5 have shown that positive reinforcement can be employed to increase approach behaviors in children identified as fearful, phobic, or anxious (e.g., Ayllon, Smith, & Rogers, 1970; Leitenberg & Callahan, 1973; Patterson, 1965; Vaal, 1973).

Interestingly, operant researchers have tended to avoid even the traditional terminology in this area, preferring to use labels such as approach behaviors, avoidance behaviors, behavior deficit, and behavior excess in treatment of child problems. For example, Gelfand (1979) entitled a chapter "Behavioral Treatment of Avoidance, Social Withdrawal and Negative Emotional States," which reflects this more operant perspective. An examination of the *Journal of Applied Behavior Analysis* (*JABA*) over its first 13 years of publication contains few studies focusing on "fear," "phobia," or "anxiety" in children as reflected in the title of the articles. The exception appeared in the Fall, 1981 issue with an article by Matson (1981). Yet, a number of studies which appeared in *JABA* during this time (e.g., Stokes & Kennedy, 1980) could easily be regarded as focusing on these types of problems. For example, Stokes and Kennedy (1980) reduced child "uncooperative behavior" during dental treatment through modeling and reinforcement. An examination of their study shows that their measurement system focused on both behavioral (motor) and self-report (child statements) that could be used to define a fear or anxiety. As a case in point, uncooperative behavior in the verbalization category was defined as follows:

child cried, complained, or moaned about dental procedures, the dental setting, or pain, e.g., "I don't like the needle," "Will it take long?" [p. 44].

Thus, many operant researchers have expressed a preference for direct measures of overt behaviors, and some have avoided traditional labels in this area. In part, this has been due to the avoidance of constructs that the terms "fear," "phobia," and "anxiety" sometimes imply. The issue of the use of different channels or response modes has been captured by Cone (1979) who noted that the question is:

> whether behavioral assessors should be talking about modes or channels at all. The "behavior as sign" implications of such terminology are discomforting and seem to be an unnecessary holdover from the old days of measuring traits and constructs. Does it make sense to speak of three modes of expressing a single emotion, especially in view of the ambiguity surrounding even the definition of such emotions? Have not behavioral assessors eschewed traits, constructs, and global terms in favor of specific responses? And, have not they done so in reaction to the limited evidence forthcoming for the generality of traits despite years of searching? To speak of modes and channels seems to beg the very question that so-called "triple response mode assessment" is seeking to answer [p. 87].

Other approaches within the behavioral camp consider a wider range of behaviors, as is the case in the mediational S-R model, social learning theory, and cognitive behavior modification. For example, in the mediational S-R approach, intervening variables and hypothetical constructs have played a major role. Illustrative is the two-factor theory of Mowrer (1939) discussed in Chapter 1.

Even with the diversity within behavioral models, some authors have noted that they are not sufficient to explain phobias (e.g., Graziano et al., 1979). Mavissakalian and Barlow (1981) noted that the necessary ingredient of a useful treatment for phobias is exposure, but little controlled empirical work has occurred with children having clinically relevant fears or phobias. Especially lacking in behavioral models are (1) the role of cognitions in the origin, maintenance, and reduction of fears and related problems, and (2) the influence of developmental issues (Graziano et al., 1979).

Recommendations.   The terms fear, phobia, and anxiety have been used in a variety of ways both across and within various therapeutic models. Yet we believe that a major goal of any definition of a problem should be stated within the context of the frequency, intensity, duration, and social and developmental appropriateness of the behavior. These data should be gathered across a number of different stimulus situations in which the child functions (e.g., home, school, community, etc.). Such measurement should further focus on direct samples of behavior, subjective self-report of stress, and psychophysiological measures where possible. We are aware that there are problems with the three-mode response assessment approach, but at this stage of knowledge in this area we would strongly support its use in future treatment/research activities. Some of the problems with its use and some corresponding recommendations are noted below.

Therapeutic Outcome Measures

A major concern that can be raised in the research on fears and phobias in children relates to the methodological criteria for measuring therapeutic outcome. The use of traditional test or outcome measures is a case in point. There is growing evidence to suggest that both traditional tests and global ratings are quite misleading in assessment of therapeutic outcomes (e.g., Kazdin, 1980e; Kazdin & Wilson, 1978; Mischel, 1968, 1973; Peterson, 1968). As noted in Chapter 3, many traditional assessment procedures lack the reliability and validity necessary to qualify as sound measurement instruments. Such devices are also subject to a number of sources of bias and artifact (Anastasi, 1976). Also, such procedures as objective and projective tests depend heavily on verbal abilities of the child. Perhaps their major limitation is the lack of a firm relationship with direct measures of behavior (Kazdin, 1980).

Several specific limitations of global ratings can also be identified (Kazdin, 1980):

1. It is not clear what global ratings actually measure since criteria for completing the ratings are frequently absent.

2. Based on the lack of criteria for completing the ratings, it is possible that the meaning attached to the rating may change over time independent of the client's characteristics.

3. Global ratings make it difficult to make comparisons across different studies.

4. Global ratings lack sensitivity in the type of questions they ask (e.g., "how fearful is this child?").

5. Global ratings are quite susceptible to various sources of bias [pp. 224–227].

Another problem with both traditional tests and many global ratings is that they do not easily lend themselves to ongoing repeated measurement over various phases of the study (Kratochwill, 1978). This is problematic since it is important to know the effect of the treatment in a relatively continuous fashion.

Specific Recommendations.   Several specific recommendations can be advanced that have utility in improving clinical research in the area of children's fears and related problems. This area is exceedingly complex and it is important to emphasize that no one outcome measure may adequately reflect the nature of these problems. Yet we recommend *direct measurement* as the preferred strategy for therapeutic outcome evaluations. Direct measures refer to the use of such assessment strategies as self-monitoring and direct observation across the three-response channels (Cone, 1978). Generally, the direct measurement strategy is supportable from the considerable research suggesting that a client is best understood by determining what he/she does, thinks, or feels in various situations (Mischel, 1973). Indeed, the tactic of using direct measures of behavior would avoid many of the past validity problems in psychotherapy research. Fiske (1979) noted:

> Investigators interested in understanding behaviors can directly observe their phenomena: these investigators are trying to understand the rapidly changing events they see before them. In contrast, those studying characteristics of people cannot observe these characteristics directly, but only as reported by some observer. These investigators postulate that persons possess various characteristics in some degree and then try to assess the degree. Since they assume their data are indicants of the unobserved characteristics, they must confront the problems of estimating the characteristics from undependable data that are affected by the individual observer and by various aspects of the method used to elicit the observer's report. The poor reliability of such data imposes a low ceiling on their maximum possible validity [p. 37].

Such direct measurement strategies have also been recommended after reviewing the general psychotherapeutic research literature (e.g., Kazdin & Wilson, 1978) and the specific literature on treatment of adult phobias (Agras & Jacob, 1981).

Another major rationale for the use of direct measures is to facilitate comparisons across different studies. For example, Ayllon et al. (1970) used direct measures of the number of hours in school and the percentage of voluntary attendance, among other measures, in their study of "school phobia." Such direct measures reduce much of the subjective bias and other problems associated with traditional tests and clinical ratings.

Aside from this advantage, direct measures are typically less affected by the various methodological problems than many traditional outcome measures. This is not to suggest that direct measures are free from various methodological problems. Indeed, as we noted in Chapter 3, the researcher must take into account a variety of factors when such measures are used (e.g., Kazdin, 1977a, 1980e; Kent & Foster, 1977; Kratochwill, 1982).

A second recommendation is that direct measurement procedures should be continuous whenever possible (Hersen & Barlow, 1976; Kratochwill, 1978). The use of repeated measurement over various phases of the study has the advantage of showing trends in the data generated. When problems in treatment emerge, the researcher is able to modify therapeutic procedures to improve client functioning. Our review of the clinical literature suggests that repeated measurement is not a common characteristic across studies, although many of the time series studies do use this strategy.

Many direct measurement strategies can be employed in clinical research, and we have reviewed a large number of these in Chapter 3. Particularly useful are those that involve direct observation of behavior (e.g., Ciminero et al., 1977; Cone & Hawkins, 1977; Goldfried & Davidson, 1976; Haynes & Wilson, 1979; Hersen & Barlow, 1976; Kazdin, 1980e), those sometimes regarded as analogue (e.g., Haynes & Wilson, 1979; Nay, 1977; McFall, 1977a; Haynes, 1978), self-monitoring (e.g., Nelson, 1977), and psychophysiological measures (e.g., Hersen & Barlow, 1976; Kallman & Feuerstein, 1977).

Use of such direct measures as those noted above has the important potential to provide the most useful strategy to establish the differential efficacy among various therapeutic techniques (Kazdin & Wilson, 1978). In the past, research on clinical fears and phobias in children using global ratings has obscured the treatment outcome differences in various studies.

A third recommendation relates to the use of at least three measures in therapeutic research. There appears to be adequate justification on both theoretical and methodological grounds that researchers should use measures of avoidance behavior, physiological arousal, and self-report of stress, anxiety, and related cognitions. Such a perspective is based on the assumption that no single measurement system is inherently valid (cf. Campbell & Fiske, 1959; Kazdin & Wilson, 1978). The focus on the three response systems has important implications for therapeutic research in that the effects of a particular intervention may be specific to a certain channel or mode (Barlow & Mavissakalian, 1981). Moreover, generalization of the treatment from one mode to the other may occur and should be documented. The conceptualization of outcome measures in the three modes or channels can help elucidate the degree of external validity of therapeutic research (e.g., Cook & Campbell, 1976; Kratochwill, 1979).

Because the issue of three-mode response assessment is a prime issue in research on childhood fears and related problems, we discuss some of the specific methodological issues in this area in more detail below.

Triple Response Mode Assessment: Patterns of Desynchrony

A rather large number of research and theoretical papers have addressed the issue of measuring fears and related emotions in therapeutic research (e.g., Barlow & Mavissakalian, 1981; Cone, 1979; Hersen, 1973; Hersen & Barlow, 1976; Hodgson & Rachman, 1974; Hugdahl, 1981; Kozak & Miller, 1982; Lang, 1968, 1977; Mills, Agras, Barlow, & Mills, 1973; Rachman & Hodson, 1974; Skinner, 1975). Numerous problems have been raised with this form of assessment. For example, Cone (1979) noted three different problem areas including (1) the lack of consensus as to what is meant by the "modes," (2) the relevance of the mode conceptualization, and (3) problems in research using modes in measuring outcomes.

Characterization of the Three Systems.   One major issue in use of the three system conceptualization is the fact that authors define the modes differently (e.g., Craighead, Kazdin, & Mahoney, 1976; Lang, 1971; Paul & Bernstein, 1976; Staats, 1975). Although Lang (1968, 1978a) directed researchers away from a total reliance on personal experience in fear assessment, the equating of fear as a *response* has possibly deprived the term "fear" of the status of a hypothetical construct (Kozak & Miller, 1982). As Kozak and Miller (1982) note:

> . . . the three-systems view deprives the term "fear" of the logical status of a hypothetical construct by failing to distinguish data and construct. This identification of data with the construct inferred from these data creates a serious practical difficulty for the assessor: one cannot specify principles of inference to bridge the gap between the data and the fear construct. In other words, given a particular set of data, we cannot know how or when to conclude that a person is afraid [p. 348].

Another problem in this area relates to different interpretations of the categories. This has been especially evident in the "cognitive" "verbal" or "self-report" mode. Whereas Paul and Bernstein (1976) refer to the self-report channel, indicating that it is "a response system under direct voluntary control" used to report experience or other behaviors, Lang (1977a) refers to a language system and describes three primary functions that language can serve in emotion: expressive, perceptual, and control. Other examples of different uses have emerged with Borkovec (1976) including unobserved cognitive activity, and Melamed and Siegel (1975) equating observed verbal behavior with unobserved cognitive activity.

The difficulties are not limited to client self-report, but can also occur within the motor and psychophysiological modes. Fears, phobias, and related problems in children have been measured along a limited number of dimensions. Aside from the relatively few numbers of studies using the three response channels, a rather limited range of measures have been used *within* the modes or channels. A major problem is that researchers may still want to focus on *three* measures, rather than considering that there are a number of measures within each category (Kozak & Miller, 1982). A behavioral avoidance measure in a clinic setting may not correspond to a direct measure of approach behavior in the natural environment. Likewise, different psychophysiological measures (e.g., heart rate, GSR) may not correspond. Van Hasselt et al. (1979) found that except for the heart rate change scores on the ladder climb, physiological indices of fear (i.e., heart rate and finger pulse volume) did not respond with introduction of the treatment. The authors speculated that the client might have shown physiological arousal in noncardiac response channels (e.g., skin resistance, muscle tension). Nevertheless, despite the number of measures that could be employed, few studies have employed multiple measures.

Use of Hypothetical Constructs.   Many recent advances in the assessment of fears and phobias have occurred in the behavioral literature. Individuals in this area have tended to avoid constructs sometimes associated with the three-mode response assessment (Cone, 1979). As noted by Kozak and Miller (1982), the three-mode respond system has frequently resulted in a methodological strategy rather than a definition. Yet, deciding if a child is anxious, fearful, or phobic is still problematic since the question of what observations under what conditions allow one to conclude that the child is experiencing these emotions is still unknown. As the authors note, "One finds *relevant* characteristics described in the three-systems approach, but one finds no *defining* characteristics" (Kozak & Miller, 1982). As an alternative Kozak and Miller (1982) propose that fear be viewed as a hypothetical construct referring to and describing a particular kind of functional state. In this approach, cognitive events are inferred from verbal and other behavior. Fear would then be recognized by varied response patterns in varied situations. The authors preserve

> the original three-systems notion as a methodological approach to fear assessment but removes from it the burden of defining fear, which, we have argued, it has not carried well. We would not claim, as have a number of writers, that fear is merely a response, nothing more than a constellation of observed data; rather that observed responses can evidence fear, which has hypothetical construct status. We are not yet persuaded of the need to exorcise unobserved events, such as fear, cognition, or even experience, from a scientific psychology. Rather, we reiterate Lang's caveat about the fallacy of treating private events as primary data and advocate clear distinctions between data and psychological constructs bearing on hypothesized events. The propriety of an inference, at a given point in time for a particular organism, would depend on the configuration of observed organismic events. In this case, three-systems data, broadly sampled, would undergrid the inference of fear as a characteristic of psychological functioning [pp. 356–357].

This approach has three implications. First, it appears to help resolve a conflict between adherence to observed data and the explanation of a mediational hypothesis in accounting for fear. A major advantage here is that cognitive processes may be employed to account for observed phenomena. Attempts to specify a relationship between various terms employed in this area could begin.

In addition to this possible benefit, the focus on multiple measurement and fear as a construct may facilitate a broader approach to therapeutic outcome across the various behavioral models reviewed in this text. The three system model may be useful for individually tailoring methods for treatment (Hugdahl, 1981). Such a perspective would also expand the stereotypic behavioral position as focusing only on observable behavior and accompanying downplay of subjective personal experience (Kazdin & Wilson, 1978).

Ultimately, however, the merits of this approach will be determined by research focused on the issue. For example, the relative status of each response system as an index of fear and emotion will still have to be empirically addressed, independent of whether a hypothetical construct approach is adopted.

Methodological Considerations. As noted above, research directed at the relationships among the three response systems is needed. This is usually accomplished by examining the correlational relationships among the content areas. Yet, when this is done, researchers must be careful not to vary both the method of assessment and content area when computing correlations (Cone, 1979). For example, an error would occur when self-report of cognitive content (e.g., a child states that he/she is afraid) is correlated with direct observations of motor and physiological contents (e.g., child's approach behavior or heart rate).

Consider the situation in which a researcher is interested in the relationships among various motoric responses in children who are afraid to go to school. In order to demonstrate that the relationships are not the result of a common measuring method, the same behaviors would be assessed differently. If the two motoric behaviors were trembling and approach toward school, self-report rating measures could also be employed (e.g., "I tremble when approaching school," "I am able to walk toward school"). Assuming that the children could be observed for both behaviors and that the self-report measures could be administered concurrently, the two content areas could be analyzed in a multimethod-multibehavior matrix. The researcher would then be able to represent the correlations between behaviors within and across methods.

In this strategy of assessing self-report and direct observation only the *method* has changed. Thus, the same specific behaviors within the content area were measured by two different measures. Such a methodological strategy represents a contrast to procedures in which self-report measures of cognitive content (fear of school) are correlated with direct observation measures in the presence of the school facility. In such a case, the self-report strategy requires the client to provide information on internal feelings around school, whereas the direct observation assesses motoric approach behavior. As Cone (1979) notes:

> Failure to find relationships among the measures may be due to content differences, method differences, or to content-method interactions. The investigator

is faced with ignoring the multitrait-multimethod implications of the data and interpreting resulting heterotrait-homomethod correlations as though relationships "really" existed, or he/she can conclude that different ways of measuring snake phobias lead to different types of data which are unrelated. Either conclusion would be unwarranted from the analysis, yet both are common enough in the literature [p. 89].

An important methodological implication raised by Cone (1979) from this strategy is that the common conclusion that response systems are independent may be premature. To help sort out some of these possible problems, Cone (1979) proposed that a third dimension be added to the analysis. This dimension would include a multicontent-multimethod-multibehavior (MC-MM-MB) matrix which represents correlations that could be computed where at least two behaviors in each of at least two content areas are assessed by at least two different methods. Although it is beyond the scope of the current presentation to review the intricacies of this approach, several considerations can be advanced in the context of this strategy. First, the addition of the content dimension allows the unconfounding of the relationships among the three major systems referred to above. Second, the use of the MC-MM-MB matrices is premised on a large enough sample size to establish reliability assumptions of the approach because measures would have to be established on groups of clients with certain specified disorders. Yet, specific measures across the content disorders may be unique to certain clients based on environmental characteristics, among others. In some respects, this is a matter of generalization of these measures across these characteristics.

ANALOGUE AND CLINICAL RESEARCH

Many different classes of research strategies have been employed in the evaluation and treatment of childhood fears and phobias. Usually a distinction has been made between analogue and clinical research in psychotherapy. Much research in the area of children's fears and phobias might be regarded as analogue in that it is conducted under conditions analogous to those in a clinical setting (clinic, home, or school). As an example of research that might be regarded as analogue, consider the study conducted by Leitenberg and Callahan (1973) on children who were afraid of the dark (see Chapter 5). In the study 14 preschool children who refused to sleep unless a light was on in (or near) their room were selected as subjects. It should again be emphasized that the childrens' parents had not requested help for the problem, but rather had agreed to participate in the experiment after a questionnaire had been circulated in nursery schools and kindergartens. The authors found that following eight sessions, children in the treatment condition were able to remain in a dark laboratory room significantly longer than a matched control group.

Concerns have been raised over this type of analogue research for clinical treatment. Ross (1981), for example, noted that while the "rigor" in such studies may be high, the relevance for clinical treatment is low. Thus, the Leitenberg and Callahan (1973) study might be faulted for not using a population that typically seeks help from professionals for a severe fear. Also, the authors did not provide data on whether the children were able to sleep in their bedrooms with the lights out.

In contrast to this study, we reviewed many studies in which a child was referred for a rather severe fear or phobia and treated by a therapist in the setting in which the problem occurred (e.g., Ayllon et al., 1970; Kirby & Toler, 1970; Luiselli, 1977; Simkins, 1971; Voal, 1973; Wayne, 1979; White & Davis, 1974). Research of this type has typically been referred to as clinical because it is focused on a clinical problem in a clinical setting.

A major issue that has been raised over the research conducted in applied and therapeutic areas of psychology is that it is too analogue and does not generalize to clinical treatment. Yet where research is conceptualized as either analogue or nonanalogue, the generalization problem may be obscured in at least two ways (Kazdin, 1980e). First of all, the distinction overlooks the "analogue" nature of all research, even that conducted in the "clinical" setting. Second, the typical dichotomy does not provide guidelines for distinguishing among types of analogue studies. Kazdin (1980e) notes: *"Virtually all psychological experimentation with human subjects is analogue research insofar as it constructs a situation in which a particular phenomenon can be studied"* [p. 112]. Thus, evaluating the effects of certain treatments through the various assessment procedures is typically removed from the phenomenon to which the therapist wishes to generalize. Also, the participation of subjects in an experiment introduces various influences (e.g., bias, demand characteristics) that make the situation only an analogue of the setting to which the therapist might wish to generalize. This view of research has implications for the work on children's fears and phobias.

> Viewing almost all psychological research with humans as analogues of situations to which one would like to generalize has important implications for conceptualizing treatment research. To begin with, it is essential to keep in mind that investigators invariably are interested in extrapolating the findings to some area, problem, or setting that itself is not studied directly. There is always the possibility that the extrapolation does not apply to the natural phenomenon. The difference between the natural and experimental situation precisely along those (usually unknown) dimensions might lead to different findings for a given variable. A second implication is that it may not be useful to speak of analogue versus nonanalogue research. Rather, research can be viewed on the basis of the extent to which it resembles the situation to which one wishes to generalize the experimental findings [Kazdin, 1980e, pp. 112–113].

In order to conceptualize the dimensions from which results might be generalized, Kazdin (1980e) suggested a continuum for this activity. Table 6.1 shows some dimensions along which studies may vary and the degree of resemblance to the clinical situation across each dimension. Each dimension is described within the context of the childhood fear and phobia area.

Target Problem.   As noted in Chapter 2, the recurring issue in the literature on childhood fears is the severity of the problem. Unfortunately we do not know a lot about childhood fears of high intensity, long duration, and highly disturbing content (Graziano et al., 1979). Given some of the incidence data on clinical fears that meet the above criteria (e.g., Rutter, Tizard, & Whitmore, 1970) very few children have had severe fears. Our review of the literature suggests that few studies have actually been conducted on clinical fears. In addition to the Leitenberg and Callahan (1973) study mentioned above, other studies attempting to eliminate fear of the dark have even eliminated subjects who displayed intense fear reactions. Yet, such children who were eliminated are those typically dealt with in clinical practice (Ross, 1981). The point is that such problems may have little generality to clinical settings, and the type of problem studied may have little resemblance to clinical settings.

Clients.   Various characteristics of the clients used in research can contribute to the degree to which the results generalize to the clinical situation. The population dimension as conceived refers to a variety of factors (e.g., age, sex, SEC, etc.) that differ between the experiment and the clinical setting. As Kazdin (1980e) notes, the generality of a particular study to the clinical situation may depend on the characteristics of the clients in the two domains.

Manner of Recruitment.   The manner in which the clients for a study are recruited may have an important bearing on generalization from the study to the clinical setting. For example, a number of studies (e.g., Bandura, Grusec, & Menlove, 1967; Bandura & Menlove, 1968; Kanfer, Karoly, & Newman, 1975; Leitenberg & Callahan, 1973; Melamed & Siegel, 1975; Ritter, 1968) made active attempts to recruit subjects for the experiment. Leitenberg and Callahan (1973) circulated a questionnaire in various settings asking parents to participate. Presumably, the contingencies operating with subjects who are recruited may be different from those who actively seek out treatment. For example, solicited subjects might be paid to participate and even fined for dropping out of therapy. This typically contrasts with clients who have severe problems and who may pay to receive treatment and make decisions on when to terminate treatment.

Therapists.   Our review of the child fear and phobia literature suggests that some studies have not used trained therapists to implement the interventions

Table 6.1. Select Dimensions Along Which Studies May Vary and the Degree of Resemblance to the Clinical Situation Across Each Dimension

Dimension	RESEMBLANCE TO THE CLINICAL OR NONRESEARCH SITUATION		
	Identity with or Great Resemblance	Moderate Resemblance	Relatively Low Resemblance
Target problem	Problem seen in the clinic, intense or disabling	Similar to that in clinic but less severe	Nonproblem behavior or experimental task
Population	Clients in outpatient treatment	College students with nontreatment interest	Infrahuman subjects
Manner of recruitment	Clients who seek treatment	Individuals recruited for available treatment	Captive subjects who serve for course credit
Therapists	Professional therapists	Therapists in training	Nontherapists or nonprofessionals
Client set	Expect treatment and improvement	Expect "experimental" treatment with unclear effects	Expect experiment with nontreatment focus
Selection of treatment	Client chooses therapist and specific treatment	Client given choice over few alternative procedures in an experiment	Client assigned to treatment with no choice for specific therapist or condition
Setting of treatment	Professional treatment facility	University facility that may not regularly offer treatment	Laboratory setting
Variation of treatment	Treatment as usually conducted	Variation to standardize treatment for research	Analogue of the treatment as in infrahuman equivalent of treatment
Assessment methods	Direct unobtrusive measure of the problem that the client originally reported	Assessment on psychological devices that sample behaviors of interest directly	Questionnaire responses about the behaviors that are a problem

Source: Kazdin, A. E. *Research design in clinical psychology*. New York: Harper & Row, 1980. Reprinted with permission.

(e.g., Ayllon et al., 1970; Neisworth, Madle, & Goeke, 1975; Stableford, 1979). In the vast majority of studies, trained psychotherapists have been employed but this does not mean that they are a homogeneous group who apply treatments in the same manner. Therapists differ across many different dimensions even though they might administer the same treatment. Such factors as expectations for treatment effectiveness and commitment to client change may vary considerably from the experiment to the clinical setting (Kazdin, 1980e). In addition, several variables have an important bearing on therapist effectiveness and the outcome of therapy. These include therapist warmth, expertise, attractiveness, and status (Goldfried & Davidson, 1976; Goldstein, 1971, 1980; Morris & Suckerman, 1974a, 1974b; Morris & Magrath, 1979). Another consideration is that therapists in various applied settings typically become somewhat eclectic in their therapeutic approaches, thereby deviating from a pure form of therapy. Such factors clearly limit the degree of generalization from the experiment to the clinical setting.

Set, Selection, and Setting of Treatment.   The set that the client has when participating in therapy is likely to be quite different than the subject participating in therapeutic research. Usually the client comes to therapy expecting to be cured. The experimental subject may be paid for participating or even informed that the treatment may not work. Also, the client usually seeks treatment from a particular therapist (through previous contact or recommendations from friends), whereas the experimental subject does not usually have this choice. Finally, the client setting might be a comfortable office or clinic, while the experimental subject participating in therapeutic research may receive the treatment in a research setting (e.g., experimental lab).

Variation of Treatment.   In many research studies, particularly in between-group studies, subjects receive a relatively standardized intervention. Yet, in clinical research, and usually in single case studies, the treatment is individualized for the client. Variations in clinical research are usually made to maximize therapeutic change. The manner in which results generalize will differ as variations in the treatment are conducted.

Assessment Methods.   The degree to which results of a study generalize is based, in part, on the type of assessment method employed. Even though measures may be taken in self-report, behavioral, and physiological areas, the measures may not reflect the problem in the situation that it usually occurs. Moreover, the setting in which the assessment is taken usually influences the results (Kazdin, 1979b). These factors make generalizations from laboratory studies to clinical studies somewhat tenuous.

Considerations.   As is apparent in the studies reviewed in this text, there is an analogue character in all of them. The several dimensions along which therapy studies can vary allow us to perceive both advantages and limitations in the existing literature. First of all, analogue studies can help investigators conduct research on therapeutic variables that might otherwise be impossible to investigate in clinical settings. As Kazdin (1981) has noted:

> The priority of analogue research is the experimental question rather than treatment delivery. Thus, conditions can be arranged in ways that usually would not be feasible in clinical settings. Because of obstacles of clinical research, much of what is known about therapeutic processes and behavior changes is learned from analogue studies. Analogue research provides opportunities to evaluate mechanisms of therapeutic change and to dismantle treatment by looking at basic elements and their contribution to outcome. The ability to control multiple conditions of the experiment and consequently to minimize variability in the data permit analogue research to evaluate questions that would otherwise be difficult to study [p. 34].

Although there are clear merits to analogue studies, a treatment literature based only on this type of work is unlikely to be of great clinical utility or is what Ross (1981) has called "relevance-low" to clinical practice. Most of all the generalizations that can be made from analogue studies to the clinical setting are limited. Nevertheless, the degree of generalization that can be made from analogue studies is a matter of empirical evidence of which there is very little (Kazdin, 1981e).

Research Design

As is evident from reading Chapters 4 and 5 in this text, many different research procedures have been employed to evaluate the therapeutic programs implemented for children's fears, phobias, and related problems. Several specific methods have been employed including case studies, single case or time series experiments, and large N-group designs. In this section we review the advantages and limitations of these strategies within the context of the fear and phobia treatment literature.

Traditional Large-N Studies.   The research literature in the area of childhood fears and phobias contains a number of studies based on large N-group comparisons. These strategies include *randomized experimental* and *quasi-experimental*. In the case of randomized experimental, random assignment is used as a basis for inferring the specific intervention effects. The randomization serves two primary functions (Cook & Campbell, 1979). First, the researcher draws random samples that are representative of some known or defined population. Second, samples are drawn so that the groups are comparable to each other. When the groups are comparable at the beginning of the experiment, effects can typically be attributed to the intervention. In contrast, group quasi-experimental designs do not use randomization to draw inferences for an intervention effect (Cook & Campbell, 1979; Kratochwill, Schnaps, & Bissell, in press).

Within each of these general domains a variety of specific design strategies are possible. It is beyond the scope of the present discussion to review in detail the options that might be employed. For an excellent review of the randomized between-group and within-subject design options the reader should consult Kazdin (1980e). Cook and Campbell (1979) should be reviewed for quasi-experimental designs. Generally, between-group randomized designs allow the researcher to control many threats to the internal validity of the study and are preferred over quasi-experimental procedures where certain controls are not possible. Also, randomized between-group strategies allow the researcher to investigate the effect of a treatment (e.g., modeling) independent of that group having experienced the treatment previously. There are many "good" examples of group research in treatment of children's fears (e.g., Kanfer et al., 1975; Leitenberg & Callahan, 1973; Miller, Barrett, Hampe, & Noble, 1972a) and there are important reasons, as noted above, for using this type of research. Yet the limitations of this approach for clinical research and practice should also be recognized. First of all, it is probably no accident that many of the group studies have been of an analogue type (see above discussion). *It should be emphasized that analogue characteristics are not limited to group studies, but rather are associated with a variety of methodological approaches.* Nevertheless, researchers employing group designs have in many cases attempted to embrace the rigor of the laboratory (e.g., random assignment, specific and homogeneous fears or phobias, and standardized treatment).

Several other specific problems with group studies can be identified (Hersen & Barlow, 1976; Kratochwill, 1978). There is the *ethical* problem of withholding treatment in a no-treatment control group or providing subjects a treatment known to be less effective than another treatment. This is especially apparent with subjects who are experiencing clinical or severe fears. Second, it is a practical difficulty to find subjects with a homogeneous problem. When the problem is homogeneous, the question is frequently raised as to whether it is a clinical problem (Ross, 1981), as was possibly the case in the Leitenberg and Callahan (1973) study.

A third problem that occurs in group research is obscuring individual differences in focusing primarily on group averages. Researchers using group designs may not always obscure individual differences. As an example, Miller, Barrett, Hampe, and Noble (1972a) randomly assigned phobic children (age 6 to 15) to one of three treatment groups. The results demonstrated that phobic reduction strategies were as effective as no treatment at all. At this point, the authors could have terminated the analysis. Yet, when they analyzed data for the younger children separately, it was determined that the treatment group had a better outcome than those in the no-treatment control group. A subsequent conclusion after a two-year follow-up (Hampe, Noble, Miller, & Barrett, 1973) was that treatment of children's phobias is justified in that differential treatment should be devised for different age groups. Certainly this study demonstrates that it is possible to examine individual differences in group research. Yet, the issue of whether age is the primary individual difference factor remains to be determined. Making treatment groups homogeneous by age may still obscure true individual differences. Child "phobics" are truly heterogeneous and the researcher should be cautious in grouping clients on broad descriptive variables.

Fourth, the averaging of results from a group study may not be easily generalized to the individual client, as was noted in our discussion of analogue studies. As Hersen and Barlow (1976) note:

> In ignorance of the responses of individual patients to treatment, the clinician does not know to what extent a given patient under his care is similar to patients who improved or perhaps deteriorated within the context of an overall group improvement. Furthermore, as groups become more homogeneous, which most researchers agree is a necessary condition to answer specific questions about effects of therapy, one loses the ability to make inferential statements to the population of patients with a particular disorder since the individual complexities in the population will not have been adequately sampled. Thus, it becomes difficult to generalize findings at all beyond the specific group of patients in the experiment [p. 16].

A final issue that has been problematic in group research is achieving differences of clinical significance in addition to statistical significance. In some cases, researchers have not been especially sensitive to obtaining differences that are truly meaningful for the clients. Groups that differ by a mean of one minute in the presence of a fear stimulus might be statistically significant but of questionable social validity. Specific issues in establishing clinical or therapeutic significance in research are discussed later in the chapter.

Case study investigation.   Case studies continue to play a primary role in treatment investigation in the area of children's fears and phobias. In addition to the classical case descriptions presented in earlier chapters (e.g., Little Hans, Little Albert), a large percentage of studies across each of the behavioral areas discussed in this text employed case study methodology. Yet, case studies have been criticized for a number of shortcomings. For example, Wolpe and Rachman (1960) have provided a critical analysis of the case of Little Hans, and other authors have been critical of the case of "Little Albert" (e.g., Harris, 1979; Samelson, 1980). Harris (1979) notes that "it seems time, finally, to place the Watson and Rayner data in the category of 'interesting but uninterpretable results' " (p. 158).

There certainly seems to be justification for the criticism of case studies. As traditionally conceived they have been conducted without the usual controls that are imposed on experimental research (Kazdin, 1980e), designed to control major threats of the validity of the experiment (e.g., history, maturation, and testing).[1] In the case where controls are absent, an investigator should not make firm statements about the treatment effect, yet such statements are frequently made.

Despite the limitations of the case study, there are some good reasons for supporting this type of research in some instances (Kazdin, 1980e, 1981a, 1981b; Hersen & Barlow, 1976; Kratochwill, in press). Case studies have several positive features (Kazdin, 1980e). First, they provide ideas and hypotheses about behavior. Kazdin (1980e) noted:

> Both cases, Little Hans and Little Albert, are important because they suggested theoretical notions about how fear develops. Neither case establishes that parental relationships relate in some symbolic way to fear or points out how everyday fears are acquired. Yet, the case demonstrations provide important hypotheses about theories of personality and behavior and ideas that can be tested more adequately in research [p. 17].

This has certainly been the case with work in psychoanalytic therapy and behavior therapy. Second, case studies serve as sources of therapeutic techniques and therapeutic applications (e.g., Jones, 1924b). Particularly important in this context is the degree to which case studies have served as examples of the extent and type of treatments that can be applied in clinical settings. Case studies allow this application under natural settings where other methodologies might not be possible, such as group designs and single subject research.

Third, case studies allow the study of rare disorders or problems. Many of the fears and phobias described in this text would not be in the clinical treatment literature if case studies were considered unacceptable as a method of reporting data.

Fourth, case studies may provide a counterinstance of a treatment otherwise regarded as universally acceptable. For example, in certain reports, systematic desensitization has not been found particularly successful in treating children (e.g., Tahmisian & McReynolds, 1971). This should lead the investigator to explore treatment variations with a client. Such variations could then be explored in future research to help gauge their contribution.

Fifth, case studies may have persuasive or motivational value in therapeutic research (Kazdin, 1980e). Case study reports may seem convincing to both the author and readers of the report, especially those who are of the same theoretical persuasion. While this may prove advantageous for stimulating the spread of the particular "effective" technique and promote further research, it may also limit the acceptance of a technique due to the application of case study methods.

Aside from these positive aspects of the case study method, a major reason for continued support of such strategies is that they are frequently conducted with subjects experiencing clinical problems in clinical settings. This typically contrasts with group and even well-controlled single case or time-series methods that are conducted under more analogue conditions, as described in the previous section. Yet case studies can help document what does happen under conditions that more closely reflect the realities of clinical practice.

Case studies do not need to be conceptualized as completely uncontrolled and lacking in credible research strategies. Various factors can be taken into account in evaluation of case studies on dimensions of internal validity (Kazdin, 1981). First, the data collected in a case study can be gathered in an objective fashion (e.g., self-report, self-monitoring, direct observation). Second, in some cases the credibility of a case study can be improved when it is very likely that the problem would have continued or gotten worse without intervention of some type. Generally, a chronic problem may allow more inference for an intervention than an acute or transient fear or problem. Thus, past and future predictions about a particular problem are important in establishing inference for an intervention effect. Third, the type of effect may increase inference for the study, as when the change is sudden and large (see also, Glass, Wilson, & Gottman, 1975). Such a situation would contrast with treatment that shows small changes over the period of several months or every year. In the latter case, it is difficult to attribute change in the problem to the treatment. Fourth, the case study may be stronger when the intervention is replicated across more than one subject. Moreover, when the cases differ (i.e., are heterogeneous on a number of dimensions, such as type of fear, intensity of fear, setting, therapist, etc.) a stronger case can be made for a treatment effect. In general, the case study can make an important contribution to experimental work, especially when the aforementioned issues are considered. The interested reader is referred to Kazdin (1980d, 1981e) for a more detailed presentation of these issues.

Single Case or Time Series Designs.   Case study methodology, as described above, has been employed with one or a few cases. As an improvement over the typical case study procedure, numerous writers have advocated that single case or time-series designs be employed in therapeutic research (Hersen & Barlow, 1976; Jarantyne & Levy, 1979; Kazdin, 1980e, 1982; Kratochwill, in press). Single case studies typically represent an improvement over case methods in that they use formal measurement schemes, formal designs, and replication, among other features (Kratochwill, 1979), which give them an advantage in addressing various internal validity threats.

A number of researchers in the behavioral field have described variations of these designs, and the interested reader is referred to some original sources for details (e.g., Hersen & Barlow, 1976; Kazdin, 1982; Kratochwill, 1978). Generally, a few basic design elements serve as the building blocks for these designs. Three basic formats can be devised including within-, between-, and combined-series (Hayes, 1981). In the within-series type of design, effects are examined within a single series across time. In these designs, simple and complex phase changes can be made. In the simple phase change the researcher can alternate between a baseline (A) and treatment (B), i.e., A/B or A/B/A or A/B/A/B. In complex phase changes, treatments can be added or subtracted across phases (e.g., A/B+C/A/B+C). A number of authors have used within-series design strategies in evaluating treatments for fears and related problems (e.g., Ayllon et al., 1970; Wulbert, Nyman, Snow, & Owen, 1973).

In the between-series design, two or more data series are compared across time. The treatment comparisons are made between these series. The alternating treatments design presents an example of this type of strategy (Barlow & Hayes, 1979). In this design, the subject experiences each treatment for the same amount of time while assessment continues. The specific schedule of administering treatments is also predetermined, and there is a counterbalancing of treatment administration. Our review of the childhood fear literature did not turn up any examples of this design. However, this is a recently employed design, and one would not expect to find frequent applications. Nevertheless, this design and its variations would be quite useful because it is one of the few strategies that can be used to compare two or more treatments in a single case.

In the combined design options, combined sets of comparisons are made both between and within series of measurements (Hayes, 1981). A design that falls into this category is the multiple baseline design which can be implemented across subjects, settings, or behaviors (Hersen & Barlow, 1976; Kratochwill, 1978). As in the within-series designs, several baseline observations are made prior to the treatment being implemented in the first series. The other baseline series are maintained under no treatment until each series successively and independently receives the intervention. There are a few applications of the multiple baseline design in the treatment literature on children's fears and phobias (e.g. Matson, 1981; Van Hasselt et al., 1979).

Considerations. The widespread use of single subject or time-series designs in therapeutic research suggests that they have made a major contribution to evaluation of treatment effectiveness. Like between-group research strategies, the time-series designs have promoted a degree of rigor in research not possible with the more traditional case study. Several advantages of time-series strategies can be advanced (Hersen & Barlow, 1976; Kazdin, 1982; Kratochwill, 1979). Single case research generally shares all the advantages of case studies (e.g., allows research on a single client and analysis of individual variability) but generally can provide an improvement over these strategies in establishing that the treatment produced behavior change. That is, these designs allow a degree of internal validity in the experiment.

Single case designs do have limitations and should be used within the context of major methodological and conceptual issues raised in this form of research. A major issue in research in this area relates to the generalizability of the results. It is sometimes difficult to generalize results from one or a few studies in a particular area. For example, if it is found that contact desensitization is effective with a nine-year-old female child severely phobic of dogs, it is difficult to generalize to other children who have different phobic problems. To help deal with this concern, most researchers advocating these types of strategies have recommended replication of results (Hersen & Barlow, 1976). Such replication should occur across subjects, settings, and target problems.

Formal single subject designs have been advocated as a strategy suitable for the evaluation of clinical practice (Hayes, 1981). The position is that these designs bring a degree of rigor to clinical practice that may be an empirical approach to each treatment evaluation. However, it is our position that the demands of regular clinical practice are far too complex to routinely allow the methods of single case research to be used (cf. Kratochwill & Piersel, in press). For example, the methods of clinical research are typically costly, time consuming, and difficult to implement. Moreover, ethical and legal issues might be raised if such clinical treatment is conceptualized as treatment research (e.g., informed consent and withholding treatment for design purposes).

Directions for Clinical Research

Each of the above methodologies has made relevant contributions to the treatment literature on children's fears and phobias. Yet, the question that may emerge is what type of research should be conducted in the future and under what conditions (e.g., group versus case study). No general statement can be made in response to this question. A number of different methodological strategies might be appropriate at different stages of knowledge or development in an area. Moreover, because there will be many restrictions and costs on certain types of research, compromises will be necessary.

Recently, several perspectives have been offered on clinical research that have relevance for future direction in the childhood fear and phobia area (e.g., Agras & Berkowitz, 1980; Kazdin, 1981e; Ross, 1981). Agras and Berkowitz (1980) have presented a "progressive model of clinical research" (see Figure 6.1). These authors note that clinical research is perceived as an accumulation of studies that shape the future course of research when disseminated. The beginning of the model is development of a novel intervention. Research may then involve short-term between-group comparisons of clinical problems. Next, both analogue and single case studies emerge. The authors note that such strategies may be particularly useful in defining the components of therapy that are useful. Beyond these short-term issues, the model moves into short-term comparative outcome studies where aspects of treatment and treatment generalization are addressed. Thereafter, long term outcome studies are addressed. Agras and Berkowitz (1980) note:

> By this time the procedure may have become quite complex, perhaps taking the form of a decision tree, in which a particular response to therapy calls for one procedure to be applied while another response leads to the application of a different procedure. Issues such as the relative cost effectiveness of different treatments or reductions in morbidity (and even mortality if appropriate) may become salient at this point in research. Such studies, since they may require large numbers of participants, may have to be carried out in several centers, denoting the phase of the multicenter clinical trial [p. 479].

Obviously, such a model will seldom occur in actual research practice. For example, research will be going on at each stage, sometimes quite independently. Some research at a particular level may or may not influence other research. However, the important point is that the interrelationships of different types of research must be used to evaluate the state of knowledge in an area.

An important issue in this model is the dissemination of findings to practitioners so that treatments can be implemented in practice. A critical issue here is whether or not the treatment is effective in actual clinical practice. Ross (1981) has advocated an approach for clinical research to be both rigorous and relevant to clinical practice. He notes that an approach that combines detailed study of individual cases with group comparison approaches in the context of comprehensive research programs would be most useful. He has also advocated a *tracer method*, which refers to gathering extensive information on each individual client after data from group-comparison studies have been analyzed. A *deviant case analysis* is then conducted. Ross (1981) notes:

> To do this, one first investigates a research question with one of the traditional experimental designs that employs groups of subjects and requires data analysis by appropriate statistical methods. Immediately after the data have been analyzed, while the subjects can still be identified and contacted, the results are examined for deviant cases, that is, for subjects whose performance did not "fit"

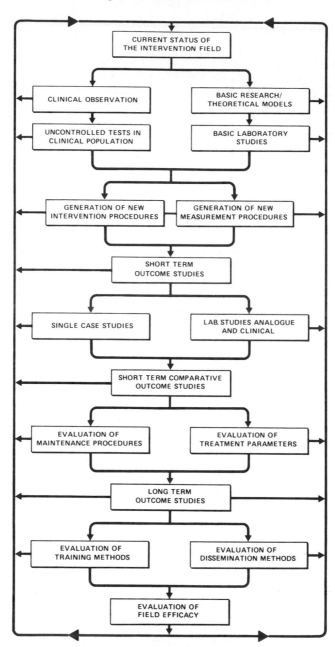

Figure 6.1. A progressive model of clinical research.
Source: Agras, W. S., & Berkowitz, R. Clinical research in behavior therapy: Halfway there? *Behavior Therapy*, 1980, **11**, 472–487. Copyright 1980 by the Association for Advancement for Behavior Therapy. Reproduced by permission.

the tested hypothesis. Depending on how many of these deviant cases are found, either all, or a sample, or the most extreme of them are then called back to the laboratory where they are examined by whatever case-study method is appropriate. Given time and resources, one can even go one step further and subject individuals whose performance was close to the mean of the group to similar individual scrutiny. By doing this, one can seek an answer to the question in what ways the deviant cases differed from the group. I suspect that this approach would generate new and interesting hypotheses that could then once more be tested in a well-controlled group design, thus leading to an ever greater refinement in our knowledge [pp. 325–326].

This approach appears to have some potential of advancing knowledge in the area of treatment of children's fears and related problems. Nevertheless, neither the Ross nor the Agras and Berkowitz models completely address the issue of the efficacy of a treatment in actual clinical practice. As a further alternative, Kazdin (1981e) has proposed *clinical replication* as a way to obtain information on treatment efficacy. A clinical replication refers to a procedure in which treatment is introduced into an actual clinical setting without the typical controls imposed in research (e.g., design, therapist training, monitoring of treatment and the client). In this activity, it is assumed that the internal validity in research on a particular treatment will already have been established. Clinical replication is focused on establishing the generalizability or external validity of a particular treatment. The clinical replication procedure is itself subject to empirical evaluation as a method of value in outcome evaluation. Unfortunately, there has been no work of this kind in the children's fear and phobia literature.

CRITERIA FOR EVALUATION OF OUTCOMES

Traditional criteria for evaluation of therapeutic outcome in children's fear and phobia research have included a rather limited range of measures. In this text and specifically in this chapter we have argued for measures that take into account cognitive, motor, and physiological channels. Yet even when these are employed in therapeutic research, they represent a rather limited source of information on the efficacy of psychotherapy. Recently, several criteria have been recommended that take into account a broader conceptual and methodological picture of behavior change (Kazdin, 1980e; Kazdin & Wilson, 1978; Rachman & Wilson, 1980). The criteria discussed in this section include experimental and therapeutic criteria, client-related criteria, efficiency and cost-related criteria, and criteria for generalization and follow-up.

Experimental and Therapeutic Criteria

In therapeutic research two criteria should be considered. Experimental criteria are used in group and single case research, but differ in some respects between the two types. In group research appropriate inferential statistical tests are usually employed to help establish that the intervention had an effect. Choice of an appropriate data analysis technique is a statistical conclusion validity issue (Cook & Campbell, 1979), and researchers should be careful to adhere to assumptions of the test employed. Beyond the more conventional criteria, an important issue to consider is the power and sample size needed to determine a treatment effect (Cohen, 1977; Levin, 1975). It is beyond the scope of this presentation to deal fully with the methodological and conceptual aspects of statistical power [the interested reader is also referred to Agras and Jacob (1981) for a discussion of power and sample size in the adult phobia literature]. Nevertheless, we would recommend the following in future group research. First of all, researchers should report the power and desired effect size for their study. For example, a power (1-B) of .80 means that the Type II error rate is .20. The effect size refers to the magnitude of the difference relative to variability. When the effective size is large, the probability of finding a significant difference is increased. However, no formal statement can be made as to what power should be, since it depends on such factors as variability in the measures, difference between groups, sample size used, design, number of conditions compared, statistical test used (e.g., *a priori* tests will be more powerful), and the alpha level chosen (.05 vs. .01). However, if the effect size is small, variability is large, and a small sample is employed, the findings may be doomed to nonsignificance. Questions should then be raised over the efficacy of conducting the study. Also, comparing five treatment groups will require many subjects to increase power. If few subjects are available, the researcher should consider a different type of methodology. Finally, consideration of a meaningful effect size has implications for the therapeutic significance of the results. Small effects obtained through large sample sizes may be statistically significant, but not clinically meaningful. Further considerations here relate to whether research is basic or clinical. A small effect might be relevant in more basic research in the context of development of a treatment technique.

In single case or time-series, the typical method of establishing the experimental criterion has been visual data analysis. Yet, this data analytic method may not be appropriate under some conditions (Kazdin, 1976; Kratochwill, 1978). When visual analysis is employed, several guidelines that make the method more formal could be employed (Parsonson & Baer, 1978). All of the single case experiments on children's fears and phobias used visual analysis to establish an experimental criterion. Yet despite advances made in visual analysis, a major problem with the approach has been the unreliability of the method (Kratochwill & Levin, 1979).

As a supplement to visual analysis, some authors have recommended several possible statistical tests for time-series experiments (cf. Kratochwill, 1978; Gottman, 1981). Traditional techniques that do not take into account the autocorrelated nature of time-series data will usually be inappropriate (e.g., ANOVA, regression).[2] Procedures that take into account this potential problem include time-series analysis (Gottman, 1981; McCleary & Hay, 1980), and a class of nonparametric randomization tests (Edgington, 1967; Levin, Marascuilo, & Hubert, 1978). However, each of these techniques may add a degree of inflexibility to the research (e.g., design and measurement restrictions), and this should be balanced against other factors surrounding the research. Also, statistical criteria may be potentially redundant if large effects are found that are visually evident.

In addition to experimental criteria, therapeutic criteria can be advocated for research on children's fears and related problems. Therapeutic criteria are usually conceptualized within the context of social validation (Kazdin, 1977; Risley, 1970; Wolf, 1978). The application of certain therapeutic criteria presupposes that the behavior selected for change is meaningful. This is an important issue in this area of children's fears, for as noted earlier, much therapeutic research has focused on nonclinical problems. When the evaluation of treatment outcomes is conducted, two considerations can be advanced. First of all, the behavior of the client is compared to that of his/her peers. This normative comparison might be difficult with the identified difficulties in the normative fear research (see Chapter 2). As an alternative, researchers could use data from peer ratings to help establish a therapeutic goal. Obviously, in cases such as spider phobias, it may be difficult to find peers who are free from this fear. In other cases, such as fear of school, peers may serve as good normative comparisons. A second procedure could involve subjective evaluations of the child's behavior by individuals in the natural environment (e.g., teachers, parents). Therapeutic changes in the child experiencing a fear can be viewed as important to the degree that the intervention brings the child's behavior within a range of socially acceptable levels when compared to the peer group and based on qualitative ratings from significant others in the natural environment.

Generally, few studies in the fear and phobia literature have employed social validation procedures in any formalized way. One notable exception is a study by Matson (1981). In this experiment, a criterion for success was established by having the teacher and teacher's aides rank order the same sex peers as the participant from their class in order of socially appropriate fear level. This behavior rating was based on the degree of fear displayed toward significant adult strangers identified as "safe" (i.e., persons who would not harm the child). After several ratings were obtained from the staff, the child with the lowest total score was labeled as the most "normal" on fear of strangers. A same age child from the same class was the only individual matched with a peer on clinical performance. Scores on the social validity assessment were used as the criterion for treatment success. As can be observed from Figure 6.2, the changes as a result of treatment placed the children within the social validity range based on assessments of their matched normal peers. Our recommendation is that researchers attempt to gather this type of information whenever possible. Examples of these tactics in other areas of research (e.g., Mahoney, Harper, Braukman, Fixsen, Phillips, & Wolf, 1975) could be applied to children experiencing a variety of problems.

In addition to these conceptual issues, social validation procedures could have important methodological implications as well. Such procedures would likely facilitate a perspective in which the researcher focuses on clinically meaningful changes in addition to the usual experimental criteria. Generally, therapeutic or clinical criteria should far surpass experimental criteria. As Kazdin and Wilson (1978) noted, "for clinical research, a major, if not *the* major, criterion for evaluating treatment is the clinical significance or overall importance of the improvement effected in the client" (p. 118).

Client-Related Criteria

Several client-related criteria have a direct bearing on future investigation in the area of children's fears and phobias. Usually the main criterion for measuring improvement in clients receiving psychological treatments in this area has been a single dependent measure (approach toward the feared object) that is evaluated by some experimental criteria. Of course, this is relevant since researchers are interested in determining if the treatment altered the problem behavior of interest. In addition, the breadth of changes produced could be applied to differentiate treatments or expand the understanding of the effects of treatment (Kazdin & Wilson, 1978). That is, two treatments might be equally effective, but one may have more desirable side effects than the other. For example, placing children on medications may reduce anxiety and promote other treatment, yet may have some unfortunate side effects. Thus, a treatment that is as effective as medication, but does not produce undesirable side effects would be preferable. The differential effectiveness of psychological treatments on this dimension must also be evaluated. Implosion therapy may create a number of undesirable side effects (increased arousal, escape behaviors) even though it is possibly as effective as another intervention. Of course, even if one form of treatment is of demonstrated superiority over another, the alternative might still be preferred when severe side effects are possible with the superior treatment.

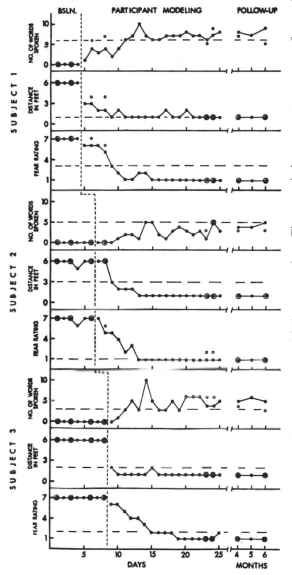

Figure 6.2. Levels of fear during baseline, treatment, and follow-up sessions. The open circles represent a measure of generalization at the children's homes. Dependent measures are represented for all three children in a multiple baseline design. The dotted horizontal lines represent scores of nonfearful children.

Source: Matson, J. L., Assessment and treatment of clinical fears in mentally retarded children. *Journal of Applied Behavior Analysis*, 1981, **14**, 287–294. Copyright 1981 by the Society for the Experimental Analysis of Behavior. Reproduced by permission.

In addition to the relative efficacy of two treatments, one treatment may produce either positive or negative behaviors which should be monitored. For example, in the case of a "school phobic" child, increased school attendance should assist development of social and academic skills that would otherwise be developing in youngsters attending school. Formal measures of academic and social competence would help describe the breadth of changes in a particular intervention program.

Efficiency and Cost-Related Criteria

The foregoing criteria greatly expand the possible ways in which a treatment program can be evaluated. In addition to these, future researchers should consider criteria related to the efficiency in duration of therapy, efficiency in the measures of administering the treatment, client costs, and cost effectiveness (Kazdin & Wilson, 1978). Each of these criteria could be applied to help make better decisions over the relative efficacy of two or more treatments or when examining the effect of any one particular treatment. The efficiency in duration of therapy implies that a certain procedure that reaches some desirable level of outcome in a relatively shorter period of time is generally preferred (when other criteria are considered). In the literature on children's fears and phobias, there is considerable variation or duration both across and within different theoretical areas. For example, some behavioral approaches extend for many months (e.g., Hersen, 1970; Luiselli, 1977). This provides a dramatic contrast to some other therapies which last only a few minutes, hours, days, or weeks (e.g., Ritter, 1968). Thus, within a particular therapeutic area, treatment time varies from one technique to another. In many cases the operant treatments were quite long (e.g. Ayllon et al., 1970). Even though two treatments might produce equally successful results, the "rapid treatment" method would be preferable, given due consideration to the other issues noted in this chapter.

In addition to the actual amount of time that is needed to implement treatment, a relevant variable to monitor is the manner in which the treatment is implemented. Treatment might be administered in group form, through reading materials, or by paraprofessionals rather than trained professionals. In the fear and phobia studies reviewed in this book, many treatments have a variety of implementation formats. For example, as noted by Kazdin and Wilson (1978), modeling treatments are quite versatile because they can be shown to large number of clients at the same time and can be used over and over again to treat children with the same type of problem. This has been true in case work of Melamed and her associates (e.g., Melamed, Hawes, Hiegy, & Glick, 1975; Melamed & Siegel, 1975; Melamed, Weinstein, Hawes, & Katin-Borland, 1975; Melamed, Yurcheson, Fleece, Hutchinson & Hawes, 1978) in treatment of dental hospital-associated fears.

There are clear contrasts between some of the treatment procedures on the dimension of efficiency in the manner in which the treatment is administered. Clearly, some behavioral treatments cannot be widely disseminated due to the mode of service delivery (individual therapy) or the years of training required to provide psychotherapy.

Kazdin and Wilson (1978) also note that an important consideration in evaluating psychotherapy is the cost of the professional training required. In some cases treatments can be carried out by individuals in the natural environment with minimal training in the treatment techniques. However, this type of treatment relationship usually necessitates careful monitoring by the more skilled professionals, and this must be included in any costs in this area. Nevertheless, treatment approaches that rely on a consultation or triadic model (e.g., Bergan, 1977; Tharp & Wetzel, 1969) in which the therapist/professional works through a mediator (e.g., teacher, parent) are likely to be more cost efficient in terms of professional expertise than strategies that do not rely on this mode of service delivery (e.g., Piersel & Kratochwill, 1981).

Various client costs should also be monitored in research on children's fears and phobias. Such costs to the client can be either monetary or "emotional" (Kazdin & Wilson, 1978). In the monetary domain, client costs are influenced by such factors as the cost of professional training of the therapist and the dissemination of the treatment. For example, systematic desensitization may be more expensive to train people in than many of the operant techniques discussed in Chapter 5. However, this remains an empirical issue.

Emotional costs to the client should routinely be evaluated in therapeutic research. For example, some studies have been run with flooding or implosive therapies (e.g., Handler, 1972; Smith & Sharpe, 1970). In these studies little information is available on the emotional side effects of treatment. Yet the nature of the treatment techniques would suggest some rather intense emotional responses would be typical. Emotional side effects to the client should be monitored in each therapeutic case, but are especially important in some programs (e.g., implosion therapy, punishment procedures). The important issue here is that clients may actually refuse treatment (or the careprovider may refuse treatment) when informed of its characteristics in advance. In short, clients may perceive the "cure" as worse than the problem.

Finally, cost effectiveness is an important issue in therapeutic research and should be considered in outcome measures (Kazdin & Wilson, 1978; McMahon & Forehand, 1980, Yates, 1981). Several conceptual features of a cost analysis have recently been described (cf. Yates, 1981; Yates, Haven, & Thoresen, 1977). A cost-effectiveness analysis requires measures of resources consumed and outcomes produced, thus developing an "input" to "output" ratio (Yates et al., 1977). A number of different variables can be included in the cost analysis, including such factors as personnel, facilities, equipment, and material in addition to the "costs" described above.

Unfortunately, no study in the childhood literature on treatment of fears and phobias conducted a comprehensive cost analysis in the context of the variables described above. We would strongly encourage researchers to provide this type of information in future investigations. When this is done the following guidelines may be quite useful for conducting this analysis (Yates, 1978; McMahon & Forehand, 1980):

1. The researcher should provide information on the amount of professional time involved in:
   (a) Training therapists to treat the case.
   (b) Assessment of the problem.
   (c) Development of the treatment material, (e.g., a manual, recording formats).
   (d) Actual contact with the client/careproviders.

2. The researcher should provide information on the amount of time needed by careproviders/consultees (e.g., parents, teachers, paraprofessionals) on:
   (a) Training to treat the case.
   (b) Assessment of the problem.
   (c) Actual contact with the client in a treatment context.
   (d) The "emotional" costs associated with treatment delivery.

3. Finally, the researcher should provide information on the amount of time needed by the client in:
   (a) Training in the implementation of the treatment (e.g., self-relaxation training).
   (b) Assessing him/herself (e.g., self-monitoring).
   (c) Actually participating in the treatment program.
   (d) Negative emotional factors that stem from participation in the treatment program.

Generalization and Follow-up

In recent years researchers have devoted increased attention to generalization and follow-up measures. This has prompted critical examinations of these concepts and offered methodological advances (e.g., Hammer & Rosenbaum, 1979; Karoly & Steffen, 1980; Kazdin & Wilson, 1978; Mash & Terdal, 1980; Stokes & Baer, 1977). Each of these issues has an important bearing on future research in the area of children's fears and phobias as well as on conclusions that can be drawn from the existing literature.

Generalization.   Generalization has several dimensions including generalization across time, settings, behaviors, and subjects. Generalization across time is usually conceptualized as a maintenance or follow-up issue and is discussed in more detail below. A useful conceptual framework called the "Generalization Map" has recently been proposed by Drabman et al. (1979). In this framework the various generalized effects of therapeutic programs can be categorized into 16 different classes (see figure 6.3). Several issues in this generalization analysis must be considered. First of all, relatively few studies in the fear and phobia literature actually took any measure of generalization. Second, our results parallel those of Drabman et al. (1979) who found that the largest number of studies occurred in class 9, or treatment off, in the same setting, behavior, and subject. Third, a considerable range of designs and assessment procedures was used to gather generalization measures. Methodological limitations of the actual measures used severely limits the conclusions that can be drawn about the generalization construct in this literature.

The finding that many reports did not assess and actively promote generalization provides a strong endorsement to pursue this area in future research. A number of issues have a bearing on generalization (Drabman et al., 1979, pp. 213–216). First of all, various designs can be used to help assess generalization. In single case research the investigator can study generalization in a systematic fashion (see Kazdin & Kopel, 1975; Rush & Kazdin, 1981; Kendall, 1981). Generalization can also be studied in large-N between group studies. For example, if the researcher includes two control groups, children who come into contact with treated children and/or parents can be assessed to determine if there is any generalization to "nontreated" subjects. Further, specific assessment of individual subjects through the "tracer" method advocated by Ross (1981) can further help to determine the degree of generalization evident.

Second, assessment measures of generalization should be taken across the three response domains through multiple measures. A number of unresolved issues remain in the area of treatment generalization from one response mode to another. For example, it is not clear whether treatment success as measured on overt behavior will generalize to the child's self-report or physiological measures. Generally we would express a preference for direct measures (e.g., observational) whenever possible. Measures should probably be qualitative as well as the usual quantitative type (Drabman et al., 1979). As Drabman et al. note, generalization typically will occur not only in the frequency of a response, but also in the quality of performance. Such qualitative performance could possibly be measured through ratings or even self-report.

Finally, generalization has typically been viewed as a passive phenomenon. Growing evidence suggests that it must be specifically programmed if it

GENERALIZATION MAP

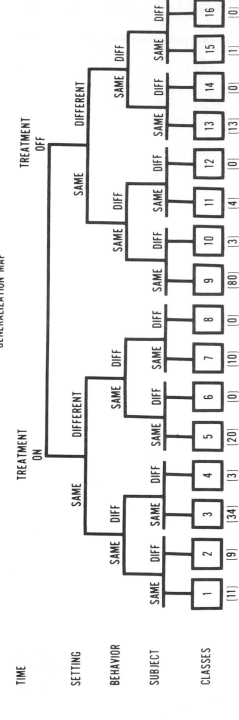

Figure 6.3. The Generalization Map depicting the 16 different classes of generalized treatment effects. The numbers in parentheses indicate the number of studies found (in the Drabman et al., 1979 review) which illustrated a particular class of generalization.
Source: Drabman, R. S., Hammer, D., & Rosenbasum, M. S. Assessing generalization in behavior modification with children: The generalization map. *Behavioral Assessment*, 1979, **1**, 203–219. Copyright 1979 by the Association for Advancement of Behavior Therapy. Reproduced by permission.

is to occur (e.g., Stokes & Baer, 1977; Wildman & Wildman, 1975). For example, Stokes and Baer (1977) presented a technology for programming generalization that is most useful in treatment of children's fears and phobias.

Follow-up and Maintenance

Follow-up is recognized as an important feature of therapeutic research in behavior therapy, yet considerable disagreement exists on the actual conceptual and methodological practices of this assessment. Questions usually associated with the follow-up concept are: "Does the treatment have a lasting impact?"; "Are the effects of treatment durable?"; "Does the client remain cured?" Implicit in the concept of follow-up is the measurement of some client variable at two or more points in time (Robbins, 1979). Yet, the passage of time between the formal treatment program and the follow-up measure(s) is but one dimension of this concept.

Several different purposes of follow-up can be outlined (Mash & Terdal, 1980):

1. *Evaluative follow-up (E-FU)*. This type of follow-up assessment is aimed at determining whether changes have occurred in relation to some interventions, and whether they continue to occur. No attempt is made to intervene.
2. *Diagnostic follow-up (D-FU)*. This type of follow-up assessment is directed at making program changes when it is determined that revised interventions could improve the services of the client.
3. *Therapeutic follow-up (T-FU)*. This type of follow-up is therapeutically oriented and is directed at enhancing therapeutic effects.
4. *Investigative follow-up (I-FU)*. In this type of follow-up, assessment is directed toward answering some type of research question. Longitudinal studies of children's fears could provide one example of this type [pp. 109–112].

Determining which type of follow-up is best is not always easy. The type of follow-up assessment used will depend on the type of problem and nature of the study, among other features. However, in clinical research on children's fears and phobias, D-FU and T-FU's will usually be used. In some respects, this is an ethical issue because determination that the client is not doing well will usually result in some type of therapeutic intervention. While different conceptual and theoretical conceptions regarding the nature of follow-up might be expected to guide the actual practice of it in divergent ways, the child fear and phobia literature shows amazing agreement on the approach used for follow-up assessment. This approach, depicted in Figure 6.4, has been labeled "treatment termination" (Mash & Terdal, 1980) and is characterized as the measurement of the "persistence" of therapeutic effects once the treatment is terminated. Several generalizations are characteristic of this approach:

1. Treatment occurs at a fixed point in time that precedes and is distinct from follow-up. This distinction is typically based on the presence or absence of regular contact with a professional therapist.

2. Treatment is directed at some target response and does not attempt to influence directly the surrounding contextual events. These targets are often conceptualized as intrapsychic personality conflicts that are not necessarily affected by environmental events and consequently may be altered directly, independent of environmental change.

3. Measures of outcome are typically restricted only to target responses, and since these are viewed as internal events, the use of indirect and discrete measures involving verbal response to personality inventories and/or projective tests is common.

4. Changes are expected to occur primarily during the time that treatment is in effect, although some later consolidation of effects within the individual is possible.

5. With effective treatment, changes will persist after termination and should continue in spite of the influence of everyday circumstances which are given a relatively unimportant role (Sargent, 1960).

6. If maintenance is not found, the inference is that the previously occurring treatment was not powerful enough in producing resolution of personality conflict.

7. Follow-up assessments are primarily evaluative in purpose (E-FU), and in the absence of maintenance provide little information relevant to treatment reformulation.

Although many of the intrapsychic or dynamic approaches to treatment of fears and phobias have been associated with these seven characteristics, the vast majority of behaviorally-oriented interventions have also used a treatment termination model. Yet current assumptions about the nature of behavior in behavior therapy would necessitate that a model based on programming generalization be used (Mash & Terdal, 1980; Stokes & Baer, 1977). In this view, it is assumed that generalization must be specifically programmed for it to occur. Thus, within the context of follow-up assessment, active attempts must be made to promote the transfer of treatment across time and other dimensions.

Consistent with the findings of Mash and Terdal (1980) on behavior therapy generally, one finding is that when generalization is programmed during fear treatment, it is not measured over time. This type of situation is depicted in Figure 6.4. As an alternative to this model of programming, the authors represent the model depicted in figure 6.4c, where measures of behavior and context are gathered. In this model, Mash and Terdal (1980) note *"Follow-up assessment is viewed simply as ongoing measurement of behavior and relevant*

FOLLOW-UP ASSESSMENT

a. Treatment Termination
   Discrete Measures: Response

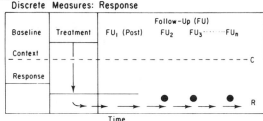

b. Programming Generalization I
   Continuous Measures: Response

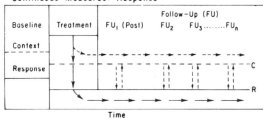

c. Programming Generalization II
   Continuous Measures: Response and Context

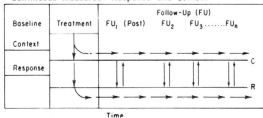

Figure 6.4. Three models for follow-up assessment: treatment termination (a), programming generalization I (b), and programming generalization II (c). Broken horizontal lines represent unmeasured events; solid horizontal lines are measured events. (C = contextual events for response; R = response).

Source: Mash, E. J., & Terdal, L. G., Follow-up assessments in behavior therapy. In P. Karoly and J. J. Steffen (Eds.), *Improving the long-term effects of psychotherapy.*

context over extended periods of time, rather than the measurement of effects following the termination of treatment" [p. 117].

An important issue that emerges in the behavior therapy model of follow-up being recommended here relates to the question of how treatment and generalization are distinguished. For example, it appears somewhat arbitrary to suggest that at some point treatment terminates and at another generalization begins. To begin with, various strategies that promote generalization might be included in the treatment program (e.g., reinforcement, self-monitoring). The client might also be instructed to begin the treatment program (e.g., exposure, positive self-statements) if the problem reoccurs. In this regard, follow-up assessment would need to focus on what is occurring and in what context. Clearly, direct ongoing measurement will help provide a clear picture of this.

SUMMARY AND CONCLUSION

A wide range of conceptual, methodological, and assessment considerations were reviewed in this chapter. After consideration of the clinical research literature on treatment of children's fears and phobias, we must unfortunately conclude that many important gaps exist in our knowledge base in this area. The problems in the field are spread across a number of different areas. First of all, there is a general lack of consensus on definition of fears, phobias, and anxiety both within and across different behavioral orientations. One recommendation that was advanced to deal with this concern is that three modes of client response be used to define the existence of fears and related problems. Even though patterns of desynchrony may emerge in therapeutic work, each system can be the focus of independent treatment efforts.

Another concern raised with therapy research in the area of children's fears and related problems is that much work is only an analogue to the actual clinical setting. In this chapter we have argued that the characterization of research as either analogue or nonanalogue has obscured the real issue that all clinical research is analogue to some degree (Kazdin, 1980d, 1980e). The important feature to consider in research in this area is a set of characteristics that may limit the degree to which the results of a study can generalize. Nevertheless, there is great need for well-controlled outcome research that is conducted on clinical fears. Much of the research literature is based on studies of children who would not usually be regarded as clinically fearful or phobic. The criteria adopted by Graziano et al. (1979) for definition of a clinical fear is useful for future research in the area.

A number of different experimental research methods have been used in outcome studies for children with fears and related problems. Three general domains of studies were discussed including traditional large-N studies, case studies, and controlled single case or time-series experiments. There are numerous examples of each type of methodology in the child literature. Each has its own positive and negative features and is best perceived as part of the knowledge building process in clinical research activity.

Increasingly, therapeutic research has been focused on a wider range of criteria for evaluation of outcome. These outcome measures include client-related criteria, efficiency, and cost-related criteria, and generalization and maintenance. Each of these criteria must be considered in future research across different methodologies and theoretical areas. Only when these criteria are employed will we truly extend our knowledge in this area of treatment.

NOTES

1. Limitations of case studies within the context of the validity threats invoked in experimental research include such factors as the failure to rule out alternative explanations, various biases of the therapist in reporting results, and generalizing to other subjects (Kazdin, 1980e).
2. In time-series experiments autocorrelation refers to a correlation (r) between the data points separated by different time-intervals (or lags) in the data series. A first order autocorrelation would be computed by pairing the initial observation with the second, second with the third, and so forth over the series (Kazdin, 1976). In the case where the data are significantly autocorrelated, traditional statistical tests that have as one assumption independence or error components (e.g., ANOVA and Regression Techniques) are inappropriate (see Levin et al., 1978).

References

Abe, K. Phobias and nervous symptoms in childhood and maturity: Persistence and associations. *British Journal of Psychiatry*, 1972, **120**, 275–283.

Achenbach, T. M. *Developmental psychopathology*. New York: Ronald Press, 1974.

Achenbach, T. M. Psychopathology of childhood: Research problems and issues. *Journal of Consulting and Clinical Psychology*, 1978, **46**, 759–776.

Achenbach, T. M., & Edelbrock, C. S. The classification of child psychopathology: A review and analysis of empirical efforts. *Psychological Bulletin*, 1978, **85**, 1275–1301.

Adams, H. B. "Mental illness" or interpersonal behavior? *American Psychologist*, 1964, **19**, 191–197.

Adams, H. E., Doster, J. A., & Calhoun, K. S. A psychologically based system of response classification. In A. R. Ciminero, K. A. Calhoun, & H. E. Adams (Eds.), *Handbook of behavioral assessment*. New York: Wiley-Interscience, 1977.

Adler, A. *Social interest: A challenge to mankind*. London: Faber & Faber, 1938.

Adler, A. *Problems of neurosis*. New York: Harper & Row, 1964. (a)

Adler, A. *Problems of neurosis: A book of case histories*. P. Mairet (Ed.) New York: Harper & Row, 1964. (b)

Adler, A. *The practice and theory of individual psychology*. Totowa, New Jersey: Littlefield, Adams, 1968.

Agras, W. S., & Berkowitz, R. Clinical research in behavior therapy: Halfway there? *Behavior Therapy*, 1980, **11**, 472–487.

Agras, W. S., Chapin, H. H., & Oliveau, D. C. The natural history of phobia. *Archives of General Psychiatry*, 1972, **26**, 315–317.

Agras, W. S., & Jacob, R. G. Phobia: Nature and measurement. In M. Mavissakalian & D. H. Barlow (Eds.), *Phobia and pharmacological treatment*. New York: The Guilford Press, 1981.

Agras, W. S., Sylvester, D., & Oliveau, D. The epidemiology of common fears and phobias. *Comprehensive Psychiatry*, 1969, **10**, 151–156.

Albee, G. W. Conceptual models and manpower requirements in psychology. *American Psychologist*, 1968, **23**, 317–320.

Algozzine, R. Biophysical perspective of emotional disturbance. In R. Algozzine, R. Schmidt, & C. D. Mercer (Eds.), *Childhood behavior disorders: Applied research and educational practice*. Rockville, Md.: Aspen, 1981.

Algozzine, B., Mercer, C. D., & Coutermine, T. The effects of labels and behavior on teacher expectation. *Exceptional Children*, 1977, **44**, 131–132.

Allen, K. E., Hart, B. M., Buell, J. S., Harris, F. R., & Wolf, M. M. Effects of social reinforcement on isolate behavior of a nursery school child. *Child Development*, 1964, **35**, 511–518.

American Psychiatric Association. *Diagnostic and statisical manual of mental disorders (DSM-I)*. Washington, D.C.: American Psychiatric Association, 1952.

American Psychiatric Association. *Diagnostic and statistical manual of mental disorders (DSM-II)*. Washington, D.C.: American Psychiatric Association, 1968.

American Psychiatric Association. *Diagnostic and statistical manual of mental disorders (DSM-III)*. Washington, D.C.: American Psychiatric Association, 1979.

American Psychological Association. *Ethical standards of psychologists.* Washington, D.C., 1972.

Anastasi, A. *Psychological testing.* (4th ed.) New York: Macmillan, 1976.

Angelino, H., Dollins, J., & Mech, E. V. Trends in the "fears and worries" of schoolchildren as related to socio-economic status and age. *Journal of Genetic Psychology,* 1956, **89**, 263–276.

Angelino, H., & Mech, E. V. Fears and worries concerning physical changes: A preliminary survey of 32 females. *Journal of Psychology,* 1955, **39**, 195–198.

Angelino, H., & Shedd, C. Shifts in the content of fears and worries relative to chronological age. *Proceedings of the Oklahoma Academy of Science,* 1953, **34**, 180–186.

Arieti, S. Psychiatric controversy: Man's ethical dilemma. *American Journal of Psychiatry,* 1974, **132**, 763–764.

Association for Measurement and Evaluation in Guidance, American Personnel and Guidance Association & National Council for Measurement in Education. The responsible use of tests: A position paper of AMEG, APGA, and NCME. *Measurement and Evaluation in Guidance,* 1972, **5**, 385–388.

Austad, C. S. Successful treatment of a case of elective mutism. *The Behavioral Therapist,* 1979, **3**, 18–21.

Ayllon, T., Smith, D., & Rogers, M. Behavioral management of school phobia. *Journal of Behavior Therapy and Experimental Psychiatry,* 1979, **1**, 125–138.

Baer, D. M., & Bushell, D., Jr. The future of behavior analyses in the schools? Consider its recent past and then ask a different question. *The School Psychology Review,* 1981, **10**, 259–270.

Bailey, K. G., Deardoff, P., & Nay, W. R. Students play therapist: Relative effects of role playing, feedback, and modeling in a simulated interview. *Journal of Consulting and Clinical Psychology,* 1974, **45**, 257–266.

Baker, B. L., Cohen, D. C., & Saunders, J. T. Self-directed desensitization for acrophobic behavior. *Research Therapy,* 1973, **11**, 79–89.

Bamber, J. H. The fears of adolescents. *Journal of Genetic Psychology,* 1974, **125**, 127–140.

Banaher, B. G., & Thoresen, C. E. Imagery assessment by self-report and behavioral measures. *Behaviour, Research, and Therapy,* 1972, **10**, 131–138.

Bandura, A. A social learning interpretation of psychological dysfunctions. In P. London & D. Rosenhan (Eds.), *Foundations of abnormal psychology.* New York: Holt, Rinehart & Winston, 1968.

Bandura, A. *Principles of behavior modification.* New York: Holt, Rinehart & Winston, 1969.

Bandura, A. Psychotherapy based upon modeling principles. In A. E. Bergin & S. L. Garfield (Eds.), *Handbook of psychotherapy and behavior change.* New York: John Wiley, 1971.

Bandura, A. Self-efficacy: Toward a unifying theory of behavioral change. *Psychological Review,* 1977, **84**, 191–215. (a)

Bandura, A. *Social learning theory.* Englewood Cliffs, N.J.: Prentice-Hall, 1977. (b)

Bandura, A. Reflections on self-efficacy. In H. J. Eysenck & S. Rachman (Eds.), *Advances in behavior research and therapy.* (Vol. 1) New York: Pergamon Press, 1978.

Bandura A., Blanchard, E. B. & Ritter, B. Relative efficacy of desensitization and modeling approaches for inducing behavioral, affective, and attitudinal changes. *Journal of Personality and Social Psychology,* 1969, **13**, 173–199.

Bandura, A., Grusec, J., & Menlove, F. Vicarious extinction of avoidance behavior. *Journal of Personality and Social Psychology,* 1967, **5**, 16–23.

Bandura, A., Jeffrey, R., & Wright, C. Efficacy of participant modeling as a function of response induction aids. *Journal of Abnormal Psychology,* 1974, **83**, 56–64.

Bandura, A., & Menlove, F. Factors determining vicarious extinction of avoidance behavior through symbolic modeling. *Journal of Personality and Social Psychology,* 1968, **8**, 99–108.

Bandura, A., & Rosenthal, T. Vicarious classical conditioning as a function of arousal level. *Journal of Personality and Social Psychology,* 1966, **3**, 54–62.

Bandura, A., & Walters, R. H. *Social learning and personality development*. New York: Holt, Rinehart & Winston, 1963.

Barabasz, A. Group desensitization of test anxiety in elementary schools. *Journal of Psychology*, 1973, **83**, 295–301.

Barlow, D. H. President's message. *the Behavior Therapist*, 1979, **2**, 14.

Barlow, D. H. (Ed.) *Behavioral assessment of adult disorders*. New York: Guilford Press, 1981. (a)

Barlow, D. H. On the relation of clinical research to clinical practice: Current issues, new directions. *Journal of Consulting and Clinical Psychology*, 1981, **49**, 147–155. (b)

Barlow, D. H., & Hayes, S. C. Alternating treatments design: One strategy for comparing the effects of two treatments in a single subject. *Journal of Applied Behavior Analysis*, 1979, **12**, 199–210.

Barlow, D. H., & Mavissakalian, M. Directions in the assessment and treatment of phobia: The next decade. In M. Mavissakalian & D. H. Barlow (Eds.), *Phobia: Psychological and pharmacological treatment*. New York: Guilford Press, 1981.

Barlow, D. H., Mavissakalian, M. R., & Schofiel, L. D. Patterns of desynchrony in agoraphobia: A preliminary report. *Behaviour, Research and Therapy*, 1980, **18**, 441–448.

Barlow, D. H., & Wolfe, B. E. Behavioral approaches to anxiety disorders: A report on the NIMH-SUNY, Albany, Research Conference. *Journal of Consulting and Clinical Psychology*, 1981, **49**, 448–454.

Barrios, B. A., Hartmann, D. P., & Shigetomi, C. Fears and anxieties in children. In E. J. Mash & L. G. Terdal (Eds.), *Behavioral assessment of childhood disorders*. New York: Guilford Press, 1981.

Barrios, B. A. & Shigetomi, C. C. Coping skills training: Potential for prevention of fears and anxieties. *Behavior Therapy*, 1980, **11**, 431–439.

Barrios, B. A. & Shigetomi, C. C. Behavioral assessment of children's fears: A critical review. In T. R. Kratochwill (Ed.), *Advances in school psychology*. Vol. 4. Hillsdale, N.J., Lawrence Erlbaum, in preparation.

Bauer, D. H. An exploratory study of developmental changes in children's fears. *Journal of Child Psychology and Psychiatry*, 1976, **17**, 69–74.

Bauermeister, J. M., & Jamail, J. A. Modification of elective mutism in the classroom setting: A case study. *Behavior Therapy*, 1975, **6**, 246–250.

Baum, C. G., Forehand, R., & Zegiob, L. E. A review of observer reactivity in adult-child interactions. *Journal of Behavioral Assessment*, 1979, **10**, 312–120.

Bedell, J., & Roitzsch, J. The effects of stress on state and trait anxiety in emotionally disturbed, normal, and delinquent children. *Journal of Abnormal Child Psychology*, 1976, **4**, 173–177.

Bednar, R. A. A behavioral approach to treating an elective mute in the school. *Journal of School Psychology*, 1974, **12**, 326–337.

Begelman, D. A. Misnaming, metaphors, the medical model, and some muddles. *Psychiatry*, 1971, **34**, 38–58.

Begelman, D. A. Ethical and legal issues of behavior modification. In M. Hersen, R. M. Eisler & P. H. Miller (Eds.), *Progressive behavior modification*. (Vol. 1.) New York: Academic Press, 1976.

Bellack, A. S., & Hersen, M. *Behavior modification: An introductory textbook*. Baltimore: Williams & Wilkins, 1977. (a)

Bellack, A. S. & Hersen, M. The use of self-report inventories in behavioral assessment. In J. D. Cone & R. P. Hawkins (Eds.), *Behavioral assessment: New directions in clinical psychology*. New York: Brunner/Mazel, 1977. (b)

Bellack, A. S., & Hersen, M. Assessment and single-case research. In M. Hersen & A. S. Bellack (Eds.), *Behavior therapy in the psychiatric setting*. Baltimore: Williams & Wilkins, 1978.

Benjamin, L. S. Structural analysis of social behavior. *Psychological Review*, 1974, **81**, 392–425.

Bentler, P. M. An infant's phobia treated with reciprocal inhibition therapy. *Journal of Child Psychology and Psychiatry*, 1962, **3**, 185–189.

Bergan, J. R. *Behavioral consultation.* Columbus: Charles E. Merrill, 1977.

Bergin, A. E. The evaluation of therapeutic outcomes. In A. E. Bergin & S. L. Garfield (Eds.), *Handbook of psychotherapy and behavior change: An empirical analysis.* New York: Wiley, 1971.

Bergin, A. E., & Lambert, M. J. The evaluation of therapeutic outcomes. In S. L. Garfield & A. E. Bergin (Eds.), *Handbook of psychotherapy and behavior change.* (2nd ed.) New York: Wiley, 1978.

Bergin, A. E., & Suinn, R. M. Individual psychotherapy and behavior therapy. *Annual Review of Psychology,* 1975, **26,** 509–556.

Bergland, B. W., & Chal, A. H. Relaxation training and a junior high behavior problem. *The School Counselor,* 1972, **20,** 288–293.

Bernstein, D. A. Behavioral fear assessment: Anxiety or artifact? In H. Adams & P. Unikel (Eds.), *Issues and trends in behavior therapy.* Springfield, Ill.: C. C. Thomas, 1973.

Bernstein, D. A., & Nietzel, M. T. Procedural variation in behavioral avoidance tests. *Journal of Consulting and Clinical Psychology,* 1973, **41,** 165–174.

Bernstein, D. A., & Nietzel, M. T. Behavioral avoidance tests: The effects of demand characteristics and repeated measures of two types of subjects. *Behavioral Therapy,* 1974, **5,** 184–192.

Bernstein, D. A., & Paul, G. L. Some comments on therapy analogue research with small animal "phobias." *Journal of Behavior Therapy and Experimental Psychiatry,* 1971, **2,** 225–237.

Bersoff, D. N., & Grieger, R. M. An interview model for the psychosituational assessment of children's behavior. *American Journal of Orthopsychiatry,* 1971, **41,** 483–493.

Betts, G. H. The distribution and functions of mental imagers. Teacher's College, Columbia University, 1909. In A. Richardson (Ed.), *Mental imagery.* New York: Springer Publishing Co., 1969.

Biglan, A., Villwock, C., & Wick S. The feasibility of a computer controlled program for the treatment of test anxiety. *Journal of Behavior Therapy and Psychiatry,* 1979, **10,** 47–49.

Bijou, S. W., & Grimm, J. A. Behavioral diagnosis and assessment in teaching young handicapped children. In T. Thompson & W. S. Dockens III (Eds.), *Applications of behavior modification.* New York: Academic Press, 1975.

Bijou, S. W., & Redd, W. H. Child behavior therapy. In S. Arieti (Ed.), *American handbook of psychiatry.* (Vol. 5.) New York: Basic Books, 1975.

Bijou, S. W., & Peterson, R. F. Functional analysis in the assessment of children. In P. McReynolds (Ed.), *Advances in psychological assessment.* (Vol. 2.) Palo Alto, Calif.: Science and Behavior Books, 1971.

Blanchard, E. B. The relative contributions of modeling, information influences, and physical contact in the extinction of phobic behavior. *Journal of Abnormal Psychology,* 1970, **76,** 55–61.

Boer, A. P., & Sipprelle, C. N. Elimination of avoidance behavior in the clinic and its transfer to the normal environment. *Journal of Behavior Therapy and Experimental Psychiatry,* 1970, **1,** 169–174.

Borkovec, T. D., Weerts, T. C., & Bernstein, D. A. Assessment of anxiety. In A. R. Ciminero, K. A. Calhoun & H. E. Adams (Eds.), *Handbook of behavioral assessment.* New York: Wiley, 1977.

Bornstein, P. H., & Knapp, M. Self-control desensitization with a multi-phobic boy: A multiple baseline design. *Journal of Behavior Therapy and Experimental Psychiatry,* 1981, **12,** 281–285.

Bosma, B. The NEA testing moratorium. *Journal of School Psychology,* 1973, **11,** 304–306.

Bowlby, J. *Attachment.* New York: Basic Books, 1969.

Bowlby, J. *Attachment and loss.* Vol. 2. New York: Basic Books, 1973.

Boyd, L. T. Emotive imagery in the behavioral management of adolescent school phobia: A case approach. *School Psychology Digest,* 1980, **9,** 186–189.

Brady, J. B. Brevital relaxation treatment of frigidity. *Behaviour Research and Therapy,* 1966, **4,** 71–77.

Brady, J. P. Systematic desensitization. In W. S. Agras (Ed.), *Behavior modification: Principles and clinical applications.* Boston: Little, Brown, 1972.

Bronson, G. W. Fear of visual novelty: developmental patterns in males and females. *Developmental Psychology,* 1969, **2,** 33–40. (a)

Bronson, G. W. Sex differences in the development of fearfulness: a replication. *Psychonomic Science,* 1969, **17,** 367–368. (b)

Brown, D. K., Kratochwill, T. R., & Bergan, J. R. Teaching interview skills for problem identification: An analogue study. *Behavioral Assessment,* 1982, **4,** 63–73.

Brunner, J. W., Goodnow, J. J., & Austin, G. A. *A study of thinking.* New York: Science Editions, 1965.

Bryan, J., & Schwarz, T. Effects of film material on children's behavior. *Psychological Bulletin,* 1971, **75,** 50–59.

Bued, K. S., & Baer, D. M. Behavior modification and the law: Implications of recent judicial decisions. *Journal of Psychiatry and Law,* 1976, **4,** 171–244.

Buhler, C., Keith-Spiegel, T., & Thomas, K. Developmental psychology. In B. B. Wohman (Ed.), *Handbook of general psychology.* Englewood Cliffs, N.J.: Prentice-Hall, 1973.

Burke, J. P., & Demers, S. T. A paradigm for evaluating assessment interviewing techniques. *Psychology in the Schools,* 1979, **16,** 51–60.

Burns, G. L. Indirect measurement and behavioral assessment: A case for social behaviorism psychometrics. *Behavioral Assessment,* 1980, **2,** 197–206.

Campbell, D. T., & Fiske, D. W. Convergent and discriminant validation by the multitrait-multimethod matrix. *Psychological Bulletin,* 1959, **56,** 81–105.

Canadian Psychological Association *Ethical standards of psychologists.* (1978 rev.) Ottawa, Ontario: Canadian Psychological Association.

Carr, A. T. The psychopathology of fear. In W. Sluckin (Ed.), *Fear in animals and man.* New York: Van Nostrand Reinhold, 1979.

Cartlege, G., & Milburn, J. F. *Teaching social skills to children: Innovative approaches.* New York: Pergamon Press, 1980.

Cass, L. K., & Thomas, C. B. *Childhood pathology and later adjustment. The question of prediction.* New York: Wiley, 1979.

Castaneda, A., McCandless, B., & Palermo, D. The children's form of the Manifest Anxiety Scale. *Child Development,* 1956, **27,** 317–326.

Cautela, J. R. *Behavior analysis forms for clinical intervention.* Champaign, Ill.: Research Press, 1977.

Cautela, J. R., & Groden, J. *Relaxation. A comprehensive manual for adults, children, and children with special needs* Champaign, Ill.: Research Press, 1978.

Cautela, J. R., & Upper, D. *A behavior coding system.* Paper presented at the meeting of the Association for Advancement of Behavior Therapy, Miami, December 1973.

Chalk, R., Frankel, M. S., & Chafer, S. B. *AAAS professional ethnics project: Professional ethics activities in the scientific and engineering societies.* Washington, D.C.: American Association for the Advancement of Science, 1980.

Chazan, M. School phobia. *British Journal of Educational Psychology,* 1962, **32,** 209–217.

Children's Defense Fund. *Portrait of unequality: Black and white children in America.* Washington, D.C., Author, 1980.

Ciminero, A. R. Behavioral assessment: An overview. In A. R. Ciminero, K. S. Calhoun & H. E. Adams (Eds.), *Handbook of behavioral assessment.* New York: Wiley, 1977.

Ciminero, A. R., Calhoun, K. S., & Adams, H. E. (Eds.) *Handbook of behavioral assessment.* New York: Wiley, 1977.

Ciminero, A. R., & Drabman, R. S. Current developments in the behavioral assessment of children. In B. B. Lahey & A. E. Kazdin (Eds.), *Advances in clinical child psychology.* (Vol. 1.) New York: Plenum Press, 1977.

Ciminero, A. R., Nelson, R. O., & Lipinski, D. P. Self-monitoring procedures. In A. R. Ciminero, K. S. Calhoun, & H. E. Adams (Eds.), *Handbook of behavioral assessment*. New York: Wiley, 1977.

Clark, M. A. *An exploratory investigation of the interaction of internal-external locus of control and therapy type with snake-avoidant preschool children*. Unpublished doctoral dissertation, Syracuse University, 1979.

Clayton, W. T. The use of positive reinforcement and stimulus fading in the treatment of an elective mute. *Behavioural Psychotherapy*, 1981, **9**, 25–33.

Clement, C. W., & Milne, D. C. Group play therapy and tangible reinforcers used to modify the behavior of eight year old boys. *Behaviour Research and Therapy*, 1967, **5**, 301–312.

Clement, P. W., Roberts, P. V., & Lantz, C. E. Mothers and peers as child behavior therapists. *International Journal of Child Psychotherapy*, 1976, **26**, 335–359.

Cohen, J. *Statistical power analysis for the behavioral sciences*. New York: Academic Press, 1970.

Coleman, J. C., & Broen, W. E. *Abnormal psychology and modern life* (4th ed.) Glenview, Ill.: Scott, Foresman, 1972.

Cone, J. D. The relevance of reliability and validity for behavioral assessment. *Behavior Therapy*, 1977, **8**, 411–426.

Cone, J. D. The behavioral assessment grid (BAG): A conceptual framework and taxonomy. *Behavior Therapy*, 1978, **9**, 882–888.

Cone, J. D. Confounded comparisons in triple response mode assessment research. *Behavioral Assessment*, 1979, **1**, 85–95.

Cone, J. D. Psychometric consideration. In M. Hersen & A. S. Bellack (Eds.), *Behavioral assessment: A practical handbook*. (2nd ed.) New York: Pergamon, 1981.

Cone, J. D., & Hawkins, R. P. (Eds.), *Behavioral assessment: New directions in clinical psychology*. New York: Brunner/Mazel, 1977.

Conger, J. C., & Keane, S. P. Social skills intervention in the treatment of isolated or withdrawn children. *Psychological Bulletin*, 1981, **90**, 478–495.

Conrad, R. D., Delk, J. L., & Williams, C. Use of stimulus fading procedures in the treatment of a situation specific mutism: A case study. *Journal of Behavior Therapy and Experimental Psychiatry*, 1974, **5**, 99–100.

Cook, T. D., & Campbell, D. T. The design and conduct of quasi-experiments and true experiments in field settings. In M. D. Dunnette & J. P. Campbell (Eds.), *Handbook of industrial and organizational research*. Chicago: Rand McNally, 1976.

Cook, T. D., & Campbell, D. T. *Quasi-experimentation: Design & analysis issues for field settings*. Chicago: Rand McNally, 1979.

Coolidge, J. C., Hahn, P. B., & Peck, A. L. School phobia: Neurotic crisis or way of life. *American Journal of Orthopsychiatry*, 1957, **27**, 296–306.

Cormier, W. H., & Cormier, L. S. *Interviewing strategies for helpers: A guide to assessment, treatment and evaluation*. Belmont, CA: Wadsworth, 1979.

Corter, C., The nature of the mother's absence and the infant's response to brief separation. *Developmental Psychology*, 1976, **12**, 428–434.

Costello, C. G. Dissimilarities between conditioned avoidance responses and phobias. *Psychological Review*, 1970, **77**, 250–254.

Colter, S., & Palmer, T. The effects of test anxiety, sex of subject, and type of verbal reinforcement on maze performance of elementary school children. *Journal of Personality*, 1970, **38**, 216–234.

Craghan, L., & Musante, G. J. The elimination of a boy's high-building phobia by *in vivo* desensitization and game-playing. *Journal of Behavior Therapy and Experimental Psychiatry*, 1975, **6**, 87–88.

Craighead, W. E., Kazdin, A. E., & Mahoney, M. J. *Behavior modification: Principles, issues, and applications*. Boston: Houghton-Mifflin, 1976.

Croake, J. W. Fears of children. *Human Development*, 1969, **12**, 239–247.

Croake, J. W. Adolescent fear. *Adolescence*, 1967, **2**, 459–468.

Croake, J. W., & Knox, F. H. A second look at adolescent fears. *Adolescence*, 1971, **6**, 279–284.

Croake, J. W., & Knox, F. H. The changing nature of children's fears. *Child Study Journal*, 1973, **3**, 91–105.

Cronbach, L. J. *Essentials of psychological testing*. (2nd ed.) New York: Harper & Row, 1960.

Cummings, J. D. A follow-up study of emotional symptoms in school children. *British Journal of Educational Psychology*, 1946, **16**, 163–177.

Cummings, J. D. The incidence of emotional symptoms in school children. *British Journal of Educational Psychology*, 1944, **14**, 151–161.

de Silva, P., Rachman, S., & Seligman, M. E. P. Prepared phobias and obsessions: Therapeutic outcome. *Behavior Research and Therapy*, 1977, **5**, 65–77.

Deffenbacher, J. L. Relaxation *in vivo* in the treatment of test anxiety. *Journal of Behavior Therapy and Experimental Psychiatry*, 1976, **7**, 290–292.

Deffenbacher, J. L., & Kemper, C. C. Counseling test-anxious sixth graders. *Elementary School Guidance & Counseling*, 1974, **7**, 22–29. (a)

Deffenbacher, J. L., & Kemper, C. C. Systematic desensitization of test anxiety in junior high students. *The School Counselor*, 1974, **22**, 216–222. (b)

Deffenbacher, J., & Michaels, A. Two self-control procedures in the reduction of targeted and nontargeted anxieties—A year later. *Journal of Counseling Psychology*, 1980, **27**, 9–15.

Deffenbacher, J. L., Mathis, H., & Michaels, A. C. Two self-control procedures in the reduction of targeted and nontargeted anxieties. *Journal of Consulting Psychology*, 1979, **26**, 120–127.

Deffenbacher, J. L., & Rivera, N. A behavioral self-control treatment of test anxiety in minority populations: Some cases and issues. *Psychological Reports*, 1976, **39**, 1188–1190.

Deffenbacher, J. L., & Snyder, A. L. Relaxation as self-control in the treatment of test and other anxieties. *Psychological Reports*, 1976, **39**, 379–385.

Deitz, S. M. Current status of applied behavior analysis: Science versus technology. *American Psychology*, 1978, **33**, 805–814.

Delprato, D. J. Hereditary determinants of fears and phobias: A critical review. *Behavior Therapy*, 1980, **11**, 79–103.

Denney, D. R. Self control approaches to the treatment of test anxiety. In I. G. Sarason (Ed.), *Test anxiety: Theory, research, and application*. New York: Lawrence Erlbaum Associates, Inc., 1980.

Dickson, C. R. Role of assessment in behavior therapy. In P. McReynolds (Ed.), *Advances in psychological assessment* (Vol. 3). San Francisco: Jossey-Bass, 1975.

Diener, E., & Crandall, R. *Ethics in social and behavioral research*. Chicago: University of Chicago Press, 1978.

DiNardo, P. A., & DiNardo, P. G. Self-control desensitization in the treatment of a childhood phobia. *The Behavior Therapist*, 1981, **4**, 15–16.

Doris, J., McIntyre, J. R., Kelsey, C., Lehman, E. Separation anxiety in nursery school children. *Proceedings of the 79th Annual Convention of the American Psychological Association*, 1971, **79**, 145–146.

Dorkey, M., & Amen, E. W. A continuation study of anxiety reactions in young children by means of a projective technique. *Genetic Psychology Monographs*, 1947, **35**, 139–183.

Drabman, R. S., Hammer, D. & Rosenbaum, M. S. Assessing generalization in behavior modification with children: The generalization map. *Behavioral Assessment*, 1979, **1**, 203–219.

Dreikurs, R., & Soltz, V. *Children: The challenge*. New York: Hawthorn Books, Inc., 1964.

Dreikurs, R. *Social equality: The challenge of today*. Chicago: Henry Regnery Co., 1971.

Dunn, J. A. Factor structure of the test anxiety scale for children. *Journal of Consulting Psychology*, 1964, **28**, 92.

Dunn, J. S. Stability of the factor structure of the test anxiety scale for children across age and sex groups. *Journal of Consulting Psychology*, 1965, **29**, 187.

Dyer, H. S. The menace of testing reconsidered. *Educational Horizons*, 1964, **43**, 3–8.

Edehman, M. W. Who is for children? *American Psychologist*, 1981, **36**, 109–116.

Edelberg, R. Electrical activity of the skin: Its measurement and uses in psychophysiology. In N. S. Greenfield & R. A. Sternbach (Eds.), *Handbook of psychophysiology*. New York: Holt, Rinehart & Winston, 1972.

Edington, E. S. Statistical inference from N=1 experiments. *Journal of Psychology*, 1967, **65**, 195–199.

Eikeland, T. A case of conditioned fear in a two-year-old boy after tonsillectomy. *Acta Oto-Laryngologica*, 1973, **76**, 377–380.

Eisenberg, L. School phobia: A study in the communication of anxiety. *American Journal of Psychiatry*, 1958, **114**, 712–718.

Emmelkamp, P. M. G. The behavioral study of clinical phobias. In M. Hersen (Ed.), *Progress in behavior modification*. New York: Academic Press, 1979.

Emmelkamp, P. M. G., & Karpers, A. C. M. Agoraphobia: A follow-up study four years after treatment. *British Journal of Psychiatry*, 1979, **134**, 352–355.

Esveldt-Dawson, K., Wisner, K. L., Unis, A. S., Matson, J. L., & Kazdin, A. E. Treatment of phobias in a hospitalized child. *Journal of Behavior Therapy and Experimental Psychiatry*, 1982, **13**, 77–83.

Evans, I. M., & Nelson, R. O. Assessment of child behavior problems. In A. R. Ciminero, K. S. Calboun, & H. E. Adams (Eds.), *Handbook of behavioral assessment*. New York: Wiley, 1977.

Evers, W. L., & Schwarz, J. C. Modifying social withdrawal in preschoolers: The effects of filmed modeling and teacher praise. *Journal of Abnormal Child Psychology*, 1973, **1**, 248–256.

Evers-Pasquale, W., & Sherman, M. The reward value of peers: A variable influencing the efficacy of film modeling and modifying social isolation preschoolers. *Journal of Abnormal Child Psychology*, 1975, **3**, 179–189.

Eysenck, H. J. The effects of psychotherapy: An evaluation. *Journal of Consulting Psychology*, 1952, **16**, 319–328.

Eysenck, H. J. The effects of psychotherapy: An evaluation. *Journal of Consulting Psychology*, 1952, **16**, 319–328.

Eysenck, H. J. The effects of psychotherapy. In H. J. Eysenck (Ed.), *Handbook of abnormal psychology*. New York: Basic Books, 1961.

Eysenck, H. J. *The effects of psychotherapy*. New York: International Science Press, 1966.

Farnham-Diggory, S. But how do we shape up rigorous behavioral analysts? *Developmental Review*, 1981, **1**, 58–60.

Feld, S., & Lewis, J. Further evidence on the stability of the factor structure of the test anxiety scale for children. *Journal of Consulting Psychology*, 1967, **31**, 434.

Finch, A., Jr., Kendall, P., & Montgomery, L. Multidimensionality of anxiety in children: Factor structure of the Children's Manifest Anxiety Scale. *Journal of Abnormal Child Psychology*, 1974, **2**, 311–334.

Finch, A., Jr., Kendall, P., & Montgomery, L. Qualitative difference in the experience of state-trait anxiety in emotionally disturbed and normal children. *Journal of Personality Assessment*, 1976, **40**, 522–530.

Finch, A., Jr., Kendall, P., Montgomery, L., & Morris, T. Effects of two types of failure on anxiety. *Journal of Abnormal Psychology*, 1975, **84**, 583–586.

Finch, A., Jr., Montgomery, L., Deardorff, P. Children's Manifest Anxiety Scale: Reliability with emotionally disturbed children. *Psychological Reports*, 1974, **34**, 658. (a)

Finch, A., Jr., & Nelson, W. Anxiety and locus of conflict in emotionally disturbed children. *Journal of Abnormal Child Psychology*, 1974, **2**, 33–37.

Fiske, D. W. Two worlds of psychological phenomena. *American Psychologist*, 1979, **34**, 733–739.

Forehand, R., Wells, K. C., & Griest, D. L. An examination of the social validity of a parent training program. *Behavior Therapy*, 1980, **11**, 488–502.

Foster, S. L., & Cone, J. D. Current issues in direct observation. *Behavioral Assessment*, 1980, **2**, 313–338.

Frankl, S., Shiere, F., & Fogels, H. Should the parent remain with the child in dental operatory? *Journal of Dentistry for Children*, 1962, **29**, 150–163.

Freedman, A. M., & Kaplan, H. I. (Eds.) *Comprehensive textbook of psychiatry*. Baltimore: Williams & Wilkins, 1967.

Freeman, B. J., Roy, R. R., & Hemmick, S. Extinction of a phobia of physical examination in a 7-year-old mentally retarded boy: A case study. *Behaviour, Research, and Therapy*, 1976, **14**, 63–64.

Freud, A. Foreword to 'Analysis of a phobia in a five-year-old boy.' *The writings of Anna Freud (Vol. III) 1970–1980*. New York: International Universities Press, Inc., 1981.

Freud, S. (1909) The analysis of a phobia in a five-year-old boy. *Standard edition of the complete psychological works of Sigmund Freud*. Vol. 10. London: Hogarth Press, 1963.

Freud, S. The loss of reality in neurosis and psychosis. 1917. In *Collected papers*. Vol. 2. London: Hogarth Press, 1924.

Friedman, D. E. A new technique for the systematic desensitization of phobic symptoms. *Behaviour Research and Therapy*, 1966, **4**, 139–140.

Gaines-Schwartz, B., Hadley, S. W., & Strupp, H. H. Individual psychotherapy and behavior therapy. *Annual Review of Psychology*, 1978, **29**, 435–471.

Gardner, G. T. Effects of federal human subjects regulations on data obtained in environmental stressor research. *Journal of Personality and Social Psychology*, 1978, **36**, 628–634.

Garfield, S. L., & Bergin, A. E. (Eds.). *Handbook of psychotherapy and behavior change*. (2nd ed.). New York: Wiley, 1978.

Garvey, W., & Hergrenes, J. Desensitization technique in the treatment of school phobia. *American Journal of Orthopsychiatry*, 1966, **36**, 147–152.

Gelfand, D. M. Behavioral treatment of avoidance, social withdrawal and negative emotional states. In B. B. Wolman, J. Egan, & A. O. Ross (Eds.), *Handbook of Treatment of Mental Disorders in Childhood and Adolescence*. Englewood Cliffs, N.J.: Prentice-Hall, 1978.

Gelfand, D. M. Social withdrawal and negative emotional states: Behavior therapy. In B. B. Wolman, J. Egan & A. O. Ross (Eds.), *Handbook of treatment of mental disorders in childhood and adolescence*. Englewood Cliffs, N.J.: Prentice-Hall, 1978.

Genshaft, J. L. The use of cognitive behavior therapy for reducing math anxiety. *School Psychology Review*, 1982, **11**, 32–34.

Gittleman-Klein, R. Pharmacotherapy and management of pathological separation anxiety. *International Journal of Mental Health*, 1975, **4**, 255–271.

Gittleman Klein, R. Psychopharmacological treatment of anxiety disorders, mood disorders, and Tourette's disorder in children. In M. A. Lipton, A. D. Mascio & K. F. Killam (Eds.), *Psychopharmacology: A generation of progress*. New York: Raven Press, 1978.

Gittleman-Klein, R., & Klein, D. F. School phobia: Diagnostic considerations in the light of imipramine effects. *The Journal of Nervous and Mental Disease*, 1973, **156**, 199–215.

Glass, G. V., Wilson, V. L., & Gottman, J. M. *Design and analysis of time-series experiments*. Boulder: University of Colorado Press, 1975.

Glennon, B., & Weisz, J. R. An observational approach to the assessment of anxiety in young children. *Journal of Consulting and Clinical Psychology*, 1978, **46**, 1246–1257.

Glynn, E. L., Thomas, J. D., & Shee, S. M. Behavioral self-control of on-task behavior in an elementary classroom. *Journal of Applied Behavior Analysis*, 1973, **6**, 105–113.

Goldfried, M. Systematic desensitization as training in self-control. *Journal of Consulting and Clinical Psychology*, 1971, **37**, 228–234.

Goldfried, M., & Davison, G. *Clinical behavior therapy*. New York: Holt, 1976.

Goldfried, M., & Goldfried, A. P. Importance of hierarchy content in the self-control of anxiety. *Journal of Consulting and Clinical Psychology*, 1977, **45**, 124–134.

Goldfried, M. R., & Goldfried, A. P. Cognitive change methods. In F. H. Kanfer & A. P. Goldstein (Eds.), *Helping people change.* (2nd ed.) New York: Pergamon Press, 1980.

Goldfried, M. R., & Merbaum, M. A perspective on self-control. In M. R. Goldfried & M. Merbaum (Eds.), *Behavior change through self-control.* New York: Holt, 1973.

Goldstein, A. P. Relationship-enhancement methods. In F. H. Kanfer & A. P. Goldstein (Eds.), *Helping people change.* (2nd ed.) New York: Pergamon, 1980.

Goldstein, A. P., Sprafkin, R. P., & Gershaw, N. J. *Skill training for community living: Applying structured learning therapy.* New York: Pergamon Press/Structured Learning Associates, 1976.

Goldstein, A. P., Sprafkin, R. P., Gershaw, N. J., & Klein, P. The adolescent: Social skills forming through structural learning. In G. Cartledge & J. F. Milburn (Eds.), *Teaching social skills to children: Innovative approaches.* New York: Pergamon Press, 1980.

Goldstein, M. K. Behavior rate change in marriages: Training wives to modify husbands' behavior. *Dissertation Abstracts International*, 1971, **32**, 559.

Gordon, R. L. *Interviewing: Strategy, techniques, and tactics.* (Rev. ed.) Homewood, Il.: The Dorsey Press, 1975.

Gottfredson, S. D. Evaluating psychological research reports: Dimensions, reliability, and correlates of quality judgments. *American Psychologist*, 1978, **33**, 920–964.

Gottman, J. M. *Time-series analysis: A comprehensive introduction for social scientists.* Cambridge: Cambridge University Press, 1981.

Graham, P. *Controlled trial of behavior therapy vs. conventional therapy: A pilot study.* Unpublished D.P.M. dissertation; University of London, 1964.

Gray, B. H. Complexities of informed concern. *Annals of the American Academy of Political and Social Sciences*, 1978, **437**, 37–48.

Gray, J. *The psychology of fear and stress.* New York: McGraw-Hill, 1971.

Graziano, A. M., & DeGiovanni, I. S. The clinical significance of childhood phobias: A note on the proportion of child-clinical referrals for the treatment of children's fears. *Behaviour, Research, and Therapy*, 1979, **17**, 161–162.

Graziano, A. M., DeGiovanni, I. S., & Garcia, K. A. Behavioral treatments of children's fears: A review. *Psychological Bulletin*, 1979, **86**, 804–830.

Graziano, A. M., & Mooney, K. C. Family self-control instruction for children's nighttime fear reduction. *Journal of Consulting Clinical Psychology*, 1980, **48**, 206–213.

Graziano, A. M., Mooney, K. C., Huber, C., & Ignasiak, D. Self-control instructions for children's fear-reduction. *Journal of Behavior Therapy and Experimental Psychiatry*, 1979, **10**, 221–227.

Greenwood, C. R., Todd, N. M., Hops, H., & Walker, H. M. Behavior change targets in the assessment and behavior modification of socially withdrawn pre-school children. *Behavioral Assessment*, in press.

Gresham, F. M., & Nagle, R. J. Treating school phobia using behavioral consultation: A case study. *School Psychology Review*, 1981, **10**, 104–107.

Grey, S., Sartory, G., & Rachman, S. Synchronous and desynchronous changes during fear reduction. *Behaviour Research and Therapy*, 1979, **17**, 137–147.

Gynther, M. D., & Gynther, R. A. Personality interviews. In I. B. Weiner (Ed.), *Clinical methods in psychology.* New York: Wiley, 1976.

Hagman, E. A study of fears of children of preschool age. *Journal of Experimental Education*, 1932, **1**, 110–130.

Hampe, E., Noble, H., Miller, L. C., & Barrett, C. L. Phobic children 1 and 2 years posttreatment. *Journal of Abnormal Psychology*, 1973, **82**, 446–453.

Handler, L. The amelioration of nightmares in children. *Psychotherapy: Theory, Research, & Practice*, 1972, **9**, 54–56.

Harris, B. Whatever happened to little Albert? *American Psychologist*, 1979, **34**, 151–160.

Hart, B. M., Reynolds, N. J., Baer, D. M., Brawley, E. R., & Harris, F. R. Effect of contingent and non-contingent social reinforcement on the cooperative play of a preschool child. *Journal of Applied Behavior Analysis*, 1968, **1**, 73–76.

Hartmann, D. P., Roper, B. L., & Bradford, D. C. Source relationships between behavioral and traditional assessment. *Journal of Behavioral Assessment*, 1979, **1**, 3–21.

Haslam, J. H. Nervous fears of children. In O'Shea, M. V. et al. (Eds.), *The child welfare manual*. Vol. 2. New York: The University Society, 1915.

Hare-Musdin, R. T., Marecek, J., Kaplan, A. G., & Liss-Levinson, N. Rights and responsibilities of therapists. *American Psychologist*, 1979, **34**, 3–16.

Hatzenbuehler, L. C., & Schroeder, H. E. Desensitization procedures in the treatment of childhood disorders. *Psychological Bulletin*, 1978, **85**, 831–844.

Hawkins, R. P. The functions of assessment: Duplications for selection and development of devices for assessing repertoires in clinical, educational, and other settings. *Journal of Applied Behavior Analysis*, 1979, **12**, 501–516.

Hay, W. H., Hay, L. R., Angle, H. V., & Nelson, R. O. The reliability of problem identification in the behavioral interview. *Behavioral Assessment*, 1979, **1**, 107–118.

Hayes, S. C. Theory and technology in behavior analysis. *The Behavior Analyst*, 1978, **1**, 35–41.

Hayes, S. C. Single case experimental design and empirical clinical practice. *Journal of Consulting Psychology*, 1981, **49**, 193–211.

Hayes, S. C., & Nelson, R. O. *Methodological problems in the use of self-monitoring*. Presented at the meeting of the American Psychological Association, San Francisco, August 1977.

Haynes, S. N. *Principles of behavioral assessment*. New York: Gardner Press, 1978.

Haynes, S. N., & Horn, W. F. Reactivity in behavioral observation: A review. *Behavioral Assessment*, in press.

Haynes, S. N., & Jensen, B. J. The interview as a behavioral assessment instrument. *Behavioral Assessment*, 1979, **1**, 97–106.

Haynes, S. N., & Wilson, C. D. *Behavioral Assessment*. San Francisco: Jossey-Bass, 1979.

Herink, R. (Ed.) *The psychotherapy handbook: The A to Z guide to more than 250 different therapies in use today*. New York: New American Library, 1980.

Hersen, M. Treatment of a compulsive and phobic disorder through a total behavior therapy program: A case study. *Psychotherapy: Theory, Research, & Practice*, 1968, **5**, 220–225.

Hersen, M. Behavior modification approach to a school phobia case. *Journal of Clinical Psychology*, 1970, **26**, 128–132.

Hersen, M. Treatment of a compulsive and phobic disorder through a total behavior therapy program: A case study. *Psychotherapy: Theory, Research, and Practice*, 1968, **5**, 220–225.

Hersen, M. Self-assessment of fear. *Behavior Therapy*, 1973, **4**, 241–257.

Hersen, M. Historical perspectives in behavior assessment. In M. Hersen & A. S. Bellack (Eds.), *Behavioral assessment: A practical handbook*. New York: Pergamon Press, 1976.

Hersen, M. Complex problems require complex solutions. *Behavior Therapy*, 1981, **12**, 15–29.

Hersen, M., & Barlow, D. H. *Single case experimental designs: Strategies for studying behavior change*. New York: Pergamon Press, 1976.

Hersen, M., & Bellack, A. S. (Eds.) *Behavioral assessment: A practical handbook*. New York: Pergamon Press, 1976.

Hersen, M., & Bellack, A. S. (Eds.) *Behavioral assessment: A practical handbook*. (2nd ed.) New York: Pergamon Press, 1981.

Hill, J. H., Liebert, R. M., & Mott, D. E. W. Vicarious extinction of avoidance behavior through films: An initial test. *Psychological Reports*, 1968, **22**, 192.

Hill, K., & Sarason, S. *Monographs*. Chicago: Society for Research in Child Development, 1966, **31**(2).

Hiscock, M., & Cohen, D. B. Visual imagery in dream recall. *Journal of Research in Personality*, 1973, **7**, 179–188.

Hodgson, R., & Rachman, S. Desynchrony in measures of fear. *Behaviour Research and Therapy*, 1974, **12**, 319–326.

Holland, C. J. An interview guide for behavioral counseling with parents. *Behavior Therapy*, 1970, **1**, 70–79.

Holmes, F. B. An experimental investigation of a method of overcoming children's fears. *Child Development*, 1936, **7**, 6–30.

Homme, L. E. Contiguity theory and contingency management. *Psychological Record*, 1966, **16**, 233–241.

Hopkins, K. D., & Stanley, J. C. *Educational and psychological measurement and evaluation*. Englewood Cliffs, N.J.: Prentice-Hall, 1981.

Horan, J. J., Layng, F. C., & Pursell, C. H. Preliminary study on effects of "in vivo" emotive imagery on dental discomfort. *Perceptual and Motor Skills*, 1976, **42**, 105–106.

Hugdahl, K. The three-system model of fear and emotion—A critical examination. *Behaviour Research and Therapy*, 1981, **19**, 75–85.

Hugdahl, K., Fredrikson, M., & Öhman, A. "Preparedness" and "arousability" as determinants of electrodermal conditioning. *Behaviour Research and Therapy*, 1977, **15**, 345–353.

Hull, C. *Principles of behavior*. New York: Appleton-Century-Crofts, 1943.

Ilg, F. L., & Ames, L. B. *Child behavior*. New York: Dell, 1955.

Ince, L. P. The use of relaxation training and a conditioned stimulus in the elimination of epileptic seizures in a child. *Journal of Behavior Therapy and Experimental Psychiatry*, 1976, **7**, 39–42.

Irwin, O. C. The distribution of the amount of motility in young infants between two nursing periods. *Journal of Comparative Psychology*, 1932, **14**, 429–445.

Jackson, H. J., & King, N. J. The emotive imagery treatment of a child's trauma-induced phobia. *Journal of Behavior Therapy and Experimental Psychiatry*, 1981, **12**, 325–328.

Jacobson, E. *Progressive relaxation*. Chicago: University of Chicago Press, 1938.

Javel, A. F., & Denholtz, M. S. Audible GSR feedback in systematic desensitization: A case report. *Behavior Therapy*, 1975, **6**, 251–254.

Jayaratne, S., & Levy, R. L. *Empirical clinical practice*. New York: Columbia University Press, 1979.

Jersild, A. T. Studies of children's fears. In R. G. Baker, J. S. Kounin, & H. F. Wright (Eds.), *Child behavior and development*. New York: McGraw-Hill, 1943.

Jersild, A. T. Emotional development. In L. Carmichael (Ed.), *Manual of child psychology*. (2nd ed.) New York: Wiley, 1954.

Jersild, A. T. *Child psychology*. (5th ed.) Englewood Cliffs, N.J.: Prentice-Hall, 1960.

Jersild, A. T. *Child psychology* (6th ed.) Englewood Cliffs, N.J.: Prentice-Hall, Inc., 1968.

Jersild, A. T., & Holmes, F. B. Children's fears. *Child Development Monographs*, 1935, No. 20. (a)

Jersild, A. T., & Holmes, F. B. Methods of overcoming children's fears. *Journal of Psychology*, 1935, **1**, 75–104. (b)

Jersild, A. T., Markey, F. U., & Jersild, C. L. Children's fears, dreams, wishes, daydreams, likes, dislikes, pleasant and unpleasant memories. *Child Development Monograph*, 1933, **12**.

Johnson, P., & Stockdale, D. Effects of puppet therapy on palmar sweating of hospitalized children. *Johns Hopkins Medical Journal*, 1975, **137**, 1–5.

Johnson, R. Maternal influence on child behavior in the dental setting. *Psychiatry in Medicine*, 1971, **2**, 221–228.

Johnson, R., & Machen, J. Modification techniques and maternal anxiety. *Journal of Dentistry for Children*, 1973, **40**, 272–276.

Johnson, S. B. Children's fears in the classroom setting. *School Psychology Digest*, 1979, **8**, 382–396.

Johnson, S. B., & Melamed, B. G. The assessment and treatment of children's fear. In B. B.

Lahey & A. E. Kazdin (Eds.), *Advances in clinical child psychology*. Vol. 2. New York: Plenum, 1979.

Johnson, S. M., & Bolstad, O. D. Methodological issues in naturalistic observation: Some problems and solutions for field research. In L. A. Hamerlynck, L. C. Handy & E. J. Mash (Eds.), *Behavior change: Methodology, concepts, and practice*. Champaign, Illinois: Research Press, 1973.

Johnson, T., Tyler, V., Thompson, R., & Jones, E. Systematic desensitization and assertive training in the treatment of speech anxiety in middle school students. *Psychology in the Schools*, 1971, **8**, 263–267.

Jones, M. C. The elimination of children's fears. *Journal of Experimental Psychology*, 1924, **7**, 382–390. (a)

Jones, M. C. A laboratory study of fear: The case of Peter. *Journal of Genetic Psychology*, 1924, **31**, 308–315. (b)

Jones, R. R., Reid, J. B., & Patterson, G. R. Naturalistic observation in clinical assessment. In P. McReynolds (Ed.), *Advances in psychological assessment*. Vol. 3. San Francisco: Jossey-Bass, 1975.

Kagan, J. *Change and continuity in infancy*. New York: Wiley, 1971.

Kallman, W. M., & Feuerstein, M. Psychophysiological procedures. In A. R. Ciminero, K. S. Calhoun & H. E. Adams (Eds.), *Handbook of behavioral assessment*. New York: John Wiley & Sons, 1977.

Kandel, H. J., Ayllon, T., & Rosenbaum, M. S. Flooding or systematic exposure in the treatment of extreme social withdrawal in children. *Journal of Behavior Therapy and Experimental Psychiatry*, 1977, **8**, 75–81.

Kanfer, F. H. Self-monitoring: Methodological limitations and clinical applications. *Journal of Consulting and Clinical Psychology*, 1970, **35**, 148–152. (a)

Kanfer, F. H. Self-regulation: Research, issues, and speculations. In C. Neringer & J. L. Michael (Eds.), *Behavior Modification in clinical psychology*. New York: Appleton-Century-Crofts, 1970. (b)

Kanfer, F. H. The many faces of self control, or behavior modification changes its focus. In R. B. Stuart (Ed.), *Behavioral self-management: Strategies, techniques, and outcomes*. New York: Brunner/Mazel, 1977.

Kanfer, F. H. Self-management methods. In F. H. Kanfer and A. P. Goldstein (Eds.), *Helping people change*. (2nd ed.) New York: Pergamon Press, 1980.

Kanfer, F. H., Karoly, P., & Newman, A. Reduction of children's fear of the dark by confidence-related and situational threat-related verbal cues. *Journal of Consulting and Clinical Psychology*, 1975, **43**, 251–258.

Kanfer, F. H., & Grimm, L. G. Behavioral analysis: Selecting target behaviors in the interview. *Behavior Modification*, 1977, **1**, 7–28.

Kanfer, F. H., & Phillips, J. S. *Learning foundations of behavior therapy*. New York: Wiley, 1970.

Kanfer, F. H., & Saslow, G. Behavioral diagnosis. In C. M. Franks (Ed.), *Behavior therapy: Appraisal and status*. New York: McGraw-Hill, 1969.

Karoly, P., & Steffen, J. J. (Eds.) *Improving the long-term effects of psychotherapy*. New York: Gardner Press, 1980.

Katz, E. R. *Beta-endorychin and acute behavioral distress in children with leukemia*. Unpublished doctoral dissertation. University of Southern California, 1980.

Katz, E. R., Kellerman, J., & Siegel, S. E. Behavioral distress in children with cancer undergoing medical procedures: Developmental considerations. *Journal of Consulting and Clinical Psychology*, 1980, **48**, 356–365.

Katz, E. R., Kellerman, J., & Siegel, S. E. Anxiety as an affective study in the clinical study of acute behavioral distress: A reply to Shachaur and Daut. *Journal of Consulting and Clinical Psychology*, 1981, **49**, 470–471.

Katz, E. R., Kellerman, J., & Siegel, S. E. *Objective and subjective measurement of behavioral distress in children with cancer.* Manuscript in preparation, 1981.

Kazdin, A. Covert modeling in the reduction of avoidance behavior. *Journal of Abnormal Psychology*, 1973, **81**, 87–95.

Kazdin, A. E. The effect of model identity and fear-relevant similarity on covert modeling. *Behavior Therapy*, 1974, **5**, 624–635. (a)

Kazdin, A. E. Self-monitoring and behavior changes. In M. J. Mahoney & C. E. Thoresen (Eds.), *Self-control: Power to the person.* Monterey: Brooks/Cole, 1974. (b)

Kazdin, A. E. Statistical analysis for single-case experimental designs. In M. Hersen & D. H. Barlow (Eds.), *Single case experimental designs: Strategies for studying behavior change.* New York: Pergamon Press, 1976.

Kazdin, A. E. Artifact, bias, and complexity of assessment: The ABC's of reliability. *Journal of Applied Behavior Analysis*, 1977, **10**, 141–150. (a)

Kazdin, A. E. Assessing the clinical or applied importance of behavior change through social validation. *Behavior Modification*, 1977, **1**, 427–452. (b)

Kazdin, A. E. Evaluating the generality of findings in analogue therapy research. *Journal of Consulting and Clinical Psychology*, 1978, **46**, 673–686. (a)

Kazdin, A. E. *History of behavior modification.* Baltimore: University Park Press, 1978. (b)

Kazdin, A. E. Fictions, factions, and functions of behavior therapy. *Behavior Therapy*, 1979, **10**, 629–654. (a)

Kazdin, A. E. Situational specificity: The two-edged sword of behavioral assessment. *Behavior Assessment*, 1979, **1**, 57–75. (b)

Kazdin, A. E. Acceptability of alternative treatments for deviant child behavior. *Journal of Behavior Analysis*, 1980, **13**, 259–273. (a)

Kazdin, A. E. Acceptability of time-out from reinforcement procedures for disruptive child behavior. *Behavior Therapy*, 1980, **11**, 329–344. (b)

Kazdin, A. E. *Behavior modification in applied settings.* (Rev. ed.) Homewood, Ill.: The Dorsey Press, 1980. (c)

Kazdin, A. E. Investigating generality of findings from analogue research: A rejoinder. *Journal of Consulting and Clinical Psychology*, 1980, **48**, 772–773. (d)

Kazdin, A. E. *Research design in clinical psychology.* New York: Harper & Row, 1980. (e)

Kazdin, A. E. Acceptability of child treatment techniques: The influence of treatment efficacy and adverse side effects. *Behavior Therapy*, 1981, **12**, 493–506. (a)

Kazdin, A. E. Behavioral observation. In M. Hersen & A. S. Bellack (Eds.), *Behavioral assessment: A practical handbook.* (2d ed.) New York: Pergamon Press, 1981. (b)

Kazdin, A. E. Behavior modification in education: Contributions and limitations. *Developmental Review*, 1981, **1**, 34–57. (c)

Kazdin, A. E. Drawing valid inferences from case studies. *Journal of Consulting and Clinical Psychology*, 1981, **49**, 183–192. (d)

Kazdin, A. E. *Methodology of psychotherapy outcome research: Recent developments and remaining limitations.* Paper presented as master lecture at the American Psychological Association, Los Angeles, California, August, 1981. (e)

Kazdin, A. E. Uses and abuses of behavior modification in education: A rejoinder. *Developmental Review*, 1981, **1**, 61–62. (f)

Kazdin, A. E. *Single-case research designs: Methods for clinical and applied settings.* New York: Oxford University Press, 1982.

Kazdin, A. E., & Hersen, M. The current status of behavior therapy. *Behavior Modification*, 1980, **4**, 283–302.

Kazdin, A. E., & Kopel, S. A. On resolving ambiguities in the multiple-baseline design: Problems and recommendations. *Behavior Therapy*, 1975, **6**, 601–608.

Kazdin, A. E., & Wilcoxon, L. A. Systematic desensitization and nonspecific treatment effects: A methodological evaluation. *Psychological Bulletin*, 1976, **83**, 719–758.

Kazdin, A. E., & Wilson, G. T. *Evaluation of behavior therapy: Issues, evidence, and research strategies.* Cambridge, Mass.: Ballinger, 1978.

Keane, T. M., Black, J. L., Collins, F. L., Jr., & Vinson, M. C. A skills training program for teaching the behavioral interview. *Behavior Assessment,* 1982, **4,** 53–62.

Keller, M. F. & Carlson, P. M. The use of symbolic modeling to promote social skills in preschool children with low levels of social responsiveness. *Child Development,* 1974, **45,** 912–919.

Kellerman, J. Rapid treatment of nocturnal anxiety in children. *Journal of Behavior Therapy and Experimental Psychiatry,* 1980, **11,** 9–11.

Kellerman, J. *Helping the fearful child.* New York: Norton, 1981.

Kelley, C. K. Play desensitization of fear of darkness in preschool children. *Behaviour Research and Therapy,* 1976, **14,** 79–81.

Kendall, P. C. Assessing generalization and the single-subject strategies. *Behavior Modification,* 1981, **5,** 307–319. (a)

Kendall, P. C. Cognitive-behavioral interventions with children. In B. B. Lahey & A. E. Kazdin (Eds.), *Advances in clinical child psychology.* Vol. 4. New York: Plenum, 1981.

Kendall, P. C., & Finch, A. J., Jr. Developing non-impulsive behavior in children: Cognitive-behavioral strategies for self-control. In P. C. Kendall & S. D. Hollon (Eds.), *Cognitive-behavioral intervention: Theory, research, and problems.* New York: Academic Press, 1979.

Kendall, P. C., & Hollon, S. D. (Eds.) *Cognitive-behavior interventions: Theory, research, and problems.* New York: Academic Press, 1979.

Kendall, P. C., Pellegrini, D. S., & Urbain, E. S. Approaches to assessment for cognitive-behavioral interventions with children. In P. C. Kendall & S. D. Hollon (Eds.), *Assessment strategies for cognitive-behavioral interventions.* New York: Academic Press, 1981.

Kennedy, W. A. School phobia: Rapid treatment of fifty cases. *Journal of Abnormal Psychology,* 1965, **70,** 285–289.

Kenny, A. *Action, emotion and will.* London: Routledge & Kegan Paul, 1963.

Kent, R. N., & Foster, S. L. Direct observational procedures: Methodological issues in naturalistic settings. In A. R. Ciminero, K. S. Calhoun & H. E. Adams (Eds.), *Handbook of behavioral assessment.* New York: John Wiley & Sons, 1977.

Kern, J. M. Relationships between obtrusive laboratory and unobtrusive naturalistic behavioral fear assessments: "Treated" and untreated subjects. *Behavioral Assessment,* in press.

Kessler, J. Neurosis in childhood. In B. Wolman (Ed.), *Manual of child psychopathology.* New York: McGraw-Hill, 1972.

Kestenbaum, J., & Weiner, B. Achievement performance related to achievement motivation and test anxiety. *Journal of Consulting and Clinical Psychology,* 1970, **34,** 343–344

Kirby, F. D., & Toler, H. C. Modification of a preschool isolate behavior: A case study. *Journal of Applied Behavior Analyses,* 1970, **3,** 309–314.

Kirkland, K. D., & Thelen, M. H. Uses of modeling in child treatment. In B. B. Lahey and A. E. Kazdin (Eds.), *Advances in clinical child psychology.* (Vol. 1). New York: Plenum, 1977.

Kissel, S. Systematic desensitization therapy with children: A case study and some suggested modifications. *Professional Psychology,* 1972, **3,** 164–168.

Klein, D. F., Gittleman, R., Quitkin, F. & Rifkin, A. *Diagnosis and drug treatment of psychiatric disorders: Adults and children.* Baltimore: Williams & Wilkins, 1980.

Klinger, E. Modes of normal conscious flow. In K. S. Pope & J. L. Singer (Eds.), *The stream of consciousness: Scientific investigations into the flow of human experience.* New York: Plenum, 1978.

Klorman, R., Hilpert, P. L., Michael, R., LaGana, C., & Sveen, O. B. Effects of coping and mastery modeling on experienced and inexperienced pedodontic patients' disruptiveness. *Behavior Therapy,* 1980, **11,** 156–168.

Klorman, R., Ratner, J., Arata, C., King, J., & Sveen, O. Predicting the child's uncooperativeness in dental treatment from maternal treatment, state and specific anxiety. *Journal of Dental*

Research, 1977, **56,** 432.

Klorman, R., Weerts, T. C., Hastings, J. E., Melamed, B. G., & Lang, P. J. Psychometric description of some specific-fear questionnaires. *Behavior Therapy,* 1975, **5,** 401–409.

Knopf, I. J. *Childhood psychopathology.* Englewood Cliffs, N.J.: Prentice-Hall, 1979.

Koenigsberg, S., & Johnson, R. Child behavior during sequential dental visits. *Journal of the American Dental Association,* 1972, **85,** 128–132.

Kohn, M. *Congruent competence and symptom factors in the preschool child.* Paper presented at the meeting of the American Psychological Association. Washington, D.C., September, 1969.

Kohn, M. *Social competence, symptoms and under-achievement in childhood: A longitudinal perspective.* Washington, D.C.: Winston, 1977.

Kohn, M., & Rosman, B. L. A social competence scale and symptom checklist for the preschool child: Factor dimensions, their cross-instrument generality, and longitudinal persistence. *Developmental Psychology,* 1972, **6,** 430–444. (a)

Kohn, M., & Rosman, B. L. Relationship of pre-school social-emotional functioning to later intellectual achievement. *Developmental Psychology,* 1972, **6,** 445–542. (b)

Kohn, M., & Rosman, B. L. Cross-situational and longitudinal stability of social-emotional functioning in young children. *Child Development,* 1973, **44,** 721–727.

Kondas, O. Reduction of examination anxiety and "stage fright" by group desensitization and relaxation. *Behaviour Research and Therapy,* 1967, **5,** 275–281.

Koppitz, E. M. *Psychological evaluation of children's human figure drawings.* New York: Grune & Stratton, 1968.

Korchin, S. J., & Schudbery, D. The future of clinical assessment. *American Psychologist,* 1981, **36,** 1147–1148.

Kornhaber, R. C., & Schroeder, H. E. Importance of model similarity on extinction of avoidance behavior in children. *Journal of Consulting and Clinical Psychology,* 1974, **43,** 601–607.

Kozak, M. J., & Miller, G. A. Hypothetical constructs vs. intervening variables: A re-appraisal of the three-systems model of anxiety assessment. *Behavioral Assessment,* 1982, **4,** 347–358.

Kraemer, H. C. Coping strategies in psychiatric clinical research. *Journal of Consulting and Clinical Psychology,* 1981, **49,** 309–318.

Kratochwill, T. R. Intensive research: A review of methodological issues in clinical, counseling, and school psychology. In D. C. Berliner (Ed.), *Review of Research in Education.* Itasca, Ill.: F. E. Peacock Publishers, 1979.

Kratochwill, T. R. *Selective mutism.* New York: Lawrence Erlbaum, 1981.

Kratochwill, T. R. Advances in behavioral assessment. In C. R. Reynolds and T. B. Gutkin (Eds.), *Handbook of School Psychology.* New York: Wiley, 1982.

Kratochwill, T. R. *Time-series research.* New York: Academic Press, in press.

Kratochwill, T. R. (Ed.). *Single subject research: Strategies for evaluating change.* New York: Academic Press, 1978.

Kratochwill, T. R., Bergan, J. R., & Mace, F. C. Practicum competencies needed for implementation of behavioral psychology in the schools: Issues in supervision. *The School Psychology Review,* 1981, **10,** 434–444.

Kratochwill, T. R., & Levin, J. R. What time-series designs may have to offer educational researchers. *Contemporary Educational Psychology,* 1979, **3,** 273–329.

Kratochwill, T. R., & Piersel, W. C. Time series research: Contributors to empirical practice. *Behavioral Assessment,* in press.

Kratochwill, T. R., Schnaps, A., & Bissell, M. S. Research design in school psychology. In J. R. Bergan (Ed.), *School psychology in contemporary society.* Columbus, Ohio: Charles E. Merrill, in press.

Kraus, P. E. *Yesterday's children: A longitudinal study of children from kindergarten into the adult years.* New York: Wiley, 1973.

Krug, S. E. The role of personality assessment in the schools: A conversation with Dr. Raymond B. Cattell. *The School Psychology Digest,* 1978, **7,** 26–35.

Kuroda, J. Elimination of children's fears of animals by the method of experimental desensitization—An application of learning theory to child psychology. *Psychologia*, 1969, **12**, 161–165.

Kushner, M. Desensitization of a post-traumatic phobia. In L. P. Ullmann & L. Krasner (Eds.), *Case studies in behavior modification*. New York: Holt, Rinehart & Winston, 1965.

Kutina, J., & Fischer, J. Anxiety, heart rate and their interrelation at mental stress in school children. *Activitas Nervos Superior*, 1977, **19**, 89–95.

Lang, P. J. Experimental studies of desensitization psychotherapy. In J. Wolpe (Ed.), *The conditioning therapies*. New York: Holt, Rinehart, & Winston, 1964.

Lang, P. J. Fear reduction and fear behavior: Problems in treating a construct. In J. M. Shlier (Ed.), *Research in psychotherapy*. Vol. 3. Washington, D.C.: American Psychological Association, 1968.

Lang, P. J. The application of psychophysiological methods to the study of psychotherapy and behavior modification. In A. E. Bergan & S. L. Garfield (Eds.), *Handbook of psychotherapy and behavior change*. New York: Wiley, 1971.

Lang, P. J. Psychophysiological assessment of anxiety and fear. In J. D. Cone & R. P. Hawkins (Eds.), *Behavioral assessment: New directions in clinical psychology*. New York: Brunner/Mazel, 1977. (a)

Lang, P. J. The psychophysiology of anxiety. In J. Akiskal (Ed.), *Psychiatric diagnosis: Exploration of biological criteria*. New York: Spectrum, 1977. (b)

Lang, P. J. Anxiety: Towards a psychological definition. In H. S. Akiskal & W. L. Webb (Eds.), *Psychiatric diagnosis: Exploration of biological criteria*. New York: Spectrum, 1978. (a)

Lang, P. J. Self-efficacy theory: Thoughts on cognition and unification. In S. Rachman (Ed.), *Advances in Behavior Research and Therapy*, 1978, **1**, 187–192. (b)

Lang, P. J. A bio-informational theory of emotional imagery. *Psychophysiology*, 1979, **16**, 495–512.

Lang, P. J., & Lazovik, A. D. Experimental desensitization of a phobia. *Journal of Abnormal and Social Psychology*, 1963, **66**, 519–525.

Lapouse, R., & Monk, M. A. Fears and worries in a representative sample of children. *American Journal of Orthopsychiatry*, 1959, **29**, 803–818.

Laxer, R. M., Quarter, J., Kooman, A. & Walker, K. Systematic desensitization and relaxation of high test-anxious secondary school students. *Journal of Counseling Psychology*, 1969, **16**, 446–451.

Lazarus, A. A. The elimination of children's phobias by deconditioning. In H. J. Eysenck (Ed.), *Behaviour therapy and the neuroses*. Oxford: Pergamon Press, 1960.

Lazarus, A. A. & Abramovitz, A. The use of emotive imagery in the treatment of children's phobias. *Journal of Mental Science*, 1962, **108**, 191–195.

Lazarus, A. A., Davison, G. C., & Polefka, D. A. Classical and operant factors in the treatment of school phobia. *Journal of Abnormal Psychology*, 1965, **70**, 225–229.

Leal, L. L., Baxter, E. G., Martin, J., & Marx, R. W. Cognitive modification and systematic desensitization with test anxious high school students. *Journal of Counseling Psychology*, 1981, **28**, 525–528.

Lehrer, P. M., & Woolfolk, R. L. Self-report assessment of anxiety: Physiological, cognitive, and behavioral modalities. *Behavioral Assessment*, 1982, **4**, 167–177.

Leitenberg, H., Agras, S., Butz, R., & Wincze, J. Relationship between heart rate and behavioral change during the treatment of phobias. *Journal of Abnormal Psychology*, 1971, **78**, 59–68.

Leitenberg, H., & Callahan, E. J. Reinforced practice and reductions of different kinds of fears in adults and children. *Behavior Research and Therapy*, 1973, **11**, 19–30.

Leton, D. Assessment of school phobia. *Mental Hygiene*, 1962, **46**, 256–264.

Levin, J. R. Determining the sample size for planned and post analysis of variance comparisons. *Journal of Educational Measurement*, 1975, **12**, 99–108.

Levin, J. R. What have we learned about maximizing what children learn? In J. R. Levin & V. I.

274 Treating Children's Fears and Phobias

Allen (Eds.), Cognitive learning in children: Theories and strategies. New York: Academic Press, 1976.

Levin, J. R., Marascuelo, L. M., & Hubert, L. N. Nonparametric randomization tests. In T. R. Kratochwill (Ed.), *Single subject research: Strategies to evaluate change.* New York: Academic Press, 1978.

Levis, D. J. Implementing the technique of implosive therapy. In A. Goldstein & E. B. Foa (Eds.), *Handbook of behavioral interventions: A clinical guide.* New York: Wiley, 1980.

Levis, D. J. Implosive therapy: A critical analysis of Morganstern's review. *Psychological Bulletin,* 1974, **81,** 155–158.

Lewis, M., & Brooks, J. Self, other, and fear: Infants reactions to people. In M. Lewis & L. A. Rosenblum (Eds.), *The origins of behavior: The origins of fear.* (Vol. 2) New York: Wiley, 1974.

Lewis, S. A comparison of behavior therapy techniques in the reduction of fearful avoidant behavior. *Behavior Therapy,* 1974, **5,** 648–655.

Lick, J. R., Unger, T., & Condiotte, M. Effects of uncertainty about the behavior of a phobic stimulus on subjects' fear reactions. *Journal of Consulting and Clinical Psychology,* 1978, **46,** 1559–1560.

Lighthall, F. Defensive and non-defensive changes in children's responses to personality questionnaires. *Child Development,* 1963, **34,** 455–470.

Lindsley, O. R. Direct measurement and prosthesis of retarded behavior. *Journal of Education,* 1964, **147,** 62–81.

Linehan, M. M. Issues in behavioral interviewing. In J. D. Cone & R. P. Hawkins (Eds.), *Behavioral assessment: New directions in clinical psychology.* New York: Brunner/Mazel, 1977.

Lippman, H. S. The phobic child and other related anxiety states. In M. Hammer & A. M. Kaplan (Eds.), *The practice of psychotherapy with children.* Homewood, Ill.: Dorsey Press, 1967.

Lipton, H. Rapid reinstatement of speech using stimulus fading with a selectively mute child. *Journal of Behavior Therapy and Experimental Psychiatry,* 1980, **11,** 147–149.

Lore, R. Palmar sweating and transitory anxieties in children. *Child Development,* 1966, **37,** 115–123.

Lotman, V. Security Mutual Life Insurance Co., F 2nd 8 68 (3rd Cir., 1973).

Love, D. W., Weise, H. J., Henson, R. E., & Parker, C. L. Teaching interviewing skills to pharmacy residents. *American Journal of Hospital Pharmacy,* 1978, **35,** 1073–1074.

Luiselli, J. K. Case report: An attendant-administered contingency management program for the treatment of toileting phobia. *Journal of Mental Deficiency Research,* 1977, **21,** 283–288.

Luiselli, J. K. Treatment of an autistic child's fear of riding a school bus through exposure and reinforcement. *Journal of Behavior Therapy and Experimental Psychiatry,* 1978, **9,** 169–172.

Luiselli, J. K. Relaxation training with the developmentally disabled: A reappraisal. *Behavior Research on Severe Developmental Disabilities,* 1980, **1,** 191–213.

Luiselli, J. K. Assessing the effects of relaxation training. *Behavior Therapy,* 1979, **10,** 663–668.

MacCoby, E. E. & Jacklin, C. N. *The psychology of sex differences.* Stanford: Stanford University Press, 1974.

MacDonald, M. L. Multiple impact behavior therapy in a child's dog phobia. *Journal of Behavior Therapy and Experimental Psychiatry,* 1975, **6,** 317–322.

MacFarlane, J. W., Allen, L., & Hozik, M. P. *A developmental study of the behavior problems of normal children between twenty-one months and fourteen years.* Berkeley: University of California Press, 1954.

Machen, J. B., & Johnson, R. Desensitization, model learning, and the dental behavior of children. *Journal of Dental Research,* 1974, **58,** 83–87.

Magrath, K. *Investigating the developmental analysis of children's fears.* Unpublished doctoral dissertation. Syracuse University, 1982.

Mahoney, D. M., Harper, T. M., Braukmann, C. J. Fixsen, D. L., Phillips, E. L., & Wolf, M. M. Teaching conversation-related skills to predelinquent girls. *Journal of Applied Behavior Analysis*, 1976, **9**, 371.

Mahoney, M. J. *Cognition and behavior modification*. Cambridge, Mass.: Ballinger Publishing Company, 1974.

Mahoney, M. J. *Abnormal psychology: Perspectives on human variance*. San Francisco: Harper & Row, 1980.

Mahoney, M. P., & Ward, M. P. *Psychological assessment: A conceptual approach*. New York: Oxford University Press, 1976.

Mallory, W. A., & Russell, R. L Behavior modification as a value-laden technology: Implications for selection of intervention strategies with developmentally handicapped clients. *Behaviorists for Social Action Journal*, 1981, **3**, 194–199.

Mandler, G., Mandler, J. M., & Uviller, E. T. Autonomic activity. *Journal of Abnormal and Social Psychology*, 1958, **56**, 367–373.

Mann, J. Vicarious desensitization of test anxiety through observation of videotaped treatment. *Journal of Counseling Psychology*, 1972, **19**, 1–7.

Mann, J., & Rosenthal, T. L. Vicarious and direct counterconditioning of test anxiety through individual and group desensitization. *Behaviour Research and Therapy*, 1969, **7**, 359–367.

Mann, I., Taylor, R., Jr., Proger, B., & Morrell, J. Test anxiety and defensiveness against admission of test anxiety induced by frequent testing. *Psychological Reports*, 1968, **23**, 1283–1286.

Marholin, D. II, & Bijou, S. W. Behavioral assessment: Listen when the data speak. In D. Marholin II (Ed.), *Child behavior therapy*. New York: Gardner Press, 1978.

Marine, E. School refusal-who should intervene? *Journal of School Psychology*, 1968–69, **7**, 63–70.

Marks, I. M. *Fears and phobias*. New York: Academic Press, 1969.

Marks, I. M. Research in neurosis: A selective review. I. Causes and courses. *Psychological Medicine*, 1973, **3**, 436–454.

Marshall, W. L., Gauthier, J., Christies, M. M., Curries, D. W., & Gordon, A. Flooding therapy effectiveness, stimulus characteristics, and the value of brief *in vivo* exposure. *Behaviour Research and Therapy*, 1977, **15**, 79–87

Martinez, L. *A comparison of self-control desensitization with systematic desensitization in the reduction of test anxiety*. Unpublished dissertation. Syracuse University, 1978.

Mash, E. J. & Terdal, L. G. (Eds.) *Behavior therapy assessment: Diagnosis, design, and evaluation*. New York: Springer, 1976.

Mash, E. J., & Terdall, L. G. Follow-up assessments in behavior therapy. In P. Karoly & J. J. Steffen (Eds.), *Improving the long term effects of psychotherapy*. New York: Gardner Press, 1980.

Mash, E. J., & Terdall, L. G. (Eds.) *Behavioral assessment of childhood disorders*. New York: The Guilford Press, 1981. (a)

Mash, E. J., & Terdall, L. G. Behavioral assessment of childhood disturbance. In E. J. Mash & L. G. Terdall (Eds.), *Behavioral assessment of childhood disorders*. New York: The Guilford Press, 1981. (b)

Mathews, A. M., Gelder, M. G., & Johnston, D. W. *Agoraphobia: Nature and treatment*. New York: The Guilford Press, 1981.

Matison, R., Cantwell, D. P., Russell, A. T., & Will, L. A comparison of DSM-II in the diagnosis of childhood psychiatric disorders: II. Interrater agreement. *Archives of General Psychiatry*, 1979, **36**, 1217–1222.

Matson, J. L. Assessment and treatment of clinical fears in mentally retarded children. *Journal of Applied Behavior Analysis*, 1981, **14**, 287–294.

Mavissakalian, M., & Barlow, D. H. (Eds.), *Phobia: Psychological and pharmacological treat-*

ment. New York: The Guilford Press, 1981. (a)

Mavissakalian, M., & Barlow, D. H. Phobia: An overview. In M. Mavissakalian & D. H. Barlow (Eds.), *Phobia: Psychological and pharmacological treatment*. New York: The Guilford Press, 1981. (b)

Maurer, A. What children fear. *Journal of Genetic Psychology*, 1965, **106**, 265–277.

McCleary, R. M., & Hay, R. A., Jr. *Applied time series analysis for the social sciences*. Beverly Hills: Sage, 1980.

McFall, R. M. Analogue methods in behavioral assessment: Issues and prospects. In J. D. Cone & R. P. Hawkins (Eds.), *Behavioral assessment: New directions in clinical psychology*. New York: Brunner/Mazel, 1977. (a)

McFall, R. M. Parameters of self-monitoring. In R. B. Stuart (Ed.), *Behavioral strategies, techniques, and outcomes*. New York: Brunner/Mazel, 1977. (b)

McLemore, C. W. Factorial validity of imagery measures. *Behaviour Research and Therapy*. 1972, **14**, 399–408.

McLemore, C. W., & Benjamin, L. S. Whatever happened to interpersonal diagnosis?: A psychosocial alternative to DSM-III. *American Psychologist*, 1979, **34**, 17–34.

McMahon, R. J., & Forehand, R. Self-help behavior therapies in parent training. In B. B. Lahey & A. E. Kazdin (Eds.), *Advances in clinical child psychology*. (Vol. 3) New York: Plenum, 1980.

McNally, R. J., & Reiss, S. The preparedness theory of phobias and human safety-signal conditioning. *Behaviour Research and Therapy*, 1982, **20**, 153–159.

McReynolds, W. P. DSM-III and the future of applied social science. *Professional Psychology*, 1979, **10**, 123–132.

McReynolds, W. T. Anxiety as fear: A behavioral approach to one emotion. In M. Zuckerman & C. Spielberger (Eds.), *Emotions and anxiety*. New York: Wiley, 1976.

Meichenbaum, D. Self-instructional methods. In F. H. Kanfer & A. P. Goldstein (Eds.), *Helping people change*. New York: Pergamon Press, 1974.

Meichenbaum, D., & Gerest, M. Cognitive behavior modification: An integration of cognitive and behavioral methods. In F. H. Kanfer and A. P. Goldstein (Eds.), *Helping people change*. (2nd ed.) New York: Pergamon Press, 1980.

Meisel, A., Roth, L. H., & Lidz, C. W. Toward a model of the legal doctrine of informed consent. *American Journal of Psychiatry*, 1977, **134**, 285–289.

Melamed, B. Behavioral approaches to fear in dental settings. In M. Hersen, R. Eisler & P. Miller (Eds.), *Progress in behavior modification*. Vol. 7. New York: Academic Press, 1979.

Melamed, B. G., & Siegel, L. J. *Behavior medicine*. New York: Springer, 1980.

Melamed, B. G., Yurcheson, R., Fleece, E. L., Hutcherson, S., & Hawes, R. Effects of film modeling on the reduction of anxiety-related behaviors in individuals varying in level or previous experience in the stress situation. *Journal of Consulting and Clinical Psychology*, 1978, **46**, 1357–1367.

Melamed, B., Hawes, R. R., Heigy, E., & Glick, J. Use of filmed modeling to reduce uncooperative behavior of children during dental treatment. *Journal of Dental Research*, 1975, **54**, 797–801.

Melamed, B., & Siegel, L. Reduction of anxiety in children facing hospitalization and surgery by use of filmed modeling. *Journal of Consulting and Clinical Psychology*, 1975, **43**, 511–521.

Melamed, B., Weinstein, D., Hawes, R., & Katin-Borland, M. Reduction of fear related dental management problems using filmed modeling. *Journal of the American Dental Association*, 1975, **90**, 822–826.

Meyer, V., Liddell, A., & Lyons, M. Behavioral interviews. In A. R. Ciminero, K. S. Calhoun & H. E. Adams (Eds.), *Handbook of behavioral assessment*. New York: Wiley, 1977.

Milgram, R., & Milgram, N. The effect of test content and context on the anxiety-intelligence relationship. *Journal of Genetic Psychology*, 1977, **130**, 121–127.

Miller, A. M. & Kratochwill, T. R. Reduction of frequent stomachache complaints by time-out. *Behavior Therapy*, 1979, **10**, 211–218.

Miller, B., & Wolpe, J. Automated self-desensitization: A case report. *Behaviour Research and Therapy*, 1967, **5**, 133–135.

Miller, L. C. Louisville Behavioral Check List for males 6–12 years of age. *Psychological Reports*, 1967, **21**, 855–896.

Miller, L. C., Barrett, C. L., & Hampe, E. Phobias of childhood in a prescientific era. In A. Davids (Ed.), *Child personality and psychopathology: Current topics*. New York: Wiley, 1974.

Miller, L. C., Barrett, C. L., Hampe, E., & Noble, H. Revised anxiety scales for the Louisville Behavior Check List. *Psychological Reports*, 1971, **29**, 503–511.

Miller, L. C., Barrett, C. L., Hampe, E., & Noble, H. Comparison of reciprocal inhibition, psychotherapy and waiting list control for phobic children. *Journal of Abnormal Psychology*, 1972, **79**, 269–279. (a)

Miller, L. C., Barrett, C. L., Hampe, E., & Noble, H. Factor structure of childhood fears. *Journal of Consulting and Clinical Psychology*, 1972, **39**, 264–268. (b)

Miller, P. M. The use of visual imagery and muscle relaxation in the counterconditioning of a phobic child: A case study. *Journal of Nervous and Mental Disease*, 1972, **154**, 457–460.

Mills, H. L., Agras, W. S., Barlow, D. H., & Mills, J. R. Compulsive rituals treated by response prevention: An experimental analysis. *Archives of General Psychiatry*, 1973, **28**, 524–529.

Mischel, W. *Personality and assessment*. New York: Wiley, 1968.

Mischel, W. Toward a cognitive social learning reconceptualization of personality. *Psychological Review*, 1973, **80**, 252–283.

Mischel, W. Cognitive appraisals and transformations in self-control. In B. Weiner (Ed.), *Cognitive views of human motivation*. New York: Academic Press, 1974.

Mischel, W. On the interface of cognition and personality: Beyond the person-situation debate. *American Psychologist*, 1979, **34**, 740–754.

Montgomery, L., & Finch, A., Jr. Validity of two measures of anxiety in children. *Journal of Abnormal Child Psychology*, 1974, **2**, 293–296.

Morgan, G. A. Children who refuse to go to school. *Medical Officer*, 1959, **103**, 221–224.

Morganstern, K. P. Implosive therapy and flooding procedures: The critical review. *Psychological Bulletin*, 1973, **79**, 318–334.

Morganstern, K. Behavioral interviewing: The initial stages of assessment. In M. Hersen & A. Bellack (Eds.), Behavioral assessment: *A practical handbook*. New York: Pergamon Press, 1976.

Morris, R. J. Shaping relaxation in the unrelaxed client. *Journal of Behavior Therapy and Experimental Psychiatry*, 1973, **4**, 343–353.

Morris, R. J. *Behavior modification with children: A systematic guide*. Cambridge, Mass.: Winthrop, 1976.

Morris, R. J. Fear reduction methods. In F. H. Kanfer & A. P. Goldstein (Eds.), *Helping people change*. (2nd ed.) New York: Pergamon Press, 1980.

Morris, R. J., & Dolker, M. Developing cooperative play in socially withdrawn retarded children. *Mental Retardation*, 1974, **12**, 24–27.

Morris, R. J., & Dolker, M. A constituent analysis of contact desensitization with snake fearful children. *Education and Treatment of Children*, in press.

Morris, R. J., & Magrath, K. Contribution of therapist warmth to the contact desensitization treatment of acrophobia. *Journal of Consulting and Clinical Psychology*, 1979, **47**, 786–788.

Morris, R. J., & Magrath, K. The therapeutic relationship in behavior therapy. In M. Lambert (Ed.), *Therapeutic relations in psychotherapy*. Homewood, Ill.: Dow-Jones-Irwin, 1982.

Morris, R. J., & Suckerman, K. R. The importance of the therapeutic relationship in systematic desensitization. *Journal of Consulting and Clinical Psychology*, 1974, **42**, 148. (a)

Morris, R. J., & Suckerman, K. R. Therapist warmth as a factor in automated systematic desensitization. *Journal of Consulting and Clinical Psychology*, 1974, **42**, 244–250. (b)

Morris, R. J., & Suckerman, K. R. Studying therapist warmth in analogue systematic desensitization. *Journal of Consulting and Clinical Psychology*, 1976, **44**, 285–289.

Mosak, H. H. Adlerian psychotherapy. In R. J. Corsini (Ed.), *Current psychotherapies*. Itasca, Ill.: F. E. Peacock Publishers, 1979.

Mowrer, O. H. A stimulus-response analysis of anxiety and its role as a reinforcing agent. *Psychological Review*, 1939, **46**, 553–565.

Mowrer, O. H. *Learning theory and behavior*. New York: John Wiley & Sons, 1960.

Muller, S. D. & Madsen, C. H. Group desensitization for "anxious" children with reading problems. *Psychology in the Schools*, 1970, **7**, 184–189.

Murphy, C. M., & Bootzin, R. R. Active and passive participation in the contact desensitization of snake fear in children. *Behavioral Therapy*, 1973, **4**, 203–211.

Nalven, F. B. Manifest fears and worries of ghetto versus middle class suburban children. *Psychological Reports*, 1970, **27**, 285–286.

Nathan, P. E. Symptomatic diagnosis and behavioral assessment: A synthesis? In D. A. Barlow (Ed.), *Assessment of adult disorders*. New York: Guilford Press, 1981.

Nawas, M. M. Standardized scheduled desensitization: Some unstable results and an improved program. *Behaviour Research and Therapy*, 1971, **9**, 35–38.

Nay, W. R. Analogue measures. In A. R. Ciminero, K. S. Calhoun, & H. E. Adams (Eds.), *Handbook of behavioral assessment*. New York: John Wiley & Sons, 1977.

Neisworth, J. T., Madle, R. A., & Goeke, K. E. Errorless elimination of separation anxiety: A case study. *Journal of Behavioral Therapy and Experimental Psychiatry*, 1975, **6**, 79–82.

Nelson, R. O. Assessment and therapeutic functions of self-monitoring. In M. Hersen et al. (Eds.), *Progress in behavior modification*. Vol. 5. New York: Academic, 1977.

Nelson, R. O. Realistic dependent measures for clinical use. *Journal of Consulting and Clinical Psychology*, 1981, **49**, 168–182.

Nelson, R. O., & Barlow, D. H. Behavioral assessment: Basic strategies and initial procedures. In D. H. Barlow (Ed.), *Assessment of Adult Disorders*. New York: Guilford, 1981.

Nelson, R. O., & Bowles, P. E. The best of two worlds—Observation with norms. *Journal of School Psychology*, 1975, **13**, 3–9.

Nelson, R. P., Hayes, S. C. The nature of behavioral assessment: A commentary. *Journal of Applied Behavior Analysis*, 1979, **12**, 491–500.

Nelson, R. O., & Hayes, S. C. Some current dimensions of behavioral assessment. *Behavioral Assessment*, 1979, **1**, 1–16.

Newstatter, W. L. The effect of poor social conditions in the production of neurosis. *Lancet*, 1938, **234**, 1436–1441.

Nietzel, M. T., & Bernstein, D. A. Assessment of anxiety and fear. In M. Hersen & A. S. Bellack (Eds.), *Behavioral assessment: A practical handbook*. (2nd ed.) New York: Pergamon, 1981.

O'Connor, R. D. Modification of social withdrawal through symbolic modeling. *Journal of Applied Behavior Analysis*, 1969, **2**, 15–22.

O'Connor, R. D. Relative efficacy of modeling, shaping and the combined procedures from modification of social withdrawal. *Journal of Abnormal Psychology*, 1972, **79**, 327–334.

Oden, S. A child's social isolation: Origins, prevention, intervention. In G. Cartledge & J. F. Milburn (Eds.), *Teaching social skills to children*. New York: Pergamon Press, 1980.

Oden, S., & Asher, S. R. Coaching children in social skills for friendship making. *Child Development*, 1977, **48**, 495–506.

O'Farrell, T. J., Hedlund, M. A., & Cutter, H. S. G. Desensitization for a severe phobia of a fourteen year old male. *Child Behavior Therapy*, in press.

Öhman, A., Eriksson, A., & Olofsson, C. One-trial learning and superior resistance to extinction of autonomic responses conditioned to potentially phobic stimuli. *Journal of Comparative and Physiological Psychology*, 1975, **88**, 619–627.

Öhman, A., Erixon, G., & Löfberg, I. Phobias and preparedness: Phobic versus neutral pictures as conditioned stimuli for human autonomic responses. *Journal of Abnormal Psychology*, 1975, **84**, 41–45.

O'Leary, K. D., & Johnson, S. B. Psychological assessment. In H. C. Quay & J. S. Werry (Eds.), *Psychopathological disorders of childhood*. (2nd ed.) New York: John Wiley & Sons, 1979.

Ollendick, T. H. Behavioral treatment of anorexia nervosa: A five year study. *Behavior Modification*, 1979, **3**, 124–135.

Ollendick, T. H. Assessment of social interaction skills in school children. *Behavioral Counselling Quarterly*, 1981, **1**, 227–243.

Ollendick, T. H., & Gruen, G. E. Treatment of a bodily injury phobia with implosive therapy. *Journal of Consulting and Clinical Psychology*, 1972, **38**, 389–393.

O'Reilly, P. Desensitization of fire bell phobia. *Journal of School Psychology*, 1971, **9**, 55–57.

O'Toole, W. Effects of practice and some methodological considerations in training counseling interviewing skills. *Journal of Counseling Psychology*, 1979, **26**, 419–426.

Paivio, A., Baldwin, A., & Berger, A. A measurement of children's sensitivity to audiences. *Child Development*, 1961, **32**, 721–730.

Parsonson, B. S., & Baer, D. M. The analysis and presentation of graphic data. In T. R. Kratochwill (Ed.), *Single subject research: Strategies for evaluating change*. New York: Academic Press, 1978.

Patterson, G. R. A learning theory approach to the treatment of the school phobic child. In L. P. Ullmann & L. Krasner (Eds.), *Case studies in behavior modification*. New York: Holt, Rinehart, and Winston, 1965.

Paul, G. L. *Insight vs. desensitization in psychotherapy*. Stanford, California: Stanford University Press, 1966.

Paul, G. L., & Bernstein, D. A. *Anxiety and clinical problems: Systematic desensitization and related techniques*. Morristown, N.J.: General Learning Press, 1973.

Paul, G. L., & Bernstein, D. A. Anxiety and clinical problems: Systematic desensitization and related techniques. In J. T. Spence, R. C. Carson, & J. W. Thibaut (Eds.), *Behavioral approaches to therapy*. Morristown, N.J.: General Learning Press, 1976.

Pavlov, I. P. *Conditioned reflexes*. Translated by G. V. Anrep. London: Oxford University Press, 1927.

Pennington, L. W. Provision of school psychological services. *The School Psychology Digest*, 1977, **6**, 50–57.

Perry, M. A., & Furukawa, M. J. Modeling methods. In F. H. Kanfer and A. P. Goldstein (Eds.) *Helping people change*. (2nd ed.) New York: Pergamon Press, 1980.

Peterson, D. R. *The clinical study of social behavior*. New York: Appleton-Century-Crofts, 1968.

Peterson, L., & Shigetomi, C. *The use of a self-control procedure to minimize pain and anxiety in hospitalized children*. Unpublished manuscript, University of Utah, 1978.

Peterson, L., & Shigetomi, C. The use of coping techniques in minimizing anxiety in hospitalized children. *Behavior Therapy*, 1981, **12**, 1–14.

Petrie, P., Brown, D. K., Piersel, W. C., Frinkfrock, S. R., Schelble, M., LeBlanc, C. P., & Kratochwill, T. R. The school psychologist as behavioral ecologist. *Journal of School Psychology*, 1980, **18**, 222–233.

Phillips, B. N. *An analysis of causes of anxiety among children in school*. (Final Rep., Proj. No. 2616, U.S.O.E. Cooperative Research Branch) Austin, Texas: University of Texas, 1966.

Phillips, B. N. *School stress and anxiety: Theory, research, and intervention*. New York: Human Sciences Press, 1978.

Phillips, C. A psychological analysis to tension headache. In S. J. Rachman (Ed.), *Contributions to medical psychology*. Oxford: Pergamon Press, 1977.

Phillips, D., & Wolpe, S. Multiple behavioral techniques in severe separation anxiety of a 12-yr-old. *Journal of Behavior Therapy and Experimental Psychiatry*, 1981, **12**, 329–332.

Phillips, L., & Draguns, J. G. Classification of the behavior disorders. *Annual Review of Psychology*, 1971, **22**, 447–482.

Phillips, L., Draguns, J. G., & Bartlett, D. P. Classification of behavior disorders. In N. Hobbs (Ed.), *Issues in the classification of children*. Vol. 1. San Francisco: Jossey-Bass, 1975.

Piersel, W. C., & Kratochwill, T. R. A teacher-implemented contingency management package to assess and test selective mutism. *Behavioral Assessment*, 1981, **3**, 371–382.

Pomerantz, P. B., Peterson, N. T., Marholin, D., & Stern, S. The *in vivo* elimination of a child's water phobia by a paraprofessional at home. *Journal of Behavior Therapy and Experimental Psychiatry*, 1977, **8**, 417–421.

Porter, R. B., & Cattell, R. B. *The Children's Personality Questionnaire*. Champaign, Ill.: Institute of Personality & Abilities Testing, 1963.

Poznanski, E. O. Children with excessive fears. *American Journal of Orthopsychiatry*, 1973, **43**, 428–348.

Pratt, K. C. The study of the "fears" of rural children. *Journal of Genetic Psychology*, 1945, **67**, 179–194.

Pratt, K. C., Nelson, A. K., & Sun, K. H. The behavior of the newborn infant. *Ohio State University Studies Contributions in Psychology*, 1930, no. 10.

Pressley, M. Imagery and children's learning: Putting the picture in developmental perspective. Review of Educational Research, 1977, **47**, 585–622.

Prokasy, W. F., & Raskin, D. C. (Eds.), *Electrodermal activity in psychological research.* New York: Academic Press, 1973.

Quay, H. C. Classification. In H. C. Quay & J. S. Werry (Eds.), *Psychopathological disorders of childhood.* (2nd ed.) New York: Wiley, 1979.

Rachlin, H. Self-control. *Behaviorism.* 1974, **2**, 94–107.

Rachman, S. Studies in desensitization: II flooding. *Behaviour Research and Therapy,* 1966, **4**, 1–6.

Rachman, S. *Phobias: Their nature and control.* Springfield, Ill.: Charles C. Thomas, 1968.

Rachman, S. Observational learning and therapeutic modeling. In M. P. Feldman & A. Broadhurst (Eds.), *Theoretical and empirical bases of the behavior therapies.* London: Wiley, 1976. (a)

Rachman, S. The passing of the two-stage theory of fear and avoidance: Fresh possibilities. *Behaviour Research and Therapy*, 1976, **14**, 125–134. (b)

Rachman, S. The conditioning theory of fear-acquisition: A critical examination. *Behaviour Research and Therapy*, 1977, **15**, 375–387.

Rachman, S. *Fear and courage.* San Francisco: Freeman, 1978.

Rachman, S. & Hodgson, R. Synchrony and desynchrony in fear and avoidance. *Behaviour Research and Therapy*, 1974, **12**, 311–318.

Rachman, S. J., & Wilson, G. T. *The effects of psychological therapy.* (2nd ed.) Oxford: Pergamon Press, 1980.

Rakover, S. S. Generalization from analogue therapy to the clinical situation: The paradox and the dilemma of generality. *Journal of Consulting and Clinical Psychology*, 1980, **48**, 770–771.

Rasbury, W. C. Behavioral treatment of selective mutism: A case report. *Journal of Behavior Therapy and Experimental Psychiatry*, 1974, **5**, 103–104.

Raskin, D. C. Attention and arousal. In W. F. Prokasy & D. C. Raskin (Eds.), *Electrodermal activity in psychological research.* New York: Academic, 1973.

Ray, R. L., & Kimmel, H. D. Utilization of psychophysiological indices in behavioral assessment: Some methodological issues. *Journal of Behavioral Assessment*, 1979, **2**, 107–122.

Ray, W. J., & Raczynski, J. M. Psychophysiological assessment. In M. Hersen & A. S. Bellack (Eds.), *Behavioral assessment: A practical handbook.* (2nd ed.) New York: Pergamon, 1981.

Redd, W. H., Porterfield, A. L., & Andersen, B. L. *Behavior modification.* New York: Random House, 1979.

Reeves, J. L. & Maelica, W. L. Biofeedback—assisted cue controlled relaxation for the treatment of flight phobias. *Journal Behavior Therapy in Experimental Psychiatry*, 1975, **6**, 105–109.

Reid, J. B., Hawkins, N., Keutzer, C., McNeal, S. A., Phelps, R. E., Reid, K. M., & Meas, H. L. A marathon behavior modification of a selectively mute child. *Journal of Child Psychology and Psychiatry,* 1967, **8**, 27–30.

Reschly, D. J. Psychological testing in educational classification and placement. *American Psychologist,* 1981, **36**, 1094–1102.

Reynolds, C. R. *A bibliography of research employing the Children's Manifest Anxiety Scale: 1956–1977.* Unpublished manuscript, 1977.

Reynolds, C. R. Concurrent validity of What I Think and Feel: The Revised Children's Manifest Anxiety Scale. *Journal of Consulting and Clinical Psychology,* 1980, **48**, 774–775. (a)

Reynolds, C. R. Long-term stability of scores on the revised children's manifest anxiety scale. *Perceptual and Motor Skills,* 1981, **53**, 702.

Reynolds, C. R. *Convergent and divergent validity of What I Think and Feel: The Revised Children's Manifest Anxiety Scale.* Manuscript in preparation.

Reynolds, C. R., & Paget, K. D. Factor analysis of the revised Children's Manifest Anxiety Scale for Blacks, Whites, Males and Females with a National Innovative Sample. *Journal of Consulting and Clinical Psychology,* 1981, **49**, 352–359.

Reynolds, C. R., & Paget, K. D. *National normative and reliability data for the Revised Children's Manifest Anxiety Scale.* Paper presented to the annual meeting of The National Association of School Psychologists, Toronto, March, 1982.

Reynolds, C. R., & Richmond, B. O. What I Think and Feel: A revised measure of children's manifest anxiety. *Journal of Abnormal Child Psychology,* 1978, **6**, 271–280.

Richards, C. S., & Siegel, L. J. Behavioral treatment of anxiety states and avoidance behaviors in children. In D. Marholin II (Ed.), *Child behavior therapy.* New York: Gardner Press, 1978.

Rimm, D. C. Personal communication, 1967.

Rimm, D. C., & Masters, J. C. *Behavior therapy: Techniques and empirical findings.* New York: Academic Press, 1974.

Rimm, D. C., & Masters, J. C. *Behavior therapy: Techniques and empirical findings.* (2nd ed.) New York: Academic Press, 1979.

Ritter, B. The group desensitization of children's snake phobias using vicarious and contact desensitization procedures. *Behaviour Research and Therapy,* 1968, **6**, 1–6.

Ritter, B. Treatment of acrophobia with contact desensitization. *Behaviour Research and Therapy,* 1969, **7**, 41–45. (a)

Ritter, B. The use of contact desensitization, demonstration-plus-participation and demonstration-only in the treatment of acrophobia. *Behaviour Research and Therapy,* 1969, **7**, 157–164. (b)

Risley, T. R. Behavior modification: An experimental-therapeutic endeavor. In L. A. Hamerlynck, P. O. Davidson, & L. E. Acker (Eds.), *Behavior modification and ideal mental health services.* Calgary, Alberta, Canada: University of Calgary Press, 1970.

Robins, L. N. Follow-up studies. In H. C. Quay & J. S. Werry (Eds.). *Psychopathological disorders of childhood.* (2nd ed.) New York: John Wiley & Sons, 1979.

Robson, K. S., Pedersen, F. A., & Moss, H. A. Developmental observations of diadic gazing in relation to the fear of strangers of social approach behavior. *Child Development,* 1969, **40**, 619–627.

Rogers, C. *Client-centered therapy: Its current practice, implications and theory.* New York: Houghton Mifflin, 1951.

Rogers, C. R. *Counseling and psychotherapy.* New York: Houghton Mifflin, 1942.

Rogers, C. R. A theory of therapy and personality change as developed in the client-centered framework. In E. Koch (Ed.), *Psychology: A study of science.* Vol. III. New York: McGraw-Hill, 1959.

Romanczyk, R. G., Diament, C., Goren, E. R., Trunell, G., & Harris, S. L. Increasing isolate and social play in severely disturbed children: Intervention and postintervention effectiveness. *Journal of Autism and Childhood Schizophrenia,* 1975, **5**, 57–70.

Rosen, A., & Proctor, E. K. Distinctions between treatment outcomes and their implications for treatment evaluation. *Journal of Consulting and Clinical Psychology*, 1981, **49**, 418–425.

Rosen, G. *Don't be afraid. A program for overcoming your fears and phobias*. Englewood Cliffs, N.J.: Prentice-Hall, 1976.

Rosen, G. M., Glasgow, R. E., & Barrera, M. Jr. A controlled study to assess the clinical ethics of total self-administered systematic desensitization. *Journal of Consulting and Clinical Psychology*, 1976, **44**, 208–217.

Rosenbaum, E., & Kellman, M. Treatment of a selectively mute third-grade child. *Journal of School Psychology*, 1973, **11**, 26–29.

Rosenthal, T. L. Modeling approaches to test anxiety and related performance problems. In I. G. Sarason (Ed.), *Test anxiety: Theory, research, and applications*. New York: Lawrence Erlbaum Associates, 1980.

Ross, A. O. *Psychological disorders of children: A behavioral approach to theory, research and therapy*. (2nd ed.) New York: McGraw-Hill, 1980.

Ross, A. O. Of rigor and relevance. *Professional Psychology*, 1981, **12**, 318–327.

Ross, D. M., Ross, S. A., & Evans, T. A. The modification of extreme social withdrawal by modeling with guided participation. *Journal of Behavior Therapy and Experimental Psychiatry*, 1971, **2**, 273–279.

Rush, F. R., & Kazdin, A. E. Toward a methodology of withdrawal designs for the assessment of response maintenance. *Journal of Applied Behavior Analysis*, 1981, **14**, 131–140.

Russell, G. W. Human fears: A factor analytic study of three age levels. *Genetic Psychology Monographs*, 1967, **76**, 141–162.

Russell, P. A. Fear evoking stimuli. In W. Sluckin (Ed.), *Fear in animals and man*. New York: Van Nostrand Reinhold, 1979.

Rutter, M., Lebocici, S., Eisenberg, L., Sneznevskij, A. V., Sadoun, R., Brooke, E., & Lin, T. Y. A tri-axial classification of mental disorders in childhood: An international study. *Journal of Child Psychology and Psychiatry*, 1969, **10**, 41–62.

Rutter, M., Shaffer, D., & Shepherd, M. *A multi-axial classification of child psychiatric disorders*. Geneva: World Health Organization, 1975.

Rutter, M., Shaffer, D., & Sturge, C. *A guide to a multi-axial classification for psychiatric disorders in childhood and adolescence*. London: Institute of Psychiatry, 1975.

Rutter, M., Tizard, J., & Whitmore, K. *Education, health and behavior*. New York: Wiley, 1970.

Ryall, M. R., & Dietiker, K. E. Reliability and clinical validity of the children's fear survey schedule. *Journal of Behavior Therapy and Experimental Psychiatry*, 1979, **10**, 303–310.

Saal, F. E., Downey, R. G., & Lahey, M. A. Rating the ratings: Assessing the psychometric quality of rating data. *Psychological Bulletin*, 1980, **88**, 413–428.

Samelson, F. J. B. Watson's Little Albert, Cyril Burt's Twins, and the need for a critical science. *American Psychologist*, 1980, **35**, 619–625.

Salzen, E. A. The ontogeny of fear in animals. In W. Slukin (Ed.), *Fear in animals and man*. New York: Van Nostrand Reinhold Co., 1979.

Salzinger, K. A behavioral analysis of diagnosis. In R. L. Spitzer & D. F. Klein (Eds.), *Critical issues in psychiatric diagnosis*. New York: Raven Press, 1978.

Sarason, S., Davidson, K., Lighthall, F., & Waite, R. A test anxiety scale for children. *Child Development*, 1958, **29**, 105–113.

Sarason, S., Davidson, K., Lighthall, F., Waite, R., & Ruebush, B. *Anxiety in elementary school children*. New York: Wiley, 1960.

Sargent, H. D. Methodological problems of follow-up studies in psychotherapy research. *American Journal of Orthopsychiatry*, 1960, **30**, 495–506.

Sartory, F., Rachman, S., & Gray, S. An investigation of the relation between reported fear and heart rate. *Behavior Research and Therapy*, 1977, **15**, 435–438.

Saunders, D. G. A case of motion sickness treated by systematic desensitization and in vivo relaxation. *Journal of Behavior Therapy and Experimental Psychiatry*, 1976, **7**, 381–382.

Sax, G. *Principles of educational and psychological measurement and evaluation.* (2nd ed.) Belmont, Calif.: Wadsworth, 1980.

Scarr, S., & Salapatek, P. Patterns of fear development during infancy. *Merrill-Palmer Quarterly of Behavior and Development,* 1970, **16**, 53–90.

Schacht, T., & Nathan, P. E. But is it good for the psychologists? Appraisal and status of DSM-III. *American Psychologist,* 1977, **32**, 1017–1025.

Schaffer, H. R. & Parry, M. H. Perceptual-motor behaviour in infancy as a function of age and stimulus similarity. *British Journal of Psychology,* 1969, **60**, 1–10.

Scherer, M. W., & Nakamura, C. Y. A Fear Survey Schedule for Children (FSS-FC): A factor analytic comparison with manifest anxiety (CMAS). *Behaviour Research and Therapy,* 1968, **6**, 173–182.

Schwartz, G. E. Psychobiological foundations of psychotherapy and behavior change. In S. L. Garfield & A. E. Bergin (Eds.), *Handbook of psychotherapy and behavior change: An empirical analysis.* (2nd ed.) New York: Wiley, 1978.

Schwartz-Gould, M., Wunsch-Hitzig, R., & Dohrenwend, B. P. Formulation of hypotheses about the prevalence, treatment, and prognostic significance of psychiatric disorders in children in the United States. In B. P. Dohrenwend et al. (Eds.), *Mental illness in the United States.* New York: Praeger, 1980.

Schwitzgabel, R. L., & Schwitzgabel, R. K. *Law and psychological practice.* New York: John Wiley & Sons, 1980.

Seligman, M. E. P. On the generality of the laws of learning. *Psychological Review,* 1970, **77**, 406–418.

Seligman, M. E. P. Phobias and preparedness. *Behavior Therapy,* 1971, **2**, 307–320.

Seligman, M., & Johnston, J. A cognitive theory of avoidance learning. In J. McGuigan & B. Lumsden (Eds.), *Contemporary approaches to conditioning and learning.* New York: Wiley, 1973.

Semenoll, B., Park, C., & Smith, F. Behavior interventions with a six-year-old elective mute. In J. B. Krumboltz & C. E. Thoreson (Eds.), *Counseling methods.* New York: Holt, Rinehart & Winston, 1976.

Severson, R. A. *The rationale and development of teacher-completed behavior rating scales.* Paper presented in the symposium "Assessment and Management of Aggressive and Disruptive Behavior in the Classroom." Annual meeting of the National Council on Measurement in Education, New York, February, 1971.

Shachaur, S., & Daut, R. Anxiety or pain: What does the scale measure? *Journal of Consulting and Clinical Psychology,* 1981, **49**, 468–469.

Shapiro, A. H. Behavior of kibbutz and urban children receiving an injection. *Psychophysiology,* 1975, **12**, 79–82.

Shepherd, M., Oppensheim, B. & Mitchell, S. *Childhood behaviour and mental health.* London: University of London Press, 1972.

Shields, J. Genetic factors in neurosis. In H. M. van Pragg (Ed.), *Research in neurosis.* New York: SP Medical & Scientific Books, 1978.

Siegel, L. J., & Peterson, L. Stress reduction in young dental patients through coping skills and sensory information. *Journal of Consulting and Clinical Psychology,* in press.

Simkins, L. The reliability of self-recorded behavior. *Behavior Therapy,* 1971, **2**, 83–87.

Skinner, B. F. *The behavior of organisms.* New York: Appleton-Century-Croft, 1938.

Skinner, B. F. *Science and human behavior.* New York: Macmillan, 1953.

Skinner, B. F. *Cumulative record.* (Rev. Ed.) New York: Appleton-Century-Croft, 1961.

Skinner, B. F. *Contingencies of reinforcement: A theoretical analysis,* New York: Appleton-Century-Croft, 1969.

Skinner, B. F. The steep and thorny way to a science of behavior. *American Psychologist,* 1975, **39**, 42–49.

Skinner, H. A. Toward an integration of classification theory and methods. *Journal of Abnormal*

Psychology, 1981, **90**, 68–87.

Sloane, R. B., Stables, F. R., Cristol, A. H., Yorkston, N. J., & Whipple, K. *Psychotherapy versus behavior therapy*. Cambridge: Harvard University Press, 1975.

Sluckin, A., & Jehu, D. A behavioral approach in the treatment of elective mutism. *British Journal of Psychiatric Social Work*, 1969, **10**, 70–73.

Sluckin, W. (Ed.) *Fear in animals and man*. New York: Van Nostrand Reinhold, 1979.

Smith, P. K. The ontogeny of fear in children. In W. Sluckin (Ed.), *Fear in animals and man*. New York: Van Nostrand Reinhold, 1979.

Smith, M. L., & Glass, G. V. Meta-analysis of psychotherapy outcome studies. *American Psychologist*, 1977, **32**, 752–760.

Smith, R. E., & Sharpe, T. M. Treatment of a school phobia with implosive therapy. *Journal of Consulting and Clinical Psychology*, 1970, **35**, 239–243.

Snyder, A. L., & Deffenbacher, J. L. Comparison of relaxation and self-control and systematic desensitization in the treatment of test anxiety. *Journal of Consulting and Clinical Psychology*, 1977, **45**, 1202–1203.

Sokolov, V. N. *Perception and the conditioned reflex*. New York: Macmillan, 1963.

Spiegler, M., & Liebert, R. Some correlates of self-reported fear. *Psychological Reports*, 1970, **26**, 691–695.

Spielberger, C. *Manual for the State-Trait Inventory for Children*. Palo Alto, Cal.: Consulting Psychologists Press, 1973.

Spinetta, J. J. The dying child's awareness of death: A review. *Psychological Bulletin*, 1974, **81**, 256–260.

Spinetta, J. J., Rigler, D., & Karou, M. Anxiety in the dying child. *Pediatrics*, 1973, **52**.

Spitzer, R. L., & Klein, D. F. *Critical issues in psychiatric diagnosis*. New York: Raven Press, 1978.

Spitzer, R. L., Sheehy, M., & Endicott, J. DSM-III: Guiding principles. In V. M. Rakoff, H. C. Stancer, & H. B. Kedward (Eds.), *Psychiatric diagnosis*. New York: Brunner/Mazel, 1977.

Spitzer, R. L., & Williams, J. B. W. Classification of mental disorders and DSM-III. In H. I. Kaplan, A. M. Freedman, & B. J. Sadock (Eds.), *Comprehensive textbook of psychiatry/III*. (Vol. 1) Baltimore: Williams & Wilkins, 1980.

Spivack, G., & Swift, M. Classroom behavior of children: A critical review of teacher-administered rating scales. *Journal of Special Education*, 1973, **1**, 55–89.

Sroufe, L. A. Wariness of strangers and the study of infant development. *Child Development*, 1977, **48**, 731–746.

Staats, A. W. *Social behaviorism*. Homewood, Ill.: Dorsey Press, 1975.

Stableford, W. Parental treatment of a child's noise phobia. *Journal of Behavior Therapy and Experimental Psychiatry* 1979, **10**, 159–160.

Stampfl, T. G. *Implosive therapy: A learning theory derived psychodynamic therapeutic technique*. Paper presented at the University of Illinois, 1961.

Stampfl, T. G., & Levis, D. J. Essentials of implosive therapy: A learning-based-psychodynamic behavioral therapy. *Journal of Abnormal Psychology*, 1967, **72**, 496–503.

Stampfl, T. G., & Levis, D. J. Implosive therapy—a behavioral therapy? *Behaviour Research and Therapy*, 1968, **6**, 31–36.

Stanford, D., Dember, W., & Stanford, L. A children's form of the Alpert-Haber achievement anxiety scale. *Child Development*, 1963, **34**, 1027–1032.

Sternbach, R. Assessing differential autonomic patterns in emotions. *Journal of Psychosomatic Research*, 1962, **6**, 87.

Stokes, T. F., & Baer, D. M. An Implicit Technology of Generalization. *Journal of Applied Behavior Analysis*, 1977, **10**, 349–367.

Stokes, T. F., & Kennedy, S. H. Reducing child uncooperative behavior during dental treatment through modeling and reinforcement. *Journal of Applied Behavior Analysis*, 1980, **13**, 41–49.

Strain, P., Cooke, T., & Apolloni, T. *Teaching exceptional children: Assessing and modifying social behavior.* New York: Academic Press, 1976.

Strain, P. S., Shores, R. E., & Timm, M. A. Effects of peer social initiations on the behavior of withdrawn preschool children. *Journal of Applied Behavior Analysis,* 1977, **10,** 289–298.

Strain, P. S., & Timm, M. A. An experimental analysis of social interaction between a behaviorally disordered preschool child and her classroom peers. *Journal of Applied Behavior Analysis,* 1974, **7,** 583–590.

Stuart, R. B. *Trick of treatment: How and when psychotherapy fails.* Champaign, Ill.: Research Press, 1970.

Sturge, C., Shaffer, D., & Rutter, M. *The reliability of diagnostic categories for child psychiatric disorders in ICD-9.* Paper presented at the Royal College of Psychiatrists Section of Child Psychiatry Meeting, Stirling, Scotland, September 1977.

Suckerman, K. R. *The role of imagery and mode of presentation in systematic desensitization.* Unpublished dissertation, Syracuse University, 1977.

Swan, G. E., & MacDonald, M. L. Behavior therapy in practice: A national survey of behavior therapists. *Behavior Therapy,* 1978, **9,** 799–807.

Szasz, T. S. The myth of mental illness. *American Psychologist,* 1960, **15,** 113–118.

Szasz, T. S. *The myth of mental illness.* New York: Harper & Row, 1974.

Tahmisian, J., & McReynolds, W. The use of parents as behavioral engineers in the treatment of a school phobic girl. *Journal of Counseling Psychology,* 1971, **18,** 225–228.

Tal, A., & Miklich, D. Emotionally induced decreases in pulmonary flow rates in asthmatic children. *Psychosomatic Medicine,* 1976, **38,** 190–200.

Tarler-Benlolo, L. The role of relaxation in biofeedback training: A critical review of the literature. *Psychological Bulletin,* 1978, **85,** 727–755.

Tasto, D. L. Systematic desensitization, muscle relaxation and visual imagery in the counter-conditioning of a 4-year-old phobic child. *Behaviour Research and Therapy,* 1969, **7,** 409–411.

Tasto, D. L. Self-report schedules and inventories. In A. R. Ciminero, K. S. Calbourn, & H. E. Adams (Eds.), *Handbook of behavioral assessment.* New York: John Wiley & Sons, 1977.

Taylor, C. B., & Agras, S. Assessment of phobia In D. H. Barlow (Ed.), *Assessment of adult disorders.* New York: Guilford, 1981.

Taylor, D. W. Treatment of excessive frequency of urination by desensitization. *Journal of Behavior Therapy and Experimental Psychiatry,* 1972, **3,** 311–313.

Taylor, J. H. Curnate emotional responses in infants. *Ohio State University Studies, Contributions in Psychology,* 1934, **12,** 69–81.

Tennes, K. H., & Lampl, E. E. Stranger and separation anxiety in infancy. *Journal of Nervous and Mental Disease,* 1964, **139,** 247–254.

Tharp, R. G., & Wetzel, R. J. *Behavior modification in the natural environment.* New York: Academic Press, 1969.

Thoresen, C. E., & Mahoney, M. J. *Behavioral self-control.* New York: Holt, Rinehart, & Winston, 1974.

Thornson, R. The concept of fear. In W. Sluckin (Ed.), *Fear in animals and man.* New York: Van Nostrand Reinhold, 1979.

Tramontana, M. G. A critical review of research on psychotherapy outcome with adolescents: 1967–1977. *Psychological Bulletin,* 1980, **88,** 429–450.

Ullmann, L. P., & Krasner, L. (Eds.) *Case studies in behavior modification.* New York: Holt, 1965.

Ullmann, L. P., & Krasner, L. *A psychological approach to abnormal behavior.* Englewood Cliffs, N.J.: Prentice-Hall, 1969.

Ullmann, L. P., & Krasner, L. A. *A psychological approach to abnormal behavior.* (2nd ed.) Englewood Cliffs, N.J.: Prentice-Hall, 1975.

Unn, J. A. Factor structure of the test anxiety scale for children. *Journal of Consulting Psychol-*

ogy, 1964, **28**, 92.

Vaal, J. J. Applying contingency contracting to a school phobic: A case study. *Journal of Behavior Therapy and Experimental Psychiatry*, 1973, **4**, 371–373.

Van der Ploeg, H. M. Treatment of frequency of urination by stories competing with anxiety. *Journal of Behavior Therapy and Experimental Psychiatry*, 1975, **6**, 165–166.

Van Hasselt, V. B., Hersen, M., Bellack, A. S., Rosenblum, N. D., & Lamparski, D. Tripartite assessment of the effects of systematic desensitization in a multi-phobic child: An experimental analysis. *Journal of Behavior Therapy and Experimental Psychiatry*, 1979, **10**, 51–55.

Van Hoose, W. H., & Kottler, J. A. *Ethical and legal issues in counseling and psychotherapy*. San Francisco: Jossey-Bass, 1977.

Venham, L., Bengston, D., & Cipes, M. Children's responses to sequential dental visits. *Journal of Dental Research*, 1977, **56**, 454–459.

Vernon, D. Use of modeling to modify children's responses to a natural, potentially stressful situation. *Journal of Applied Psychology*, 1973, **58**, 351–356.

Vernon, D., Foley, J. L., & Schulman, J. L. Effect of mother-child separation and birth order on young children's responses to two potentially stressful experiences. *Journal of Personality and Social Psychology*, 1967, **5**, 162–174.

Vernon, D., Schulman, J. L., & Foley, J. M. Changes in children's behavior after hospitalization. *American Journal of the Diseases of Children*, 1966, **3**, 581–593.

Vernon, V. T., & Bailey, W. C. The use of motion pictures in the psychological preparation of children for induction of anesthesia. *Anesthesiology*, 1974, **40**, 68–72.

Voeltz, L. M., & Evans, I. M. The assessment of behavioral interrelationships in child behavior therapy. *Behavioral Assessment*, 1982, **4**, 131–165.

Wade, T. C., Baker, T. B., & Hartmann, D. P. Behavior therapist's self-reported views and practices. *The Behavior Therapist*, 1979, **2**, 3–6.

Waechter, E. H. *Death anxiety in children with fatal illness*. Unpublished doctoral dissertation. University of Michigan, 1968.

Waechter, E. H. Children's awareness of fatal illness. *American Journal of Nursing*, 1971, **71**, 1168–1172.

Wahler, R. G., & Cormier, W. H. The ecological interview: A first step in out-patient child behavior therapy. *Journal of Behavior Therapy and Experimental Psychiatry*, 1970, **1**, 279–289.

Walk, R. D. Self-ratings of fear in a fear-invoking situation. *Journal of Abnormal and Social Psychology*, 1956, **52**, 171–178.

Walker, C. E., Hedberg, A., Clement, P. W., & Wright, L. *Clinical procedures for behavior therapy*. Englewood Cliffs, N.J.: Prentice-Hall, 1981.

Walls, R. T., Werner, T. J., Bacon, A., & Zane, T. Behavior checklists. In J. D. Cone & R. P. Hawkins (Eds.), *New assessment: New directions in clinical psychology*. New York: Brunner/Mazel, 1977.

Wasik, B. H., & Loven, M. D. Classroom observational data: Sources of inaccuracy and proposed solutions. *Behavioral Assessment*, 1980, **2**, 211–227.

Watson, J. B. Psychology as the behaviorist views it. *Psychological Review*, 1913, **20**, 158–177.

Watson, J. B. *Psychology from the standpoint of a behaviorist*. Philadelphia: Lippincott, 1919.

Watson, J. B. *Behaviorism*. New York: W. W. Norton, 1924.

Watson, J. B., & Rayner, R. Conditioned emotional reactions. *Journal of Experimental Psychology*, 1920, **3**, 1–14.

Wayne, M. F. Behavioral treatment of a child displaying comic-book mediated fear of hand shrinking: A case study. *Journal of Pediatric Psychology*, 1979, **4**, 43–47.

Weissbrod, C. S., & Bryan, J. H. Filmed treatment as an effective fear-reduction technique. *Journal of Abnormal Child Psychology*, 1973, **1**, 196–201.

White, W. C., & Davis, M. T. Vicarious extinction of phobic behavior in early childhood. *Journal of Abnormal Child Psychology*, 1974, **2**, 25–37.

Whitehill, M. B., Hersen, M., & Bellack, A. S. Conversation skills training for socially isolated children. *Behavior Research and Therapy*, 1980, **18**, 217–225.

Wiggins, J. S. *Personality and prediction: Principles of personality assessment*. Reading, Mass.: Addison-Wesley, 1973.

Wildman, B. G., & Erickson, M. T. Methodological problems in behavioral observation. In J. D. Cone & R. P. Hawkins (Eds.), *Behavioral assessment: New directions in clinical psychology*. New York: Brunner/Mazel, 1977.

Wildman, R. W., II, & Wildman, R. W. The generalization of behavior modification procedures: A review—with special emphasis on classroom applications. *Psychology in the Schools*, 1975, **12**, 432–448.

Williamson, D. A., Jewell, W. R., Sanders, S. H., Haney, J. N., & White, D. The treatment of reluctant speech using contingency management procedures. *Journal of Behavior Therapy and Experimental Psychiatry*, 1977, **8**, 151–156.

Wilson, G. T., & Evans, I. M., The therapist-client relationship in behavior therapy. In A. S. Gurman & A. M. Razin (Eds.), *Effective psychotherapy: A handbook of research*. New York: Pergamon Press, 1977.

Wilson, G. T., & Evans, I. M. Goal specification and the reliability of target behavior selection in behavioral assessment. *Behavioral Assessment*, in press.

Wine, J. D. Test anxiety and evaluating threat: Children's behavior in the classroom. *Journal of Abnormal Child Psychology*, 1979, **7**, 45–59.

Wines, A. N. The assessment interview. In I. B. Weiner (Ed.), *Clinical methods in psychology*. New York: Wiley, 1976.

Wiselli, J. K. Case report: An attendant-administered contingency management program for the treatment of a toileting phobia. *Journal of Mental Deficiency Research*, 1977, **21**, 283–288.

Wish, P. A., Hasazi, J. E., & Jurgela, A. R. Automated direct deconditioning of a childhood phobia. *Journal of Behavior Therapy and Experimental Psychiatry*, 1973, **4**, 279–283.

Wolf, M. F. Social validity: The case for subjective measurement or how applied behavior analysis is finding its heart. *Journal of Applied Behavior Analysis*, 1978, **11**, 203–214.

Wolpe, J. *Reciprocal inhibition therapy*. Stanford, California: Stanford University Press, 1958.

Wolpe, J. The experimental foundations of some new psychotherapeutic methods. In A. J. Bachrach (Ed.), *Experimental foundations of clinical psychology*. New York: Basic Books, 1962.

Wolpe, J. The comparative clinical status of conditioning therapies and psychoanalysis. In J. Wolpe, A. Salter & L. J. Reyna (Eds.), *The conditioning therapies*. New York: Holt, 1964.

Wolpe, J. *The practice of behavior therapy*. New York: Pergamon Press, 1969.

Wolpe, J. *The practice of behavior therapy*. (2nd ed.) New York: Pergamon Press, 1973.

Wolpe, J., & Lazarus, A. A. *Behavior therapy techniques*. New York: Pergamon Press, 1966.

Wolpe, J., & Rachman, S. J. Psychoanalytic evidence: A critique based on Freud's case of Little Hans. *Journal of Nervous and Mental Disorders*, 1960, **131**, 135–145.

Wright, G., & Alpern, G. Variables influencing children's cooperative behavior at the first dental visit. *Journal of Dentistry for Children*, 1971, **38**, 124–128.

Wright, G., Alpern, G., & Leake, J. The modifiability of maternal anxiety as it relates to children's cooperative dental behavior. *Journal of Dentistry for Children*, 1973, **40**, 265–271.

Wulbert, M., Nyman, B. A., Snow, D., & Owen, Y. The efficacy of stimulus fading and contingency management in the treatment of elective mutism: A case study. *Journal of Applied Behavior Analysis*, 1973, **6**, 435–441.

Yates, A. G. *Behavior therapy*. New York: Wiley, 1970.

Yates, B. T. Improving the cost-effectiveness of obesity programs: Three basic strategies for reducing the cost per pound. *International Journal of Obesity*, 1978, **2**, 249–266.

Yates, B. T. The theory and practice of cost-utility, cost-effectiveness, and cost-benefit analysis in behavioral medicine: Toward delivering more health care for less money. In J. Ferguson

& B. Taylor (Eds.), *Advances in behavioral medicine.* Englewood Cliffs, N.J.: Spectrum, in press.

Yates, B. T., Haven, W. G., & Thoresen, C. T. Cost-effectiveness analyses at Learning House: How much changes for how much money? In J. S. Stumphauzer (Ed.), *Progress in behavioral therapy with delinquents.* Vol. 2. Springfield, Ill.: Charles C. Thomas, 1977.

Young, F., & Brown, M. Effects of test anxiety and testing conditions on intelligence test scores of elementary school boys and girls. *Psychological Reports,* 1973, **32,** 643–649.

Yule, W. The epidemiology of child psychopathology. In B. B. Lahey & A. E. Kazdin (Eds.), *Advances in clinical child psychology.* Vol. 4. New York: Plenum, 1981.

Yule, W., & Fernando, P. Blood phobia-beware. *Behaviour, Research and Therapy,* 1980, **18,** 587–590.

Yule, W., Sacks, B., & Hersov, L. Successful flooding treatment of a noise phobia in an 11 year old. *Journal of Behavior Therapy and Experimental Psychiatry,* 1974, **5,** 209–211.

Ysseldyke, J. E., & Weinberg, R. A. (Eds.). The future of psychology in the schools: Proceedings of the Spring Hill Symposium. *The School Psychology Review,* 1981, **10,** 112–318.

Zimmerman, B. J. Modeling. In H. L. Hom, Jr. & P. A. Robinson (Eds.), *Psychological processes in early education.* New York: Academic Press, 1977.

Author Index

Subject Index

About the Authors

Richard J. Morris (Ph.D., Arizona State University, 1970) is Professor of Special Education, College of Education, The University of Arizona. He was also Assistant to Associate Professor of Psychology, Clinical Psychology Training Program, Syracuse University and Clinical Assistant Professor of Pediatrics, Upstate Medical Center, State University of New York at Syracuse. He has authored and edited several books including *Behavior modification with children: A systematic guide* and *Perspectives in abnormal behavior*, and is co-editor with Thomas R. Kratochwill of *The practice of child therapy: A textbook of methods*. He has published numerous journal articles and chapters on fear reduction methods and in the area of behavior therapy. He is a member of several professional associations, serves on the editorial boards of *Applied Research in Mental Retardation, Mental Retardation*, and *Rehabilitation Psychology*, and has been a consultant to several publishing companies, mental health and developmental disabilities treatment facilities, and schools.

Thomas R. Kratochwill (Ph.D., The University of Wisconsin, 1973) is Professor of Educational Psychology, College of Education, The University of Arizona. He has authored and edited several books including *Single subject research: Strategies for evaluating change, Selective mutism: Implications for research and treatment, The practice of child therapy: A textbook of methods* (with Richard J. Morris), and *Advances in school psychology*, an annual series. He has published numerous journal articles and chapters on behavior therapy and assessment, and research methodology. In 1977 he received the Lightner Witmer award from Division 16 of the American Psychological Association. He is an associate editor of *Behavior Therapy* and serves on the editorial boards of *Behavioral Assessment, Journal of School Psychology, Journal of Learning Disabilities, Behavioral Counseling Quarterly, Psychoeducational Assessment*, and the *Journal of Applied Behavior Analysis*. In addition, he has been a consultant to several publishing companies, child treatment facilities, and schools.

Pergamon General Psychology Series

Editors: Arnold P. Goldstein, Syracuse University
Leonard Krasner, SUNY at Stony Brook

618.92
M877T